**On the occasion of the
10th anniversary of the European Society of Anaesthesiologists**

this special edition has been made possible through the generous sponsorship of the following ESA Partner Companies

The ESA Board of Directors acknowledges their sincere gratitude for this gesture.

I Awaken To Glory

*Essays Celebrating the Sesquicentennial of
The Discovery of Anesthesia by*

HORACE WELLS

December 11, 1844–December 11, 1994

Edited by

Richard J. Wolfe and Leonard F. Menczer

Published by the Boston Medical Library in
The Francis A. Countway Library of Medicine, Boston
In Association With
The Historical Museum of Medicine and Dentistry, Hartford
1994

Sole commercial distributor: Science History Publications/USA
P.O. Box 493, Canton, Massachusetts 02021   Tel. (617) 828-8450

ISBN: 0-88135-161-X

This Work Is Dedicated To
Louise ("Billie") Archer

And To The Memory Of
W. Harry Archer
and
Leonard F. Menczer

Contents

List of Illustrations ix

Introduction and Acknowledgments xiii

1. Who was the Discoverer of Surgical Anesthesia?
   A Brief for Horace Wells. *Richard J. Wolfe* 1

2. Horace Wells and His Dental Practice.
   Malvin E. Ring and Leonard F. Menczer 73

3. Horace Wells's "Day Book A:" a Transcription
   and Analysis. *Leonard F. Menczer* 97

4. The Shop on Main Street: Horace Wells's Hartford.
   Sarah H. Gordon 182

5. "I Sleep To Awaken:" a Profile of Elizabeth
   Wales Wells. *Richard J. Wolfe* 216

6. "Genius, the Result of Original Mental Superiority:"
   John M. Riggs and Horace Wells.
   David A. Chernin 255

7. Christopher Starr Brewster: American Dentist in Paris
   and Patron of Horace Wells. *Jaques Fouré* 275

8. Recognition from Britain: the Horace Wells
   Testimonial Fund, 1871–1873. *J.A.W. Wildsmith* 301

9. W. Harry Archer, D.D.S., Biographer of
   Horace Wells. *C. Richard Bennett*   312

10. The Charles Noel Flagg Posthumous Portrait of
    Horace Wells: an Examination of Its Documentation
    and Sources and of the Iconography of Horace
    Wells. *Richard J. Wolfe and Leroy D. Vandam*   320

11. The Redemption of Horace Wells Through Public
    Art. *Shirley Stallings and Michael Montagne*   358

12. Horace Wells and his Paris Statue. *Jacques Fouré*   404

Notes on Contributors   419

Index   421

ILLUSTRATIONS

1. Apparatus for evolving and preserving nitrous oxide gas developed by Dr. Robert Hare of the University of Pennsylvania   15

2. A Depiction of "laughing gas sniffing" in London in the late 1830s   17

3. An instrument case similar to one probably used by Horace Wells   81

4. Dental drill invented by John Lewis in 1838   81

5. Hand drills typical of those used by Horace Wells   82

6. The highly popular "ring drill" of Amos Wescott   82

7. The first commercially produced dental chair, invented by James Snell of London in 1832   83

8. An extraction forceps of the type used by Horace Wells   84

9. Individual porcelain denture teeth with platinum pins embedded in them   84

10. A gold swaged denture base with individual porcelain teeth soldered to it   85

11. A gold foil packet of 1850   85

12. Front cover and page 3 of "Day Book A"   99

13. Main Street, Hartford, in the 1890s   184

14. Map of Horace Wells's Hartford   207

15. Map of Main Street, Hartford, 1839–1850   208

16. Photograph of Elizabeth Wales Wells in mid-life 241

17. Charles Thomas Wells in later life   246

18. Bronze casting of a plaster death mask of
    Horace Wells, made by John M. Riggs on
    January 27, 1848, the day of Wells's burial   263

19. John M. Riggs in later life   270

20. Passport granted to Horace Wells on December 19,
    1847   281

21. Jacques Fouré at the grave of Christopher Starr
    Brewster in Notre Dame Cemetery in Versailles
    in 1991   289

22. Facsimiles of pages one and three of the
    holograph "Memoir" by Wells that was read
    before the Académie des Sciences, Paris, on
    March 8, 1847   299

23. Resolution of the medical and dental professions of
    Britain, 1871, awarding Wells credit for the
    discovery of anesthesia   308

24. W. Harry Archer, photographed in his University
    of Pittsburgh dental school office about 1970,
    with the portrait of Horace Wells, by Verona
    Kiralfy, in the background   318

25. Life-size portrait of Horace Wells painted by
    Charles Noel Flagg in 1899   323

26. Original silhouette of Horace Wells, presumed to
    have been made by him   326

27. Tintype portrait of Horace Wells, copied from
    an original daguerreotype reportedly made by
    him ca. 1840   327

28. Reproductions of two silhouettes by Auguste
    Edouart   332

29. Advertisement for Truman Smith's *An Inquiry into
    the Origin of Modern Anesthesia* with
    Horace Wells's portrait by Henry Bryan Hall   336

30. Miniature oil portraits on ivory of Horace and
    Elizabeth Wales Wells by an unidentified artist   337

31. The portrait of Horace Wells that hung in his son
    Charles's house until Charles's death in 1909   338

32. Silhouette of Horace Wells by an unidentified
    artisan, now in the Historical Museum of
    Medicine and Dentistry in Hartford   339

33. Oil portrait of Horace Wells in the Historical
    Museum of Medicine and Dentistry, thought
    to have been painted by Charles Hine   342

34. Oil portrait of Elizabeth Wales Wells by an
    unknown artist, possibly Jared Flagg or
    Charles Hine   343

35. Oil portrait of Horace Wells by his son Charles   346

36. X-ray photograph of the picture in Illustration 35,
    showing the portrait of a woman, appearing to be
    Elizabeth Wales Wells, beneath   348

37. Front and side views of the statue of Horace Wells
    by Truman Howe Bartlett that stands in Hartford's
    Bushnell Park   359

38. Horace Wells's birthplace at Hartford, Vermont   368

39. The Wells's homestead in Westminster, Vermont   368

40. The Abiather Shaw, Jr. homestead at Westmoreland,
    New Hampshire, where Wells grew up   369

41. The schoolhouse on the Shaw property which Horace
    Wells attended and where he probably taught
    writing   369

42. Commemorative plaque by Enoch S. Woods placed
    at the site of Horace Wells's dental office in 1895   390

43. The stained glass window by Tiffany Studios, Inc.,
    placed in the Center Church, Hartford, in 1903 to
    commemorate Horace and Elizabeth Wells   390

44. Church pew at Trinity College chapel dedicated to
    Horace Wells in 1937   394

45. Brass relief on the stone memorial at Horace and
    Elizabeth Wells's gravesite in Cedar Hill Cemetery,
    Hartford   394

46. Bronze reliefs on the side of Wells's memorial   396

47. Front and side views of the statue of Horace Wells
    placed in 1910 in the Place des Etats Unis in Paris   405

48. Ceremonies marking the restoration of Horace
    Wells's statue on December 10, 1994, following
    the liberation of Paris   410

49. Photograph made for Howard R. Raper in 1972
    of the Horace Wells monument in Paris   415

Introduction

This book was begun because its editors felt that Horace Wells has not been judged fairly by history. Not only was it generally not recognized that Wells was first to realistically grasp the concept of inhalation anesthesia—that is, analgesia brought about by a gas and not a solid; it was also little appreciated that it was he who, by immediately putting theory to the test, began the journey which led directly to the introduction of painless surgery. Wells's unfortunate death by suicide left him at a disadvantage in the rancorous debate that afterwards erupted over credit for the discovery of anesthesia, and the confused and fragmentary literature that resulted has left us with an incomplete and misinterpreted picture of the man. For example, descriptions of Wells by recent commentators on the history of anesthesia as "volatile," "errant" and "wayward" do not accord with the picture of him that the editors had formed over the years from the evidence they had seen; such views indicate how misunderstood Wells has remained nearly a hundred and fifty years after his death.

It was the desire to dig deeper into the literature on Wells and on the so-called "ether controversy" and to present a realistic picture of Wells and of his achievement in this, the sesquicentennial year of his discovery, that prompted the decision to attempt this work. Although the late Dr. Harry Archer had done a very creditable job of portraying Well's life and work fifty years ago when the centennial was celebrated, we felt that, by digging even deeper than he had done, a more accurate account of Wells's life and character and his role in ushering in modern anesthesia might emerge. The successful conclusion of this project is due to the fact that we were able to find other interested and enthusiastic individuals who not only shared our view of Wells, but also had knowledge of various aspects of his life and role in introducing surgical anesthesia. They contributed new facts and insights and reassessments which helped answer many questions about Wells that had not appeared answerable previously; they joined with the editors in collectively sketching out a truer picture of Horace Wells than any seen before, one which now shows him in a clearer and more discernible light, and one which we believe justifies us in awarding him the credit he deserves.

Unhappily, Leonard Menczer, coeditor of this volume and long one of the most active supporters of Horace Wells's claim, died just after the last essay had been received and as we were about to undertake final editing preparatory to seeing the work through press. (It is for this reason that Dr. Menczer's name appears on the book's dedication page as well as on its title page.) This unfortunate circumstance left the undersigned editor the task of writing this introductory statement alone and has also relegated to him the lonely duty of acknowledging the help of others whose contributions in one way or another made it possible.

Nevertheless, he takes comfort in knowing that Leonard Menczer, who was a good friend as well as a close collaborator, had read every essay in near final form and was able to realize that the research we had initiated did indeed result in answering many questions about Wells and his circle that had long puzzled or troubled him. For example, Menczer's question to me, "Is it possible that Horace Wells could have known about Humphry Davy's allusion to the analgesic powers of nitrous oxide?", prompted the undersigned to research and compile the first essay in this volume. And that type of questioning occurred many times more. Dr. Menczer thus knew in the final days of life that we had at last achieved a more balanced picture of Wells. He knew that by looking more deeply into the literature than had ever been done before, we finally had at hand, nearly a century and a half after Well's death, a clear and perhaps definitive composite sketch of Wells the discoverer, Wells the scientist, Wells the inventor, Wells the dentist, Wells the idealist, Wells the humanist and—while last, not least—Wells the man.

In the planning and execution of this work Leonard Menczer played a dual role, in addition to that of author. Because of his extensive knowledge of Horace Wells and of the history of dentistry, acquired over nearly forty years of research and sharpened during his twenty-year tenure as Curator of the Historical Museum of Medicine and Dentistry in Hartford, he was able to suggest and enlist many of the authors whose essays appear here. And his questioning and skeptical mind challenged new ideas as they arose or appeared or were introduced by others, which led in many cases to re-evaluations, further research, new views, and final answers. It was a great pleasure as well as a privilege to have worked with Leonard and to have helped him achieve his long-cherished ambition.

The undersigned served as author and also co-organizer, co-planner and general editor of the volume, writing, re-writing, copy-editing, indexing and performing and coordinating all of those services which make up the duties of an editor. One of the main problems to be confronted was the repetition that appeared in twelve separate essays written by ten authors who focused their attention on a single individual and theme and who were forced to depend on a limited amount of documentation. While I have tried to eliminate as much repetition as possible, I could not do away with all of it, because it was sometimes necessary to the telling of an individual story. Since each essay referred to a particular aspect of Wells's life or work, or to his association with specific individuals, it was often necessary to repeat facts that had been related in a previous article in order to round out the subsequent essay and give continuity to it as well as to make it readable and understandable.

The assistance provided by the many people who worked together to bring this book to fruition falls roughly into five categories: those who participated directly in its writing and compilation; those who helped provide information and documentation; those who lent advice or contributed constructive criticism, or assisted in similar ways; individuals and institutions allowing quotations from documents in their possession or reproductions of illustrations in their collections; and, finally, organizations which advanced funds to underwrite publication costs and individuals who solicited such funds.

In the first category are the nine authors who worked untiringly to dig into scattered sources and from them create this reevaluation of Horace Wells and his remarkable achievement. It was a great pleasure for the editor to work with these dedicated and exceptional people who never objected when criticism, interpolation, cutting or re-writing was called for. Their enthusiasm never dimmed in any way. In the second category are individuals such as Mrs. W. Harry ("Billie") Archer of Pittsburgh who, with her husband, helped preserve the critical documents relating to Horace Wells's life, work and family. As is pointed out in the article on Dr. Archer within, had it not been for the efforts of the Archers, we would know pitifully little about Horace Wells today, and this volume would not have been possible. Mrs. Archer allowed the undersigned complete freedom to examine and work with all of the materials that she and her husband had collected and preserved. Another important contributor to this cause was Jeanne McKenzie, formerly with the Anesthesia Department of the University of Pittsburgh's School of Dental Medicine. Mrs. McKenzie collaborated closely with Mrs. Archer in making these documents available to me and was helpful in other and innumerable ways; she was, in fact, an essential cog that kept the wheels spinning time and again. Dr. A. Moneim El-Attar of Pitt's Department of Oral Surgery contributed reminiscences, pictorial materials and other information on Dr. Archer and his intellectual love affair with Horace Wells and thereby made our work easier.

Diane G. Neumann, who assisted Leonard Menczer in caring for the Historical Museum of Medicine and Dentistry, has also been an integral part of this endeavor, serving as Mrs. McKenzie's counterpart in Hartford; she was especially helpful in solving all sorts of problems which arose understandably following Dr. Menczer's untimely death. Others lending advice, criticisms, or other services are Dr. Robert J.T. Joy of the school of Medicine of the Armed Services University of the Health Sciences in Bethesda, Maryland; Elizabeth R. McClintock of the Wadsworth Atheneum in Hartford; Dr. Henry Epstein of the Harvard School of Dental Medicine; Dr. Alan Van Poznak and Adele A. Lerner of the New York Hospital-Cornell

Medical Center in New York City; and Dr. Lester L. Luntz of Hartford and John A. Woods of South Windsor, Connecticut, both of whom assisted with photography. Special thanks must be tendered to Estrellita Karsh of Ottawa, Canada, who helped the Boston Medical Library acquire the silhouette by and of Horace Wells which forms an integral part of the documentation within, and to Dr. John Bockstoce of South Dartmouth, Massachusetts, and his mother, Mrs. Clifton Bockstoce of Bloomfield, Connecticut, for donating it.

Individuals, institutions and organizations allowing the quotation or reproduction of documents or pictorial materials in their possession or charge are: the Boston Medical Library in The Francis A. Countway Library of Medicine; the *Bulletin of the History of Medicine* in Baltimore; the Connecticut Historical Society, the Historical Museum of Medicine and Dentistry, the Connecticut State Library, and the Wadsworth Atheneum in Hartford; the archives of the Smithsonian Institution (through Judy Chelnick, its Museum Specialist); Dr. Philip S. Moran of West Hartford, Connecticut; Robert H. Hirst, General Editor of the Mark Twain Project at the University of California at Berkeley; and the University Press of Virginia.

Organizations and individuals assisting in funding this publication are: the Aetna Life & Casualty Foundation, Hartford; the American Association of Oral and Maxillofacial Surgery, and its President, Dr. Ronald B. Marks; the McManus Fund of the Hartford Dental Society; and the Ordre National des Chirurgiens-Dentistes of Paris, France, and its president Dr. E. Saint-Eve; the Jean A. Curran-James F. Ballard Publication Fund of the Boston Medical Library; and the American Fund for Dentistry of the American Dental Society of Anesthesiology, Inc., and its officers, Mr. Peter C. Goulding, Dr. Robert J. Klaus, and Dr. Christopher LoFrisco. Special thanks must be extended to Dr. Peter Jacobsohn of the Department of Oral and Maxillofacial Surgery at Marquette University in Milwaukee, who interceded and worked hard to have the American Society of Dental Anesthesiology, Inc. make its significant contribution.

Richard J. Wolfe

1

Who Was the Discoverer Of Surgical Anesthesia? A Brief for Horace Wells

Richard J. Wolfe

It is a well known fact that in 1799, while investigating the applicability of "factitious air" (synthetic gases) to the prevention and cure of disease, the twenty-one year old chemist Humphry Davy studied the effects of the inhalation of nitrous oxide in both man and animals and discovered its analgesic properties. Moreover, in a subjective report published the following year, *Researches, Chemical and Philosophical, Chiefly Concerning Nitrous Oxide, or Dephlogisticated Nitrous Air, and Its Respiration,* a work which made his reputation, Davy suggested that because "nitrous oxide in its extensive operation appears capable of destroying physical pain, it may probably be used with advantage during surgical operations in which no great effusion of blood takes place."[1] As a recent biographer has observed, however, "nobody took any notice of this recommendation. Instead, breathing nitrous oxide for the delightful feeling of intoxication became the rage."[2]

It is also well known that forty-four years later, on the night of December 10, 1844, Horace Wells, a young but well-established dentist of Hartford, Connecticut, escorted his wife Elizabeth to Union Hall in that city to witness a grand exhibition by Gardner Quincy Colton of the exhilarating effects produced by the inhalation of nitrous oxide. While there, he observed Samuel Cooley, a young pharmacist who (along with Wells and others) had volunteered to inhale the laughing gas and had become intoxicated with it, run into and knock over several settees, thereby severely bruising his knees, but yet appeared oblivious to any pain.[3] "Reasoning by analogy," Wells would later write, "I was led to believe that surgical operations might be performed without pain."[4]

On the very next day, December 11, 1844, less that fifteen hours later, Wells had his troublesome wisdom tooth extracted by John Riggs, a fellow dentist, while under the influence of nitrous oxide gas supplied by Colton, without suffering the agony that normally accompanied such an operation. These circumstances set off a chain reaction which resulted just less than two years later in the introduction of anesthesia into medical practice and brought about the inestimable benefit of painless surgery.

The objectives of this study are twofold. First, it will explore why it took forty-five years for Davy's observation to be turned to practical use, and it will attempt to determine whether Wells might have had some prior knowledge of Davy's researches and, because of this, may have gone to Union Hall that night for purposes other than entertainment. Secondly, we will examine the literature—some of it veiled, much of it confused, conflicting and contradictory, and until now most of it ignored—which followed in the wake of Well's discovery. This will show the Hartford dentist to be far more deserving of credit for the discovery of anesthesia than history has previously accorded him.

The Path from Davy to Horace Wells

Humphry Davy conducted his researches on nitrous oxide while employed at Thomas Beddoes's Pneumatic Institution at Clifton, a well-to-do residential suburb of Bristol. Beddoes, eighteen years

Davy's senior, had become interested in chemistry while reading medicine at Pembroke College, Oxford. Convinced that true medical science must have a chemical basis, in 1798 he set up a Pneumatic Institute for treating diseases by the administration of gases, appointing Davy, then nineteen, superintendent. While self-taught in chemistry, Davy had a genius for it, for within five years of reading his first book on chemistry, he became professor of chemistry at the Royal Institution in London. Although Beddoes was well known in his day for his popular works on preventive medicine and his investigations into the use of gases, probably his most important contribution to science was his discovery of Humphry Davy, who went on to become one of England's greatest scientists and discoverer of several chemical elements.

At the time Davy began working for Beddoes, knowledge of some of the gases vital to life was only a quarter of a century old, and many of their properties and physiological effects remained unknown. Joseph Priestley had only discovered oxygen in 1774 and nitrous oxide two years earlier, which he concluded to be not respirable, an opinion that a group of Dutch chemists (who called it gaseous oxide of azote) substantiated in 1793.[5] Davy reportedly began his researches on nitrous oxide because Samuel Latham Mitchill of New York had in 1795 suggested that this gas was the principle of contagion;[6] Davy's work not only disproved Mitchill's theory but proved that the gas, to which he gave the name nitrous oxide, was indeed respirable, a conclusion that was soon confirmed by others who duplicated his experiments. Davy also concluded that nitrous oxide was a powerful diffusible stimulant.

In a much overlooked article which he published in William Nicholson's *Journal of Natural Philosophy, Chemistry, and the Arts* in 1801, outlining his observations on nitrous oxide, Davy summed up his findings on the action of the gas on living bodies.[7] Pointing out that nitrous oxide is respirable, he related that the sensations it occasions are in general analogous to those connected with intoxication from fermented liquors. He also noted that its respiration by healthy persons for a minute or two causes exhilaration and strong pleasurable sensations, with quickened circulation and a sense of warmth; while in unhealthy persons, its effects are less pleasant and in some cases hysterical affections result. Finally, he observed, after being breathed for more than three minutes, nitrous oxide produces violent excitement, which generally ends in momentary loss of sensation. Davy made no reference in this article to the gas's ability to relieve or obliterate pain or to its possible employment in surgery.

As was noted before, Davy's studies on nitrous oxide were quickly noticed and some of his experiments were corroborated by chemists and other interested parties, and information on the gas began to appear almost immediately in contemporary English works on chemistry and in other pertinent literature. As early as 1799 and 1801, Dr. James Parkinson (memorialized today by the debilitating neurologic disease that bears his name) provided brief accounts of Davy and his researches in his *Chemical Pocket-Book, or Memoranda Chemica;*[8] and in 1801, William Henry devoted a page to the "Gaseous Oxyd of Azote—Nitrous Oxyd of Davy" in his *An Epitome of Chemistry,* a work which in its day achieved the status of a "best seller;"[9] information on Davy and nitrous oxide also appeared in the 1802 and subsequent editions of Thomas Thomson's comprehensive textbook on chemistry;[10] in 1804, the English physician John Bostock took notice of Davy's work and referred to his experiments numerous times in his *Essay on Respiration;*[11] in 1806, Samuel Parkes included a nearly three-page discussion of the gas in his *The Chemical Catechism, with Notes, Illustrations, and Experiments;*[12] and chemists on the continent duplicated and substantiated Davy's novel observations at this early time as well.[13]

Finally, before the 1801–1810 decade had run its course, nitrous oxide had also entered the popular literature. In 1806, Mrs. Jane Marcet (1769–1858), an English author who wrote familiarly on scientific subjects for the young female sex, included an account of the gas in her *Conversations on Chemistry,* which appeared initially at London that year. Mrs. Marcet taught the rudiments of chemistry to young ladies by having two fictitious characters, Emily and Caroline, pose questions to "Mrs. B.", who answered them. During their discussion of the combinations of oxygen and nitrogen, the subject of nitrous oxide was raised. Mrs. B. told Caroline that only lately had Mr. Davy examined the properties of this gas, which had also obtained the name of exhilarating gas, and that when it was inhaled into the lungs, something like delirium or intoxication resulted. In answer to Caroline's question as to how one breathed it, Mrs. B. described how it was collected in a bladder and applied to the mouth with one hand, while the nostrils were kept closed with the other. But she would not consent to Caroline making the experiment, for, she explained, the nerves were sometimes unpleasantly affected by it, and she would not run any risk of that kind.

Like Mrs. Marcet's other books, *Conversations on Chemistry* passed through a great many editions, nearly thirty of them appearing in Great Britain and the United States by 1844. In her description of Mrs. Marcet in the *Dictionary of National Biography,* Elizabeth Lee relates that 160,000 copies of this work, her first book, were said to have been sold in the United States before 1853, and the *National Union Catalog* indicates that editions of it appeared at Hartford in 1822, 1826, 1828, 1829, 1830, 1831, 1835, 1836, 1839, 1841 and 1844.[14]

Each commentator discussed Davy's researches in relation to his own particular subject or interest; no one paid any attention to Davy's casual (and terminal; it appeared on page 556 of a 580-page book) allusion to the pain-destroying capability of the gas and its possible use in surgery. Indeed, Davy's allusion can hardly be termed the "recommendation" that was mentioned before; his use of the words "appears" and "may probably" with reference to the gas's ability to destroy pain and its applicability to surgery shows the matter to be on a most indefinite and theoretical plane and indicates that Davy was merely suggesting a possibility rather than recommending a fact. (Davy was probably led to make this suggestion because of his apprenticeship to an apothecary-surgeon in the 1795–1797 or 98 period.)

Furthermore, Beddoes was a physician and Davy was a chemist; in a few years, Beddoes would give up his researches on gases and turn to preventive medicine, and Davy would transfer his attention to other areas of chemistry and never really work with nitrous oxide again.[15] Thus, neither was in a position to carry the observation further, if, indeed, they ever thought of doing so; and there is no evidence that Davy's book on nitrous oxide was noticed in the surgical world at all. In any event, the medical and surgical world of the early nineteenth century was hardly prepared for painless surgery; taking Davy's suggestion a step ahead was inhibited by the medical thought of the period, which was still securely anchored into concepts and theories of the eighteenth century and earlier.

F. F. Cartwright has pointed out in his volume on *The English*

Pioneers of Anaesthesia why it is not remarkable that Davy's suggestion of anesthesia fell upon deaf ears.[16] The outlook of the ordinary eighteenth-century man upon the subject of pain, Cartwright observed, made Davy's idea an entirely new concept. Such an idea, obliterating pain during surgical operations, was opposite to the eighteenth-century attitude to suffering. While attempts had been made in the past to find pain-allaying drugs, pain, Cartwright has reasoned, "was regarded as an inevitable, and even beneficial, concomitant of surgery . . . pain and suffering were held to be of no account; what mattered was not the degree of pain inflicted, but the fortitude with which it could be borne."

Furthermore, the idea that pain could be obliterated or lessened through the inhalation of a gas—a non-solid—was an entirely new concept, one that at the beginning of the nineteenth century would be little understood or accepted. And, as Cartwright has also observed, any suggestion coming from the Pneumatic Institute would have been little heeded by the contemporary medical profession. Pneumatic medicine was by all intents and purposes dead; the wild claims that Beddoes had made had destroyed any faith that the average practitioner might ever have held in the powers of the gases.

Let us now turn our attention to America and see how Davy's researches were received there, for it was here that the young chemist's casual observation would in time advance beyond the theoretical phase. The first notice of nitrous oxide following Davy's experiments with it that I have found in an American book appeared in Dr. Stephen Jacobs's *The Student's Chemical Pocket Companion*, which was first printed for its author at Philadelphia in 1802. (This work would be reprinted in 1807.)[17] Jacobs devoted a little over a page to "Nitrous oxyde," or the gaseous oxide of azote of Dr. Mitchill, or the dephlogisticated nitrous air of Dr. Priestley, summing up its chemical constituents and properties, but nowhere mentioning Davy or his investigations, although, strangely enough, he now referred to the agent by the name that Davy had given to it. (Nor would Davy or his experiments be mentioned in the 1807 edition, which was a word-for-word reprinting of the earlier one.)

Nonetheless, cognizance was taken of Davy's experiments in 1802 when Dr. James Woodhouse, professor of chemistry at the University of Pennsylvania, began trying to duplicate them. Woodhouse, however, did not publish his findings until 1807, when he devoted several pages to Davy and nitrous oxide gas in his edition (the fourth American one) of M.I.A. Chaptal's *Elements of Chemistry,* to which he had made additions, the most important of which, for our purposes, were the inclusion of his experiments and experiences with nitrous oxide gas.[18] Woodhouse devoted almost all of the first five pages of Chapter IV, "Concerning the Muriatic Acid," to reporting on nitrous oxide and the results he had obtained when administering it to a great many students in his chemical class, first in 1802 and again in 1806. As a result of these experiments, which he described in detail, Woodhouse related that, "I am now convinced the gas produces all the effects ascribed to it, by the justly celebrated Mr. Davy; and I am happy in having this opportunity of confirming his experiments." Woodhouse concluded his notice of nitrous oxide by reprinting a letter on the subject which he had received from professor Benjamin Silliman of Yale College. Silliman reported that he too had lately given the gas a full and fair trial and, as a result, was able "to confirm in the most satisfactory manner, Mr. Davy's account of the effects of this wonderful agent."

In the following year, Woodhouse repeated some of his findings in an article, "Observations on the Effects of Nitrous Oxide, When Taken into the Lungs," which he published in John Redman Coxe's *Philadelphia Medical Museum.*[19] And in that same year, 1808, was published an even more extensive account of nitrous oxide and its effects, the most extensive report to appear after Davy's original one, when William P.C. Barton, one of the students who had inhaled the gas during Woodhouse's experiments with it, chose nitrous oxide as the subject of his medical dissertation. In this work, which he titled *A Dissertation on the Chymical Properties and Exhilarating Effects of Nitrous Oxide Gas; and Its Application to Pneumatick Medicine,* Barton described how he had repeated Davy's experiments, and he provided a vivid description of the sensations experienced during its inhalation.[20]

Barton, whose early work and publications were oriented toward the fields of materia medica and medical botany, never referred in his dissertation to Davy's concluding remark about the potential use of nitrous oxide in surgery, not did Woodhouse or any other early commentator whose works I have examined. However, when describing how he had inhaled the gas after he had accidentally struck his head violently on the edge of a door, Barton stated that "I am decidedly of the opinion with Mr. Davy, that his gas has the power of removing intense physical pain,"[21] indicating that he was aware of Davy's observation; but, like Davy, he did nothing to exploit the idea of using the gas as a surgical anesthetic.

When describing its properties, Dr. Barton related that nitrous oxide gas was respirable for a limited time, producing exhilaration of spirits and increased muscular strength, which were not followed by somnolency or languor. When breathed too long, it induced fainting, and in its most extensive operation was capable of extinguishing life, both in man and in animals. One of his most important observations was the following:

> When Mr. Davy first respired nitrous oxide, he breathed it only in small quantities, and mingled with common air. In these trials, though not decided in his opinion, he inclined to the idea that it acted as a depressing power. This suspicion received a temporary support from the result of the experiments made by other persons, who, in consequence of their fears were at first temporarily affected. Subsequent and satisfactory trials, however, made by numerous persons with the pure gas, entirely exploded this opinion, and it is now proved to be a powerful stimulant, and one entirely *sui generis*.[22]

Although Fulton and Stanton assert that Barton's thesis did much to rouse interest in the use of nitrous oxide inhalations,[23] I have found little evidence that any special attention was paid in America to nitrous oxide in the decade following the publication of Barton's studies on it. No one, in Europe or in America, seemed to know what to do with the gas. It continued to be described in chemistry textbooks that were published into the 1820s, such as Henry's,[24] Thomson's,[25] Parkes',[26] Orfila's,[27] Gorham's,[28] and Brande's,[29] but only in a brief and usual way. It was not mentioned at all in the London or Edinburgh pharmacopoeias, or in other early nineteenth-century dispensatories, with the exception of Andrew Duncan's *The Edinburgh New Dispensatory*, beginning with the 1803 edition, the first to be issued following Davy's work with nitrous oxide,[30] and, in America, John Redman Coxe's *The American Dispensatory*, which professed to derive much of its information from Duncan's work. Information on nitrous oxide in *The Edinburgh New Dispensatory* was extremely brief, amounting to a single paragraph devoted to a chemical description alone; however, while the first edition of Coxe's work, published in 1806, basically reprinted Duncan's description, in the second, 1810 edition of *The American Dispensatory,* Coxe did add the comment, possibly influenced to do so by Barton's and Woodhouse's work with the gas, "when perfectly pure, or mixed with atmospheric air, [it] produces the highest excitement of which the animal frame seems capable." This added comment continued to be reprinted in all successive editions of Coxe's *American Dispensatory* until 1831, when the last one appeared.[31] Nonetheless, no one in medicine seemed to know what to employ nitrous oxide for or for what purpose it might be used.

A somewhat lengthy description of the "protoxyde of azote" appeared in the second edition of the English translation of M.P. Orfila's well known treatise on poisons, published at London in 1818.[32] No mention was made, however, of its pain-inhibiting action or of its possible use in surgery or even in medicine, for that matter, despite the fact that the translator of this edition, John Augustine Waller, identified himself on its title-page as "Surgeon." Orfila merely discussed research that had gone on in Europe, primarily before 1810, on the effects of the gas on the animal economy. He paid special attention to the experiments conducted in France by P.H. Nysten, who, in following out Xavier Bichat's physiological researches upon life and death, was injecting animals with differing amounts of nitrous oxide and other chemical substances in order to determine tolerance and other reactions. Nysten had reported his results in 1811.[33]

When Andrew Ure published the first edition of his *Dictionary of Chemistry* at London in 1821, he included a page-and-a-half description of nitrous oxide or protoxide of azote in it, summarizing its chemical aspects and reporting in detail from Davy's 1800 treatise many of the strange effects that occurred after it had been inspired. However, he provided no new information on the gas and said absolutely nothing about any applicability it may have had to medicine— in fact, the subjects medicine and surgery were not mentioned at all.[34]

Interest in nitrous oxide seems to have continued in the 1820 decade, with notice of it appearing in new editions of the textbooks of Henry and Parkes and in many other works in the field of chemistry that were noted before.[35] The descriptions that were printed in ill-fated Harvard professor John White Webster's 1826 *Manual of Chemistry*,[36] Edward Turner's 1827 *Elements of Chemistry*,[37] and Jacob Green's *Textbook of Chemical Philosophy*,[38] are typical of how the new gas had come to be considered and treated. Webster devoted three-and-a-half pages to the chemistry of the gas, making a brief allusion to Davy and its respiration; Turner followed suit; and Dr. Green, professor of chemistry at Jefferson Medical College in Philadelphia, provided a page-and-a-half resume of its physical and chemical properties and noted that Davy had discovered that nitrous oxide could be taken into the lungs with safety, describing some of the reactions that followed its inhalation, such as feelings of excitement similar to the early stages of intoxication, a strong propensity to laughter (hence the alternative name "laughing gas"), a rapid flow of vivid ideas, and an unusual disposition to muscular exertion.

As in the past, little or no attention was paid to nitrous oxide in works on materia medica and therapeutics, and it was left entirely unnoticed in most pharmacopoeias and dispensatories that appeared during the first three decades of the nineteenth century.[39] Works that did mention it indicated that no use had yet been found for it in medicine. However, events occurring at the beginning of the 1830 decade were to bring about a temporary change of view.

Cholera, which became epidemic in India in 1817 and pandemic in the decade following, reached England in 1831 and North America in the following year, leaving widespread death in its path. Dr. Eugene H. Conner, an anesthesiologist, has observed in an article on "Anesthetics in the Treatment of Cholera" how a number of anesthetic agents, such as nitrous oxide, diethyl ether, and chloroform, were tried in attempts to treat patients afflicted with the disease.[40] Since the contagiousness of cholera was not then recognized, Conner observed, direct therapeutic approach to control the disease was not possible; and while the use of anesthetics might seems ridiculous in light of our present knowledge, their use as a response to cholera could be rationalized in the 1830s on the basis of prevalent eighteenth-century medical concepts. Dr. Conner has argued that the rationale for the use of nitrous oxide and similar anesthetic agents in the treatment of cholera found justification in the system of medicine proposed by Dr. John Brown (1735–1788) in 1780, which, even as late as the 1830s, was still embraced by many practitioners.

"The Brunonian system," Conner relates, "is quite simple. 'The indication for the cure of sthenic diathesis, [he quoted from the 1791 Philadelphia edition of Brown's *Elements of Medicine,* which reprinted an English one] is to diminish, that for the cure of asthenic diathesis is to encrease the excitement, and to continue to encrease it . . .'." No patient, Conner observes, could be better characterized as manifesting an asthenic diathesis or showing "depression of vital spirits" than a victim in the third stage of cholera or the stage of collapse. The patient was dehydrated to such an extent that his skin was wrinkled and discolored with scattered areas of lividity; his lips and nailbeds were cyanosed; his pulse was barely, if at all, palpable; and he was too weak to cry out. This appearance of the victim of cholera was so frequent that the term "cholera asphyxia" came to be applied. The application of Brunonian concepts to such a moribund patient clearly demanded the use of a drug that would stimulate the vital spirits and counteract the apparent state of asphyxia, and the bulk of knowledge available in the early 1830s indicated that nitrous oxide, which was looked upon as a powerful stimulant, would be ideal for this purpose.

The exhilarating properties of nitrous oxide, as evidenced by the hilarious and boisterous behavior of those inhaling it, were widely known. Conner has written

> That medical and scientific thought in the early decades of the 19th century was completely oriented toward considering nitrous oxide as a stimulant is also apparent from the disregard of the temporary unconsciousness sometimes produced by inhalation of the gas. Loss of consciousness was simply ascribed to 'a faint,' and such occasional observations failed to interfere with the predominance of Brunonian thinking.

As one example of how earlier medical thought still prevailed in this period, Conner has cited Dr. Samuel Jackson's system of therapeutics, as enunciated in his *Principles of Medicine* issued at Philadelphia in 1832, which fully embraced the principles of John Brown.[41] Furthermore, Conner refers to a number of writings published in 1831 and 1832 which recommend the use of nitrous oxide as a specific to counteract the depression of strength brought about by cholera. Noting that reports of the use of nitrous oxide in the treatment of cholera became less frequent by 1833 as physicians learned that it was not effective, Conner iterates that its use in the treatment of cholera was predicted on the erroneous concept that, as a stimulant, Brunonian theory dictated its use in counteracting such a depressing disease, and he concluded by saying:

> It is not strange then that Humphry Davy's statement that nitrous oxide was a powerful diffusible stimulant[42] should have received world-wide trial and his recommendation for the employment of the same gas for the relief of pain in surgical operations went unheard, although printed in the same monograph, and but a few pages further on.

When, in 1833, George B. Wood and Franklin Bache of Philadelphia issued the first of a long run of editions of the *Dispensatory of the United States*, the largest compilation of its type to be issued in America to that time, they said nothing about nitrous oxide—in fact, the gas would not be described in this work until the tenth edition of 1854.[43] However, cognizance had been taken of nitrous oxide gas, and the strange behavior it elicited, on a wider scale, outside of the fields of chemistry and medicine, when, in the previous year, Sir David Brewster, a well-known natural scientist who made original contributions to the field of optics, published a book he called *Letters on Natural Magic*, a work intended for popular reading.[44] Brewster's book took the form of letters addressed to Sir Walter Scott, who, in the first one, Brewster acknowledged, had suggested that he undertake a popular account "of those prodigies of the material world which have received the appellation of *Natural Magic.*"

In effect, Brewster's letters were intended to show how phenomena, which had been looked upon as magical in former times, were really attributable to natural causes and could be explained through later scientific discoveries and inventions. Brewster used various branches of science—optics, hydrostatics, acoustics, mechanics, chemistry, etc.—to expose deceptions and impostures and explain matters that had been viewed as magic, by providing a scientific basis for them instead of the magical ones that had been attributed to them through ignorance and superstition. At the very end of his book of over 300 pages, Brewster discussed, among the wonders of chemistry, "the remarkable effects produced upon the human frame by the inhalation of *paradise* or *intoxicating gas,* as it has been called . . . known to chymists as *nitrous oxide,* or the *gaseous oxide of azote,* or the *protoxide of nitrogen.*"

Brewster devoted a full seven pages to nitrous oxide, explaining briefly its background and chemistry. But the bulk of his attention was focused on Humphry Davy and the experiments he had conducted on it. Brewster concluded from Davy's reports that the gas affected different people in different ways. In the gravest and most phlegmatic persons its effect was to produce the highest degree of exhilaration and happiness, unaccompanied by languor or depression. In some, it created an irresistible disposition to laugh, and in others a propensity to muscular exertion; in others, it impaired the intellectual functions; and in several it had no sensible effect, even when it was breathed in its purest state and in considerable quantities.

Although Sir (he had by this time long been knighted) Humphry Davy experienced no unpleasant effects from nitrous oxide, Brewster reported, such effects were nonetheless produced. As examples, he related two cases which had been reported by Professor Silliman of Yale College. Silliman's students had been in the habit of preparing this gas and administering it to one another, and in two cases, the only remarkable ones that had been observed, the gas had brought about strange effects. In one student, it caused violent behavior. The student later reported that his feelings alternated between perfect happiness and consummate misery, and this effect remained for a period of three days. In the other, it had a remarkable effect upon the organs of taste, with the student manifesting a craving for everything that was sweet and using such articles of food in inordinate ways, for example, pouring molasses over beef, fish, potatoes, cabbage, and whatever was placed before him, and this he continued to do for eight weeks or more.

Brewster derived his information on Silliman's remarkable cases from an article that had appeared in Silliman's *American Journal of Science and the Arts* in 1822.[45] Just short of a decade later, Silliman would devote a full eight pages to nitrous oxide or the protide of nitrogen in his *Elements of Chemistry, in the Order of the Lectures Given in Yale College.*[46] His account here is one of the most complete reports of the composition, physical and chemical properties, and actions and effects of this gas which I have noticed in a textbook, and especially an American textbook, to this time. And it was accompanied by an illustration of the "Apparatus for evolving and preserving nitrous oxide Gas" (Illustration 1) which Dr. Hare of the University of Pennsylvania had included along with an account of the "Protoxide of Nitrogen, or Nitrous Oxide" in his *Compendium of the Course of Chemical Instruction in the Medical Department of the University of Pennsylvania,* a work that went through four editions between the years 1828 and 1840.[47] Silliman remarked that

> Although we can offer no satisfactory theory to account for the action of the nitrous oxide [i.e., its causing exhilaration or, in other cases, fits, swoons, fainting, troubled dreams, and even violent delirium, as he mentioned before], it cannot but be regretted, that so powerful a stimulus both in our physical and in[t]ellectual powers should remain a subject of mere curiosity or merriment. Differing from every other stimulus, in not producing depression correspondent to the excitement; why should it not be employed as a general tonic and as a comforting reviving remedy? In cases of great debility, it clearly ought not to be used in such doses, as to produce violent effects, but rather such as are gentle and longer continued, which might then be more frequently renewed. It would be proper to begin with diluting the gas one half or more, with common air, and the strength and quantity might thus be graduated to the state and strength of the patient.

From the early 1830s, until the mid 1840s, when Horace Wells made his momentous discovery, nitrous oxide was discussed in almost every chemistry book that came into print and in an occasional book on materia medica. As before, information provided was restricted to its chemistry, its manufacture, Davy's experiments with it, and the strange behavior that it provoked. Such discussions appeared in an edition of Turner's *Elements of Chemistry* which Franklin Bache edited and which was published at Philadelphia in 1830,

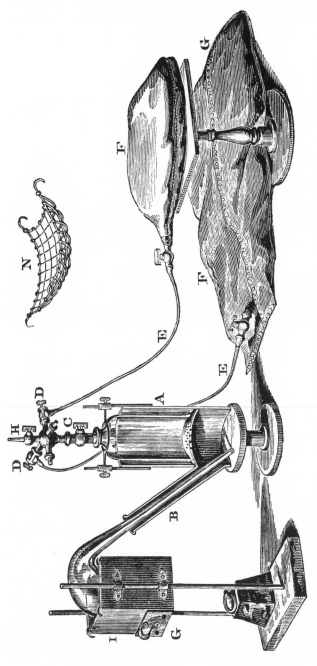

Illustration 1. Apparatus for evolving and preserving nitrous oxide gas that was developed by Dr. Robert Hare of the University of Pennsylvania. This illustration accompanies the discussion of nitrous oxide in Benjamin Silliman's *Elements of Chemistry in the Order of the Lectures Given in Yale College*, 1830 (v. 1, opposite p. 482). The same wood engraving was previously published in Hare's *Compendium of the Course of Chemical Instruction in the Medical Department of the University of Pennsylvania*, which came out in four editions between 1828 and 1840. Courtesy of the Boston Medical Library in the Francis A. Countway Library of Medicine.

1832, and 1840; [48] in Lewis C. Beck's *Manual of Chemistry* that first appeared at Albany in 1831 and in a fourth edition at New York by 1844;[49] in the many editions of Mrs. Marcet's *Conversations on Chemistry* that appeared at Hartford and elsewhere during this time;[50] in James Renwick's *First Principles of Chemistry*, which Harper and Brothers issued at New York in 1842;[51] and in the American edition of Sir Robert Kane's *Elements of Chemistry* that Harper reprinted in 1843 from its Dublin edition in 1842 or 1843;[52] as well as in editions of Henry's book and in other standard chemical texts that were also issued during this interval.

Of course, experiments with nitrous oxide continued to be carried on and demonstrated in medical and chemical classes like Silliman's—indeed, it was while studying medicine at the College of Physicians and Surgeons in New York City that Gardner Colton learned about the exhilarating effects of the gas and began to give lectures and demonstrations in New York and neighboring communities—but its use by the lay public as a curiosity at "nitrous oxide sniffing parties" supposedly went on at this time also.

Although it is unlikely that Horace Wells ever saw a copy of it, an English book somewhat akin to Brewster's popular work provides a delightful insight into the manner in which nitrous oxide sniffing was carried on in the late 1830s, and furnishes a humorous illustration of it by George Cruikshank (Illustration 2). The book is made up of a series of popular lectures on chemistry by John Scoffern which were published in 1839 under the title *Chemistry No Mystery; or, A Lecturer's Bequest*.[53] Scoffern, who listed himself on the title page as "Surgeon; and Late Assistant Chemist at the London Hospital, and Aldergate School of Medicine," devoted several pages to laughing gas and the scene that ensued after it was inhaled.

After a number of bladders had been handed around, Scoffern related, the lecture room was broken by deep-drawn inspirations of those breathing the gas. Everybody seemed to be enjoying the extreme of happiness; they puffed and pulled as if they could not get enough. Shortly thereafter, they cast the bladders from their faces with a jerk, and unmindful of the ridiculous figures they made, kept breathing laboriously, their mouths thrown wide open, their noses still tightly clenched. Some jumped over tables and chairs; some were bent upon making speeches; some were inclined to fight; and one

Illustration 2. A depiction of "laughing gas sniffing" in London in the late 1830s. Drawn or painted by George Cruikshank and engraved on wood by E. Evans, and added as a preliminary title-page to John Scoffern's *Chemistry No Mystery; or, A Lecturer's Bequest*, published at London in 1839. Courtesy of the Harvard Medical Library in The Francis A. Countway Library of Medicine.

young man persisted in attempting to kiss the ladies. (The last described, it was insinuated, had breathed little of the gas and knew very well what he was doing.)

A few minutes served to restore the maniacs to their senses, and they afterwards felt as if nothing had occurred; for, as Scoffern remarked, it is a peculiarity of this gas that it does not act like intoxicating liquors in producing depression or other unpleasant effects. Such antics, of course, were probably mostly confined to chemical and medical lecture rooms and to demonstrations like Scoffern's and Colton's; because of the danger involved, and the difficulty in making and preserving the gas, it is unlikely that, with few exceptions, they went on at parties in the parlors of private homes, as might be supposed.

Accounts of nitrous oxide undoubtedly appeared in other popular works as well. One such American publication that has come to the author's attention is James Pilkington's *The Artist's and Mechanic's Repository, and Working Man's Informant; Embracing Chemistry, Abstracts of Electricity, Galvanism, Magnetism, Mechanics, Pneumatics, Optics, and Astronomy,* which was issued at Philadelphia in 1841.[54] Over half of Pilkington's text is devoted to the subject of chemistry, into which he has woven a page and a half on nitrous oxide. After providing the essentials of the gas's chemistry, Pilkington devotes most of its attention to its respiration, observing that

> It may be respired for a few minutes; and the extraordinary effects it produces on the system, during its respiration, and for a short time after, occasions it to be frequently made for this purpose, which is the only use (if it may be called use,) to which it may be applied.

After reviewing the involuntary physiological and psychological reactions it produces, and the enjoyment that many derive from inhaling it, Pilkington relates that there are others on whom it produces less favorable effects and cautions those who have never breathed it or who are not in perfect health to take it for the first time in only a small dose. He also advises those intending to inhale it to make sure that it is perfectly pure, and he gives directions for making certain that it is properly prepared.

Some of the works on materia medica that came out in the 1830s paid a little more attention to the gas, but the information provided was still quite limited. For example, Jonathan Pereira's *Elements of Materia Medica,* issued at London in 1839, told about the history, preparation, properties, characteristics and physiological effects of the gas but said little different from the information provided in other works on this subject or in the field of chemistry. It did tell, however, that while it was employed in only a few cases of disease, it was found beneficial in the treatment of paralysis and spasmodic asthma.[55]

Information on poisoning by nitrous oxide was reported in Robert Christison's *Treatise on Poison,* which was printed at Edinburgh in four editions between 1829 and 1845, but was limited to but a single page.[56] Christison related, when referring to experiments that had been carried out by Thenard in France earlier in the century, that two of Thenard's assistants, on making experiments with nitrous oxide, had fainted away, and remained for some seconds motionless and insensible.[57] (A report of the unpleasant sensations and injurious and alarming effects produced by the inhalation of nitrous oxide, due probably to impurities in the gas, had been made by Michael Faraday in 1820; and, in late 1842, on the eve of Horace Wells's discovery, there appeared an account of the poisoning of three students who had inhaled an impure state of the gas.)[58] Christison also observed that

> It is a remarkable circumstance in the operation of this gas, that, unlike other stimulants, it does not lose its virtues under the influence of habit. Neither does the habitual use of it lead to any ill consequences. *Sir H. Davy,* in the course of his researches, which were continued above two months, breathed it occasionally three or four times a-day for a week together, at other periods four or five times a-week only; yet at the end his health was good, his mind clear, his digestion perfect, and his strength only a little impaired.[59]

We have seen that none of the works on chemistry or on materia medica and pharmacy cited before took notice of nitrous oxide for its pain-obliterating qualities, or of Davy's reference to its possible use in surgery. Nonetheless, a few attempts were made from the 1820s on to find a means of alleviating pain during surgical operations, and they should be mentioned here, despite the fact that none of them involved nitrous oxide gas or chemical agents which later came to be employed as anesthetics, and none of them led to or resulted in surgical anesthesia.

The first such attempt was carried out by Henry Hill Hickman, a young English surgeon who conceived the idea of employing carbonic acid gas (carbon dioxide) to suspend animation during surgery. Cartwright devotes a sizable part of his book on the English pioneers of anesthesia to Hickman and the experimental operations he performed on animals under the influence of this agent. Although Hickman reported his experiments in 1824 in a small pamphlet of fourteen pages which reportedly survives in but a single known copy today, and afterwards attempted to make his work better known in England and France, he met with no success. He died a few years later at the age of thirty, and his researches slipped into oblivion, only to be renoticed a century after his death.[60]

While Hickman carried on part of his experiments at Shifnal, the place where the pneumatic physician Thomas Beddoes had been born, he appears to have known little or nothing of Beddoes's work and did not have any knowledge of Humphry Davy's researches with nitrous oxide. As Cartwright has observed, Hickman's experiments were performed only on animals; they did not aim to produce anesthesia as we know it today, but were designed to produce insensibility by means of controlled asphyxia. Hickman attempted only to produce a temporary and reversible suspension of life and freedom from pain during which swift and less bloody operations could be carried out. In 1829, another Englishman, William Wright, recommended the use of carbonic acid gas for relieving pain caused by inflammation of the middle ear. And, interestingly enough, he began his description of the use of the gas with the comment:

> Such has been the quackery relative to the medical administration of aërial fluids, that it has disgusted most of the medical profession, and caused agents that are probably very useful, under proper modifications, to be abandoned. My object in noticing this gas here, is, that it may be applied, if there be deep-seated pain in the auditory passage . . . [61]

Other attempts at carrying out surgery under painless or less painful circumstances were made in the early 1840s by several English surgeons (John Elliston, James, Esdaile, and James Braid) who resorted to mesmerism or hypnosis to effect anesthesia during operations. These, as well as the Hickman and Wright use of gas, are described and discussed in the Fulton-Stanton catalog. They must be looked upon merely as interesting sidelights in the history of anesthesia and signs of a growing recognition by surgeons or some surgeons, at least, of the need to combat the pain of surgery. All of these methods were uncertain in their action and met only with a limited degree of success; and they exerted no influence on the events that transpired at Hartford on December 10 and 11, 1844.

This concludes our survey of nitrous oxide from Humphry Davy's researches with the gas in the 1798–1800 period to the eve of Horace Wells's employment of it on December 11, 1844 for the purpose of painless dentistry. Quite naturally, the question arises as to how much Wells might have known about nitrous oxide prior to attending Colton's grand demonstration of its strange effects. Could he have been aware of Davy's allusion to its pain-inhibiting power and its possible application to surgical operations when going to Union Hall on December 10, 1844 to observe its remarkable action?

We find no clues in the fragments of Well's library that have survived. The only two works on chemistry among the books which he is known to have owned—with the exception of Amos Eaton's *Botanical Grammar,* and a few later publications acquired by his family, all are non-medical and non-scientific—[62] are Joseph Black's *Lectures on the Elements of Chemistry,* issued at Philadelphia in 1806, and David Blair's (i.e. Sir Richard Phillip's) *Grammar of Chemistry,* published at Philadelphia in 1823.

Dr. Black died in 1799 and his lectures first were published posthumously at Edinburgh in 1803.[63] While he does discuss azotic gas, it is only with relation to Cavendish's and Lavoisier's work with it; Humphry Davy had only begun publishing on nitrous oxide in 1799, and it seems likely that Black knew little or nothing of his researches. Phillips's *Grammar* provided only the barest information about nitrous oxide, namely, the manner in which it was procured, that it supports combustion better than oxygen does, and that when breathed into the lungs it communicates a pleasurable or intoxicating sensation.[64] Clearly, Phillips's book was an elementary text, intended for beginners, and no more. The fact that Well's copy contains the date "1831" along with his signature indicates that Phillips may have introduced him to the science of chemistry when he was sixteen years old.

Nonetheless, Well's study and practice of dentistry from about 1835 on must have brought him into closer contact with chemistry and with the advanced texts available at that time. Furthermore, he was a scientific and resourceful man, as is proved by his investigation of daguerrotypy soon after its discovery had been announced, a matter which is discussed at another place in this book (see p. 328), and by his invention of dental instruments, a coal-sifter and a shower bath. The dental instruments he contrived are mentioned in the article by Drs. Ring and Menczer on Wells's dentistry, and the patents he obtained for the latter two inventions are described and discussed in W. Harry Archer's "Life and Letters of Horace Wells."[65] Clearly, his was an original, inventive, and creative mind.[66]

Whether Wells knew about Brewster's and Silliman's books, or about the other works on chemistry and materia medica that have been mentioned here, we can only conjecture. Brewster's book was a popular one, oriented toward mass reading. (And the fact that he addressed his letters to Sir Walter Scott, whose works were in great vogue at that time, could not have but helped sell copies.) The series title, "Harper's Family Library, No. L," which its American publishers J. & J. Harper printed on its pasteboard cover (and its English publisher also, who used a similar series note), is indicative of the audience they intended it for. *The National Union Catalog of Pre-1956 Imprints* [67] shows that between 1832, the date of its first English edition, and 1842, it had appeared in five London editions; J. & J. Harper of New York brought out its first American edition in 1832 also, stereotyped it (which indicates that many printings would ensue) and reissued it in 1833, 1835, 1836, 1838, 1839 and 1842, and the book continued to be printed here and abroad until at least 1883. Between 1832 and 1844, when Wells ushered in painless dentistry, at least 10,000 copies must have been printed, and it is likely that production was many times that number. As for Silliman's book, we have only to remember that it appeared at neighboring New Haven, about forty miles removed from Hartford, and was within Well's easy reach.

One important point stands out, however. Regardless of whether or not Wells knew about Humphry Davy's researches, from one or more of the many references mentioned here, the fact remains—and it must be emphasized—that following Barton's dissertation on nitrous oxide back in 1808, no published work associated the gas with the obliteration of pain. Davy's casual observation seems to have been noticed by Barton and by Barton alone, who, like Davy, had no idea then of exploiting its possible use in surgery. Afterwards, reference was made to the gas mainly in works outside of medicine— its use in cholera excepted, which was an experimental affair, based on incorrect medical thought, and soon proved to be of little value. Discussion of it was confined almost entirely to the field of chemistry and to a few works on materia medica. However, none of this literature mentioned the gas's ability to mitigate or temporarily abolish pain. As the Silliman and other chemical texts indicate, nitrous oxide was demonstrated to medical and chemistry students as a curiosity; they breathed it for the exhilaration it produced and to gain first-hand knowledge of the curious behavior that resulted. In short, it portrayed the role of the court jester in that era's chemical kingdom.

Taking all of these circumstances into account, it seems certain that Horace Wells had no knowledge of the pain-alleviating property of nitrous oxide when he escorted Elizabeth to Union Hall on the night of December 10, 1844. This, of course, does not rule out the strong probability that he was acquainted with much or some of the literature that we have discussed and, being aware of the strange behavior that the gas provoked, wished to see more of its interesting effects and allow his wife to be entertained in the process, for after all, this matter was discussed in just about all the chemistry books then at hand. Thus, the deduction that Wells made when observing Samuel Cooley to be without pain from his injury *was an original one*. He made the same observation that Humphry Davy did forty-four or forty-five years before. In effect, he rediscovered the analgesic power of nitrous oxide after a long period of disregard, or, otherwise stated, *he discovered it anew*. However, unlike Davy, Wells had the surgical background and clinical imagination to immediately put his deduction to the test; and within fifteen hours or so after the Colton demonstration, inhalation anesthesia would be born.

There is another argument to be made that Well's deduction was an original one. Had he had available a copy of Davy's *Researches* and read it, it seems likewise certain that, given his imaginative and creative mind, he would have immediately have put Davy's suggestion to the test. After all, it took him only a little more that half a day to translate his observation of Cooley's painless injury into painless dentistry. From the 1830s on, dentistry had been making great strides, particularly mechanical dentistry in the hands of Nathan Cooley Keep of Boston, who may have been Well's teacher. Dentistry was being held back, however, by the pain and suffering that accompanied it. Dentists, working in the sensitive mouth and directly underneath the brain, were acutely aware—probably even more than surgeons were—of the pain they caused and of patients' reluctance to undergo dental procedures because of the intense pain and suffering that resulted.

Clearly, dentists had to find some aid to help them perform their work with less pain resulting, or, ideally, with no pain at all, a matter that must often have been on Well's mind.[68] So that when Wells observed young Cooley to be without pain, despite the fact that his knees and legs had been severely injured, he was able to make the instant transference of thought that brought about this desired result.[69] Wells, in effect, possessed that particular requisite that all the others before him did not, that element that Pasteur would later refer to when, while discussing the nature of scientific discovery, he observed that "chance only favors the prepared mind."[70]

The Path from Wells to
William Thomas Green Morton

Horace Wells claimed to have quickly followed up the December 11 operation with twelve or fifteen more, with the same results, and the later testimony of patients and other participants and witnesses backs him up. However, despite his initial success, when the Boston surgeon Henry J. Bigelow announced the discovery of painless surgery to the world on November 18, 1846,[71] less than two years afterward, the chemical agent identified with bringing it about was not nitrous oxide, but sulfuric ether; and the person credited with the discovery was not Horace Wells, but William

Thomas Green Morton, Wells's former preceptee, and, in 1843, his partner in a short-lived dental practice.[72] And less than fifteen months later, Horace Wells would be dead at the age of thirty-three, the victim of his own hand.

The dramatic success of the three ether trials conducted at the Massachusetts General Hospital between October 16 and November 7, 1846, and the support of Morton and ether by the prestigious Boston medical community, swept Horace Wells and nitrous oxide into the background; and in the ensuing bitter debate over who was the discoverer of anesthesia, as others came forward to press their claims, and because he was no longer alive to advance his, Wells and nitrous oxide were obliterated even more. As a result of the dramatic events of late 1846, credit for the discovery of painless surgery would henceforth revolve not around the question of who was the discoverer of inhalation anesthesia, but who was the discoverer of ether anesthesia.

From the time of its introduction as an anesthetic in late 1846, ether proved to be the more viable agent for achieving deep muscle relaxation, and the more reliable one and the one more easily prepared as well. It also maintained and controlled the unconscious state for a longer time, and hence was the one better suited to surgical operations. In time, however, nitrous oxide would be resurrected by Gardner Quincy Colton for use in dental operations (which were of shorter duration), in the performance of which it has served admirably ever since. When discussing the introduction of surgical anesthesia in his *English Pioneers of Anesthesia*, F.F. Cartwright came close to hitting the center of the target when, in referring to the merits of the rival claimants, he observed,

> Two to me stand out: Horace Wells who employed nitrous oxide, and William Thomas Green Morton who used ether. Of one thing there can be no possible doubt; the general acceptance of anaesthesia dates from Morton's successful demonstration of October 16, 1846. But Morton did not himself think of anaesthesia and immediately employ ether; he already knew that Wells had had a limited success with nitrous oxide, for he was a friend and perhaps at one time a partner of Wells, and he had himself used nitrous oxide which he discarded as being too unreliable for general use. That Wells introduced anesthesia into limited use is certain; Morton's claim to fame lies in the

fact that he introduced the only feasible method of administering a reliable anaesthetic with the primitive apparatus at his command. It was, in fact, not the men Wells and Morton who introduced anaesthesia into general use, but the drug Ether.[73]

While it is impossible to deny Wells his original discovery, a careful study of the evidence leads to the conclusion that his loss of favor early in the anesthesia story is attributable to the fact that he backed the wrong drug. We have to realize, however, that he was traveling an untrodden trail—the very first person to do so—and could not judge the pitfalls ahead. Furthermore, he appears to have been the victim of poor advice from those he was associating and consulting with, although it is obvious that they, too, were walking the same blind path that he was. On the other hand, Morton came later and built on the experience of Wells and others, and, initially, enjoyed the best of luck and got good advice—and good luck and good advice, it appears, played a leading role in the initial ether drama.

There is ample evidence attesting that soon after his initial discovery, Wells considered employing sulfuric ether in his operations, but rejected the option, and, under the circumstances, did so for valid reasons. Contrary to the situation with nitrous oxide, ether, in its various forms, was described in the pharmacopoeias and materia medicas from early on. By the early nineteenth century, a great deal was known about ether, and it had been included in the pharmaceutical and chemical literature for quite a long time. Silliman, in his 1830–1831 textbook, devoted nearly a dozen pages to it, describing in depth the properties and manufacture of ether in its various varieties: sulfuric ether, oleum aethereum (or oil of wine), phosphoric ether, muriatic ether, hydriodic ether, and nitric ether, of which the first was the most important, the purest, and the one most frequently used in medicine.[74] Silliman related that sulfuric ether was used, in relation to the animal economy, either as a diffusible stimulant or is inhaled as a vapor in cases of difficult breathing, in which case, it provided instantaneous relief.

Jonathan Pereira's 1839 *Elements of Materia Medica* also devoted considerable space and attention to this agent, and to its various forms.[75] Pereira provided more than a full page of information on sulfuric ether and its medical uses. Ether could be taken internally in small amounts for various ailments, or it could be inhaled for relief in cases of spasmodic asthma, chronic catarrh (hay fever), dyspnoea, and whooping cough, and for relief of the effects caused by the accidental inhalation of chlorine gas. Commonly used for such purposes from early in the nineteenth century, and sometimes even before, ether was readily available from dealers in pharmaceuticals and over the counter in drug stores. However, forms other that sulfuric ether—nitric ether, for example—were less pure, and when used indiscretely, sometimes caused serious problems and even death. Thus, ether was employed cautiously and was considered by many a dangerous drug. Finally, ether was demonstrated along with nitrous oxide in classes on chemistry in academies, colleges and medical schools, and its similarity to nitrous oxide in causing exhilaration and lessening sensation was pointed out and was well known.

Shortly after Bigelow's announcement in mid-November 1846 of the discovery of ether anesthesia, Pinckney Webster Ellsworth, a Hartford surgeon, rushed to Wells's defense. Ellsworth, a maternal grandson of the lixicographer Noah Webster and son of ex-governor of Connecticut William W. Ellsworth, had, a year previously, actually published the very first reference to the use of nitrous oxide as an anesthetic, but unfortunately it was a veiled one. In an article that was printed in the *Boston Medical and Surgical Journal* on June 18, 1845 (about six months after Wells's discovery), "On the Modus Operandi of Medicines," Ellsworth related that "The nitrous oxide gas has been used in quite a number of cases by our dentists, during the extraction of teeth, and has been found, by its excitement, perfectly to destroy pain. The patients appear very merry during the operation, and no unpleasant effects follow."[76] Now, in a second communication to the *Boston Medical and Surgical Journal* in early December 1846, Ellsworth was attempting to give a fuller account of the discovery.[77] (Ellsworth's second communication, coincidentally, appeared in print on the same day, December 9, 1846, that the *Hartford Courant* published Well's own account of his discovery.)[78]

Ellsworth related in his December 9 article that the first announcement of painless surgery had been made by himself more than a year previously, and he now revealed that the original discoverer was Horace Wells, who tried the first experiment upon himself. (Archer regretted in his "Life and Letters" article that Ellsworth did not specifically mention the names of the dentists in his 1845 article, but subsequent congressional testimony indicates that he was referring to Wells, Riggs, J.B. Terry, C.C. Marcy, L.B. Beresford, and others, as well as himself.)

Continuing on, Ellsworth introduced a theme that would recur throughout the testimony of other participants in the initial scene of this drama, namely, that

> After the idea suggested itself to him, he [Wells] debated for some time which to use, the gas or ether, but preferred the former as he thought it less likely to injure the system.

Ellsworth now asked, "Is there any merit in using ether in place of nitrous oxide gas?" To which he replied, "Certainly not, for the properties of the two things are so alike in this respect, that for months I supposed our dentists were using both.[79]

In his *Courant* letter, Wells recounted that when deciding what exhilarating agent to use for relieving pain in surgery, it immediately occurred to him that it would be best to use nitrous oxide gas or sulfuric ether. " I advised with Dr. Marcy, of this city, and by his advice I continued to use the former, as being the least likely to do injury, although it was attended with more trouble in its preparation." Wells also described in detail his early (1844–1845) experiments with ether as an anesthetic in his *History of the Discovery of the Application of Nitrous Oxide Gas* and in an article, "The Discovery of Ethereal Inhalation," which he published in the *Boston Medical and Surgical Journal* on May 12, 1847.[80]

Marcy himself, in his "Statement No. 4" which was published in the 1853 congressional volume relating to the claim of Morton,[81] recounted an incident that occurred just after Well's initial use of nitrous oxide gas:

> Knowing that the inhalation of sulphuric ether gave rise to precisely the same effects as those of the gas [nitrous oxide], from numerous former trials with both these substances, I suggested to Dr. Wells the employment of the vapor of rectified sulphuric ether . . . Our first impression was that it possessed all the anaesthetic properties of nitrous oxyd—was equally safe, and could be prepared with less trouble; thus affording an article which was not expensive, and could always be kept at hand.

Marcy then related that at this time he told Wells that he would prepare some ether and furnish him some to administer, and also make a trial of it himself in a surgical case he expected to operate on in a few days. "Not long after this conversation," Marcy related,

> I administered the vapor of rectified sulphuric ether, in my office, to the young man above alluded to [the surgical case mentioned before], and after he had been rendered insensible to pain, cut from his head an encysted tumor, of about the size of an English walnut. The operation was entirely unattended with pain, and demonstrated to Dr. Wells and myself, in the most conclusive manner, the anaesthetic properties of ether vapor. Very little was thought of this particular case, at that time, by Dr. Wells or myself, as neither we or Dr. Riggs, Ellsworth, &c., had entertained the slightest doubt of the efficacy of ether vapor.

Marcy afterwards stated that Dr. Wells now wished him to determine whether ether was as safe as nitrous oxide gas. Wells reported that Dr. Riggs had informed him that he had inhaled both of these substances while in Washington (now Trinity) College, and had the impression, from the effects of the two agents upon him, as well as from the views of Professor Rogers in his lectures upon these substances before the class, that the inhalation of ether was more dangerous than that of nitrous oxide gas. Whereupon, Marcy informed Wells that the nitrous oxide was more agreeable and easier to inhale than ether, and was safer and equally efficacious as an anesthetic agent.

Dr. Marcy referred once more to the use of the vapor of rectified sulfuric ether by Wells in late 1844 or early 1845 when writing another supportive letter to the New York *Journal of Commerce,* which was published on January 8, 1847,[82] and again in an article entitled "Inhalation of Ether to Prevent Pain," this appearing in the *Boston Medical and Surgical Journal* the following July 21.[83] In the latter report, Marcy iterated that he had suggested to Wells the use of the vapor of pure sulfuric ether as a substitute for the gas, "at the same time showing my entire belief in its efficacy, and my firm determination to make a trial of it for the performance of a surgical operation." Relating, as he had before, that a small tumor was cut from the head of a young man, Marcy went on to say that "On account of the disagreeable smell which necessarily attends the use of ether, the choking sensation which it is apt to cause, and from an opinion which I then formed, that the after-effects were more unpleasant than those of the gas, I gave the nitrous oxide the preference, and I have not since had reason to alter this opinion."

Thus, ample evidence exists to conclude that ether was not only tried by Wells and his associates in the weeks or months following Well's discovery, but that they rejected it for seemingly valid reasons. It must be remembered that these individuals were then dealing almost entirely with dental cases, in which nitrous oxide later proved to be the drug of choice. The use of anesthesia in serious operations, requiring longer and more controlled unconsciousness and better muscle relaxation, for which ether later proved to be the better agent, were still a thing of the future. As a result, Dr. Marcy, who appears to have associated more closely with Wells at this time than did the others, and had his confidence, made the wrong decision and recommendation for the right reasons, at least under those circumstances.

From his testimony and letters, Marcy appears to have had an aversion to strong drugs, which may account for the fact that he soon afterwards deserted regular medicine to espouse homeopathy. Born in Greenville, Massachusetts, in 1822, Marcy attended Amherst College and was trained in surgery by Amariah Brigham, who initially practiced surgery in Hartford before turning to the field of mental diseases, and by George McClellan of Philadelphia, graduating from the Jefferson Medical College in 1838. Marcy moved to New York City and in 1848 became a member of the American Insititute of Homeopathy, nonetheless remaining loyal to Wells and supporting the claim later entered on his behalf for the discovery of anesthesia.[84]

Both Drs. Marcy and Ellsworth employed nitrous oxide for serious operations—at least they were considered serious under the standards of the day—following the introduction of ether by Morton in late 1846, and both reported their cases to the *Boston Medical and Surgical Journal*. In the issue for August 26, 1847, Marcy described the removal of a scirrhous testicle from a man under the influence of nitrous oxide;[85] and in the January 19, 1848 issue, Ellsworth reported that amputation of a leg at the thigh while the patient, a boy, was under the influence of nitrous oxide also.[86]

Ellsworth concluded his article, saying, "I am particular in recounting the effects of the gas similar in so many respects to that of ether, because, although it has been freely used in slighter cases, it it has never before to my knowledge been used in a capital [i.e., major] operation." In both cases, Horace Wells was on hand to administer the anesthesia, the second one, which took place during the first week of January 1848, occurring less than a month before his death, while he was on a visit from New York City, to which he had previously moved with the intention of introducing nitrous oxide into dental practice there. And during this same visit he anesthetized another patient whom J.B. Beresford operated on.[87]

After the third ether trial at the Massachusetts General Hospital on November 7, 1846, in a dramatic and convincing amputation operation, the acceptance of ether and Morton were so overwhelming that the reports of the earlier work of Wells, Ellsworth and Marcy with ether were hardly noticed. They mattered little now. The success of ether and Morton literally swept Wells and nitrous oxide from the scene; little attention was paid to them afterward, except to belittle the protestations of Wells and his supporters. Gardner Colton would, in 1896, when replying to claims that Mrs. Morton had made on behalf of her husband, contend that in the controversy which arose in 1849 over who was the discoverer of anesthesia, Morton quashed the claim that was entered on behalf of the dead Wells by arguing that nitrous oxide was *not* an anesthetic and that insensibility could not be produced by it, and, therefore, he, Morton, was the discoverer of anesthesia; and he added, "this was an admission, that if the gas *was* an anesthetic, Wells was the discoverer."[88] Colton lamented that

> No one took up the matter in defense of Dr. Wells, and the claim of Morton, that the gas was *not* an anaesthetic was generally allowed. Thus the gas lay dead and forgotten as an anaesthetic for seventeen years, from the time Wells went to Europe [from late December 1846 to mid-March 1847] till I revived its use in 1863, and proved that it was the *best* and *safest* anaesthetic known for short operations. This took place in New Haven, Conn., in June 1863.

Indeed, following Ellsworth's report, nitrous oxide would not be mentioned in the medical literature as a viable anesthetic until well after Colton reintroduced it in 1863 as an aid in dental extractions.[89] As the *Index-Catalogue of the Library of the Surgeon General's Office* clearly shows,[90] articles on nitrous oxide and its applicability in dental operations and operations of short duration only began to appear about 1869, and by the 1880s references to the employment of nitrous oxide in dentistry had become considerable. In a sense, nitrous oxide was discovered a third time, but this time it was here to stay, and it has remained a mainstay in dentistry to the present time. In his 1896 reply to Mrs. Morton, Colton also said that

> After I proved that the gas *was* an anaesthetic, Morton was compelled to change his ground. He could no longer say that nitrous oxide was not an anaesthetic, and that, therefore, *he* was the discoverer of anaesthesia. So he took the ground that Wells *abandoned his discovery!* He abandoned it only while traveling on the continent of Europe, where he could not speak the language.

The operations of Ellsworth and Bereford at Hartford the first week of 1848 indicate clearly that Wells had not abandoned his discovery; indeed, these operations and another, which we shall now discuss, show that he was continuing to employ nitrous oxide in operations outside of the field of dentistry as well as within it.[91] In a paper on "The History of Anesthesia at the New York Hospital," delivered at the Third International Symposium on the History of Anesthesia at Atlanta in 1992, Alan Van Poznak and Adele A. Lerner reported that they had recently uncovered a case in the Hospital's patient's records in which Wells had administered nitrous oxide in an operation performed on January 9, 1848, just two weeks before his tragic and untimely death. The operation was performed by Dr. John Kearney Rogers on an eleven year old girl for an ectropion of the upper lid of her right eye, which had resulted from an attack of erysipelas about four months before.[92] While Van Poznak and Lerner did not refer to the quality of anesthetic given at this operation, a brief notice of it in a contemporary document related that "pain diminished, patient excited and uncontrollable."[93]

Van Poznak and Lerner were not aware that this case had been discussed nearly a hundred years earlier, in 1895 to be exact, by William R. Hayden, a surgeon of Bedford Springs, Massachusetts, and a supporter of Morton, who referred to it in a four-part article in an attempt to degrade Wells's claim and substantiate Morton's.[94] Dr. Hayden related that the operation (which was incorrectly reported to have occurred in 1847 and not early 1848) took place at the New York Hospital in the presence of Dr. Valentine Mott and other eminent surgeons.[95] As proof, he reprinted a letter of an eyewitness, the eminent New York surgeon William H. Van Buren, then professor of surgery at the Bellevue Hospital Medical College and Mott's son-in-law:

> New York, Oct. 1, 1858
>
> I recollect distinctly having been present in the operating theatre of the New York Hospital in 1847, to witness the operation by the late Dr. John Kearney Rodgers. Dr. Horace Wells was present and administered nitrous oxide gas to the patient, with the object of producing insensiblity to the pain of the operation; but the attempt was unsuccessful, as the patient seemed to suffer as much pain as might have been anticipated under ordinary circumstances. A large number of surgeons and physicians were present, among whom was Dr. Valentine Mott, and other prominent members of the profession. As the supply of the supposed anaesthetic agent was apparently ample, judging from the large size of the bags containing it, and its administration conducted fairly and fully, the general impression upon the spectators seemed to me to be decidedly unfavorable as to its power of producing insensibility to pain.

In his *Manual of Etherization,* compiled from the experiences of others and issued in 1861, at the beginning of the Civil War, Charles T. Jackson referred disparagingly to Wells's 1844 experiments with nitrous oxide and stated that "in 1847 he met with a similar failure in the hospitals of New York," a matter that is alluded to in Trumen Smith's 1867 *Inquiry into the Origin of Modern Anaesthesia.*[96] In light of this, it is possible that Wells was involved in other as yet unnoticed demonstrations in New York hospitals as well. Smith stated in the same work that Wells went to New York a few weeks before his death for the purpose of introducing anesthetics in the hospitals and in dentistry.[97]

This report points out the disadvantages of nitrous oxide vis-á-vis ether in serious or protracted surgical cases, and experiences like the one Van Buren described must have brought about a growing awareness of this fact. Despite what Marcy and Ellsworth believed, there *was* a difference between the two drugs: nitrous oxide could not provide the sustained and controlled unconsciousness and the proper physiological conditions that ether could in cases of protracted surgery. And this came to be realized each time that ether was used. Let us now examine the relationship that existed between Horace Wells and William T. G. Morton during the fateful period following Wells's momentous discovery of December 11, 1844.

It may have been Horace Well's impetuosity, arising from his first blush of success, that was responsible for starting him on his downward spiral. As he related in his letter of December 7, 1846 to the editor of the *Hartford Courant* three weeks after Bigelow's announcement, when attempting to put the facts of his prior discovery onto the record, "I was so much elated with this discovery, that I started immediately for Boston, resolving to give it into the hands of the proper persons, without expecting to derive any pecuniary benefit therefrom." The unhappy events that followed have often been told. His attempt to demonstrate nitrous oxide in a dental case before the Harvard medical class was frustrated when the gas bag was removed too soon by mistake and the student who had volunteered to have his aching tooth extracted cried out and later related that he had experienced some pain, causing several other students to denounce the demonstration as "a humbug affair."

Well's subsequent erratic behavior indicate how depressing this experience was on the idealistic, nervous, and sensitive dentist. As a result, he desisted from performing dentistry for six months or more, during which time he amused himself by giving lectures or entertainments at Hartford's City Hall on ornathology, a branch of natural history of which he was fond and in which he was knowledgable, advertising them as "Wells' Panorama of Nature."[98]

It was through the help of Morton, Well's former student and business associate, now attending medical lectures at Harvard,[99] that the demonstration had been arranged. John Collins Warren, Harvard's Professor of Anatomy and Surgery, would later recall that Wells came to Boston "and in the company of Dr. Morton visited me at the Medical College for the purpose of requesting that the Medical Class should have an opportunity of hearing some of the remarks on the use of nitrous oxide for the prevention of pain."[100] It was at the time of this demonstration, Wells would later relate in his *Courant* letter and elsewhere, that he conversed with Drs. Charles T. Jackson and Morton upon the subject of painless surgery. Both, he reported, "admitted that it to be entirely new to them." Furthermore, he added, "Dr. Jackson expressed much surprise that severe operations could be performed without pain."[101]

Archer reports that in July of 1845, while Wells was still depressed over the debacle of the previous January, Morton traveled to Hartford and conferred with him and John Riggs concerning the manufacture of nitrous oxide gas. As Wells would relate, "After relinquishing my professional business in consequence of this illness, Dr. Morton requested me to prepare some gas for him. I told him to go to Dr. Jackson, as he was a chemist, and get it."[102] In a deposition he made in March 1847, which is printed in the Congressional volume relating to Morton's claim,[103] John Riggs also stated that

> Dr. W. T. G. Morton . . . a former pupil of Dr. Wells, during the spring and summer of 1845, called at two different times, at the latter's office, which was adjoining my own, in the city of Hartford, and requested Dr. Wells to inform his as to the manner of preparing the nitrous oxyd gas for use, and said Morton was by him referred to me, (Dr. Well's apparatus being at the time in my possession), and also to Dr. Charles T. Jackson, of Boston, as professional chemist, for said information.

Morton never admitted in print to talking with Wells on the subject of nitrous oxide gas. In his official biography, *Trials of a Public Benefactor,* which he and his supporters commissioned Nathan P. Rice to write in late 1856, when Morton's fortunes were flagging, and which was published in early 1859, the matter was explained thus:[104]

> While Dr. Morton was still a student of medicine . . . there were occasional exhibitions before the students on Nitrous Oxide Gas. It was exhibited in the presence of the whole class, for the purpose of extracting a tooth without pain. The patient screamed, the students laughed and hissed, and the experiment was looked upon as a failure of course.
>
> But one good effect was produced by this failure; it rejuvinated in the mind of Morton, that idea which had always remained nestled there, asleep part of the time, but with its vigor in no wise extin-

guished, that some agent existed, and would in time be found, which would be safely taken, and would deaden all feelings of pain.[105]

Wells's last direct contact with Morton came when, following the second trial with ether in an operation at the Massachusetts General Hospital on October 17, 1846, Morton wrote to Wells, telling him that he had discovered a preparation which, when inhaled, put the person in a sound sleep; that while in this state, the severest surgical and dental operations could be performed without the patient experiencing the slightest pain; and that he had patented the preparation and was sending out agents to dispose of the right to use it; and he asked Wells if he would not want to dispose of rights in New York and other cities. After warning Morton that his plan might defeat his objective, Wells visited Boston and observed the administration of Morton's disguised compound to several patients for the extraction of teeth. Later, in response to his wife's question whether Morton had discovered anything new, Wells replied "No! it is my old discovery and he does not know how to use it."[106]

If W. T. G. Morton's first piece of good luck was his association with Horace Wells, as his student, his partner in practice, and lastly, learning about nitrous oxide from him, his second stroke of good luck may have been in taking Well's advice and going to Charles T. Jackson for information. Whether Wells told Morton about ether as well as about nitrous oxide is unknown; however, since Wells had rejected ether as an anesthetic, his advice about it probably would have been negative. But Jackson had had a different experience with ether than had Wells. Jackson would later claim that he had known about the pain-extinguishing capability of ether as early as the winter of 1841–42, when, after having accidentally inhaled chlorine gas, he afterwards inhaled sulfuric ether for relief, and later, on a similar occasion, he repeated the experience until complete insensibility resulted.

When Morton came to him—in late September 1846, by his account—and asked for the loan of an India rubber bag for administering nitrous oxide in tooth extractions, Jackson suggested that he employ the vapor of sulfuric ether instead. And he gave the dentist instructions regarding the degree of purity requisite for the purpose and assured him that complete insensibility would result if the application was properly carried out. Morton's second stroke of good luck would later prove a curse for him, for it was on the basis of this contact and suggestion that Jackson would later argue his own claim to the discovery, provoking an internecine battle for priority that lasted more than two decades and brought no satisfaction or real benefit to anyone involved. Thus, Cartwright's conclusion that Morton discarded nitrous oxide for being too unreliable for general use is not exactly the way the matter seems to have occurred.

In Rice's *Trials of a Public Benefactor,* Jackson's role in the affair would be dismissed in about the same manner as had Wells's. It was related here that Morton learned about the exhilarating effect of ether from a contact who had inhaled it while a student, and Morton afterwards began making trials with it, first on himself, then on a goldfish and his dog, for which experiments he had obtained a high-quality supply of the drug. When afterwards attempting to obtain more ether from another supplier, in order not to bring too much attention to what he was up to, Morton got hold of a chemically impure product which caused problems, and he had to search for a pure one. As it was explained in the *Trials* book,

> Unfortunately for Dr. Morton, the investigations which his slight knowledge of chemistry rendered necessary to discover this fact, threw him into communication with others [Jackson], who, taking advantage of the character of the questions asked, the uncommunicative manner of their being put, and induced by the credit subsequently thrown around the discovery by its disclosure, have since stated that it was by suggestion that he made all his experiments, and have involved him in a constant and unhappy controversy.[107]

That something must have transpired between Morton and Jackson seems well established by the fact that, soon after the successful trials of late 1846, Morton agreed to patent his discovery jointly with Jackson.

Morton's third piece of good luck—as important a stroke as any, if indeed, not even more so—came on October 1, 1846 when Henry Jacob Bigelow, a twenty-eight year old Boston surgeon, read in the *Boston Daily Journal* of that date a brief announcement of the extraction of an ulcerated tooth by Morton without the slightest pain occuring. His curiosity aroused, Bigelow paid a visit to Morton, and, during the next two weeks, witnessed Morton performing many such dental operations. (In reporting a number of such cases, *Trials of a Public Benefactor* relates that they were taken from Bigelow's notes.)[108] Then, fifteen days later, the first public demonstration of ether anesthesia in a surgical case took place at the Massachusetts General Hospital. However, based on the following account, it is possible that Bigelow's participation in the events after October 1 went far beyond the taking of notes.

In 1911, while attending a medical meeting in Boston, Dr. William J. Morton, the son of W. T. G. Morton and by now a successful New York practitioner of long standing, was asked to comment on a paper that had been delivered on the uses and limitations of anesthesia. Dr. Morton's remarks, which have largely remained unnoticed until now, were as follows:

> It is not generally known that previous to the first use of ether anesthesia at the Massachusetts General Hospital (in late 1846) my father, Dr. Morton, had employed this for thirty-seven private operations done by Dr. Henry J. Bigelow, and that, before beginning the administration of ether, he was accustomed to give large doses (40 minims) of laudanum.[109]

Although we will probably never know whether or not these operations actually took place, there can be little doubt that young Bigelow was a major player in the drama that led up to the proving of sulfuric ether as the best agent for surgical anesthesia; and there are grounds for believing that he not only helped bring about the ensuing trials but helped orchestrate them to a successful conclusion, also making the first public announcements of the successful proving of ether anesthesia. When Bigelow encountered Morton on October 1, 1846, Morton was little known dentist and medical student, employing ether in dental procedures, and no more; less than six weeks later, due in large part to his association with Bigelow, Morton had become the hero of surgery. To his everlasting credit, however, Bigelow, unlike some other participants in the drama, never claimed credit for the discovery for himself, and, in fact, throughout his life was an unwavering supporter of Morton's claim. (And the same can be said of Colton and John Riggs in their support of Wells.)

A fourth stroke of good fortune for Morton was his association with Augustus Addison Gould, a forty-one year old former House Physician at the Massachusetts General Hospital. Gould had befriended Morton, and Morton and his family had been taken as boarders into the Gould home. Gould also helped Morton develop his ether inhaler, which initially had proved ineffectual. Indeed, on the eve of the October 16 operation which would test ether in surgery for the first time under hospital teaching conditions, Gould had devised and sketched out a valve for the inhaler, and it was the delay occasioned by having this device fabricated that caused Morton to arrive late for the operation and nearly miss the opportunity of his life.

And during and after the trials, Gould was a constant advisor to Morton, helping him avoid some of the pitfalls and embarassments that his limited education and unpolished character might have involved him in. When reflecting on the importance of Gould in this affair, one has only to think of what would have happened had the valve failed or had the apparatus not performed correctly. Morton probably would have been subjected to the same accusations of humbuggery and the same derisions that Wells had suffered about eighteen months before, and, like Wells, probably would have been summarily dismissed from the scene.

The controlling efforts of Bigelow and Gould in the overall proving of ether anesthesia is attested to by the fact that it was they who, even more than Morton, were instrumental in devising the term "anesthesia." After the child had been born, there still remained to christen it. It was deemed desirable to find a single word that would describe this new phenomenon of painless surgery. To do so, Morton's son would later report,[110] a meeting was held in Gould's house, at which he, Bigelow, Morton and Oliver Wendell Holmes were present. After Gould read aloud a list of names he had prepared, and Morton had expressed his preference for "Letheon," the name he had initially given to his preparation when disguising its color and odor so that he might later patent his discovery, he was voted down by Bigelow and Gould; afterwards, when Holmes suggested the term "anesthesia," that word was accepted by all concerned. As Holmes pointed out in a subsequent letter, the term had been used in the literature of materia medica since the time of Linnaeus and William

Cullen to signify insensibility to objects of touch and therefore seemed an appropriate term for producing a temporary loss of sensation and insensibility to pain. And so it was that anesthesia was born linguistically as well as in actuality.

Another smile from Dame Fortune which favored Morton at this time was the fact that these events took place in Boston. Unlike Wells, Morton did not come on the scene as a stranger. Wells's discovery had taken place in Hartford, which, unlike Boston, lacked a hospital, a medical school, and a medical press; and, unlike Hartford, Boston's physicians were united in cohesive groups that gathered together at eating clubs and in the rooms of learned societies, united by common bonds of upbringing, education, and blood ties. Wells's friend, Riggs, would later express this situation and its effects in bitter terms:

> If Hartford possessed a hospital, or ample surgical facilities which Boston possesses . . . the discovery of Dr. Wells would have been more minutely and fully carried out in its details, in 1844. It must be remembered that surgical cases, in Hartford, are 'few and far between,' and that we have, comparatively, no opportunities for the general or common introduction of any article like the one under consideration. Boston, with its array of surgeons, its hospitals, its medical and other journals, all eager to secure credit of the discovery to the Athens of America, was the first city, after *Hartford*, where Wells communicated his wonderful discovery. There he met with a reception so cold, that after a single imperfect trial of the gas, amidst the sneers of those around him, he left Boston in disgust and sick at heart, at the unfair disposition manifested towards him.[111]

Within a few months of Bigelow's historic announcement of November 18, 1846, surgery now made painless through the inhalation of ether was being performed in England and throughout the European continent. And well before the year 1847 was out, surgeons in France (like F.A. Longet, who published his researches on the effect of ether on the nervous system as early as February 1847), in Germany (like the renowned J.F. Dieffenbach), and even in far away Russia (in the person of N.I. Pirogov) were writing on ether and their experiences when using it for carrying out operations and in other ways.[112] However, because he had immediately jumped in and sent claims for the discovery to Europe ahead of Morton, many publications which discussed its recent history (like Dieffenbach's) would credit Jackson with the discovery or at least give him greater credit than Morton. Already, Morton's initial good fortune had begun to take an alternate turn!

We have now traveled the path leading from Humphry Davy in 1800 to Horace Wells in 1844 and to W. T. G. Morton in 1846. These three names are the principal markers on the road that terminated in the discovery and introduction of surgical anesthesia. There are other signposts along the way—Hickman and Crawford Long, to mention two—but the others mark *cul-de-sacs*—blind alleys and close-ended pathways—that did not lead to the actual discovery. They are merely part of the scenic and interesting panorama along the way.

Nonetheless, Crawford Long and his claim are deserving of additional comment before we conclude our journey across this landscape. For reasons of regional pride, Long has been credited by some with the discovery of anesthesia. However, while it is true that he probably employed ether for anesthetic purposes before any of the others, as early as March, 1842 by his own account, his experience contributed nothing to the story we have just reviewed—the introduction of anesthesia into everyday surgery. Born and raised in Georgia, Long returned to his native state following his graduation in medicine at the University of Pennsylvania in 1839 and settled into practice in the small country town of Jefferson, far removed from railroads and in the midst of a farming community that was centered around the cotton gin.

Long's priority in the use of anesthesia rests upon the report he published in 1849—following Morton's petition to Congress for a cash reward for his discovery—and an account he made to the Georgia Medical Society in 1852, both coming well after ether had been proved to the world as a viable anesthetic agent and had for several years been accepted into everyday surgical practice.[113] His priority is backed up by the testimony of three patients and one of his students, and by some hearsay evidence and no more; the operations he reported were for the removal of two superficial tumors in 1842 and for the amputation of two fingers in 1844, and Long did no operations with ether afterwards. Nor did he report his experiences concurrently so that others could test them and build on them.

It was only after ether had been fully tested and proved under public trials that Long came forward with his claim. And the evidence that supports it—the affidavits of patients who were asleep at the time and a medical preceptee—pale when compared with the testimony of those who supported Horace Wells: practicing physicians such as Drs. Ellsworth and Marcy and the dentist John Riggs, who is memorialized today through the medical eponym "Riggs' Disease," and contemporary publications of their operations in the *Boston Medical and Surgical Journal!*

Also interesting are the circumstances under which Long made his discovery, for, as in the real ether story, it all started with nitrous oxide sniffing. Long reported to the Georgia Medical Society in 1852 that a number of young men, who had assembled in the village at night, asked him to prepare some nitrous oxide for them, the subject of inhaling it for its exhilarating effects having come up. Long informed them that he did not have the proper apparatus for making or preserving the gas, but that ether would produce the same effects (having learned about this during chemistry demonstrations at medical school). Whereupon, ether was produced and inhaled by all, the experience was repeated several times and "ether sniffing" became fashionable in that area of the country.

Long related that he also inhaled it on occasion and noticed sometimes afterwards that there were bruised or painful spots on his person which he had no recollection of receiving. From this, he concluded that ether might prove useful for obliterating pain during surgical operations. Thus, Long made the same deduction that Horace Wells would do nearly three years later. But unlike Wells, Long took his experience no further, and nothing of value to mankind (other than to the few patients involved) issued from it. Wells, on the other hand, built on his observation and thus forged the first link in the chain that would extend to Morton and to the eventual introduction of anesthesia into the practice of surgery. While Wells's discovery came after that of Long, his was the catalyst which began the reaction that brought about painless surgery and therefore constituted a key element in the process.

In the search for priorities in this drama, the name of William E. Clarke has also been mentioned, along with the claim that he administered ether in a dental operation which occurred a few months prior to Crawford Long's first experience with ether in surgery. In 1882, Henry Munson Lyman, a medical teacher and long-time practicioner in Chicago, published a book, *Artificial Anaesthesia and Anaesthetics,*[114] in which he reported that in January 1842 Clarke (who later practiced medicine in Chicago) administered ether to a young woman in Rochester, New York, after which one of her teeth was extracted without pain by a dentist. According to Lyman, who knew him personally, Clarke had learned about the pain-obliterating ability of ether while attending the Berkshire Medical Institution in Pittsfield, Massachusetts during the winter of 1841–1842, where he and his companions had inhaled ether for entertainment and frolics. This episode has been the subject of a recent article by the late Dr. John B. Stetson, a Chicago anesthesiologist and teacher.[115]

While Dr. Stetson lamented that Clarke's attendance at the Berkshire college could not be verified because the student rolls were unavailable to him, I have located the name of "Wm. E. Clarke, Rochester, N.Y.," in the list of "Juniors," the first year in class, in the Berkshire Medical Institution's printed catalog for the year 1841, published in October of that year,[116] bestowing further credibility upon this account of the use of ether in dentistry about two month's before Crawford Long's employment of it in surgery. As is the case with Long, however, nothing lasting flowed from this early experience, and it was reported only decades after ether anesthesia had been proved and introduced into medicine. Clarke's experience, like Long's, was just another close-ended affair which, while enriching the history of anesthesia, contributed nothing to bringing it into existence as a practical, everyday affair.

Nathan P. Rice, who in the late 1850s wrote Morton's "official" biography, came away from this experience (as Henry Viets has observed)[117] an unhappy man. In the same month that his *Trials of a Public Benefactor,* was published,—February 1859—the *Knickerbocker, or New York Monthly Magazine* carried an article by Rice on the ether discovery in which he gave Wells and not Morton the major credit for introducing anesthesia, although Morton was unmistakably recognized as the first to publicly demonstrate it.[118] While it may appear, at first glance, that Rice published his article out of vindictiveness or rancor, having formed a dislike for Morton while compiling this book, a careful reading of his article, which he titled "A Grain of Wheat from a Bushel of Chaff," gives an entirely different impression; it is a well-reasoned and not overly emotional evaluation of a situation which he had come to learn about first-hand from Morton and from Morton's documents. And despite some flowery language, it has something of a modern flair which makes reading it today a pleasure.

Rice began his account by metaphorically and allegorically reviewing the history of the use of narcotic substances, pointing out that from ancient times to the time of Humphry Davy, the drugs which were tried and applied for their narcotic or pain relieving power were *solid* substances, although three steps along the way pointed toward the right direction. It was Humphry Davy, Rice argued, who made the first important step, the fourth one in the overall story, by showing that a *gas* inhaled into the system would bring about insensibility and that it might be used with advantage during surgical operations. But, as Rice also points out, "This was only a suggestion—a proposition which was never put by him to the test of experimentation; its death was coincident with its birth as far as any real benefit accrued from it to mankind." Rice next retold the incidents of Horace Wells's discovery asserting that when Wells inhaled nitrous oxide himself and allowed one of his teeth to be extracted, "This was the fifth step, the demonstration of an invaluable principle—in fact, the discovery."

Rice then explained how Wells searched for other less troublesome agents and came up with ether, a drug then sold in every druggist's shop and a common item of medicine. This, Rice concluded, was the sixth step, "the step which left us as our present state of knowledge." But although Wells anticipated much from ether, he did not consider it wholly satisfactory and ultimately returned to his first agent, nitrous oxide gas. "And during a visit made by him to Boston that same winter," Rice continued, "he communicated his discovery to an old friend and partner, named Morton," who ultimately went on to prove the matter.

Rice stated that three men have stood before the world as claimants to the honor of the discovery: Horace Wells, for his acknowledged use of nitrous oxide gas in 1844; William T. G. Morton, upon the undisputed ground of his public demonstration of ether in 1846; and Charles T. Jackson, who made the positive personal assertion that he had in 1842, through inhaling an excessive amount of ether to obtain relief from the very unpleasant sensations caused by the accidental inhalation of chlorine gas (a treatment Jonathan Pereira has suggested in 1839), and had continued to inhale it until he passed out, discovered that ether would produce insensibility, and communicated this information to Morton.

Pointing out that although Morton, "who evidently considers the pen mightier than the sword, substituting a multiplicity of documents for weakness of proof," denied receiving information from Wells, Rice noted that

> Yet it is allowed that two years before his [Morton's] public appearance, he knew that Wells was experimenting with nitrous oxyd, and that he conversed with him concerning it. Some corroborative testimony is evidently needed to show when he [Morton] formed and experimented upon the theory. The claim of Wells rests upon testimony showing that from 1844 to 1846, he used both ether and nitrous oxyd gas, to produce anesthesia; upon testimony showing that he communicated his knowledge directly to Morton, and probably indirectly to Jackson. Could more be required to establish any demand? Should not the grain of truth picked from the bushel of chaff with which the antagonism of others has enveloped it, be sufficient, under the benign influence of honest investigation, to produce a harvest of honor to the memory of that man [Horace Wells], who died unnoticed and unrewarded, after bestowing one of the greatest blessings ever conferred on suffering man?

Rice thus made his final comment on the discovery of surgical anesthesia, by singling out Horace Wells as the key player in the drama that was acted out.

William Osler, who seems to have had an opinion on just about everything that ocurred in the medicine of his period, and before, also voiced his thoughts on who was responsible for the introduction of surgical anesthesia. When remarking on the early development of anesthesia at a meeting of the Royal Society of Medicine on May 15, 1918, a year and a half before his death, Osler asserted:[119]

> Before October 16, 1846, surgical anaesthesia did not exist; within a few months it became a world-wide procedure; and the full credit for its introduction must be given to William Thomas Green Morton, who, on the date mentioned, demonstrated at the Massachusetts Gen-

eral Hospital the simplicity and safety of ether anaesthesia. On the priority question, let me quote two appropriate paragraphs: 'He becomes the true discoverer who establishes the truth; and the sign of the truth is the general acceptance'. . .'In science the credit goes to the man who convinces the world, not to the man to whom the idea first occurs . . . Morton convinced the world; the credit is his.'[120]

Nonetheless, just as William T. G. Morton cannot and should not be denied the honor for introducing surgical anesthesia to the world—the evidence is irrefutable on the matter—Horace Wells, by the same token, cannot and should not be denied the honor for discovering it—for the evidence is just as weighty on his behalf. It must be affirmed and emphasized that the success story we have just observed (albeit a tragic one for all of the principals involved) which terminated at Boston on the morning of October 16, 1846, had its beginning at Hartford on the night of December 10, 1844, notwithstanding the view voiced by Henry J. Bigelow in the survey of modern anesthesia which he published in 1876 in connection with the centennial celebration of the United States as a nation.

When upholding Morton's claim in *A Century of American Medicine*,[121] Bigelow attributed Wells's lack of success to the fact that he had, through Colton, who was following Davy's instructions, made use of the traditional gas bag when administering nitrous oxide, and had applied only Davy's prescribed dose. "This volume of gas," Bigelow argued, "is inadequate to produce anaesthesia with any certainty; and Wells failed to suggest a larger dose. This small omission closed his chances. He narrowly missed a great invention. Inventors, by thousands, have missed inventions as narrowly." Bigelow went on to say that modern dental insensibility by nitrous oxide is unfailing, because the volume employed is much larger, and it is also usual to exhale it into the atmosphere. In a form of argumentation that is reminiscent of Morton's type of reasoning, Bigelow concluded that

> From all this it will be seen that Wells did not, as has been claimed for him, "discover that the inhalation of a gaseous substance would *always* render the body insensible to pain during *surgical operations*," but only that it would *occasionally* do so, and until long after the ether discovery, his experiments were *not "surgical operations," but only tooth-pulling.*

Dr. Bigelow failed to point out that before *he* arrived on the scene, Morton's activity was likewise only restricted to *toothpulling*, (and his expectations appeared to have been as well.)

Finally, Charles F. Heywood, the surgical house officer at the Massachusetts General Hospital at the time of Morton's initial ether demonstrations in October and November 1846, would, in 1853, write a long letter in which he presented his thoughts on the controversy that had arisen over the honor of discovery.[122] Heywood, who, as a Harvard medical student in 1845, could also have been in attendance at Wells's unsuccessful demonstration in January of that year, related that "the question of priority may be easily settled." He observed that the great advance from the use of solid agents such as opium and methods such as animal magnetism to the inhalation of intoxicating agents was beyond all dispute made by Horace Wells. While acknowledging the contributions made by Morton for introducing sulfuric ether and Simpson for chloroform, Heywood stated that,

> but before all, let full and ample justice be done to that noble genius which first conceived the grand idea, which has been the basis of all the experiments, and the father of all the discoveries. To the spirit of Dr. Horace Wells belongs the honor of having given to suffering humanity the greatest boon it ever received from science.

Having directly participated in the dramatic events that ushered in ether anesthesia, Heywood's support of Wells over Morton is unexpected and somewhat surprising.

When one looks into the early anesthesia story in depth, and reads the polemical writings of the claimants and their supporters, the original congressional documents that were compiled, and especially W. Harry Archer's "Life and Letters of Horace Wells," one is left with the strong impression that of all of those who trod across that uneven stage, Horace Wells was the most idealistic, humane, generous, and morally correct—unlike others, for example, he contended from the first that anaesthesia could not and should not be patented. Wells also comes across as the most sensitive, creative, inventive, and probably the best educated of the whole cast of players. Nonetheless, one also detects in his character or personality some flaws as well: a tendency to mood swings to either extreme, flightiness, oversensitivity, and a propensity to be easily discouraged. There can be no doubt that his failure in Boston in January 1844 acted as a strong depressent on Horace Wells, and Morton's claims further deflated his spirit.

While, as Archer shows, Wells resumed his dental practice in the fall of 1845, he soon stopped practicing again, turning his attention instead to the development of his shower bath, a matter that primarily concerned him into the following spring. His few surviving letters from this period show that he still found it difficult to work, but by September 1846 had opened up his old office and was again engaged in the practice of dentistry. Then, on October 19, came news from Morton of the success of "his new compound" for putting patients to sleep during surgical operations and Morton's offer to help him dispose of shares in "his invention."

Late in December, Horace sailed for France and was away from home for nearly three months, returning to Hartford in mid March of 1847[123] and taking up once more the defense of his priority as the discoverer of anesthesia. Although he resumed administering anesthesia and conducted self-experimentation with various agents for producing it, the record indicates that he was ill-disposed in doing so. Following his tragic suicide in New York on January 23, 1848, one of his Hartford obituaries related that "some of his friends supposed he was somewhat deranged when he left Hartford. His mind had been a great deal excited for some time past, and he has personally experimented to a great extent in gases, prepared in different forms."[124] Indeed, Wells would say, at the very conclusion of the letter he addressed to the editors of the *Journal of Commerce,* which he left behind when taking his life and which was published in this obituary and is reprinted in Archer,[125] "My brain is on fire.[170]

It would be naive to think that the so-called "ether controversy" will ever have an ending. Born out of jealousy and greed, and nourished with rancor and venom, it seems to go on as heatedly today as it did in the mid-1850's and after, although today it is motivated more by regional pride than the by the quest for fame and fortune. Nevertheless, to anyone who has taken the time and made the effort to look at *all* the evidence closely, and impartially, there can be no controversy about the key role played by Horace Wells in bringing about surgical anesthesia. He made the critical deduction that altered the course to the right direction, and he influenced Morton, who traveled the journey beyond. It would only come about following Wells's critical deduction and demonstration that, by inhaling a synthetic gas, patients could be rendered insensible to the painful aspects of surgery and relieved of the shock and horror that accompanied surgical operations. Thus, Wells stands along with Humphry Davy and William Thomas Green Morton, as one of the trio—and undoubtedly its most contributing member—that brought to mankind one of the greatest benefits it has ever received.

Notes

1. Humphry Davy, *Researches, Chemical and Philosophical, Chiefly Concerning Nitrous Oxide, or Dephlogisticated Nitrous Air, and Its Respiration* (London, Printed for J. Johnson, 1800). Davy's observation on the pain destroying property of nitrous oxide appears on p. 556, among the concluding remarks in the volume.
2. David M. Knight, "Davy, Humphry," in *Dictionary of Scientific Biography* (New York, Charles Scribner's Sons [1971]), v. 3, p. 600.
3. Accounts differ as to how Samuel Cooley injured himself that evening, and on the nature and extent of his injuries. His own testimony on the matter related that after running against and knocking over several settees, he was thrown down, causing several bruises upon his knees and other parts of his person. After the influence of the gas had subsided, his friends asked him if he had not injured himself and directed his attention to what had occurred. Upon examining his knees, he found them severely injured, with the skin severely abrased and broken. His testimony appears in United States Senate, *Statements, Supported by Evidence, of Wm. T. G. Morton, M.D. on His Claim to the Discovery of the Anaesthetic Properties of Ether, Submitted to the Honorable the Select Committee Appointed by the Senate of the United States. 32d Congress, 2d Session, January 21, 1853* (Washington 1853), on the first page of the appendix, which contains testimony relating to the claims entered on behalf of Horace Wells for the discovery of surgical anesthesia.
4. Horace Wells, *A History of the Discovery of the Application of Nitrous Oxide Gas, Ether, and Other Vapors, to Surgical Operations* (Hartford, J. Gaylord Wells, 1847), 5.
5. J. R. Deiman, P. van Troostwik, P. Nieuwland, N. Bondt, and

A. Lauwerenburgh published two articles on the subject in 1793 which are referenced in Eugene H. Conner's "Anesthetics in the Treatment of Cholera" in Note 40.

6. Samuel Latham Mitchill, *Remarks on the Gaseous Oxyd of Azote or of Nitrogene, and on the Effects it Produces When Generated in the Stomach, Inhaled into the Lungs, and Applied to the Skin: Being an Attempt to Ascertain the True Nature of Contagion, and to Explain Thereupon the Phenomena of Fever* (New York, T. and J. Swords, 1795).

7. Humphry Davy, "Outlines of Observations Relating to Nitrous Oxide, or Dephlogisticated Nitrous Air," *A Journal of Natural Philosophy, Chemistry, and the Arts* 5 (November 1801): [281]-287.

8. I have not been able to examine a copy of the first 1799 London edition of James Parkinson's *The Chemical Pocket-Book,* which cited information on nitrous oxide from an article Davy published in Nicholson's *Journal* in May 1799. However, the information in it was reprinted in a pirated Dublin edition I have seen, entitled *The Chemical Pocket-Book; or, Memoranda Chemica: Arranged in a Compendium of Chemistry, According to the Latest Discoveries with Bergman's Table of Singular Elective Attractions, Improved by Dr. G. Pearson, and also Mr. Kirwan's Elective Attractions . . .* (Dublin, Printed for Gilbert and Hodges, 1801), 18–22. A somewhat different account of nitrous oxide, reflecting Davy's continued work on it, as reported in his 1801 *Researches, Chemical and Philosophical,* appeared in the second London edition of *The Chemical Pocket-Book,* which C. Wittingham printed for H. D. Symonds, Murray and Highley, Cox, Boosey, and Callow in 1801, pp. 23–25.

9. *William Henry, An Epitome of Chemistry, in Three Parts. Part I. Intended to Facilitate to the Student, the Acquisition of Chemical Knowledge, by Minute Instructions for the Performance of Experiments. Part II. Directions for the Analysis of Mineral Waters; of Earths and Stones; of Ores; of Metals; and of Mineral Bodies in General. Part III. Instructions for Applying Chemical Tests and Reagents to Various Useful Purposes* (London, J. Johnson, 1801; 2d ed., corrected, London, J. Johnson, 1801). This was reprinted at Philadelphia by James Humphreys in 1802 and at New York by Collins and Perkins in 1808, and it went through five English editions by 1809, appearing in its sixth edition under a new title, *The Elements of Experimental Chemistry* at London in 1809, of which more will be said later.

10. Thomas Thomson, *A System of Chemistry* (Edinburgh, [Printed by J. Brown], 1802); a third edition had appeared by 1807, and a fourth by 1810; it was reprinted by Abraham Small in Philadelphia in 1818.

11. John Bostock, *An Essay on Respiration* (Liverpool, Printed by J. M'Creery for Messrs. Longman and Rees, London, 1804).

12. Parkes's book became a popular one, appearing in England and America in numerous editions into the 1820s. The first edition of 1806 was issued by the author at London. A listing of editions can be found in the *National Union Catalog of Pre-1956 Imprints* ([London] Mansell, 1972), v. 442, pp. 533–534. Parkes also issued other similar works, one entitled *An Essay on the Utility of Chemistry to the Arts and Manufactures,* and another, *The Rudiments of Chemistry,* which are likewise listed in the *National Union Catalog.*

13. Some of these studies are mentioned in W. P. C. Barton's dissertation, cited in Note 20, and in Eugene Conner's article on anesthesia and cholera, cited in Note 40 .

14. Jane Hallimand Marcet, *Conversations on Chemistry, In Which the Elements of That Science are Familiarly Explained and Illustrated by Experiments, and Plates* (London, Printed for Longman, Hurst, Rees, and Orme, 1806), 2 v. Mrs. Marcet's biography can be found in v. 12, pp. 1007–1008 of the *Dictionary of National Biography* (reprint ed., Oxford, Oxford University Press, 1921–1922). It is stated here that her books fulfilled a need for information at a time when simple scientific textbooks were almost unknown. The large number of editions of *Conversations on Chemistry* can be ascertained by referring to the *National Union Catalog of Pre-1956 Imprints* ([London] Mansell, 1974), v. 360, pp. 609–611.

15. In 1812, when issuing his *Elements of Chemical Philosophy, Vol I, Part I* (no more was published), which was printed at London for J. Johnson, Davy did devote about nineteen pages of azote, or nitrogene gas. His discussion, however, was purely technical, outlining its chemistry up to that time. He said nothing about the physiological or psychological effects it produced, nor was its analgesic capability mentioned.

16. F. F. Cartwright, *The English Pioneers of Anesthesia (Beddoes, Davy, and Hickman),* (Bristol, John Wright & Sons Ltd.; London, Simpkin Marshall Ltd., 1952). This and other matters alluded to here comes from the concluding essay, and mainly from pp. 312–313.

17. William Stephen Jacobs, *The Student's Chemical Companion* (Philadelphia, Printed for the Author, by S. W. Conrad, 1802; reprint

edition: Philadelphia, Printed by M. Carey, and Kimber, Conrad & Co., 1807). Information on "nitrous oxyde" appears on pp. 20–21 of the 1802 edition and on pp. 26–27 of the later one.

18. M. I. A. Chaptal, *Elements of Chemistry. The Fourth American Edition, with Great Additions and Improvements, by James Woodhouse, M.D.* (Philadelphia, Published by Benjamin & Thomas Kite, 1807), 179–183. Chaptal's *Élemens de Chemie* first appeared in three volumes in 1790, and was translated into English by William Nicholson in 1795. American editions were printed at Philadelphia in 1801 and 1806, and at Boston in 1806. None of these pre-1807 American editions paid any attention to nitrous oxide or Humphry Davy's experiments with it. A discussion of the "Oxyde of azot", however, also appeared in volume 3 of a four-volume edition printed by Richard Phillips at London in 1807.

19. James Woodhouse, "Observations on the Effects of Nitrous Oxide, When Taken into the Lungs," *The Philadelphia Medical Museum* 4 (1808): 179–188.

20. William Paul Crillon Barton, *A Dissertation on the Chymical Properties and Exhilarating Effects of Nitrous Oxide Gas; and Its Applications to Pneumatick Medicine* (Philadelphia, Printed for the Author, at the Lorenzo Press, 1808). Barton is best known for his *Vegetable Materia Medica*, which Mathew Carey issued at Philadelphia in two volumes in 1817–1819.

21. Ibid, 72–74.

22. Ibid, 22.

23. John F. Fulton and Madeline E. Stanton, *The Centennial of Surgical Anesthesia; an Annotated Catalogue of Books and Pamphlets Bearing on the Early History of Surgical Anesthesia, Exhibited at the Yale Medical Library October 1946* (New York, Henry Schuman, 1946), 11.

24. In 1808, 1810 and 1814, Benjamin Silliman of Yale College brought out three editions of Henry's *Epitome of Chemistry* (the first anonymously , and the last under its new title *The Elements of Experimental Chemistry,* to which he added notes of his own. The 1808 edition was issued by Collins and Perkins in New York, while the last two appeared at Boston, the 1810 edition under the imprint of William Andrews and the 1814 edition under the imprint of Thomas and Andrews. The description of "Azotic or Nitrogen Gas" was the standard chemical one, but in his supplementary notes Silliman provided information on preparing nitrous oxide for the purpose of respiring it (which he had students do in his classes). Other American

editions of Henry's book were brought out in Philadelphia by John Redman Coxe in 1817 and Robert Hare in 1819, while London editions continued to be issued into the early 1830s.

25. The fifth London edition of Thomson's book had appeared in 1817, and it was reprinted for the first time in America at Philadelphia the next year (see Note 10). A succeeding edition, the sixth printed at Edinburgh in 1820, would be the last.

26. Editions of Parkes's *Chemical Catechism* were published at London in 1812, 1816, 1818 and 1819, with a New York edition issuing from the press of Collins and Company in 1818.

27. P. M. Orfila, *Practical Chemistry, or a Description of the Processes by Which the Various Articles of Chemical Research, in the Animal, Vegetable and Mineral Kingdoms, Are Procured: Together with the Best Method of Analysis. Translated from the French of P. M. Orifla by John Redman Coxe* (Philadelphia, Published by Thomas Dobson and Son, 1818). A brief description of "Gaseous Protoxyde of Azot" is printed on pp. 18–19, with an illustration of the apparatus in which it was made appearing on plate 4.

28. John Gorham of Harvard issued his *Elements of Chemical Science* (Boston, Cummings and Hilliard) in two volumes in 1819 and 1820. Volume 1 contained a more than three-page (pp. 321–325) resume of nitrous oxide, mostly of its chemistry; about a page-and-a-half was devoted to an exposition of how it was respired and its ensuing physiological effects.

29. William Thomas Brande, *A Manual of Chemistry; Containing the Principal Facts of the Science, Arranged in the Order in Which They Are Discussed and Illustrated in the Lectures at the Royal Institution of Great Britain* (London, John Murray, 1819; 2d ed., 1821). The first American edition, 3 volumes in 1 from the 2d London edition, with added notes and emendations by William James Macneven of New York, was published by George Long in that city in 1821. A description of the "Protoxide of Nitrogen, or Nitrous Oxide," can be found on pp. 39–40 of the American edition.

30. Andrew Duncan, *The Edinburgh New Dispensatory: Containing, I. The Elements of Pharmaceutical Chemistry. II. The Materia Medica . . . III. The Pharmaceutical Preparations and Compositions . . .* (Edinburgh, Printed for Bell & Bradfute, 1803), 17. The description continued to be reprinted in successive editions—1804, 1806, 1808, 1810, etc. By 1831, when the twelfth edition came into print, reference to nitrous oxide gas has been dropped out altogether. Duncan became responsible for editing this work with the edition of 1791, continuing

a long series of editions that had been initiated by William Lewis in the early 1750s.

31. John Redman Coxe, *The American Dispensatory, Containing the Operations of Pharmacy; Together with the Natural, Chemical, Pharmaceutical and Medical History of the Different Substances Employed in Medicine* . . . (Philadelphia, Printed by A. Bartram, for Thomas Dobson, 1806), 498; second edition, Published by Thomas Dobson, 1810, 471–472. Additional editions appeared in 1814, 1817, 1818, 1822, 1830, and 1831. Like the description that was contained in the Duncan work, no medical use for nitrous oxide was provided.

32. M. P. Orila, *A Treatise on Mineral, Vegetable, and Animal Poisons, Considered as to Their Relations with Physiology, Pathology, and Medical Jurisprudence; Translated from the French, by John Augustine Waller, Surgeon. Second Edition, Corrected* (London, Printed for E. Cox and Son, and Burgess and Co., 1818), 169.

33. P. H. Nysten, *Recherches de Physiologie et de Chimie Pathologiques, pour Faire a Suite á Celles de Bichat sur la Vie et la Mort* (Paris, Chez J. A. Brosson, 1811), 131–139. Bichat's work had appeared in print in 1800.

34. Andrew Ure, *A Dictionary of Chemistry, on the Basis of Mr. Nicholson's; In Which the Principles of the Science Are Investigated Anew, and Its Applications to the Phenomena of Nature, Medicine, Mineraolgy, Agriculture, and Manufactures Detailed* (London, Printed for Thomas Tegg, and T. G. Underwood, J. Cox, Simpkin & Marshall, and also R. Griffin & Co., Glasgow, and J. Coming, Dublin [1821]). The first American edition appeared in Philadelphia in 1821, and additional London editions were published in 1823, 1824, 1827, 1828 and afterwards.

35. In 1822, Robert Desilver of Philadelphia issued Henry's *Elements of Experimental Chemistry* in two volumes containing additional material by Robert Hare of the University of Pennsylvania, and in 1823 Desilver published a supplemental volume by Hare, while London editions appeared in 1826 and 1829; Collins and Company of New York issued an edition of Parkes' *Chemical Catechism* in 1821, with editions appearing at London in 1822, 1824, and 1826 (Parkes *Chemical Essays, Principally Relating to the Arts and Manufactures of the British Dominions,* which appeared at London in its second edition in 1823 and again in 1825, contained no information at all on nitrous oxide); and Turner's *Elements of Chemistry* was published at Edinburgh in 1827 and was reissued at Philadelphia by John Grigg in 1828.

36. John W. Webster, *A Manual of Chemistry on the Basis of Professor Brande's Containing the Principal Facts of the Science, Arranged in the Order in Which They Are Discussed and Illustrated in the Lectures at Harvard University, N.E. Compiled from the Works of Brande, Henry, Berzelius, Thomson and Others. Designed as a Text Book for the Use of Students, and Persons Attending Lectures of Chemistry* (Boston, Richardson and Lord, 1826), 120–122. The same publishers issued a second edition in 1828, and in 1839 Marsh, Capen, Lyon and Webb published a third. In 1850, Webster was hanged for the murder of Dr. George Parkman.

37. Edward Turner, *Elements of Chemistry, Including the Recent Discoveries and Doctrines of the Science* (Edinburgh, Printed for William Tait, and Charles Tait, London, 1827). John Grigg of Philadelphia issued the first American edition in 1828.

38. Jacob Green, *A Text Book of Chemical Philosophy. On the Basis of Dr. Turner's Elements of Chemistry; in Which the Principal Discoveries and Doctrines of the Science Are Arranged in a New Systematic Order* (Philadelphia, R. H. Small, 1829), 112–113.

39. John Ayrton Paris, a London physician who issued a work entitled *Pharmacologia* in 1812, and reissued it in a third edition by 1820 and a ninth edition by 1843, said nothing on the subject of nitrous oxide; and indeed, when publishing another work which he called *The Elements of Medical Chemistry*—I have examined the American edition issued at New York by Collins & Hannay, Collins & Co., and Stacy B. Collins in 1825—he provided (pp. 249–250) only the barest chemical details on azote or nitrogen and again said nothing about nitrous oxide.

40. Eugene H. Conner, "Anesthetics in the Treatment of Cholera," *Bulletin of the History of Medicine* 40 (January-February 1966): 52–58.

41. Samuel Jackson, *The Principles of Medicine Founded on the Structure and Functions of the Animal Organism* (Philadelphia, Carey and Lea, 1832), 520. On the title page of this work, Jackson listed himself as Assistant Professor of the Institutes and Practice of Medicine and Clinical Medicine in the University of Pennsylvania; Lecturer on Therapeutics and Materia Medica in the Medical Institute of Philadelphia; Vice President of the Philadelphia Medical Society; and Vice President of the College of Pharmacy.

42. On page 548 of his *Researches, Chemical and Philosophical*, Davy related that "the immediate effects of nitrous oxide upon the living system, are analogous to those of diffusible stimuli."

43. George B. Wood and Franklin Bache, *The Dispensatory of the United*

States (Philadelphia, Published by Grigg & Ellior, 1833). Subsequent editions appeared in 1833, 1836, 1839, 1845, 1847, 1849 and 1851 (the ninth), all omitting reference to nitrous oxide. The tenth edition, appearing in 1854, included a brief description of it and noted that it was capable of producing anesthetic effects. It also reported that the late Horace Wells of Connecticut tried to introduce it as an anesthetic but his first experiments were unsuccessful, and further attempts were superseded by the discovery of etherization.

44. Sir David Brewster, *Letters on Natural Magic. Addressed to Sir Walter Scott, Bart.* (London, J. Murray, 1832).

45. "Two Singular Cases of the Nitrous Oxide, or Exhilarating Gas," *American Journal of Science and the Arts* 5 (1822): 194–196.

46. Benjamin Silliman, *Elements of Chemistry, in the Order of Lectures Given in Yale College* (New Haven, Printed by Hezekaih Howe, 1830–1831), 2 v. The section dealing with nitrous oxide appears in v. 1, pp. 476–484.

47. Robert Hare, *A Compendium of the Course of Chemical Instruction in the Medical Department of the University of Pennsylvania* (Philadelphia, J. G. Auner, 1828). Auner issued a second edition in 1834, a third in 1836, and a fourth in two volumes between 1840 and 1843. The plate here showing the apparatus for making and preserving nitrous oxide gas was reprinted by Benjamin Silliman in 1830, from which illustration 1 was taken. Hare restricted his discussion of the gas to its chemical make-up and properties and to methods for evolving and collecting it. He did note, however, that "When respired it stimulates then destroys life. Its effects on the human system, when breathed, are analogous to a transient, peculiar, various, and generally very vivacious ebriety."

48. Edward Turner, *Elements of Chemistry, Including the Recent Discoveries and Doctrines of That Science. Third American, from the Second London Edition, with Notes and Emendations by Franklin Bache* (Philadelphia, John Grigg, 1830; fourth American edition, from the third London edition, 1832). The 1840 edition was reprinted by Thomas, Cowperthwait & Co. at Philadelphia in 1840. The eleventh edition of Henry's earlier *Elements of Experimental Chemistry* had been issued by the Philadelphia publisher Robert Desilver in 1831.

49. Lewis C. Beck, *A Manual of Chemistry; Containing a Condensed View of the Present State of the Science, with Copius References to More Extensive Treatises, Original Papers, &c. Intended as a Text-Book for Medical Schools, Colleges and Academies* (Albany, Webster and Skinners, 1831); the fourth edition, revised, was issued by W. E. Dean of New York in 1844.

50. Many of the editions of the Marcet book which came out at this time contained additonal explanations and directions by James Lee Comstock, M.D., and a new and extensive series of questions by the Rev. J. L. Blake. I have seen such an edition issued at Hartford by Oliver D. Cooke and Sons as early as 1824; and another which was issued at New York by Collins, Kease & Co. in 1836; there were a great many, for it was obviously a popular work.

51. James Renwick, *First Principles of Chemistry; Being a Familiar Introduction to the Studies of That Science. For the Use of Schools, Academies, and the Lower Classes of Colleges* (New York, Harper & Brothers, 1842).

52. Robert Kane, *Elements of Chemistry, Including the Most Recent Discoveries and Applications of the Science to Medicine and Pharmacy and to the Arts; An American Edition, with Additions and Corrections, and Arranged for the use of the Universities, Colleges, Academies, and Medical Schools of the United States, by John William Draper* (New York, Harper & Brothers, 1842; reissue, 1843). Editions had been published earlier by Hodges and Smith at Dublin in 1841 and 1842.

53. John Scoffern, *Chemistry No Mystery; or, A Lecturer's Bequest; Being the Subject-Matter of a Course of Lectures. Delivered by an Old Philosopher, and Taken in Short-Hand by One of the Audience, Whose Name is Not Known* (London, Harvey and Darton, 1839). Laughing gas is discussed on pp. 109–115. A second edition of this work appeared in 1848.

54. This first edition was issued by its author, a trained mechanic, with a second edition appearing at Philadelphia under the imprint of J. M. Brown that same year. It was reissued by M. Kelly of Philadelphia in 1840, and in 1841 it appeared at New York and Boston under the revised title, *The Artist's Guide and Mechanic's Own Book, Embracing the Portion of Chemistry Applicable to the Mechanic Arts, with Abstracts on Electricity, Galvanism, Pneumatics, Optics, Astronomy, and Mechanical Philosophy.* The New York edition was issued by A. V. Blake, and the Boston one by Bazin and Ellsworth. Later editions appeared in 1851, 1853, 1856 and 1871.

55. Jonathan Pereira, *The Elements of Materia Medica; Comprehending the Natural History, Preperation, Properties, Composition, Effects, and Uses of Medicines* (London, Longman, Orme, Brown, Green, and Longmans, 1839), pt. 1, pp. 155–156.

56. Robert Christison. *A Treatise on Poisons, in Relation to Medical Jurisprudence, Physiology, and the Practice of Physic* (Edinburgh, Printed for Adam Black, and Longman, Rees, Orme, Brown, & Green,

London, 1829), 604–605; second edition, 1845, 828–829. Interestingly enough, Christison did not provide any information on nitrous oxide in his *Dispensatory, or Commentary on the Pharmacopoeias of Great Britain*, which was issued at Edinburgh by Adam and Charles Black in 1842.

57. Christison was quoting from L. J. Thenard, *Traité de Chimie Élementaire* (Paris, Crochard, 1813–1816), v. 3, p. 675.

58. Faraday's report, entitled "nitrous oxide" and signed "M. F.," appeared in *The Quarterly Journal of Science, Literature, and the Arts* 6 (1820): 360–361; the latter, a report by F. Stanley on "Poisoning by the Inhalation of Impure Nitrous Oxide Gas," appeared in *The Chemist* 4 (n.s. 1) (1843): 85–86, being reprinted from *The Lancet* of December 10, 1842.

59. Davy discusses these matters on p. 462 of his *Researches, Chemical and Philosophical*.

60. Cartwright devotes Chapter X, pp. 265–305, of his *The English Pioneers of Anesthesia* to Hickman and his work with carbonic acid gas. Hickman's 1824 pamphlet, *A Letter on Suspended Animation, Containing Experiments Showing That It May Be Safely Employed during Operations on Animals, With a View of Ascertaining Its Probable Utility in Surgical Operations on the Human Subject* (Ironbridge, Printed at the Office of W. Smith, 1824), is also described and discussed in Fulton and Stanton's *The Centennial of Surgical Anesthesia*, 12–13. In early 1847, following the announcement of the successful employment of ether as an anesthetic, an English physician, Dr. Thomas Dudley of Kingwinford, remembered Hickman's pamphlet and began a campaign to award him credit for the idea of producing insensibility during surgical operations; and although James Young Simpson, who introduced chloroform as an anesthetic in late 1847, acknowledged Hickman's experiments in an article he wrote for the *Encyclopaedia Britanica* in 1870, Hickman remained unrecognized until the twentieth century. In 1930, a century after the surgeon's death, the Welcome Historical Museum in London reissued Hickman's pamphlet from the single known copy in its possession under the title *Souvenir, Henry Hill Hickman Centenary Exhibition*.

61. William Wright, *On the Varieties of Deafness, and Diseases of the Ear, with Proposed Methods of Relieving Them* (London, Hurst, Chance, and Co., 1829), 161–163.

62. In 1974, a collection of sixteen books from the library of Horace Wells came on the market and was purchased by the Hartford Public Library for its Hartford Collection. In addition to the Black and Blair

(i.e. Phillips) volumes, titles within are: Thomas Boston, *Human Nature and Its Fourfold State* (London, 1809), with signature and stamp of Horace Wells; A. G. Collot, *Progressive Pronouncing French Reader* (Philadelphia 1838), signature and stamp of Horace Wells; Amos Eaton, *Botanical Grammar and Dictionary, Translated from the French of Bulliard and Richard* (Albany 1828, 3rd ed.), with signature and stamp of Horace Wells; Joel Hawes, *Character, Every Thing to the Young, or a Pastor's Gift to the Youth of His Charge* (Hartford 1843), signature and stamp of Horace Wells; John A. Clark, *The Christian Keepsake and Missionary Annual* (Philadelphia 1838), signature and stamp of Horace Wells; A.G. Collot, *Progressive Pronouncing French Reader* (Philadelphia 1844), stamp of Horace Wells; James Hervey, *Meditations and Contemplations* (London 1808), signature of Horace Wells; Thomas Hooker, *Poor Doubting Christian, Drawn to Christ* (Hartford 1845), signature of Horace Wells; Thomas Mallory, *La Mort d'Arthur* (London 1816), stamp of Horace Wells; John Milton, *Paradise Lost* (New York, n.d.), unmarked; John M'Leod, *Voyage of His Majesty's Ship Alceste to China, Corea, and the Island of Lechew* (London 1820), stamp and signature of Horace Wells; Alexander Fraser Tytler, *Elements of General History, Ancient and Modern* (Concord, N.H., 1824–1825), signature of Horace Wells, with marginal notes in his hand; United States House of Representatives, *Annual Report of the Commissioner of Patents for the Year 1847* (Washington 1848), autograph of Joseph Wales, brother of Horace Wells's widow, Elizabeth Wales Wells; United States Patent Office, *Improvement in Surgical Operations, Specifications Forming Part of Letters Patent No. 4,808, November 12, 1846* (Washington 1846), petition for the award of a patent to C. T. Jackson and William T. G. Morton for the use of ether in surgical anesthesia. Also present in the collection is a copy of Truman Smith's *An Examination of the Question of Anaesthesia, Arising in the Memorial of Charles Thomas Wells* (New York, 1858). The last named is inscribed by the author to James Y. Simpson, 10 March 1870, "at the request of the widow of Horace Wells, Discoverer of Anaesthesia," and laid in is a leaflet addressed by Smith to the "Ladies of Hartford, Connecticut," concerning the anaesthesia controversy.

63. Joseph Black, *Lectures on the Elements of Chemistry, Delivered in the University of Edinburgh by the Late Joseph Black, Published from His Manuscripts by John Robinson. First American from the Last London Edition* (Philadelphia, Printed for Mathew Carey, by B. Graves, 1806), 2 v. Aziotic gas is discussed on pp. 250–251.

64. [Sir Richard Phillips], *A Grammar of Chemistry; Wherein the Principles of the Science Are Explained and Familiarized by a Variety of Experiments. To Which Are Added, Interrogarory Exercises; and a Glossary of Terms Used in Chemistry, By the Rev. D. Blair* [pseud.]. *Corrected and Revised by Benjamin Tucker. Fourth Edition, Improved and Adapted to the President State of the Science* (Philadelphia, Published and Sold by David Hogan, 1823). Nitrous oxide is discussed on pp. 107–108.

65. W. Harry Archer, "Life and Letters of Horace Wells, Discoverer of Anesthesia, Chronologically Arranged with an Appendix," *Journal of the American College of Dentists"*, no. 2 (June 1944): [77]-210. The patents are discussed on pp. 192–197. The coal-sifter was patented in 1839, and the shower bath in 1846.

66. Senator Truman Smith of Connecticut in the 1850s championed Wells's claim in Congress and, as a means of documenting it, compiled the Congressional report, *An Examination of the Question of Anaesthesia,* which is discussed in Note 68. In 1858, he republished the report in slightly enlarged and rewritten form as a monograph, listing himself as author (New York, John A. Gray, printer), and in 1859 reissued it (either from standing type or stereotype plates), with an inserted label containing a brief notice of Joseph Wales, Elizabeth Wales Wells's brother, and with an additonal appendix containing the most recent material. In 1867, Smith rewrote the work and published it in its final edition under the abbreviated title, *An Inquiry into the Origin of Anaesthesia* . While the 1858 and 1859 editions are, like the original report, mainly documentary, the 1867 edition is written descriptively, although incorporating most of the information contained in the earlier editions, but with some new material as well. When referring to the true character of Horace Wells on page 75 of the 1858 edition, Smith described him as of a "lofty and generous spirit" and of an "acute, inventive, ingenious, and truly philosophical mind." Similar encomiums were pronounced by Marcy, Ellsworth and others who were well acquainted with Horace Wells, in the various depositions they made on his behalf.

67. *The National Union Catalog, Pre-1956 Imprints* (London, Mansell, 1970), v. 754, pp. 26–27.

68. The only information I have noticed which indicates that Horace Wells might have been aware of nitrous oxide prior to his encounter with it at Colton's December 10, 1844 demonstration appears in a deposition which Linus P. Brockett, M.D., of Hartford, Connecticut, made in January of 1853 and which first appeared in a 103-page pamphlet

issued by the United States Senate under the title *An Examination of the Question of Anaesthesia, Arising on the Memorial of Charles Thomas Wells, Presented to the United States Senate, 2d Session, 32d Congress, and Referred to a Select Committee, of Which the Hon. Isaac P. Walker Is Chairman. Prepared for the Information of Said Committee* ([Washington 1853]), 11–12. As is pointed out in Note 66, this document was prepared by Truman Smith and in 1858 and 1859 reprinted under his name with approximately the same title. Brockett states here that he had been a resident of Hartford since December 1846, but in the year 1840 had resided there from March or April until the first day of September, while attending medical lectures in New Haven. Brockett related he knew Horace Wells intimately in that earlier period and was in the habit of calling on him frequently. Early in the spring of 1840 he had had a molar tooth extracted by Wells, which caused him much pain. In July or about August 1 following, Brockett deposed, he called at Wells's office and found him engaged in some experiment, which led to a conversation between him and Wells "respecting nitrous oxyd gas." Dr. Wells first spoke of the gas and asked whether Brockett had seen it administered. Brockett replied that he had seen two or three people inhale the gas and described the effects he had observed. According to Brockett, Wells then remarked that he believed a man might be made so drunk by the gas or some similar agent that dental and other operations might be performed without any sensation of pain on the part of the patient. "Dr. Wells' mind seemed to me at that time to be impressed with the idea that some discovery would yet be made to prevent pain in dental operations." Brockett added that he left Hartford in September 1840 and did not encounter Wells again until December 1846, thus establishing the early date of this episode. Brockett's deposition was reprinted in the 1858 and 1859 editions of Truman Smith's *Examination of the Question of Anaesthesia,* and the rewritten 1867 edition as well.

69. In the testimony presented to Congress, which is referred to in Note 3, Samuel Cooley (who later claimed that it was he who had discovered surgical anesthesia) related that following the examination of his injured knees, he remarked "that he believed a person might get into a fight with several persons and not know he was hurt" and also that "if a person would be restrained, that he could undergo a severe surgical operation, without feeling any pain at the time." Whereupon, he further testified, "Dr. Wells remarked, 'that he believed that a person could have a tooth extracted while under its influence and not

experience any pain'." Gardner Quincy Colton, in a pamphlet published fifty years after the event, *A True History of the Discovery of Anesthesia, a Reply to Mrs. Elizabeth Whitman Morton* (New York, A. G. Sherwood & Co., 1896), relates that after Cooley had inhaled the gas, he ran against some wooden settees on the stage and bruised his legs badly. On taking his seat next to Dr. Wells, the latter said to him, "You must have hurt yourself." "No." Then he began to feel some pain, and was astonished to find his legs bloody; he said he felt no pain until after the effects of the gas passed off. Colton afterwards related that Wells came to him, and said, "Why cannot a man have a tooth extracted under the gas, and not feel it?" After Colton replied that he did not know, Wells said that he believed it could be done and that he would try it himself if Colton would bring a bag of the gas to his office. Colton was replying to an article Mrs. Morton had published in *McClure's Magazine* in September 1896 (v. 7, pp. 311–318) in which she attempted to support her husband's claim to the discovery of anesthesia.

70. Quoted from Maurice B. Strauss, *Familiar Medical Quotations* (Boston, Little, Brown and Company [1968]), 108.

71. Henry Jacob Bigelow, "Insensibility during Surgical Operations Produced by Inhalation," *Boston Medical and Surgical Journal* 35 (1846): 309–317. On December 9, the *Journal* printed on pp. 279–382 additional remarks by Bigelow on this subject, in answer to a prior communication on ether by the Boston dentist J. F. Flagg.

72. Information on the Wells-Morton partnership, including the reprinting of six letters from Wells to Morton with regard to terminating it, are discussed by Henry K. Beecher and Charlotte Ford in "Some New Letters of Horace Wells Concerning an Historic Partnership," *Journal of the History of Medicine and Allied Sciences* 9 (1954): 9–20. These letters, and a few others emanating from W. T. G. Morton's family, regarding the documentation of his claim for priority as discoverer of anesthesia, are now in the Francis A. Countway Library of Medicine in Boston.

Senator Truman Smith of Connecticut, who appears to have been an upright man and who worked with Wells's widow in attempting to prove that Wells was the discoverer of anesthesia, quotes John Riggs (who in this entire episode comes off as another upright man) regarding Morton's relationship and short-lived partnership with Wells:

I knew Dr. Morton when settled in the town of Farmington, Connecticut, in the practice of dentistry; he had little knowledge of his profession, was illiterate, and generally an ignorant man. He was a pupil of Dr. Wells in the years 1841 and 1842, and was in the habit of coming to Hartford to recite to Dr. Wells, and to obtain his assistance in getting up work.

Some time before Dr. Wells made his discovery, he (Dr. Wells) entered into co-partnership with Dr. Morton, to open an office in Boston, and went there for that purpose and staid several weeks. On his return he told me he should dissolve the partnership, as he found that Dr. Morton was not qualified for the profession, and it was dissolved accordingly.

This appears on p. 27 of the 1858 edition of Smith's *An Examination of the Question of Anaesthesia.*

73. F. F. Cartwright, *The English Pioneers of Anaesthesia*, 318.
74. Benjamin Silliman, *Elements of Chemistry, in the Order of the Lectures Given in Yale College*, v. 2, pp. 522–531.
75. Jonathan Pereira, *The Elements of Materia Medica*, pt. 1, pp. 206–218.
76. In June of 1845 Ellsworth published two articles—actually, one long one that appeared in two parts—which he entitled "On the Modus Operandi of Medicine." (P. W. Ellsworth, "On the Modus Operandi of Medicines," *Boston Medical and Surgical Journal* 32, June 11, 18, 1845: [369]-377, [389]-400.) Dr. Ellsworth's stated design in publishing this long essay was to show that there is a fixed principle which should govern physicians in the selection of remedies, and his article reviewed the applicability and effect of a variety of drugs then in use for subduing specific diseases. In the second part of his essay, published on June 18, when discussing the effect of various drugs in remitting or preventing pain, Ellsworth made the statement about the current use of nitrous oxide in Hartford. According to Archer ("Life and Letters," p. 112), Ellsworth lived in the same house with Wells at this time: he occupied the north and Wells the south side. The best account of Dr. Ellsworth's life that I have found was written by H. P. Stearns, "Pinckney Webster Ellsworth, M.D., of Hartford," *Proceedings of the Connecticut Medical Society* 1897, pp. [330]-335. W. P. Ellsworth was born at Hartford on December 5, 1814. After graduating from Yale College in 1836, he tried his hand at law before studying medicine, graduating from the College of Physicians and Surgeons of New York in 1839. After a short period as House Physician in Bellevue Hospital, he practiced for a while in Hartford and, in the early 1840s, visited Europe for the study of general surgery and surgery of the eye. About the time he returned from Europe, Amariah Brigham, with whom he

had formerly associated, abandoned the general practice of medicine and surgery to become Superintendent of the Retreat for the Insane in Hartford, leaving open a broad field which Dr. Ellsworth was quick to enter. During the first ten years of his practice, Stearns relates, when he was between twenty-five and thiry-five years of age, Ellsworth did no less than 175 surgical operations, not counting many minor ones, a large experience in those days. Ellsworth died at Hartford on November 29, 1896.

77. P. W. Ellsworth, "The Discoverer of the Effects of Sulphuric Ether," *Boston Medical and Surgical Journal* 35 (December 9, 1846): 397–398. Ellsworth's December 9, 1846 communication was reprinted in the *New York Dental Recorder,* 1, no. 5 (January 1, 1847): [49]-50.

78. Wells's *Courant* letter was reprinted in the Appendix to the United States Senate, *Statements Supported by Evidence, of Wm. T. G. Morton* volume, 10–12; in Archer's "Life and Letters," 119–121; and in facsimile in Fulton and Stanton's *Centennial of Surgical Anesthesia,* [31].

79. Truman Smith included in the 1853 congressional document he had assembled to support Wells claim (Note 68) the views of Willard Parker, John W. Francis, and Richard S. Kissam, distinguished medical men of New York, as well as the depositions of distinguished physicians of Philadelphia, on the similar effects of nitrous oxide and ether prior to and at the time of Wells's discovery. Parker related (p. 6) that he became acquainted with the effect of nitrous oxide on the human system in 1831 while a student at Harvard College and later prepared it for his class at the Vermont Medical College at Woodstock, making use of sulfuric ether as well for his demonstrations. He related that any one who had knowledge of the two substances would know that ether produced the same effect as nitrous oxide did. In the deposition that followed, Dr. Francis told that he had become acquainted with the effects of the two substances on the human system early in his medical career and that the well known seditive effects of ether might readily suggest to the scientific mind its substitution for nitrous oxide. Finally, Kissam attested that "When in Washington [now Trinity] college I frequently inhaled and saw others inhale the nitrous oxyd gas and the vapor of sulphuric ether. The effects on the mental manifestations and in the abolition of sensation were so similar as to render them almost identical as Pharmaceutical agents; if any preference was observed the nitrous oxyd appeared the most efficacious anaesthetic."

80. Horace Wells, *History of the Discovery of the Application of Nitrous Oxide Gas,* 13; Horace Wells, "The Discovery of Ethereal Inhalation,"

Boston Medical and Surgical Journal 36 (May 12, 1847): 298–301. Wells relates here (p. 299) that "When I first made the discovery, rectified ether was used, as well as nitrous oxide gas. This is clearly proved by affidavit; but I preferred the latter as being more agreeable to inhale and less liable to do injury."

81. "Statement No. 4, of Dr. Marcy," United States Senate, *Statements, Supported by Evidence of Wm. T. G. Morton*, Appendix, 110–112.

82. Marcy's letter is reprinted in the Congressional volume, *Statements, Supported by Evidence of Wm. T. G. Morton*, Appendix, 116–118. This letter followed up a prior one that Marcy had written to the *Journal of Commerce* on December 30, 1846, which appears in the same Appendix, 113–115.

83. C. C. Marcy, "Inhalation of Ether to Prevent Pain," *Boston Medical and Surgical Journal* 36 (July 21, 1847): 495–497.

84. Erastus Edgarton Marcy died at New York on December 27, 1900. The brief biography, from which the information here is taken, appeared in the *Transactions of the Fifty-Seventh Session of the American Institute of Homeopathy* 1902, p. 917. His reference to his training at Amherst appears in "Extracts from the Deposition of E. E. Marcy," which Truman Smith reprinted on pp. 30–31 of his 1858 *An Examination of the Question of Anaesthesia.*

85. C. C. Marcy, "Removal of a Large Scirrhous Testicle from a Man While Under the Influence of Nitrous Oxide Gas," *Boston Medical Surgical Journal* 37 (August 26, 1847): 97–99. This article was reprinted in the *New York Dental Recorder* 2, no. 1 (October, 1847): 7–9.

86. P. W. Ellsworth, "Amputation of the Thigh Under the Influence of the Nitrous Oxide Gas," *Boston Medical and Surgical Journal* 37 (January 19, 1848): 498–499.

87. Ellsworth carried out his amputation operation on January 1, 1848. While in Hartford, Wells, on January 4, administered nitrous oxide for another surgical case, in which L. B. Bereford removed a tumor from the shoulder of a woman, Mrs. Mary Gabriel Dr. Bereford did not report this case in a medical journal, but discussed it in an interrogation which is printed in the Appendix devoted to Wells's claim that appeared in the United States Senate, *Statements, Supported by Evidence of Wm. T. G. Morton*, Appendix, 29–30. Beresford's and Mrs. Gabriels depositions also appear in Truman Smith's *An Examination of the Question of Anaesthesia* (1858), 64–67.

88. Gardner Q. Colton, *A True History of the Discovery of Anaesthesia*, 7–9.

89. The fiftieth anniversary of the discovery of the anesthetic properties

of nitrous oxide by Horace Wells was observed by the Odontological Society of Pennsylvania on December 11, 1894. As part of the ceremonies, Gardner Colton delivered an address in which he went over the events he had experienced fifty years previously and described the episode that led to his rediscovery of the gas in 1863. When giving a talk on the gas at a private entertainment in New Haven in June 1863, Colton recalled, he was asked by a dentist present, Dr. J. H. Smith, to let him try the gas the next day. On going to Smith's office the following day, Colton encountered a wealthy patient of Smith's who had been trying to have Smith give her chloroform for the extraction of some teeth, but whom Smith had refused unless she had her physician present to take the responsibility. After Colton had talked to the lady for some time, she said that she would take the gas. Colton related that after administering a pretty strong dose of nitrous oxide, Dr. Smith took out seven of her teeth, she feeling no pain. Colton afterwards agreed with Smith to furnish the gas while he extracted teeth for one week, and they would divide the profits equally. Their success was so great that they continued for three weeks and two days, during which, Colton claimed, they extracted a little over 3,000 teeth. Having concluded that this was a better business than lecturing, sometimes to empty benches, Colton established in New York, in association with Dr. John Allen, one of the leading dentists of that city, the Colton Dental Institute for the exclusive extraction of teeth, for which he would administer the anesthesia and dentists carry out the extractions. In the thirty year interval between 1863 and 1894, he estimated, on the basis of his patient register, that he had administered the gas to 186,500 patients, without a single accident occuring. *Discovery of Anesthesia by Dr. Horace Wells. Memorial Services at the Fiftieth Anniversary* (Philadelphia, Patterson & White, 1900), 44–46. In his 1867 *Inquiry into the Origin of Modern Anaesthesia,* Truman Smith reduces the number of patients to whom Colton administered nitrous oxide at New Haven in June 1863 to 1,785 (p. 75), and estimates from Colton's patient record that Colton had administered it to 17,601 patients by the end of 1868 (p. 131).

90. *Index-Catalogue of Library of the Surgeon General's Office, United States Army* (Washington, Government Printing Office, 1888), v. 9, pp. 951–954.

91. On p. 151 of the Appendix which Truman Smith added to the 1859 edition of his *An Examination of the Question of Anaesthesia* appears the deposition of T. C. Brownell of Hartford. In this, Brownell swore that on or about January 1, 1848, his daughter, Frances J. Brownell,

had five teeth extracted by John Riggs while she was under the influence of nitrous oxide gas which was administered by Wells. Brownell also stated that she had three more teeth extracted a few weeks afterwards, this time, under ether, which she thought was less genial in its effects than nitrous oxide had been.

92. Alan Van Poznak and Adele A. Lerner, "The History of Anesthesia at the New York Hospital," in B. Raymond Fink, editor, *The History of Anesthesia, Third International Symposium, Proceedings, Atlanta, Georgia, March 27–31, 1992* ([Park Ridege, Ill.] Wood Library-Museum of Anesthesiology [1992]), 421–426. Reference to the case appears on pp. 422–423, with a facsimile reproduction of part of the case being its Fig. 3.

93. *Report No. 114, William T. G. Morton - Sulphuric Ether,* of the 30th Congress, Second Session, dated February 23, 1849, being the report of the Select Committee, to which was referred the memorial of William T. G. Morton, asking compensation from Congress for the discovery of the anesthetic or pain subduing property of sulfuric ether, contains at its end, on pp. 33–42, lists of patients who were anesthetized prior to April 1, 1848 at the Massachusetts General Hospital, the New York Hospital, the clinic of the University of Pennsylvania, and the clinic of the Jefferson Medical College. At the head of the list of operations performed under the influence of ether and chloroform in the first surgical division of the New York Hospital, (p. 38) which was furnished by Dr. John Watson, under the year "1847" and the month "January," is listed the case of the eleven year old female who was operated on for ectropion and to whom nitrous oxide was given, this being the only case among all reported for all hospitals in which this gas was administered. It is here, under the column headed "Result," where the notice of diminished pain, etc. is recorded. Since the facsimile of the case in the Van Poznak-Lerner article clearly indicates that this operation occurred on January 9, 1848, the listing of the case at the beginning of the year 1847 is incorrect; it should, instead, have been the first case listed by Dr. Watson for the year 1848.

94. William R. Hayden, "The History of Anaesthesia, or Painless Surgery," *International Journal of Surgery* 8 (1895): 143–146, 168–173, 201–206, 307–310. The second part is devoted to Horace Wells, and Van Buren's Letter appears on p. 169. Hayden republished this material in a pamphlet entitled *History of Anaesthesia; or Painless Surgery* (New York, International Journal of Surgery Co., 1896) where the Van Buren letter appears on p. 16. We do not know to whom Dr. Van Buren addressed this letter.

95. While Van Poznak and Lerner state in their article that they could not determine how and under what conditions Wells was permitted on the hospital's staff, it is entirely possible that his delivery of nitrous oxide anesthesia during this operation was arranged for by Valentine Mott. Mott's deposition that Wells had visited him in New York and made known to him the influence of nitrous oxide or sulfuric ether to obliterate all consciousness of pain in surgical operations appears on p. 60 of the compilation of materials Truman Smith assembled in 1853 and published in his congressional document supporting Wells's claim (and in the editions that followed under Smith's own name in 1858 and 1859). Mott also attested that "This interview [with Wells] was some time before any publication was made anywhere on the subject."

96. Charles T. Jackson, *A Manual of Etherization: Containing Directions for the Employment of Ether, Chloroform, and Other Anaesthetic Agents, by Inhalation in Surgical Operations, Intended for Military and Navel Surgeons, and All Who May Be Exposed to Surgical Operations; with Instructions for the Preparation of Ether and Chloroform, and for Testing Them for Impurities. Comprising Also, a Brief History of the Discovery of Anaesthesia* (Boston, Published for the Author by J. B. Mansfield, 1861), 13; Truman Smith, *An Inquiry into the Origin of Modern Anaesthesia*, 1867, [66], 68.

97. Truman Smith, *An Inquiry into the Origin of Modern Anaesthesia*, 1867, 12.

98. At the time of the celebration of Connecticut's tercentennary in 1933, Henry Wood Erving delivered a talk on "The Discoverer of Anaesthesia: Dr. Horace Wells of Hartford," which was published in *The Yale Journal of Biology and Medicine* 5 (May 1933): 421–430. While Wood did not know Horace Wells—he had died before Wood was born—he talked of knowing "the other three or four actors in the drama, and often saw them in later life, and Mr. Charles T. Wells, son of Horace, was an intimate friend." With regard to the production of entertainments and panoramas in nineteenth century America, Wood had this to say:

> With the present vast number and variety of *entertainments*, it is difficult to imagine their paucity in Hartford, at least seventy or more years ago. Lectures there were on numerous topics and were well attended. Illustrated lectures came much later. Occasionally, a "panorama" was to be seen. One illustrating *Pilgrim's Progress*, for instance, was freely advertised in Sunday and week-day schools. The "panorama" consisted of scenes painted with more or less art on long strips of canvas, eight or ten feet in width, which were attached

to vertical rollers and exhibited in a large open space on the stage, a person in front with a long pointer being the lecturer . . . These halls were equipped with long movable wooden benches or settees, with spindle backs and a wide top-rail, the edge of which was square and as sharp as possible.

99. According to Albert H. Miller, "Prelude to Surgical Anesthesia," *Connecticut State Medical Journal* 7 (March 1943): 176–189, when William T. G. Morton proposed marriage with Elizabeth Whitman, the beautiful young daughter of a prominent and well-connected citizen of Farmington, Connecticut, the Whitman family objected because of Morton's lack of prospects. The marriage was eventually approved on condition that Morton take the course of study at the Harvard Medical School and became a regular practicioner. In November 1844, Morton matriculated at the Harvard Medical School, choosing Dr. Charles T. Jackson as his preceptor, while continuing his successful dental practice, his manufacture of artificial teeth, and his study of dentistry with Dr. Nathan C. Keep. Due to his involvement in introducing and promoting ether anesthesia, Morton dropped out of medical school about two months before graudation and never did receive his Harvard medical degree.

100. Quoted from W. Harry Archer's "Life and Letters of Horace Wells," 109–110. Archer cites as his source, "Index of Inventors - 1790 to 1847," by which he meant, the United States Patent Office's *List of Patents for Inventions and Designs, Issued by the United States, from 1790 to 1847, with the Patent Laws and Notes of Decisions of the Courts of the United States for the Same Period: Compiled and Published under the Direction of Edmund Burke* . . . (Washington, J. & G. S. Gideon, 1847). The passage appeared intially in John C. Warren's *Etherization; with Surgical Remarks* (Boston, William D. Ticknor & Co., 1848), 85–86; it was reprinted in full in the second part of a two part article entitled "Etherization and Chloroform" which appeared in the *New York Dental Recorder* 2, nos. 7 and 8 (April 1 and May 1, 1848), 130–134, 151–154, with the passage appearing on p. 153. This article reportedly was reprinted from the *New York Journal of Medicine and the Collateral Sciences.*

101. In addition to the *Courant* letter of December 7, 1846, Wells also made approximately the same statements in his *History of the Discovery of the Application of Nitrous Oxide Gas,* 6, 10–11.

102. Horace Wells, *History of the Discovery of the Application of Nitrous Oxide Gas,* 8.

103. "Deposition, No. 1, of J. M. Riggs," United States Senate, *Statements, Supported by Evidence, of Wm. T. G. Morton,* Appendix, 93.

104. Nathan P. Rice, *Trials of a Public Benefactor, as Illustrated in the Discovery of Etherization* (New York, Pudney & Russell, 1859), 52.

105. Nonetheless, included in the 1853 congressional document Truman Smith prepared in defense of Wells's claim is the testimony of Elizabeth Williams of Hartford, who recalled that soon after she had taken the gas in Dr. Rigg's office on the 6th day of March 1845, she had a conversation with Dr. Morton on the subject of the gas. She related that

> Some time after this [the treatment by Dr. Riggs] I saw Dr. W. T. G. Morton at Stafford Springs, and learning that he was a dentist, I spoke of my tooth, and mentioned the fact that Dr. Wells administered gas to me. He asked about the effect and operation of the gas, and made no imitation of any acquaintance with or knowledge of the gas, or of any anaesthetic agent, and the conversation passed off by Dr. Morton's saying he had recently invented some frame work for teeth.

Her testimony appears on p. 76 of the 1853 Senate document *An Examination of the Question of Anaesthesia, Arising from the Memorial of Charles Thomas Wells*, and is reprinted in the 1858 and 1859 revised editions (p. 101) that appeared under Smith's name.

106. Archer reproduces these letters on pp. 116–117 of his "Life and Letters of Horace Wells;" they also appeared as part of Morton's evidence in United States Senate, *Statements, Supported by Evidence, of Wm. T. G. Morton*, 14, and elsewhere. Wells discussed this trip to Boston in a letter he sent to the editor of the *Boston Post* on April 19, 1847, which is reproduced in the *Statements* volume, Appendix, 120. In this letter, Wells related that while at Morton's office, he saw the compound, so called, administered to a patient. "It apparently had the same effect as the gas, which I had many times administered for the same purpose. Before I left for home, the gas was given to several other patients, but with partial success—at least, so said the patients with whom I conversed."

107. Nathan P. Rice, *Trials of a Public Benefactor*, 61.

108. Ibid., 64–65.

109. The younger Dr. Morton made this statement at the twelfth meeting of the American Therapeutic Association, held in Boston May 11–13, 1911, while discussing a paper by Dr. W. W. Babcock of Philadelphia on "The Uses and Limitations of General Anesthesia as Produced by Subcutaneous and Intravasculat Injection." The proceedings of the meeting, an abstract of Babcock's paper, and Morton's remarks were published in the *Journal of the American Medical Association* 56, no. 22 (July 11, 1911): 1677.

110. William James Morton, "Memoranda Relating to the Discovery of Surgical Anesthesia and Dr. William T. G. Morton's Relation to This Event," *Post Graduate* 20 (April 1905): 333–353.

111. "Deposition, No. 1, of J. M. Riggs," United States Senate, *Statements, Supported by Evidence, of Wm. T. G. Morton*, Appendix, 92.

112. Francois Achille Longet, *Expériences Relatives aux Effets de l'Inhalation de l'Éther Sulfurique sur les Systéme Nerveux* (Paris, Victor Masson, 1847); Johann Friedrich Dieffenbach, *Die Aether Gegen den Schmerz* (Berlin, A. Hirschwald, 1847); Nikolai Ivanovich Pirogov, *Recherches Pratiques et Physiologiques sur l'Éthérisation* (St. Pétersbourg, Imprimérie Francaise, 1847).

113. Crawford Williamson Long, "An account of the First Use of Sulphuric Ether by Inhalation as an Anaesthetic in Surgical Operations," *Southern Medical and Surgical Journal* 5 (1849): 703–713. A lengthy discussion of Long, and a reprint of his second paper, which was not published contemporaneously, appears in Hugh H. Young, "Long, the Discoverer of Anaesthesia, a Presentation of His Original Documents," *The Johns Hopkins Hospital Bulletin*, 77–78 (August-September 1897): 174–184.

114. Henry Munson Lyman, *Artificial Anaesthesia and Anaesthetics* (New York, William Wood & Company, 1881), 6. Lyman devoted only a short paragraph to Clarke. Lyman's assertion here that William T. G. Morton was a participant in the ether frolics which went on at Rochester in 1839 and afterwards has not been substantiated.

115. John B. Stetson, "William Clarke and His 1842 Use of Ether," in B. Raymond Fink, editor, *The History of Anesthesia, Third International Symposium*, 400–407. Dr. Stetson provides the fullest account of Clarke that has yet come into print.

116. Berkshire Medical Institution, *Catalogue of the Trustees, Officers, Faculty, and Students, of the Berkshire Medical Institution, for the Year 1841; and of the Graduating Class of 1840* (Pittsfield, Printed by Phinehas Allan & Son 1841), 7. A copy of the catalog is in the Countway Library, Boston.

117. Two long articles have been written on Nathan Rice and the compiling of his *Trials* book: Henry R. Viets, "Nathan P. Rice, M.D., and His *Trials of a Public Benefactor*, New York, 1859," *Bulletin of the History of Medicine* 20, no. 2 (July 1946): 232–243; and Henry K. Beecher and Charlotte Ford, "Nathan P. Rice's *Trials of a Public Benefactor*," a Commentary," *Journal of the History of Medicine and Allied Sciences*, 15, no. 2 (1960): [170]-183.

118. Nathan P. Rice, "A Grain of Wheat from a Bushel of Chaff," *The*

Knickerbocker, or New-York Monthly Magazine 53 (1859): 133–138.

119. Sir William Osler, "The First Printed Documents Relating to Modern Anaesthesia," *Proceedings of the Royal Society of Medicine* 11 (1918): 65–69; this article was reprinted in the *Annals of Medical History* 1, no. 4 (Winter, 1917): 329–332.

120. On the first point, Osler was quoting from Robert Owen, "Report on the Archtype and Homologies of the Vertebrate Skeleton," *Report of the British Association for the Advancement of Science* 9 (1846): 169–340; on the second, he quoted from Sir Francis Darwin's obituary, "Francis Galton, 1822–1911," *Eugenics Review* 6, no. 1 (May 1914): 1–17. The quote appears on p. 9.

121. Henry J. Bigelow, "A History of the Discovery of Modern Anaesthesia," in *A Century of American Medicine* (Philadelphia, Henry C. Lea, 1876), [73]-112. The material discussed can be found on p. 83. This volume contained, in addition to Bigelow's essay, essays by Edward H. Clarke, Samuel D. Gross, T. Gaillard Thomas, and John Shaw Billings.

122. United States Senate, *An Examination of the Question of Anesthesia, on the Memorial of Charles Thomas Wells,* 100–101. Heywood was addressing his remarks to Mr. Brooks of the Congressional committee investigating the question of who was responsible for the origin of anesthesia.

123. Some confusion exists as to the reason for and purpose of Wells's European trip from December 1846 to March 1847. Archer states ("Life and Letters," 122) that "The object of the trip was to purchase paintings for resale in the United States and to present his claims as the discoverer of anesthesia." Elizabeth Wells declared that "One object of my husband was to publish his discovery" (Truman Smith, *An Examination of the Question of Anaesthesia,* 1858 edition, 29). In his 1867 edition of this same work, Smith relates (p. 12) that Wells "paid a visit to Europe in 1847, partly to seek health, and also to interest Continental and English surgeons in his discovery. . . . The expenses of the trip to Europe were paid by the purchase of pictures which Wells imported and sold in the United States."

124. A five-page obituary notice was issued at Hartford, without date or imprint, with the caption title "Death of Dr. Horace Wells." It begins, "Horace Wells, late of the city, located himself, a few weeks since, at 120 Chambers street, New York." A copy of this is in the Countway Library.

125. W. Harry Archer, "Life and Letters of Horace Wells," 137–139.

2

Horace Wells and His Dental Practice

Malvin E. Ring and Leonard F. Menczer

There is no doubt that Horace Wells was one of the most well thought of and competent dentists of his era. In fact, he was ahead of his time in his thinking and in his scientific approach to the problems of dentistry. That he was financially successful in practice was due as much to his pleasing personality as to his competence. "No man ever enjoyed the confidence of a community more entirely than he did that of Hartford. Enmity did not know him, and friendship and esteem everywhere attended his footsteps," were the words of one of his early adherents.[1]

There is an abundance of documentation on Horace Wells the dentist. Information on the background and general aspects of Wells's dental practice can be gleaned from the advertisements he published in the local weekly newspaper, the *Connecticut Courant,* throughout most of his career; and, by looking at the instruments he employed (some of which he crafted himself) and the small volume on dentistry which he published in 1838,[2] we can obtain a fairly clear picture of Horace Wells's technical competence—indeed, superiority. A review of this material will, together with reference to his "Day Book," discussed elsewhere in this volume, afford us insight into Wells's professional life and will make evident the reasons for his success. It will also provide us with a clearer overview of the dentistry of the era in which he practiced.

Horace Wells's Dental Career in Hartford As Reflected by his Advertisements in the *Connecticut Courant*

At the time of Well's arrival in Hartford in 1836, at age twenty-one, the city was primarily a seaport. As a recent biographer of the Hartford theologian Horace Bushnell has observed, "It was strung along an easy fertile bend in the Connecticut River on the brink of a major economic transition from ocean going commerce to nationally recognized banking, insurance, publishing, manufacturing and merchandising enterprise."[3] In 1830, Hartford's population was approximately 10,000; by 1840, it had grown by thirty percent. Thus, Wells entered into a scene that was optimistic as well as vibrant.

Wells came to Hartford from Boston, where he had apprenticed at age nineteen and practiced briefly. From the first paid "notice" that he inserted in the *Connecticut Courant* on April 4, 1836, he demonstrated a fine writing style, full of a sense of competence and self-esteem. His notice told that

> Dr. H. Wells, from Boston, would inform the Citizens of Hartford, and the adjoining towns, that he has at length acceded to the wishes of numerous friends in this section of the country, by making arrangements for spending a short time in this City, with a view of becoming a final resident, should present patronage be sufficient to warrant future success.
>
> He offers himself as a professional Dentist, and all work in the line of his profession will be thankfully and faithfully executed. As he has embraced the new and much improved style of inserting Teeth as recently introduced into London and Paris, He pledges himself to give an acknowledged satisfaction in the most difficult cases. In soliciting a share of patronage, Dr. W. would avoid boasting of his own skill, or derogating that of others—but Ladies and Gentlemen are respect-

fully invited to call and examine his method of Inserting Mineral Teeth on Gold Plates. Particular attention paid to the preservation of Natural Teeth, by a process of cleansing and filling with gold.

Office in Main-street, nearly opposite the Connecticut Hotel, 2d door from State-street. [No. 2175, April 4, 1836]

Just who were the "numerous friends in this section of the country" who encouraged Wells to settle in Hartford, is unknown. His notice concluded with the endorsement:

This certifies that I the subscriber, a citizen of Hartford employed Dr. Wells, while in Boston, in an operation on my teeth, I am happy to say that it has answered my most sanguine expectations.

Joseph S. French

Such endorsements were "usual and customary" and lent an air of support to the skills and character of the person mentioned. Wells employed this technique periodically, we will note later.

This April 4, 1836 advertisement appeared only once. We mention this, since Wells used the public press almost weekly throughout his eleven-to-twelve year practice in Hartford. Sometimes, two or even three advertisements appeared simultaneously. Such frequent advertising by Wells contrasts with other professionals of the time, who did not engage in this practice with such regularity. Wells's second advertisement, for example, first appearing on April 11, 1836, was found seventeen times in the ensuing weeks. Brief and succinct, it read:

Horace Wells, Dentist, Office in the Exchange building on Main Street. Two doors from State Street. [No. 3716, April 11, 1836 and following].

Because of such frequent advertising, the thought occurs that its cost was inconsequential or that it might have been "purchased" on a bartered basis. Interestingly, one of Wells's patients was the Editor of the *Connecticut Courant*; he is listed variously in Wells's day book as "Mr. J. L. Boswell (Editor of Courant)" or "Mr. Boswell (Editor of Courant)." Whether or not Wells bartered for such advertising is unknown. More likely, it was purchased at a cost of twenty dollars per annum, which allowed for weekly ads throughout the year, and as many times and with as many changes as the advertiser wished.

At a cost of ten dollars, the same advertisement might appear weekly, but no changes were allowed. Apparently, it was the responsibility of the advertiser to request the deletion of an ongoing ad and the insertion of a new one. By looking at the changes which Wells made in his ads, we gain further insight into his dental practice; they mirror the changes that occurred in his career.

From the beginning of his Hartford practice, Wells appears to have been successful. On August 29, 1836, in a letter to his sister Mary, he boasted that "My business is now increasing very fast, my profits are from about 5 to 20 Dollars per day. I shall probably remain here should my health permit me to continue my business."[4] However, on November 25, 1836, he wrote his parents, "I am now here [Hartford], but expect soon to leave . . . I think it rather more probable that I shall continue the publishing business. . . ."[5] This intention, declared only three months after his note to Mary, failed to materialize, although Wells suffered periodic bouts of illness that forced him briefly to discontinue his practice and, on one occasion, he relocated to Boston to engage in a joint dental practice with W. T. G. Morton.

On October 28, 1837, Wells advertised his improved method of filling teeth and his invention of a set of instruments for doing so. This advertisement, which will be discussed more fully later on, appeared weekly for the next sixteen months. Then, in early 1839, a second ad appeared, announcing Wells's new location—"H. Wells, Dentist. Rooms under Union Hall, 162 1/2 Main Street"—and naming as references nine physicians located in eight towns in the surrounding area.[6]

The matter of opening and closing a dental office at that time was of little consequence. There was no gas light, and, of course, no electricity, or plumbing, and not much in the way of mechanical equipment, other than hand operated. The basic needs, after "rooms" with a reasonable amount of natural light had been found, were a chair for the patient, a set of dental instruments, some type of dental cabinet, and appropriate furnishings and supplies. In Hartford, gas lines were not installed until 1848, after Wells's death early in the year. At dusk and in evenings, whale oil lamps and tallow candles provided lighting needs and supplemented daylight as needed. During the day, the dentist, with back to window, would make every effort to catch the dimly reflected daylight. His choice of office would, of necessity, be above ground level, for better natural lighting; and it would face south and have as many windows as possible, allowing more continuous natural light. However, these choices were seldom available or obtainable; heating needs, which one provided oneself, necessitated small windows and only a few of them.[7]

Between 1836 and 1847, Wells's office was located at six different places, three of which opened and closed twice, for a total of nine. The gloomy prediction that Wells confided to his parents in 1836 did not come to pass, for, in a letter he wrote to them on September 21, 1838, he related that

> I am now enjoying myself right well, making money fast enough, and good friends to spend my leisure time with, week before last I made $100 clean from all expenses.[8]

In 1840 and 1841, however, the following three notices appeared in the *Connecticut Courant*. The first spoke of "ill health" and the intention of departing Hartford for a "warm climate;" the second, of having removed himself to Boston (to work in partnership with Morton); and the third announced resumption of his Hartford practice:

> H. Wells, DENTIST having resolved to remove from Hartford to a warm climate in consequence of ill health, has left his business to Drs. Cuyler and Crofoot to whom he would cheerfully refer his friends as fully worthy of their confidence. [No. 3961, December 12, 1840].

> H. Wells, Dentist having relinquished his professional business in Hartford would cheerfully refer his friends to Drs. Cuyler and Crofoot as worthy of the unlimited confidence. Dr. Wells has removed to Boston. [No. 3962, December 19, 1840].

TEETH TEETH

> H. Wells, Dentist will resume his practice in Hartford on the ninth of May. His office will be removed to No. 8 Asylum Street a few doors from Main Street. [No. 3978, April 17, 1841].

Several of the above appeared simultaneously. In all likelihood, Wells did not request the removal of one before he ordered the printing of another. In addition, the departure to Boston notice continued to appear after the others had ceased. In a new ad, dated June 12, 1841, Wells spoke of his six month absence and his resumption of business:

TEETH TEETH

H. Wells, Dentist, having resumed his professional business in Hartford, after an absence of six months is now prepared to execute all operations in the line of his profession in the best manner, at his new operating rooms, No. 8 Asylum Street. [No. 3986, June 12, 1841].

The first entry in Wells's "Day Book A" is dated May 13, 1841; whether this indicates the actual time he was again at work is difficult to ascertain since, as we note in the transcription and analysis of Wells's Day Book, entries were probably made at the completion of dental work. The above advertisement appeared weekly from its first printing on June 12, for the remainder of that year. In early 1842 and for the ensuing eleven months, we find a notice similar to the October 1837 ad, but citing the location of his "operating rooms' at No. 8 Asylum Street and containing the same list of physician references.[9]

On October 8, 1842, Wells's new advertisement referred to children's dental care "with teeth, growing irregular" and his "'new Dental Regulator' by the use of which all irregularities are completely obviated." This quaintly worded ad read in full:

Those who have the charge of children with TEETH, growing irregular are invited to call on H. Wells, No. 8 Asylum Street and experience his new Dental Regulator, by the use of which all irregularities are completely obviated if attended to in season. The operation is attended with no pain and with little trouble or expense. This is something entirely new but its simplicity cannot fail to meet the approbation of all. Come and see. [No. 4055, October 8, 1842].

As was mentioned earlier, it was not customary for professional dentists to advertise as frequently as Wells did. For example, the newspaper notices of John M. Riggs announcing the opening of his office appeared during this same period. On February 11, 1843, Riggs advertised the establishment of his office in association with Dr. C. Kirkland.[10] His notice appeared in four consecutive weekly issues of the *Connecticut Courant,* and no further notices would appear pertaining to Riggs. The advertising rates which the *Hartford Courant* published told that it was possible to insert a one-time ad for sixty cents, and a three time ad for $1.50.[11]

On the same date that Riggs's notice first appeared, Wells published a notice in the *Connecticut Courant* telling that he had "received the prize of One Hundred Dollars which was publicly offered in Hartford for the best work in dentistry."[12] Try as we may, no further information has been found pertaining to this award. However, there is no question in our minds as to the validity of Wells's statement.

The next notice referring to Wells was published on April 5, 1845, following his unsuccessful attempt in late January to demonstrate nitrous oxide anesthesia in Boston:

> John Braddock, Surgeon Dentist notifies the public that he has taken the office recently occupied by Dr. H. Wells No. 180 Main Street. [No. 4185, April 5, 1845].

And the *Hartford Courant* of April 7, 1845, carried the following item:

> DENTAL NOTICE - Having relinquished my professional business for the present, in consequence of ill health, I do with pleasure refer those who have confidence in me, to Dr. John M. Riggs, whose professional qualifications in my opinion are not surpassed by any Dentist in the country. This is strong language, but it is said solely for the benefit of my friends who may require any operations on the teeth in my absence.
>
> H. Wells[13]

The last newspaper notice that was published within the chronological span of Wells's day book appeared in the *Connecticut Courant* on August 30, 1845 and spoke of Wells resuming "his professional business on Monday, September 8, 1845."[14] Yet, his day book shows only six entries in September and three in October. The final entry on November 5, 1845 was not for dental work, but rather, related to the settlement of an account with John Riggs. Two additional advertisements appeared in the *Connecticut Courant* during Wells's practice in Hartford. The last, published on September 5, 1847, refers to Wells's "having associated with me in business Dr.

J. B. Terry, I cheerfully recommend him to my friends and patrons . . . in my absence."[15] As is well known, Wells left Hartford for New York about this time, determining to introduce nitrous oxide anesthesia there. And while Wells had an office along with his residence at 120 Chambers Street in New York, his practice thereafter appears to have been erratic and is undocumented.

The advertisements noticed here are useful in providing a background for Wells's dental practice, almost all of which took place in Hartford. In addition to filling in voids in date-recording for office work billed in his day book, they show his skills, which may account for his busy and successful practice; and they also reveal his inventiveness in solving problems in dentistry and, in several cases, devising instruments to aid him in doing so. However, advertisements cannot give a complete picture of the man. They divulge, but in many cases only hint at, something of his personality, his inner drive, his dental skills, his fertile mind, and his inventive genius. Fortunately, additional information about Wells's methods, techniques and resourcefulness can be gleaned from his various writings, and we can conjecture his probable actions in some cases from the writings of other notable dentists of his era, based upon what they have told us about their own practices.

The Instruments He Used

At the time Wells opened his practice in Hartford, there were as yet no true dental manufacturing companies in the United States. It wasn't until 1844 that Samuel S. White established his dental manufacturing business in Philadelphia, thereafter supplying dentists throughout the country with the implements and supplies needed to carry on their businesses.[16] Consequently, it was necessary for Wells to use his skill and ingenuity to construct many of his own instruments, or to commission instrument makers to fashion them after designs he had made. He also came up with novel inventions outside the field of dentistry for which he received patents.

After Horace Wells's death, an inventory was made of his office furnishings and equipment. This was done because Wells died insol-

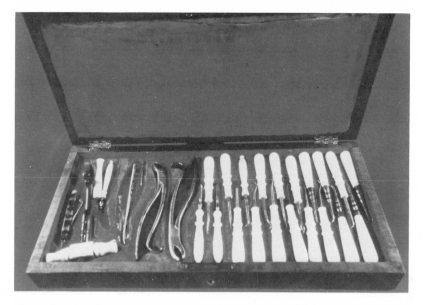

Illustration 3. An instrument case similar to one probably used by Horace Wells. This one beloged to a physician-dentist of Batavia, New York in 1840. Courtesy of the Holland Land Office Museum, Batavia.

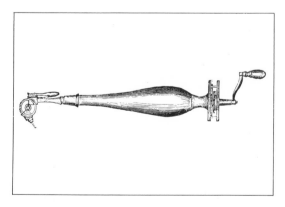

Illustration 4. Dental drill invented by John Lewis in 1838.

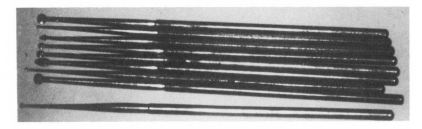

Illustration 5. Hand drills typical of those used by Horace Wells. They would be twirled between the thumb and forefinger.

Illustration 6. The highly popular "ring drill" of Amos Westcott.

Illustration 7. The first commercially produced dental chair, invented by James Snell of London in 1832.

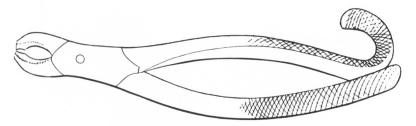

Illustration 8. An extraction forceps of the type used by Horace Wells.

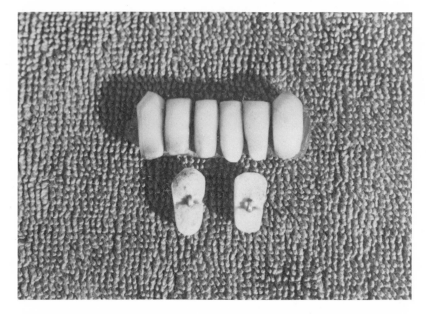

Illustration 9. Individual porcelain denture teeth with platinum pins embedded in them. These would be soldered to a swaged gold denture base.

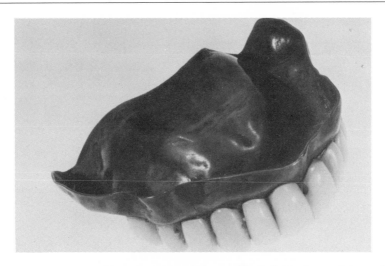

Illustration 10. A gold swaged denture base with individual porcelain teeth soldered to it. This would have been similar to those constructed by Horace Wells.

Illustration 11. A gold foil packet of 1850. Courtesy of The Francis A. Countway Library of Medicine.

vent and all that he owned, household furniture as well as office equipment, was sold at auction to pay his debts. It is from this inventory, dated March 20, 1848, and reproduced here in part, that we can get an idea of the hand instruments he used:[17]

2 Pairs Forceps(new)	$1.50	$3.00
6 Pairs Forceps	.75	4.50
1 Pair Forceps		.50
1 Pair Forceps		.25
3 Pair Forceps	.50	1.50
24 Files $1.00 per doz.		2.00
Lot gold		1.00
35 Excavators & Burrs (Square finish) 1.50 doz.		+4.25
24 Excavators & Burrs (Round finish) 1.00 doz.		+2.00
23 Excavators & Burrs (ivory handle) 1.00 doz.		+1.92
21 Pluggers, etc.(Ebony & ivory handle) 4.50 doz.		7.87
1 Spring Saw		.50
1 Drawing plate		1.00
3 Files		.50
978 Teeth (Plate & pivot)	6c.	58.68
2 Cases for tools	2.-	4.00

It is probable that Wells kept his instruments in one or more wooden boxes (noted on the inventory as "case for tools"), constructed for the purpose (Illustration 3). The first practical dental instrument case had been invented in 1840 by the New York dentist John D. Chevalier, and constructed and sold by him to the profession. It had five different instrument compartments, and when it was opened all the instruments were exposed to view at one time. On top was an additional tray which could be lifted out, and under this tray were stored such sundry items as books of gold leaf and artificial teeth. The cases were constructed of various woods, including rosewood, walnut and mahogany, and were equipped with brass or silver hinges and corner mountings.[18] It is very possible that Wells purchased one of Chevalier's cases. Nevertheless, he probably found some shortcomings in it, for he found it necessary to make one of his own, no doubt combining some features that he felt were lacking in Chevalier's case. We know this, because, in 1844, when he was in practice with William T. G. Morton, the two were awarded a special diploma by the Massachusetts Mechanics Association for an instrument case they had built and which was exhibited at the Exhibition and Fair of 1844.[19]

Indeed, when referring to the records of the Massachusetts Charitable Mechanic Association, which seems to have been overlooked by earlier biographers, one discovers that Wells not only invented such a case, along with instruments to fill it, but that Chevalier manufactured and sold it. The report of the fourth exhibition of the Association[20] contains the following entry under the category "Surgical and Dental Instruments:"

> 695. WELLS & MORTON, *Boston*. One Case of Dental Instruments, manufactured by Chevalier, New York; an Upper Set of Mineral Teeth; and Specimens of Solder. The Committee mark the Instruments as No. 1; but as they were not exhibited by the manufacturer, *the Committee* did not recommend a premium. They understand that the teeth in the case were not manufactured by Mr. Morton, and that they were only affixed to the plate by him. The plate is of silver, covered with gold. The solder, they consider, so far as they are able to judge, as *good*; but similar to that used by other dentists.
>
> Diploma.

Only a few mechanical drills existed during Wells's time. Among the more popular was a bow drill invented by J. Foster Flagg of Boston; a delicate mechanical drill invented by the Parisian dentist J. C. F. Maury in 1830; and a drill with a turn-handle at one end and a swivel head for burs at the other (Illustration 4), patented in this country in 1838 by John Lewis, and also sold by the Ash Dental Supply Company in London.[21] It is thus possible that Wells availed himself of at least one of these drills. However, all these contrivances required that both hands be used to hold and turn the drill. Consequently, most dentists relied on burs that were several inches long (Illustration 5) and could be twirled between the fingers—it is possible that these are the type of instruments referred to on the probate inventory; or else, the very popular "ring drill" invented by Amos Wescott around 1840 (Illustration 6).

From December 1844, a prominent part of Wells's armamentarium was the gas bag he used for the administration of nitrous oxide to patients for the extraction of teeth. When administering the gas to Wells on December 11, 1844, on the occasion of the first dental operation under anesthesia, Gardner Colton brought the gas to John Riggs's office in a bag made from an animal bladder.[22] Wells began using a similar bag in his practice with a capacity of only two liters; finding this insufficient, he eventually employed a larger bag. In time, gas bags were made with a capacity of thirty liters, and they had mouthpieces of wood, similar in function to the tap of a wine cask.[23] According to a deposition made by Elizabeth Wells in late 1852 or early 1853, and printed in the volume of evidence collected by Truman Smith and submitted to Congress to support the claim made on behalf of her son Charles T. Wells for his father's discovery,[24] Horace employed nitrous oxide during tooth extractions many times after December 11, 1844, and he continued to do so from time to time until his death. "In the winters of 1844 and 1845," she reported, "and repeatedly thereafter, I made bags of India (rubber) cloth for my husband, to be used in administering this gas in dental surgery, and frequently saw them in the hands of my husband when engaged in his profession."

There is no record of the equipment Wells used in his dental office, but one can speculate based on the furniture in use at the time. The first true dental chair had been invented by James Snell of London in 1832 (Illustration 7). It had a seat that could be moved forward and back and could be raised. The headrest was movable also, and the chair was supplied with a footstool that fastened to the floor. Attached to the arm of the chair was a small tray to hold the operating instruments.[25] It is likely that Wells, a very progressive dentist, would have used such a chair, but it is impossible to say one way or another, based on the terse description, "1 Dentist Chair $3.00," that appears on the inventory of his estate. As noted earlier, gas lighting was not yet available; Wells would have positioned his chair near a window so that the daylight would provide sufficient illumination for his work. Completing the office furnishings would have been a brass spittoon and a small work table on which Wells would have mixed his filling materials. The presence of "1 Looking Glass" on the inventory indicates that the patient had available a mirror in order to examine his or her appearance following the completion of dental work.

Returning to the advertisement which Wells published in the *Con-*

necticut Courant on October 28, 1837, we note that he informed his friends and the public that he had "invented a set of Instruments for FILLING TEETH, which by their construction entirely supercede those in common use." Exactly what was the nature of these implements, and who fabricated them, is unknown. Although no dental equipment or supply companies were in existence in 1837, Samuel Fitch, in his *System of Dental Surgery*, published at Philadelphia in 1835, cites Messrs. Weigand and Snowdon, "at No. 15 North Sixth Street in this city," where dental forceps might be obtained. But we have no knowledge that instruments were actually made there.[26] It was customary at that time for blacksmiths to fabricate items that were large and crude; finer instruments, such as Wells used, were more likely made by scientific and mathematical instrument makers and by die sinkers and cutters in brass, for these were the craftsmen who supplied physicians and surgeons with the precision instruments and cutlery they needed in their work.

On October 1, 1847, three months prior to Wells's death, the *New York Dental Recorder* reported, under the title "Dental Depots," that

> Nothing shows plainer the great increase in public demand for operations upon the teeth, than the number of furnishing stores which have sprung up in our large cities within the last few years. Ten years since, there was not such a thing known. If we wished the most ordinary kind of instrument, we then had to make a pattern and wait for it to be made, and so of almost every article used in the practice of Surgical and Mechanical Dentistry.

The *Recorder* then cited "ten or twelve extensive establishments" that have recently sprung up in New York.[27]

On the subject of dental instruments, Fitch, in the section of his treatise entitled "Of the Instruments required in Plugging the Teeth,"[28] describes

> two kinds of Instruments used in this operation . . . The first are those with which we clean out the cavity which is formed by the progress of the caries, or all putrid, foreign, or dead matter. These consist of small bent instruments, made of steel, with pearl, ivory, bone, or

wooden handles, or many of them to fit one handle, with which to scrape out the cavity.

He then discussed and described "a kind of hand drill," presumably for hand manipulation, since he found "very objectionable" the use of "a common drill turned with a bow and string to prepare the cavity and fit it for the plug" as being injurious to the tooth.

The Nature of Wells's Dental Practice

Preventive dentistry: First and foremost, Wells was a strong believer in preventive dentistry. He advocated regular cleaning of the teeth and, in fact, devoted a chapter on this subject in his *Essay on Teeth,* wherein he strongly advocated the use of the brush:

> I will here state one fact, which may be considered as a weighty argument in favor of the brush. Those teeth which are frequently cleansed with a brush, seldom or never decay.[29]

In his practice, he spent a fair portion of his time with that procedure. He decried the terrible measures resorted to by unethical practitioners in order to minimize their work. "Frequently . . . ignorant practitioners do not hesitate, while cleansing the teeth, to remove also a portion of the tooth itself, in order to make it perfectly white." Wells wrote in his small book, which was intended for the layman: "Acid is sometimes used for the same purpose. This for a time gives satisfaction. The teeth present a beautiful external appearance after such an operation. But a few days will effect sad changes, and the teeth assume a dead appearance."[30] As for dentifrices, he advised, "In selecting a powder, it should be remembered that it ought not to contain a particle of acid. I would recommend Peruvian Bark, pulverized."[31]

Children's dentistry: Wells had a fine reputation when it came to handling children, and his services were eagerly sought after by parents. He understood the insidious nature of sugar and cautioned that "there is nothing more destructive to teeth than a compound sold at nearly every corner of the streets, under the name of candy."[32] And he was ahead of most of his fellow dentists in appreciating the need to conserve the primary dentition. He wrote that he frequently saw the evils occasioned by premature removal of the first teeth and cautioned everyone in the care of children not to be too hasty in their removal, "but to let them remain until they are ready to fall out of themselves, unless they become too troublesome to be endured."[33] That he had a concern for teeth growing irregularly is proved by his invention of his "new Dental Regulator by the use of which all irregularities are completely obviated."

Surgery and prosthetic dentistry: A large part of Wells's practice consisted of extracting teeth and constructing full or partial dentures; this is indicated by the large number of forceps (Illustration 8) listed on the probate inventory, and in the exceptional number of artificial teeth noted there, as well as the numerous entries for extractions that appear in his day book. Furthermore, as the very first notice he inserted in the *Connecticut Courant* mentioned "his method of Inserting Mineral Teeth on Gold Plate," it is apparent that his dentures were made with swaged (hammered) gold bases to which porcelain teeth, with platinum pins embedded, were soldered (Illustrations 9, 10). Vulcanite dentures were still some twenty years in the future. Full upper and lower dentures were secured in the mouth by means of steel springs which kept the upper denture up and the lower denture down.

Operative dentistry: Treatment of carious teeth took up a large part of Wells's time. Although his treatment for this malady was efficacious, his understanding of the cause of caries was poor, except for his recognition that too much sugar would result in caries. Although he disputed a commonly held belief that caries was a *result* of inflammation, rather than its cause, he nevertheless believed that it was the composition of the saliva that determined whether or not the teeth would decay. If the saliva was "vitiated"—and to Wells, "vitiated" meant contaminated—the teeth were sure to decay, he believed. Yet he also had an inkling that more was involved in the carious process. "Another agent in this matter, may be attributed to particles of food remaining between the teeth, which soon putrify," he wrote, "thus acting with a pernicious effect upon the general health of the mouth."[34] Wells thus had some understanding of the role decomposition of food would play in the causation of caries, a theory so clearly expounded by W. D. Miller a half century later.

Wells was a very ethical dentist; with few exceptions, he used only gold foil (Illustration 11) for filling cavities, since silver amalgam was looked upon with disfavor by the leading dental authorities of his day. His day book shows that he employed other materials, such as tin, "sement," and silver, and, for temporary fillings, "Hill's stopping," on only a few occasions. The reference to tin means "tin foil" used much like gold foil. The reference to "silver" is the amalgam of today, a mixture of mercury with silver. Amalgam came into the dental armanetarium in the late 1830s, and the amalgam controversy "raged" in the middle of the 1840s as being potentially hazardous to the patient's well being.

When discussing the cases of two patients who were preparing for the Christian ministry, Samuel Fitch advised that "their carious front teeth should be plugged with gold; and more especially so, because they were intending to become public speakers, in whom the health and beauty of the teeth are indispensable to a cleanly appearance of their mouths, and perfect enunciation of language."[35] With regard to tin foil, Fitch declared that

> a gradual oxidation . . . of the tin immediately commences which gives the substance of the tooth, opposite the plug, a dark and repulsive appearance, and what is far worse, beyond comparison, that by the gradual oxidation of the tin, the caries of the tooth is suffered to go on, favored by the oxidizing metal, and ultimate destruction of the tooth is the inevitable consequence.

Regarding the use of gold (foil), Fitch states that "gold, in purity is the substance we ought to use." He continued,

> Gold, without alloy, is a substance which may be retained a century in the mouth without oxidating. It reposes upon the living substance of a tooth, and excludes all foreign natures of every kind; the saliva, the food, decayed portions of other teeth, cold air, etc. etc. and at the same time gives firmness and strength to the tooth, whilst itself remains unchanged.

Wells, in his *Essay on Teeth*,[36] explains that "gold is one of the best conductors of heat and cold there has ever been discovered," and he related that a tooth will elicit pain when exposed to "cold air or water" and because the plug "has been made quite dense by compression, giving an opportunity for a quick penetration of cold or heat. If, on the other hand, something soft, or even gold itself, were introduced without much compression, the tooth would, in all probability, remain insensible as before."

In contrast to most practitioners of his day, he recognized that filling carious teeth was the most important part of the dental art. "However simple the operation of filling the teeth may appear," he wrote,

> It is, in reality, the most complicated, as well as the most important branch of the profession. An ordinary Dentist may succeed in performing all other operations tolerably well, while this remains beyond the reach of his skill. He may truly put gold into the tooth, and perhaps it will keep its place for some length of time; but if the work is not effectually performed, the decay will proceed as before, even if the gold remains.[37]

It should be pointed out that Wells's *Essay on Teeth,* although published when he was only twenty-three years old, shows that he was not only well trained in the art and science of dentistry but was very well versed in the dental literature of his time. We have quoted from Samuel Fitch's *A System of Dental Surgery,* which was first published in 1829 and in a second edition in 1835. Fitch's text, in excess of 500 pages, may be considered the latest word on the subject of dental care at the time. Although Wells's text has no bibliography, he refers in its contents to "Mr. Fitch," to "Bunon," "Bourdet," "Hunter," "Bell," "Fox," "Longbotham," and others, all significant authors in their day, all of whom Fitch lists at the conclusion of his text.

A description of what had to be a very tedious method used by Wells's contemporaries in filling a cavity with foil was given by Robert Arthur, the inventor of cohesive gold foil. This latter product, which was easier and more satisfactory to use, became available only after Wells's time. The foil used by Wells would have been cut into strips or rolled into tapes and placed around the circumference of the cavity. More gold was then added from the center outward, and a wedge-shaped instrument was used to create more space into which more gold could be packed until sufficient density of the filling was achieved. The filling was then shaped and polished with files and abrasives.[38]

Root canal therapy was also a part of this progressive dentist's

practice. He condemned the charlatans who peddled worthless nos-
trums to an unsuspecting public desperately seeking surcease from
the pain of toothache. Wells instead offered permanent relief by his
technique of extirpating the pulp of the offending tooth:

> It is no easy matter to destroy the whole nerve of a molar tooth. The
> part exposed may be paralyzed, while the main portion of it retains
> its vigor; and in this state it cannot remain without becoming the
> subject of inflammation, at some future day, if not immediately. It may
> be said, that when it is wholly destroyed, there is an end of it, and
> consequentially an end of pain for ever from that source.[39]

Horace Wells was able to fulfill a dream that had haunted practitioners from all the ages of existence—the destruction of pain during
the carrying out of such a procedure as is described above. It was a
triumph of imagination and deductive reasoning that would lead to
one of the greatest benefits ever bestowed upon mankind, and one
going far beyond the field of dentistry. However, his discovery may
also have planted the seeds for his own destruction. With Horace
Wells's suicide on January 24, 1848, came an end to what may have
been one of the most successful and financially rewarding practices
in the country, as an analysis of Wells's day book shows. And it
brought to an end the career of one of the finest dentists of his era.

Notes

1. Truman Smith, *An Inquiry into the Origin of Modern Anaesthesia*
   (Hartford, Brown and Gross, 1867), 16.
2. Horace Wells, *An Essay on Teeth, Comprising a Brief Description of
   Their Formation, Diseases and Proper Treatment* (Hartford, Case,
   Tiffany and Co., 1838).
3. Robert L. Edwards, *Genius of Singular Grace, a Biography of Horace
   Bushnell* (Cleveland, The Pilgrim Press, 1992), 41–42.
4. W. Harry Archer, "Life and Letters of Horace Wells, Discoverer of
   Anesthesia, Chronologically Arranged, with an Appendix," *Journal of
   the American College of Dentists* 11, no. 2 (July 1944): 89.
5. Ibid, 90.
6. *Connecticut Courant*, No. 3866, January 23, 1839, and following.
7. Consider the poor quality of glass of that period (1836–1845) that

would dim and distort natural light; consider the 1,000-plus foot candles of light that can be measured in the mouth of today's patient versus the possible five to ten candles available at that time; consider the visual acuity of the dentist and the availability of better correcting glasses today.

8. W. Harry Archer, "Life and Letters of Horace Wells," 96.
9. *Connecticut Courant*, No. 4017, January 1, 1842.
10. *Connecticut Courant*, No. 4055, February 11, 1843.
11. J. Eugene Smith, *One Hundred Years of Hartford's Courant* (New Haven, Yale University Press, 1949), 198.
12. No. 4073, February 11, 1843.
13. *Hartford Courant*, April 7, 1845, v. 9, no. 81, p. 3. This is the only advertisement that Wells published in the *Hartford Courant*, which began in 1837 as a daily, concentrating on local news. The *Connecticut Courant*, in which all his other ads appeared, was a weekly reporting regional news. The two continued to be published side by side into the early 1900s.
14. *Connecticut Courant*, no. 4206, August 30, 1845.
15. No. 4311, September 5, 1847.
16. S. S. White Dental Manufacturing Company, *A Century of Service to Dentistry* (Philadelphia, 1944), 3.
17. A slightly more detailed inventory can be found in W. Harry Archer's "Life and Letters of Horace Wells," 142–143; and an inventory and appraisal of his entire estate, and a final accounting of it, appears in Ralph W. Edwards, "Horace Wells, Dentist, a Further Contribution to His Life," *Journal of the American College of Dentists* 18 (1950–1951): 91–103. The inventory was made for the Probate Court by F. A. Brown and C. L. Covell, appraisers.
18. R. A. Glenner, *The Dental Office: a Pictorial History* (Missoula, Montana, Pictorial Histories Publishing Comapny, 1984), 35.
19. W. T. G. Morton, *Remarks on the Comparative Value of Ether and Chloroform, with Hints Upon Natural and Artificial Teeth* (Boston, William A. Hall, 1850), 48.
20. Massachusetts Charitable Mechanic Association, *The Fourth Exhibition . . . at Quincy Hall in the City of Boston, September 16, 1844* (Boston, Crocker and Brewster, 1844), 105.
21. Walter Hoffman-Axthelm, *History of Dentistry* (Chicago, Quintessence Publishing Company, 1981), 301.
22. W. D. A. Smith, *Under the Influence: a History of Nitrous Oxide and Oxygen Anesthesia* (Park Ridge, Ill., Wood Library-Museum of Anesthesiology, 1982), 55.

23. Bryn, Thomas K. *The Development of Anaesthetic Apparatus* (Oxford, Blackwell Scientific Publications, 1975), 118.
24. "Further Extracts from the Deposition of Mrs. Elizabeth Wells," in United States. Senate, *An Examination of the Question of Anaesthesia, on the Memorial of Charles Thomas Wells* (Washington, 1853), 19–20. In rewritten and enlarged form, this made up the volume *An Examination of the Question of Anaesthesia* which Smith published under his name in 1858 and 1859, and in further revised and enlarged form in 1867. Mrs. Wells's testimony appears in all three later editions.
25. R. A. Glenner, *The Dental Office: a Pictorial History,* 23.
26. Samuel S. Fitch, *A System of Dental Surgery* (Philadelphia, Carey, Lea & Blanchard, 1835), 551.
27. "Dental Depots," *New York Dental Recorder* 2, no. 1, (October 1, 1848) 19–20.
28. Samuel S. Fitch, *A System of Dental Surgery,* 381–382.
29. Horace Wells, *An Essay on Teeth,* 62.
30. Ibid., 42.
31. Ibid., 62–63.
32. Ibid., 46.
33. Ibid., 22.
34. Ibid., 40.
35. Samuel S. Fitch, *A System of Dental Surgery,* 383.
36. Horace Wells, *An Essay on Teeth,* 51.
37. Ibid., 68–69.
38. Robert Arthur, *A Treatise on the Use of Adhesive Gold Foil* (Philadelphia, Jones, White & McCurdy, 1857).
39. Horace Wells, *An Essay on Teeth,* 56.

3

Horace Wells's "Day Book A:" A Transcription And Analysis

Leonard F. Menczer

Since 1928, the library of the Hartford Medical Society has been the repository of Horace Wells's "Day Book A," an account, in Wells's hand, of his billings for services rendered in his dental practice from early 1841 until late 1845. It is perhaps the most complete record extant of dental office transactions in the United States during that period. For the past sixty-six years that this volume has been on deposit, it has neither been examined closely nor has the richness of its contents been fully appreciated. Now, 150 years after Wells's momentous discovery, and approximately 147 years after his death, this document is published here in transcribed form, together with an analysis and discussion of what more it can tell us about Horace Wells the dentist and his practice.

Despite the designation he assigned to it, "Day Book A" may not have been the first such business record that Wells maintained during his Hartford practice, since it sometimes was the custom of practitioners to leave their initial volume unlettered or unnumbered and add an alphabetical or numerical designation from the second volume on. Furthermore, he may have maintained a separate ledger or ledgers to accompany it as well. Wells, we know, spent approximately five years in practice in Hartford before he commenced the record under discussion—about the same span of time as is covered in "Day Book A." Regretfully, if a previous volume existed, it has not withstood the attrition of time; indeed, few dental records of its type and period have. Had it not been for the fame of the person who maintained it, and the great discovery he made during the years it covers, it is likely that "Day Book A" would have suffered the same fate that befell the records of other dentists who practiced in America during Well's period of activity.

The physical make-up and appearance of this book are not dissimilar from other account books of its time. It is the type of volume that stationers and bookbinders made up of blank leaves which they had ruled lines across and stitched together by hand and bound in inexpensive leather to be sold as "blank books" to purchasers, who employed them for recording business transactions and memoranda, for personal journals and diaries, as scrapbooks, and for similar purposes. It measures 6 3/4 inches in width, 7 3/4 in height, and is approximately half an inch thick. In bookbinding terms, it was originally encased in a "quarter binding" of sheepskin and plain blue paper glued over wooden boards, but upon restoration in recent times, it was rebacked with modern calfskin. On its front cover is mounted a wax seal-like form at the upper center, affixing a narrow ribbon or tape beneath, and below it are the words "Day Book" and "A" (Illustration 12). On the back inside cover appears, in blue ink, the stamped mark of ownership of "Charles McManus, Hartford, Connecticut." And written in pencil at the top is the note, in Wells's hand, "H. Wells Hartford Jan. 2, 1840," this appearing to be the date on or about which Wells purchased the volume; thus he kept it on hand for about fifteen months before making his first business entry in it.

On the paste-down endpaper inside the front cover are written, in both pencil and ink, several miscellaneous notes in Wells's hand.

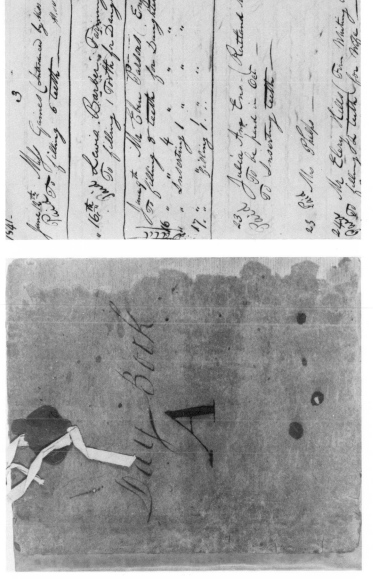

Illustration 12. Front cover and page 3 of "Day Book A" showing Wells's entries for June 1841. Courtesy of the Historical Museum of Medicine and Dentistry, Hartford.

Onto the free front endpaper has been pasted the bookplate of the Hartford Medical Society, and on the top portion of its verso appears the presentation inscription, "To the Library of the Hartford Medical Society, Sept. 10, 1928," and below this is the bookplate of Dr. James McManus. This contains the words, "Jas. McManus" and "Hartford" above and below the image of a warrior with shield and sword. On the facing flyleaf is written in pencil, in Horace Wells's hand, in two lines, "H. Wells, Hartford, May 10, 1841," and beneath this is written three times, "H. Wells" and "Hartford, Conn." On the verso of the flyleaf appears the notation, in pencil and in two lines, "May 13, 1841 - Nov. 5, 1845, and below this has been glued a small piece of paper containing the typescript library accession note:

Wells, Horace
Dr. Horace Wells' Day
book. May 13, 1841-Nov. 5, 1845
An original manuscript
Gift from:
Dr. Charles McManus (D.D.S.)

The facing page is Wells's designated page "1" and thereon appear the first entries of Wells's office records, the initial one being dated "May 13th, 1841." Office entries are found on pages numbered 1 through 65 (Illustration 12). Two additional pages, 66 and 67, are numbered but have been left blank, as is the remainder of the book, except for assorted and unrelated entries on interior pages, being recipes for preparing "Gilding Solution," "Gold Solution," "Sticking Paper," "Sealing Wax," and the like; whether these were copied from elsewhere or were ideas Wells developed is unknown. The next-to-last page in the book, numbered "148," and a page following it will be discussed later.

It is obvious that the volume was part of the library of Dr. James McManus, whose bookplate appears on the front endpaper. James McManus entered dental practice at Hartford in 1855 and died in 1920. Charles, the donor, was the older of his two sons, both of whom were in dental practice with the father. At the time the younger Dr. McManus donated Well's day book to the Hartford Medical Society, the Hartford Dental Society was twenty-three years old, having been founded in 1897, and was meeting in the Medical Society's building (and continues to enjoy this relationship with the Medical Society to this day). The Dental Society had no library and no staff at the time of Dr. McManus's gift, while the Medical Society had both. We are indebted to both Drs. James and Charles McManus for appreciating the historic value of Horace Wells's "Day Book A" and preserving it, and to the Hartford Medical Society for doing so as well.

Wells's day book served the purpose of itemizing the dental services he provided, and billed, presumably at the time of the completion of such work, and to indicate when and for whom such activities were furnished, their cost, and, finally, to record payment or other deposition, usually at a later time. It is not a record of patient care, as we understand it today, but a record of accounts for services rendered and payments due at a future time. Each entry lists the person for whom work was provided. This may be broadened to include the name of the person responsible for payment, and not necessarily the person for whom service was provided, for there often appear such notions as: "for son," "for daughter," "for wife," "for Henry," "for Miss Stanley," etc.

Starting with the entry of July 7, 1841, the letters "Dr" are regularly used following the entry name, for example, "Mr. Crocker [firm of Steel & Crocker] Dr," indicating that upon the completion of services, Wells listed Crocker as "Debtor." The book, then, is a record of services rendered for which payment was not immediately made but would be forthcoming at a future time. And when such services were paid for, presumably always at a later time, the notation "Paid" was made. In contrast, the word "By" is used with "Cr" to designate "creditor." Wells used this on a few occasions only. See, for example, page 43, March 18, 1844: "Dr. Comstock Cr By Five Dollars 5.00" and on two occasions this designation pertains to W.T.G. Morton. The use of the word "To" in entries means "to whom" and/or "for what."

In that period, a person in business usually maintained a "day book" and a "ledger." The day book listed the activities of the merchant's or businessman's day-to-day business such as sales, services, and purchases. In other words, it referenced all daily transactions which required a charge to be made, or a credit to be given to a customer or user. Its use is described by Samuel Green in his 1826 treatise *The Practical Accountant:* "In the book, termed the Day Book, are duly to be entered, daily, all the transactions of the master or mistress of the family, which require a charge to be made, or a credit to be given to any person."[1] Nicholas Harris, in his *Complete System of Practical Book-keeping,* published in 1840, closer to Wells's period of business activity, provides the following definition:

> The Day-Book, in the beginning of which is to be recorded a minute and concise statement of the Merchant's or Tradesman's affairs when he commences business; a history of his debts and effects, and afterward a record of what individuals have bought and received of the Merchant, and of what the Merchant has bought and received of individuals on account.[2]

The ledger, Harris states, is a book

> In which the Merchant, devoting one page to each person with whom he has transactions in trade, and writing his name in large round hand at the top of the page, posts to the Dr. side, all sums which the individual owes him, and on the Cr. side [the facing page] posts all sums which he has had of the individual on account.

In order to lend validity to such transactions, since the merchant could enter whatever he wished, whether valid or not, "credit slips" and "notes" were made out to the debtor at the time of each transaction (the I.O.U.s of today), signed by the debtor and held by the creditor or merchant. When payments were made, the debtor's signature was torn off, and discarded and the slip given to the debtor as proof of payment. Obviously, Horace's record under study fits the definition of a day book and not a ledger. Since only Wells's "Day Book A" is available, it is difficult to interpret how he maintained his total business accounts with additional information concerning the billing and payment notations within it.

While his method of bookkeeping may have been dissimilar from that of Horace Wells (we just don't know), John Riggs has left us some insights as to how he maintained his records. When asked, during an interrogation to "Please state the manner of keeping your books," Riggs replied as follows:

I keep no regular journal and ledger. I intend to do a cash business; when a person has work done, and does not pay, I enter it. I enter all the work for filling, whether paid or not. When I do finish the work, I make an entry, and leave a space ordinarily, if they make another engagement to come in a few days; and when they come, I enter the charge directly under the former charge, although there may be a page of charges made between the time of the two charges, which are so put together. When the space is filled up, if it don't embrace all the charges, I turn over to the next blank leaf, and give another space. If a person has any filling done, I enter it on my book; and when he pays, I balance it, and square the account.[3]

The vast majority of entries in "Day Book A" do not indicate the place of residence of the debtor. These are assumed to be Hartford residents. However, fifty-one of Wells's patients, of the approximate 250 named in the book, have entry indications of towns of residence other than Hartford. The towns from which these fifty-one patients were drawn encompasses a region in excess of 150 square miles. Forty-seven of these fifty-one patients came from fifteen of Connecticut's 169 towns; three additional patients came from Massachusetts and one from New York. A complete alphabetical list of Wells's patients whose names appear in his day book, with dates of billing and towns of residence, may be found in Appendix 1.

Wells did not, in many instances, provide first names and/or initials and he listed his patients variantly, for example, "Leonard Bacon" and "L.H. Bacon;" or "Mr. S. Bartlett" and simply "Mr. Bartlett." Many of the billing entries contain some notation as to place and/or type of employment, for example, "Case & Skinner," "Whiting Rising & Co.," "Steel & Crocker," "Editor of the Courant," "bookseller," "school teacher," "tailor," "printer." Other notations pertain to source of referral: "Introduced by Miss Francis [sic] Humphrey," "Daughter of Mrs. Strong." One entry has the word "mute" and another the description "studying law with Judge Merick of Glastenbury." These notations are not very different from those found in patient records today. Such descriptions made it easy to recall who the patient or client was.

The services Wells provided were essentially limited to those listed below, together with accompanying charges. Fees varied, but for the most part, the figure that appears in bold type is the more constant one.

Type of Service Provided	Fee
"To inserting [number of teeth]"	$3.00 & **4.00**
"To filling [number of teeth]"	.50, **1.00**, 1.50
"To extracting [number of teeth]"	.25, **.50**, .75
"To cleansing teeth"	**.50** .75
"To operations on teeth"	No price is specified. The sums that appear are total price and vary from $3.50 to $10.00.

These charges remained constant for the four/five year span of entries.

Wells's charges were essentially in line with those of other dentists of his day. For example, the *New York Dental Recorder* on December 1, 1848 (seven weeks before Wells's death) published the following fee schedule:[4]

Teeth on gold plate from	[$] 2 to 4
" silver "	1 to 2
" pivot "	.75 to 1.25
Filling with gold from	.50 to 1.00
" " cement	.50
" " tin or silver	.50
Cleaning teeth	.50 to 1.00
Separating "	.50 to 1.00
Curing toothache or extracting tooth	.50

However, it is stated here that "There is perhaps no business, either professional or purely mechanical, transacted in our city, in which the charges, for services rendered, vary so much as those of practicing dentists."

One entry in "Day Book A" shows that Wells charged for home visits. "To 2 visits at house $1.50" (see page 58, December 11, 1844). This particular entry is of further interest, since the services provided were: "To filling 3 teeth for wife," which presumably took two visits to accomplish. Two entries are for services provided at

Hartford's mental institution, the Hartford Retreat, now named the Institute for Living:

To Douglass (At Retreat)	Dr
To filling 8 teeth	8.00
To extracting 2	1.00
	9.00 [See page 32, August 1st, 1843]

And

Mrs. Haskell
To extracting 13 teeth for Daughter
At the Retreat 5.00 [See page 52, July 29, 1844]

Although most of the dental filling entries merely cite "To filling" (number of teeth), a few are listed differently:

To filling 9 teeth with Gold for Wife	$9.00
To filling 1 tooth with sement	.75
To filling with tin	.50 and .75

As for the type of filling materials Wells used, it is safe to assume that all were gold except for the few occasions where otherwise noted, such as tin, "sement" and silver. The reference to tin means "tin foil," used much like gold foil. The reference to "silver" is to the "amalgam" of today, a mixture of mercury with silver. Amalgam came into dental use in the late 1830s and the "amalgam controversy" raged from the late 1840s as being potentially hazardous to the patient's well being. With regard to tin foil, Fitch relates that a gradual oxidation of the tin immediately commences, giving the substance of the tooth opposite the plug a dark and repulsive appearance; and by the gradual oxidation of the tin, the caries of the tooth is suffered to go on and ultimate destruction of the tooth is the inevitable consequence.[5] Fitch obviously favored gold, which he claimed "may be retained in the mouth for a century without oxidating," and we can safely assume that Wells did also.

While the day book's most frequent entries are for fillings, extraction is the second most frequently recorded procedure. Wells, with few exceptions, does not indicate permanent or deciduous teeth. Exceptions appear on pages 55, 56, and 57:

To extracting permanent tooth for Daughter .50
To Extracting temporary tooth for Son .50
To Extracting temp tooth for daughter .25

While Fitch speaks of dental forceps as being of two kinds, "the Dentist Key, and Forceps," only the latter was listed on the inventory of Wells's estate. Wells's fees for "To cleansing teeth were usually $1.00.

Before concluding this brief survey of the services he provided, one entry in "Day Book A" bears particular significance because of the fee charged, for which payment was made. On page 56, under the date of October 29, 1844, appears:

Seth J. North New Britain Dr.
To Inserting whole set of teeth for Wife
$100.00

It is worth noting, at this point, that Wells frequently provided "tooth replacement services," a term which we designate today as partial and complete dentures and which he designates in his day book as "To Inserting teeth." Wells's first newspaper notice, announcing the opening of his office in Hartford, dated April 4, 1836 (and which is discussed more fully on pages 74–75) states that he has embraced the new and much improved style of inserting Teeth as recently introduced into London and Paris." On the next to last leaf of the transcription of the day book will be found, as miscellaneous outlay: "200 pivot teeth $25.00" and "250 teeth 37.00"; in addition the inventory of Wells's estate listed "978 Teeth (plate and pivot)" which further establishes the extent of such service. And, finally, on page 46, dated May 4, 1844, we find that Wells billed Morton for "1/2 doz impression cases." Throughout the day book we find reference to such dental replacements, three such references, for example, appearing on page 1, dated May 13, May 15 and May 29, 1841.

What do the dates of Wells's entries indicate? Are they the date of the last day of service? In most instances, the billings are for small sums, for work that might have been accomplished at one office visit. Was the entry made to comply with the function of a day book, that is, record credit extended and payment due, or was the word "paid" entered alongside to indicate payment at the time? More likely, the entry was made because the work was not immediately paid for, and the entry "paid" was recorded when payment was made at some later date.

Fitch states that, "as a general principle, we should not plug more than two or three teeth at one sitting. Our patient should then be dismissed, to call again in about a week, and so continue the course of operations until all teeth requiring it are plugged."[6] Fitch aside, it is inconceivable that much of the work billed for in "Day Book A" could have been provided at one sitting. The very first entry in it will serve as an example:

May 13th 1841	For Frederick
Mr. Humphrey to filling 9 teeth	$9.00
" do 1 "	*1.00*

Furthermore, we have only to recall that Wells made two home visits to provide a total of three fillings.

The first entry in Wells's day book also raises the thought that the dental work performed on Mr. Humphrey was started prior to this first entry date, i.e., prior to the inititation of this day book. Also worthy of notice are the credit by cash entries that appear in it, which represent partial payment for dental services. Of the first, on page 2, dated June 10th, 1841 for "Miss Rhonda Brown," we find two credit entries. Similar entries are found only three additional times: page 6, July 27, 1841; page 9, September 22, 1841; and page 58, December 7, 1844.

The sequence of dates, as they appear in the day book, may not divulge the whole extent of Wells's practice. Was John Riggs the only patient seen on May 14 and Miss McHinney on May 15 and no one else on the subsequent days until May 20, when appears the name of the patient John Russel and the notation "To filling 7 teeth"? How many did Wells actually fill at that time, and how many at later dates? And so on. Obviously, this day book does not serve as a complete day-to-day record and thus provides us with only partial information regarding Wells's daily activities. We must remember that dental practice in the 1840s was not like that of the 1990s, when the practitioner devotes himself to full-time office practice with advanced bookings extending into several weeks or more.

Additional notations appear in conjunction with Wells's billings. On the left side of each page and opposite most billings the word "Paid" or some equivalent appears. Where this notation is not present, an "X" is sometimes found and in a few instances there is no designation at all. It may be assumed that in the latter two events the entry "no payment" was made. In one case, the word "Settled" is found. Frequently, the letters "off" (all in lower case) appear. This notation is found independently for the first time on page 12, under the date January 15, 1842, and frequently thereafter. In addition, it is found along with the word "Paid." While Webster defines the word "off" to mean "no longer binding; out of force; at an end," in the terminology of Wells's time the notation could have meant "copied off" into a ledger. Harris notes:[7]

> When an article is posted from the Day Book into the Ledger, it will be proper, opposite the article, to note the same in the margin of the Day Book by writing the word "Entered" or making two parallel strokes of the pen.

Just what, then, Wells intended when recording "off," is left to the reader's imagination.

Appendix 1 lists the patients by name whom Wells billed over the four-to-five year span of the day book; it gives the dates of such billings; and provides towns of residence, other than Hartford. Of the approximate 300 patients (probably closer to 250 as cited earlier, since, in all probability, the same individual was counted more than once because Wells sometimes designated an individual differently), most were billed only once. Of these 250 patients, 234 were billed once; four show two billing dates; twelve, three billing dates; and the remainder were billed from four to eleven times. For example, Mr. John H. Goodwin was billed for dental care for himself as follows: 7/23/41; 8/10/41; 8/26/41; 11/21/41; 12/9/41; 3/29/42; 7/16/42; 9/2/42; 4/1/43; 10/10/43; 12/27/43.

Of the first twelve entries on pages 1 and 2 of the day book, with the possible exception of the first, Mr. Humphrey (since Wells lists three Humphreys), the remaining eleven show billing only once. The billing dates are for early 1841, and these patients do not appear again, even though the day book extends for a period of several years beyond. It would be assumed that additional dental care would be required again. There is no explanation for this. Appendix 2 shows a tabulation of the billing entries by months, along with the total number of billings for the years 1841 through 1845. No pattern can be formulated from these figures.

As to the question of who Wells's patients were, Wells's failure to write first names or initials, as noted previously, frequently makes such inquiry difficult to answer. While it cannot be stated with absolute certainty that many of Wells's patients were the prominent citizens of Hartford, it seems more than mere coincidence that thirty-four of these clients or their forebears have a street in Hartford named after them: for example, Babcock, Barnard, Bartholomew, Brinley, Kelsey, Litchfield, Loomis, etc. Robert Edwards, in his biography of Horace Bushnell,[8] Hartford's foremost Congregational minister, after whom is named Bushnell Park, the Bushnell Memorial Hall, and the Bushnell Congregational Church, lists may of Hartford's prominent citizens with whom Dr. Bushnell associated. Mentioned by him among these is Leonard Bacon (listed in Wells's day book on page 13, January 22, 1842); Henry W. Camp (Wells lists "Mr. Camp for wife," p. 51, July 12, 1844 and p. 57, November 9, 1844); John Brown (Wells lists a Mr. J. Seymour Brown on p. 14, February 25, 1842 and p. 16, May 21, 1842); and many other such examples may be found. In addition, there are Wells's own identifications alongside his billing entries: "Mr. Skinner of Case & Skinner;" "Mr. Crocker of Street and Crocker;" "Mr. Street of Street and Crocker;" "Mr. Richmond of Richmond & Coleman;" "Mr. Boswell, Editor of the Courant;" and so on.

A few names bear singling out, among them "Governor Ellsworth." Although there is no indication that Wells treated the governor, he does have seven billing entries "for Hariet," "for Miss E," "for daughter" and "for wife." Ellsworth, who served as governor from 1838–1842, was the son of Oliver Ellsworth, the third Chief Justice of the United States Supreme Court and one of the five delegates from Connecticut to the Federal Constitutional Convention. He was the father of Pinckney Webster Ellsworth, the surgeon who was a contemporary of Wells and for whom Wells provided anesthesia on more than one occasion. It was Pinckney Ellsworth who championed Wells's discovery of anesthesia and it was his sister, the Governor's daughter, whom Wells treated frequently.

John W. Bull, another well-known name of the time, was a merchant whose two-story brick home and business, located originally at Main and Charter Oak Avenue in Hartford, was relocated, in 1975, to its present site on Prospect Street, and served first as the home of the Connecticut Bicentennial Commission, and presently as the Connecticut Historical Commission. Another of Wells's patients, "Dr. Butler," was a descendant of one of the early settlers of Hartford; his homestead still stands and is known as the Butler/McCook Homestead at 394 Main Street. Its care is now under the auspices of the Connecticut Antiquarian and Landmarks Society. "Miss Cheney" was probably a member of the family that owned the Cheney Silk Mills at Manchester, Connecticut. "Dr. Crofoot," according to McManus, "commenced the practice of Dentistry in Middleton in 1835; removed to Hartford in 1840."[9] It was Drs. Cuyler and Crofoot to whom Wells referred his patients in his December 1840 advertisements, when he contemplated moving to a warmer climate and then went off to Boston. "Dr. Comstock" is listed in McManus's text as Dr. J. A. G. Comstock, who practiced dentistry in New London in 1842. Wells shows billings addressed to Dr. Comstock for February and July of 1842, and June of 1843.

The "Goodwin" name appears most prominently in Wells's day book, in various forms: "Charles L.," "James W.," John H.," "H.," and "William." Goodwin Park in Hartford's south end, encompassing, 135 acres of land, was donated to the city by this family. Lastly, there is "Dr. Terry" who located in Hartford in 1845, and whom Wells shows as having treated by a single billing, dated April 26, 1844. Terry was not only a patient, but later was an associate of Wells. His name first appeared in an advertisement which Wells inserted in the *Connecticut Courant* on September 4, 1847:

DENTIST
Notice: Having associated with me in business Dr. J. B. Terry, I cheerfully recommend him to my friends and patrons who may require Dental operations in my absence.

The second part of this ad, dated "August 28, 1847," in which Terry announced the use of nitrous oxide "to patients have teeth 'extracted,'" is especially significant because it is the first mention of the gas as an anesthetic to appear in any of these newspaper notices.

Appendix 2 (as noted earlier) contains a tabulation of the billing entries by months along with the total number of billings for the years 1841 through 1845. No pattern can be inferred from these. Wells's gross billings for these years were as follows:

1841 (the day book was initiated in May)	$559.02
1842	$458.95
1843	$506.97
1844	$758.00
1845 (no billings entries March through August)	$130.00

These figures give little indication of Wells's total income, since there is no record as to the amount Wells received from patients who paid initially and as treatment progressed. The notes held in the "Conn. River Bank," listed on the next to last page of the day book, which I will discuss shortly, imply other sources of income.[10]

It can reasonably be assumed that Wells achieved a certain monetary wealth during these years of practice, as compared with the average income of other wage earners of his era. For example, one source[11] tells us that

In 1838, the average male teacher could expect to earn $15.48 in a month . . . carpenters $40 a month . . . and bricklayers $48.00. In contrast, prominent members of the clergy might expect to receive $100 monthly, in addition to the parish house.

Accordingly, Wells's "Day Book A" has to be considered an incomplete record of the transactions encompassing his entire practice, representing only that part of it for which payment was not immediately forthcoming. For example, several of the patients who would later swear that they had had teeth extracted *by Wells* while under the influence of nitrous oxide are not billed or mentioned in it. Truman Smith's volume of evidence gathered in support of Wells contains the depositions of two such persons, H. C. Havens and Thomas Martin;[12] and the Appendix in the *Statements, Supported by Evidence, of Wm. T. G. Morton* volume mentions another, Mayo Lee.[13] Interestingly, following Wells's discovery of the powers of nitrous oxide as an anesthetic and his employment of the gas in dental operations, his day book contains no references to his use of it, since no extra charge appears to have been made for its administration.

Because the goal of this study has been to dissect and analyze Wells's "Day Book A," references to his discovery of general anesthesia have been kept to a minimum. Nonetheless, since this volume contains entries pertaining to Wells's relationship with W. T. G. Morton, perhaps it is appropriate to end it with some discussion of these. On a dozen occasions, out of the 400 or so entry billings, the notation "H. L. Rider Notary" appears at the end of an entry. Since these notations all appear in the same hand, it would seem that the debtor and Wells went to the notary's office for his formalization of the agreement they had made by the recording of his signature. Other miscellaneous entries in Wells's "Day Book A" are accompanied by this H. L. Rider notation. The page numbered "142" has twenty-one entries on it (all undated) and might be assigned the arbitrary title (where none exists) of "Cash Outlays," since it records a variety of miscellaneous expenses, such as "Box for Stove;" "Freight on Baggage from Farmington;" "Hotel board," etc. The lower portion of the same page lists "Dr. Jackson $40.00" and there are other entries of "Cash to Morton" for $10.00 and $3.00 respectively. Here, the H. L. Rider notation appears in the left hand margin, extending up the page from the last notation to include that of Dr. Jackson.

And finally, this Rider entry appears on the page adjacent to the back cover of the book. The page is titled, "Notes deposited in the Conn. River Bank for safe keeping" and lists three such notes, one against John Olmstead and Co. for $700; a second, "against Robert Trumbull for $550;" and a third which reads as follows:

1 note against W. T. G. Morton
dated August 21, 1845 - Amount $108

Only the last was notarized by H. L. Rider.

It is well known that Wells instructed Morton in dentistry. During the association of Wells and Morton at Hartford, the ever-inventive Wells devised a noncorrosive dental solder for fastening artificial teeth to gold plates, resulting in the formation of a partnership and the two young men going to Boston for the promotion of the solder.

On October 21, 1843 they opened an office at 19 Tremont Row in Boston. However, within a year the partnership was dissolved. While Henry K. Beecher and Charlotte Ford, when publishing and discussing a few of Horace Wells's letters which relate to this partnership,[14] attribute its dissolution to Wells's instability, W. Harry Archer had earlier published in his "Life and Letters" compilation a letter which indicates that Wells quickly became disillusioned with Morton.[15] Writing to his mother and sisters from Hartford on July 6, 1844, Wells devoted the first part of his letter to a report of his current good health and of his examination the previous day by "a magnetised lady," who nonetheless pronounced his lungs slightly affected. He then went on to discuss the situation with Morton. Dr. Archer dropped a sentence or two out when reprinting this letter, but because of the importance of the news contained in it, its latter portion is reprinted here in full.

"You undoubtedly feel anxious to know how I come on with my Boston business," Horace related.

I will tell you in short I was not in partnership with Morton, but about 4 weeks I found him to be a fellow without any principle whatever—you recollect when I visited Boston and came so near meeting Mother, I saw Mary—well the object of my visit then was to see if I could not influence him to persue [sic] a different course from what report told of him - it was reported here that he had taken to drinking. After I had been with him one week in Boston, I was satisfied that he possessed no self denial and I very much feared he would become a drunkard and my last words to him were when I left to be cautious and not taste of anything which might excite him, consequently I was not at all surprised when report came that he was in the daily habit of visiting grog shops. Aside from that he was the most deceitful man, I ever knew, he would not scruple to tell direct falsehoods when he knew that he must be detected in a lie within a few hours. He is now married. I attended his wedding at Farmington a few weeks since and if ever I pitied a body, I truly pitied that girl. She, however, had heard these reports about him, but it made no difference. Love they say is blind and I am sure it was in this case. He has married a fine girl and I fear she has found her mistake ere this time. By the way I am on perfectly good terms with Morton and would not on any account be otherwise; he refunded to me the money which I had expended in starting the office.

Beecher and Ford comment that as the year 1844 wore on, Wells's earlier predictions proved wrong, for large numbers of patients found their way to the office he and Morton had set up and Morton had to take on two assistants to keep up with the traffic. Wells, however, saw the situation in a different light, confiding to his mother and sisters that he was

> exceedingly sorry that I had not selected a man to conduct the business there in whom I could place confidence as our prospect for business there was far beyond our most sanguine expectations; in fact it would be easy enough to realise a fortune there [;] according to his story he is making $18000 a year or fifteen hundred dollars per month. I know he is making money fast for he keeps two workmen employed beside himself, but when he talks about making $18000 a year I am apt to think he is using his tongue in making a random statement which his is no stranger to ___ * * * * * *

While Wells, as he noted, maintained professional relations with Morton after the dissolution of their partnership, the later transactions that are reflected in his day book, he made sure, were duly notarized. Before looking at these transactions, however, we might take a few moments to follow up the notation he entered on August 21, 1845. It is well known that following his unsuccessful demonstration of nitrous oxide anesthesia in Boston in late January of that year,[16] about six months prior to that August notation, Wells became ill from the "excitement of the adventure" and did not recover for many months; as a result, there are no entries in his day book from March through August of 1845. It would not be until August 29 that Wells announced in the *Connecticut Courant* that he intended to resume his professional business on Monday September 8.

It may be assumed from the notation of August 21 on the next to last page of the day book that Morton was in Hartford on that date in order to be present before the notary public. The note for $108 recorded there probably represented a total of the sum owed to Wells by Morton following the closing of their partnership; indeed, Beecher and Ford reproduce in transcription a letter that Wells wrote to Morton the following November 28, in which Wells forwarded to Morton the note "which you have doubtless been expecting to see before this according to agreement one half ($54) was to have been paid on the 21st of this month but I have delayed sending it until now, that you can be fully prepared for it." And at the end he appended the line, "N.B. Please pay the $54 to the bearer and have it endorsed on the note."

As we can see, Morton was only one of three to be singled out by having a debit notarized; from all appearances, it seems that Morton did not honor his debts and Wells was aware of it. In Appendix 3, which lists the eleven entries in Wells's day book that pertain to Morton, each has the "H. L. Rider, Notary" signatory. Only the first and second entries, dated August 1843 and September 10, 1843, are accompanied by Wells's "Paid" notation. Of the remaining seven, two are for credit, numbers 7 and a portion of number 9; all of the remaining entries are debits, with no indication of payment.

The entries pertaining to Morton in Appendix 3 are interesting, since almost all are for the purchase (on credit) of dental supplies or for the performance of work for Morton by Wells, for example, the inserting of teeth into plates for Mrs. Smith and Mrs. Phelps, and the repairing of Mrs. Smith's teeth. The only other exception is the initial third entry, which represents the cost of dental services that Wells performed on Morton and for instructing Morton in the art of dentistry. The first nine entries span a period of one year—August 1843 to September 1844. These are found interspersed throughout the book. Morton's note of August 1845 in the safekeeping of the Connecticut River Bank and the loan of $10 and $3 found on page 142 complete the eleven entries concerning Morton. If the debit entries are added up, Morton's debt to Wells comes to $111.81. The two debit entries on page 142 total $13.00 more and the note at the bank $108. It would seem that Wells, on occasion, served as Morton's loan agent and that Morton, in turn, seemed to consider such loans as "gifts."

A word about the three notes in safe keeping, which totaled $1,358. The fee for $100 that Wells received for the "set of teeth" that was noted earlier would be equal to from $3,000 to $5,000 in today's dollars. This $1,358, then, would be equivalent to from $40,000 to $60,000 at the present time. A review of Wells's patients does not disclose the name of John Olmstead & Co., nor does the name Robert Trumbull appear. The how and why of these notes remain a mystery, as does the fact that Wells was ruled insolvent after his death.[17]

The notation that Wells made in his "Day Book A" on March 4, 1844 (see page 41 of the book) deserves some comment. It reads:

March 4, 1844, Dr. W. T. G. Morton Dr
To Operations on teeth and instruction
in the art of Dentistry per Agreement $50.00

Archer, in his "Life and Letters of Horace Wells," states that Wells "tutored Wm. T. G. Morton . . . John M. Riggs . . . and his cousin C. A. Kingsbury," the latter being one of the founders of the Philadelphia Dental College.[18] There is no question that Wells taught Morton, but nowhere in his day book does Kingsbury's name appear, and Riggs's name is found only as a patient under the billing date of May 14, 1841 (page 1), as follows:

May 14, 1841, Mr. John Riggs
To operations on Teeth $4.00

No indication of payment is found. Riggs's name appears again on page 65:

November 5th, 1845 Dr. Riggs Dr,
To Ballance Due on Act $6.71

The implication here is that further work was done or services rendered; that Riggs paid a portion thereof; and the $6.71 figure represented the new balance, which was later marked "Paid." The only other business references that Wells made to Riggs appeared in his newspaper notice of April 7, 1845, at which time he referred his patients to Riggs.

Archer, unfortunately, gives no sources or references to his statement that Wells tutored Riggs and Kingsbury. He may have taken this information from James McManus's 1896 text[19] in which McManus stated that Wells had several students, among them, Drs. John M. Riggs and W. T. G. Morton," and afterwards related, "He [C. A. Kingsbury] also received instructions from his cousin Dr. Horace Wells of Hartford."[20]

In summary, "Day Book A" shows that Wells applied his professional skills not only to Hartford's and the region's most prominent citizens, but that he also served as the "dentist's dentist." His income, according to this record, and his letters home, indicates financial success. Nonetheless, what little of his estate remained after his death was sold at auction to satisfy his creditors. While Wells reported to his mother and sister in his letter of July 6, 1844, that Morton had refunded the money which Wells had expended in starting the office, probably having taken Morton's promise to do so on face value, we can see from his letters of July 31 and November 28, 1845, written more than a year later, that he was still trying to get Morton to pay half the $108 debt, and it is possible that the debt was never repaid. Furthermore, Wells related in his letter of July 31, 1845, when discussing his ill health, which forced him to give up his business in Hartford, that "I went into a sort of speculation which used up my ready means—and I sunk the whole of it—and what is worse I now fear I shall be obliged to give up my business here for my health is no better but rather on the decline."

In light of Wells's later letters home, and what he revealed in his letters to Morton, his somewhat erratic behavior that is apparent in his constant opening and closing of his office, and the frequent references to ill health, it can safely be assumed that there was more than just a fragile soma dictating many of his actions. Restlessness, and a very active and fertile mind that might have bordered on genius, may account for his multiplicity of interests and activities that, in the scant records that remain, make him appear flighty and restless.

Nonetheless, his observation on December 10, 1844, when seeing Samuel Cooley injure himself but feel no pain, was a triumph of imagination and deductive reasoning that has been paralleled by few cases in recorded history. Now, with the perspective of 150 years since that momentous occasion, we can appreciate the enormity of Wells's accomplishment, given the little chemical and physiological information available to him at the time, and truly say that he made the great leap forward from which resulted the events that brought about the introduction of surgical anesthesia.

Notes

1. Samuel Green, *The Practical Accountant, or, Farmer's and Mechanic's Best Method of Book-Keeping, For the Easy Instruction of Youth . . . Published by Samuel Green, New London,* In Nathan Daboll, *Daboll's Schoolmaster's Assistant, Improved and Enlarged. Being a Plain, Practical Assistant, Adapted to the United States . . .* (New York, Stereotyped, Printed and published by Charles S. Baldwin, 1826), p. [2] at end.
2. Nicholas Harris, *A Complete System of Practical Book-Keeping, Exemplified in Six Sets of Books: Journalized Daily, Weekly, and Monthly; by Single and Double Entry. Applicable to All kinds of Business, Both Individual and Partnership Concerns. Accompanied with the Various Forms of Bills, Marcantile Letters, Etc., in Daily Use in the Counting Room. An Interest and Time Table; Also, a Series of Concise Rules for Performing Various Computations in Business . . . Second Edition.* (Hartford, Brown & Parsons; E. Huntington & Co., New York; W. Marshall and Co., Philadelphia, 1840), 10.
3. United States Senate, *Statements, Supported by Evidence, of Wm. T. G. Morton, M.D. on His Claim to the Discovery of the Anaesthetic Properties of Ether. Submitted to the Honorable the Select Committee Appointed by the Senate of the United States. 32d Congress, 2d Session, January 21, 1853* (Washington, 1853), Appendix, 97–98.
4. "Dentists' Fees," *The New York Dental Recorder* 3, no. 3 (December 1, 1848): [70]-72.
5. Samuel S, Fitch, *A System of Dental Surgery* (Philadelphia, Carey, Lea & Blanchard, 1835), 375–376.
6. Ibid., 391.
7. Nicholas Harris, *A Complete System of Practical Book-Keeping*, 10.
8. Robert L. Edwards, *Genius of a Singular Grace, Biography of Horace Bushnell* (Cleveland, The Pilgrim Press, 1992).
9. James McManus, *Notes on the History of Anesthesia . . . Early Records of Dentists in Connecticut* (Hartford, Chark & Smith, 1896), 80.
10. Henry W. Irving, *The Connecticut River Banking Co., 1825–1925* (Hartford, 1925) tells that "This bank was chartered by the Connecticut General Assembly in May 1824 'for the purpose of improving the boat navigation of the Connecticut River.' In 1925, it became the

Hartford National Bank & Trust Company. In 1992, it was rechartered to the Shawmut Bank."

11. "Education in the Time of Henry Barnard," *Hartford Courant*, May 25, 1993. Information reported here was taken from the records of the Connecticut Historical Society.

12. Truman Smith, *An Examination of the Question of Anesthesia, Arising on the Memorial of Charles Thomas Wells* (New York, John A. Gray, printer, 1858), 46–48.

13. United States Senate, *Statements, Supported by Evidence, of Wm. T. G. Morton, M.D.*, Appendix, 106.

14. Henry K. Beecher and Charlotte Ford, "Some New Letters of Horace Wells Concerning an Historic Partnership," *Journal of the History of Medicine and Allied Sciences* 9, no. 1 (January 1954): 9–20.

15. W. Harry Archer, "Life and Letters of Horace Wells," 106.

16. In the article he compiled with Charlotte Ford dealing with the letters Wells wrote to Morton concerning the dissolution of the partnership and his repayment for funds expended in starting it, Dr. Beecher, a preeminent anesthesiologist, added the following comment relative to Wells's unsuccessful Boston demonstration: "Anyone familiar with the vagaries of patients even under modern methods of administering N_2O would not have been duly distressed by an outcry from the patient. A little more self-assurance here might have saved the day and spared Wells the disappointment his friends believed was a contributing factor in his breakdown in health and subsequent unhappy ending."

17. In the separately-paged Appendix at the end of the *Statements, Supported by Evidence, of Wm. T. G. Morton* volume, appear a letter of G. Howell Olmstead, Jr. and the testimony of Jos. Trumbull. Morton had written to Trumbull to elicit information from him in support of his claim, and Olmstead's reply was printed on pages 12–13 of the Appendix. Olmstead wrote that he had been connected in business with Wells, "and being very intimate with him, we had a great many conversations together about the effect of the gas." Olmstead then told that after the controversy with Col. Roberts over the rights to the shower bath had been decided in Wells's favor, "I then made arrangements with Dr. Wells to travel and dispose of rights to manufacture his bath." Olmstead, then, appears to have been a lawyer, or a backer, or a financier involved in the shower bath project; but whether he was connected to John Olmstead & Co. is unknown. Jos. Trumbull, who testified (pages 36–37) that he was then seventy years old, a resident of Hartford, and not intimately acquainted with Wells,

merely gave general information concerning his scant knowledge of the discovery by Wells of the use of anesthetic agents in surgical operations. Once again, there is no known tie connecting him with the Robert Trumbull whose note for $550 Wells held in the Connecticut River Bank.

18. W. Harry Archer, "Life and Letters of Horace Wells," 99.
19. James McManus, *Notes on the History of Anesthesia*, 81.
20. Ibid., 113.

A Transcription
Of Horace Wells's
Day Book A

Horace Wells's "Day Book A", which now follows in transcribed form, has been copied just as it was written in Wells's hand. Spelling styles of his period, including misspellings, entries made and later crossed out, and other anomalies are recorded as found. The entries for the most part appear in ink, although a number are in pencil, some of which have faded considerably. And a number of pages, notably pages 11 through 16, are marred by burn marks which partially obliterate the entries made on them. A question mark in square brackets [?] has been used where the handwriting was difficult to decipher. Nonetheless, great pains have been taken to reproduce everything as it appears. When payment was made, Wells wrote "paid" or "paid in full" or "paid off" or simply "off" or "settled" in the left hand margins of accounts, and infrequently elsewhere; these latter notations appear here in bold type.

Horace Wells

[i]
Day Book, A

[ii]
H Wells
Hartford May 10 1841
          H Wells   Hartford Ct
Hartford Ct
H
          H

–1–

May 13th, 1841		for Frederick
Mr. Humphrey To filling 9 teeth		$9.00
Paid	Do 1 "	1.00
		10.00

May 13th
Mr. Skinner (Case & Skinner)

To Inserting 1 tooth for Sister					$4.00
filling	3	"	"	"	$3.00
"	2	"	"	"	2.00
Nov. 26 Inserting 1 tooth for sister					$4.00

Paid

May 14th,	Mr. John Riggs To operations on Teeth	$4.00

May 15th	Miss McHinney To Inserting one Tooth	$4.00
" "	" " " filling 8 "	8.00

Paid

20th	West Hartford	
	Mr. John Russel To filling 7 teeth	$7.00

21st	Mute	
	I. Henry Lloyd To filling Teeth	$3.00

24th	Bookseller	
Paid	Mr. Edward Reed To filling 7 teeth	$7.00

29th	Miss Phebe Smith To Inserting Teeth	$11.00
Paid		

–2–

1841		
June 7th	Miss Mary Ann Hill 64 Front St	
	To Inserting 2 teeth	8.00
	" filling 4 "	4.00
Paid	To be paid the 1st July	$12.00

~~9th~~	~~Mr Eben Parsons Enfield~~	
	~~Miss Alavina Parsons~~	8.00
	~~Warehouse Point~~	

10th	Miss Rhoda Brown	
	Newington	
	To Inserting 8 teeth	$28.00
	" filling 3 "	3.00
Paid in full		$31.00
Cr By Cash		18.00
		Due $13.00
" " "		11.00
		2.00

11th	Mr. J.N. Talcott (School Teacher)	
Paid	To filling 4 feeth	$4.00

11th	Miss mary Wells To Cash	$5.87
28th	" " " " "	$9.36
July 16	" " " " "	$5.00
29	" " " " "	.84
Paid		

–3–

1841		
June 12th	Miss Gaines (Introduced by Miss Francis Humphrey)	
Paid	To filling 6 teeth - - - $ 1.00	$6.00

16th	Lewis Barber Farmington	
Paid	To filling 1 Tooth for daughter	$1.00

June 9th	Mr. Eben Parsons (Enfield)	
	To filling 8 teeth for daughter	8.00
16th	" " 4 " " "	4.00
"	" Inserting 1 " " "	3.50
17th	" " 1 " " "	3.50
"	" filling 1 " " "	1.00
Paid		$20.00

23	Julia Ann Eno(Rutland Mass)	
	To be paid in Oct.	
	To inserting teeth - - -	$11.00
Paid		

23	Mrs. Phelps	1.00
Paid		

24	Mr. Elery Hills(Firm Whiting Rising & Co) To	
	filling 2 teeth for Wife	$2.00
Paid	Extracting 2 " " "	1.00

–4–

1841		
July 7th	Mr. Crocker (firm of Steel & Crocker) Dr	
	To filling 2 Teeth	$2.00
" 19th	" " 1 " for Niece	1.00
Paid		

9th	Henry Sage New Britain Dr	
Paid	To Inserting 8 teeth on gold @ 4.50	$36.00

11	Mr William Hudson (firm of B. & W. Hudson)	
Paid	To filling 1 tooth	$1.00

11	Mrs Donnel (Daughter of Mrs Strong)	
Paid	To filling teeth - - -	$4.00

15	Miss Cheney (at Mr Lyman Stockbridges)	
	To filling 1 tooth	1.00

15th	Mr James Noble (Tailor) Dr	
Paid	To filling 2 teeth	$2.00

14th	Mr Benning Mann Dr	
Paid	To Inserting 1 Tooth for Wife	$4.00

–5–

1841	Mr Horace Stoughn [?]	
16	East Windsor To filling 5 teeth for Daughter	5.00
	To filling 1 tooth for Self	$1.00

17	Mr Frederick W.	
	To filling 15 teeth for Wife	$15.00
20	" " 1 " " "	1.00
	Keeps a lumber yard in front St, fromerly	$16.00
Paid	kept by Niles	

19	Mr James M. Goodwin Dr	
	To filling 3 teeth	3.00
Paid	" Extracting	.50

21	Mr. Horace Robbins Dr	
Paid	To filling 2 teeth	$2.00

22	Mr W.J. Babcock Dr	
	To filling 1 tooth	1.00
Paid	" Cleansing Teeth	1.00
	July 16, 1842 Extracting 2 Teeth	$2.00
		1.00
		$3.00

23 **Paid**	Mr John Goodwin Dr To extracting 3 teeth for Charles		$1.50

| 24
Paid | Miss Candace Holcomb Simsbury
To filling 8 teeth | | 8.00 |

–6–

1841

24th	Miss Lois Curtis (Milner in Pearl St) To Inserting 1 Tooth		$4.00

| 26th

Paid | Miss Roberts Dr
To Inserting Teeth
" filling 1   " | | $10.00
1.00 |

|
Paid | Miss Butler at Mrs Strongs Dr
To Inserting 2 Teeth | | 8.00 |

27th **Paid**	Horace Wells Wethersfield To Inserting 3 teeth " filling 2 "		12.00 <u>2.00</u>
		14.00	
	Cr by cash	<u>8.00</u>	
	Paid	$6.00	

| 29th
Aug 9
" 9
" 13
Paid | Mr Steel (firm of Steel & Crocker) Dr
To filling 12 teeth for Wife
"   "   2 for Self
"   "   3 " " | | $12.00
2.00
3.00 |

| Aug. 4

Paid | Mr Ritter Dr
To Inserting 2 teeth for Wife $4.00
" [?] Wells F Dr teeth for Wife | | 8.00
<u>9.00</u>
$17.00 |

| Aug 9
" "
Paid | To extracting 1 tooth
" filling 1 " | | .50
1.00 |

–7–

1841	Aug 10	
Paid	Mr J.H. Goodwin Dr	
	To filling 7 teeth for Wife	7.00

| 12 | Mr Abner Jackson   Dr | |
| Paid | To filling 2 teeth | $2.00 |

	Mr P.B. Whitmore (Printer) Dr	
Paid	To Inserting 4 teeth	13.33
	" filling 1.	1.00

| Paid | Mr. Calvin Hatch(Farmington) | 1.00 |

26	Mr. J.H. Goodwin Dr	
Paid	To Extracting 1 Tooth for Henry	.50
27	" " 2 Teeth for Wife	1.00

	Miss Maria Dodd Dr	
	To filling 10 Teeth	10.00
	" Extracting 2 "	.75
	" Filling 1 tooth	1.50

| | Mr Gilbert Beckwith   South Glastonbury | 1.00 |

1841	–8–	
Aug 29	Mr John Warren Dr	
Paid	To filling 3 teeth for Wife	3.00

| Sept. 8 | Mr Emery Whipple E. Hartford | |
| Paid | To filling 3 teeth | 3.00 |

9	Mr W. Hudson Dr	
Paid	To Inserting 1 tooth for Wife	$4.00
	Filling 1 " " "	$1.00
13	To " 1 " " "	$1.00
		$6.00

| 11 | Mr Crooker   Dr | |
| Paid | To Extracting 1 tooth | .50 |

Mr Boswell (Courant)

Paid 10th   To Extracting tooth for Wife at house   .75

16th   Mr Lucian Burleigh
enquire of E.B. Kellogg   Dr
To be paid in April 1842
To filling 17 teeth   17.
" Extracting 1 " of Plainfield Ct   .50

Paid   17.50
$17.50

–9–

1841

22   Mr Richmond   Dr
To filling 12 teeth for Daughter   12.00
" Cleansing " " "   1.00
" filling 5 " " "   5.00

Paid   "Extracting 5 " " "   2.50

Cr by Cash $7   20.50
4
24.50

Paid   Mr Mygatt   Dr
To filling 9 teeth for Miss Catein   9.00

Miss Elizabeth Hubbard   Dr
To filling 3 teeth   3.00

Paid   Mr John Goodwin   Dr
To filling 12 teeth for Charles   12.00

Oct 11   C.P. Wells Dr
Paid   To Cleansing teeth $1.00

15   Miss I Stillman   Dr
Paid   To filling 8 teeth   8.00
Teacher of Wethersfield School
To be paid in 4 weeks

−11− [i.e. 10]

Oct 16	Miss Lucretia Ensign Dr	
	Inserting 9 teeth	$34.00
_	Cr By Cash	20.
Paid in full		Due 14.00

	Miss Cooley	1.00

17	Silas F. Cladwin [?] Dr	
	To 5 Drills	1.00
	" 1 Knife File	.75
	" 1 pr Filling Forcips	1.50
	" 2 Wood Cuts	2.00
	" 1/8 oz Gold	4.00
	" 1 Sheet "	.40
	Breaking 1 pr Forcips	$10.64
	Cr by Cash $4.40	4.40
		6.25

Nov 21	Mr John H. Goodwin Dr	
Paid	To filling 13 teeth for Henry	13.00

" 27	Samuel E. Hartwell	
	To filling 8 teeth	8.00
Paid	" Extracting 1 "	.50
	To be paid the last of Feb. 1842	8.50

Studying Law with Judge Merick of Glastenbury

−11−

1842 1

Nov 26th	Rogger Wells Dr Newington	
Paid	To filling 3 Teeth for Daughter	3.50

Dec	Miss Hariet L. Charter Dr	
	To filling 8 teeth	8.00
	Ellington	
Paid	To be paid by the 1st of February	

	Jesse	
	Miss Cornelia Savage Dr	
Paid	To Filling 9 teeth	9.00
	Church St	

| Dec 8 | Clerk at Mr Childs'   Dr | |
| Paid | To filling 3 teeth | 3.00 |

| " 9 | Mr J.H. Goodwin   Dr | |
| Paid | To filling 7 teeth for Miss Stanley | 7.00 |

| | A.B. Cobb (Bridgewater) Mass | |
| Paid | To filling teeth | 12.00 |

–12–

Dec 16	J. Seymour Brown Dr	
Settled	To filling 3 teeth for Wife	3.00
	" Extracting 1 " "	.50
		$3.50

15th	Mr Gladwin Dr	
	To gold	$9.176.04
		7.00
		2.17
		3.87
		6.04

1842 [sic]

| Jan 3 | Mr David Ritter | |
| Paid | To filling 1 tooth | 1.00 |

Jan 4	Mr Crocker Dr	
Paid	To filling 1 tooth for Neice	1.00
" 9	" " 2 " " "	2.00

" 15	Mr N. Ritter Dr	
Paid	To filling 9 teeth	9.00
	" Cleansing	1.00
		$10.00

15 **Paid** off	Mr Hamilton Dr To filling 2 teeth for Miss Pritchard	$2.00

–13–

1842

19	Mr William Jones Dr To filling 7 teeth for Maria East Hartford Cr by Cash <div align="right">Paid in full</div>	7.00 5.00 12.00

21	Mr Thompson Dr To Confectionary Cr by Cash	14.50 7.00

22 **Paid**	Mr Leonard Bacon Dr To filling 4 teeth	4.00

Paid	Charles Prentice To filling teeth for Daughter and extracting	6.75

Aug 24	Miss Lucy Chapman Dr To Operations on teeth filling 1 tooth	9.00 1.00 10.00

July 22	Rev Samuel P. Robbins East Windsor Hill To filling 8 teeth " inserting 1 " **Paid**	8.00 3.50 11.50 Paid 10 [?]

Feb 5 off	Dr Comstock To filling 9 teeth	9.00

–14–

1842

Feb 9 **Paid**	Mr Frederick Wales Dr To Cash paid for tin foil " " " " " Instruments	1.25 1.16 $2.41

Feb 10	Mr Rathbone Dr	
Paid	To Inserting 4 teeth	16.00
	" Filling 3 "	<u>3.00</u>
		$19.00
Feb 11	Mr Richmond (Richmond & Colemen)	
Paid	To filling and Cleansing teeth for Son	3.00
July 16	" filling 1 tooth for self	<u>1.00</u>
		4.00
[Feb] 16	Mr Babcock Dr	
	To Extracting 2 teeth	1.00
25	J. Seymour Brown Dr	
Paid	To filling 3 teeth	3.00
26	James H. Webb Dr	
Paid	To filling 9 cavaties	9.00
off		
March 2	Mr Henry Watson E. Windsor	
	To filling 11 teeth for Sons	11.00
9	" " 2 " " "	2.00

−15−

9th	Dr L. Wales Dr	
	To Cash	$3.00
Paid	Mr Gill (Boards with Mrs Anderson) Dr	
	To filling 5 teeth	$5.00
29	Mr J.H. Goodwin Dr	
Paid	To Extracting 2 teeth **off**	1.00
April 6	Mr Clark (Music Teacher) Dr	
	To Extracting 1 Tooth	.50
	" Filling 1 "	<u>1.50</u>
		2.00
Paid	Mrs Phelps Maria Phelps Dr	
	Enquire of Mr Joseph Langdon	
	To filling 2 teeth	$2.00

11 **Paid** **off**	Mr Boswell (Editor of Courant) Dr To filling 5 teeth	5.00
Paid	Mr Rathbun Dr To Cash———	$5.00

–16–

1842

26th **Paid**	Mr Ralph Pitkin Dr off To filling 9 teeth		$9.00
Paid	Mr Samuel Goodrich Dr To filling 5 teeth for Daughter " Cleansing		5.00 1.00
Paid	Miss Lucy A. Stillman Dr To filling 2 teeth		2.00
May 2	Irene Chapman Dr To filling 1 tooth		$1.00
" 21 **Paid**	Mr J. Seymour Brown Dr To filling 1 tooth for Wife		$1.00
22 **Paid** 23	Mr Steel (Firm of Steel & Crocker) Dr To Extracting 1 tooth for Wife at House " " " " " " " "		.75 .75 1.50
22 **off**	Mr Penfield Dr To filling 1 tooth for Daughter " Extracting 1 tooth " "		1.00 .50
Paid	Miss Mary Bartholemenu Dr To filling 1 tooth Miss Harriet To filling 1 tooth		1.00 1.00

–17–

1842

June 7 **Paid**	Mr Crocker Dr To Extracting 1 tooth	.50
10	Mr Bissell East Windsor Dr To filling 1 tooth	$1.00
off **Paid**	Mr Dimmick (Tailor) Dr To filling 2 teeth for Son	$2.00
off	Mr Norman Webster East Hartford Dr To filling 1 tooth	$1.00
	Miss Mary Jane Goodrich Dr To filling 4 teeth	$4.00
June 20 **Paid**	Mr Calvin Pomroy (Suffield Ct) To filling teeth To be paid within 3 months	$12.00
23 **Paid**	Miss Stebbins Dr To filling 7 teeth Enquire of Peter Stillman	7.00

–18–

1842

June 24 **Paid** **off**	Mr Burnham (Firm of Case Tiffany & Co) To ~~filling~~ Inserting 1 Tooth for Wife	4.00
Aug 26	" Extracting 1 " " "	.50 4.50
" 24 **Paid**	Mrs George Barnard Dr To Inserting 1 tooth	$3.00
28 **Paid** **off**	Mr Steel (firm of Steel & Crocker) Dr To filling 1 tooth	$1.00

Paid	William W. Goodrich (Wethersfield)	
	To operations on teeth	5.00
off	J.M. Loomis Dr Windsor	
Paid	To filling 2 teeth	$2.00
July 12	M J.L Boswell Dr Courant	
off	To filling 1 tooth	1.00
Paid		
July 12	A [?] Eno Tariffville	
Paid	To Inserting teeth	10.00
	To be paid within 3 months	
15th	Mr Kellogg (Clerk at A.M. Collins) Dr	
Paid	To filling 2 teeth	$2.00

–19–

1842

July 16	Mr J.H. Goodwin Dr off	
Paid	To filling teeth Amah [?] Recor	13.00
July 26	Dr Comstock Dr	
off	To Inserting 1 tooth for Wife	$4.00
Paid	Harriet Seymour Dr	
	To fitting 5 teeth	$5.00
Aug 23.	Nathaniel H. Eggleston Dr	
Paid	To filling teeth	$15.00
Sept. 2	J.H. Goodwin Dr	
	To filling 2 teeth for Wifes' Sister off	2.00
" 5	Mr William Hudson Dr (H&P)	
Paid	To Inserting 1 tooth for Wife	4.00
off		
10th	James R. Mershon Dr	
Paid	To filling 2 teeth	2.00
	Agent for New Englander	

• 135 •

–20–

1842

Sept 10   Mr Crocker   Dr   S&C
Paid   To Extracting 1 tooth for Neice   **off**   .50

"   17   Mr Whittlesey   Dr
Paid   To Operations on teeth $1.50

"   17   Elisha Gilbert   Dr
Paid   To filling 7 teeth for Lady   7.00

"   17   Benning Mann   Dr
Paid   To Extracting 1 tooth for Cyrus   **off**   .50

   29   Mr Joseph Langdon   Dr
Paid   To filling 6 teeth for Sister   6.00

   30   J.G. Smith   Dr
    To Extracting 1 Tooth   .50

off   William H. Snow   Dr
    To Inserting 1 tooth   3.00
    " Reinserting 1 "   .50
_   " Filling   2.50
    6.00

To be paid by the 1st of Jan
At Mr Denslows   (Card maker)

–21–

    1842

Paid   Miss Irving No 3 Wells St   Dr
    To filling and extracting teeth   5.50
    2.50
    8.00

Oct 17   B.W. Green   Dr (Saddler)
Paid   To Operations on teeth $2.00

Oct 22	Peter Stillman Dr		
Paid	To Extracting tooth for Girl		.50
" 22	John L. Boswell Dr		
Paid	To Extracting 1 tooth	off	.50
25	Mr Elizur Goodrich Dr		
Paid	To filling 3 teeth	off	3.00
Paid	Isaac Haden		4.00
Nov 8	G.W. Phelps		
Paid	To filling 2 teeth	off	2.00
	" Extracting		.50
" 8	Roger Wells Newington Dr		
Paid	To filling teeth for Daughter		3.50

–22–

1842			
Nov 11	Adeline Fullr Dr		
Paid	To filling 2 teeth		$2.00
	New Britain		
	Norman Webster		$1.00
" 23	Mr Elmore Dr		
Paid	To Inserting 6 teeth for Wife	off	$25.00
28	J.L. Boswell Dr Courant		
Paid	To filling 1 tooth		$3.00
off			
off	Charles L. Goodwin Dr		
Paid	To Inserting 2 teeth		10.00
—	" filling 1 "		1.00
			11.00
3d Dec	Stephen Field New York		
Paid	To filling 6 teeth for Lady		6.00
	" Extracting		.50
			$6.50

Dec 5	Mrs Lydia Irving Dr	
	To filling 9 teeth for Daughter	9.00
	" Extracting	.50
	1 Silver filling No 3 Wells St	.50
		10.00

to be paid in 9 months

–23–

6 Dec.	Mrs Lydia Irving No 3 Wells St	
	To To filling teeth	$5.50
	To be paid in 9 months	

Dec 11	Mr Kelsey Dr	
Paid	To filling 2 teeth	4.00
	" " 3 teeth	2.25
		$6.25

" 16	Mr Richmond Dr	
Paid	To Operations on teeth for Wife	6.00

Dec 28	E.B. Kellogg Dr	
Paid	To Filling 13 teeth for Wife	13.00
	" Extracting 1 " " "	.50
Jan 18	" Filling 1 " " "	1.00
	To Extracting 1 " " "	.50
		15.00

Mr Cyprian Humphrey Dr	15.00
To filling 15 teeth	

–24–

[blank]

–25–

1843

Jan 10	Mr Samuel Goodrich Dr	
off	To Cleansing teeth	1.00
Paid		

" 16 **Paid**	Mr Cyprian Humphrey Dr	
	To filling 15 teeth	$15
off June 6	” 1 "	1.00
" 7	” Extracting "	.50
		16.50
" 21	Mr Crosby (Firm Crosby White & Durham)	
off	To filling 9 teeth for Daughter	$9.00
Paid		
Feb 1.	Silas Chapman Dr	
off	To filling 3 teeth	3.00
Paid		
" 7	J.G. Smith Dr	
off	To filling 7 teeth for Sexton	7.00
Paid	" Extracting 3	1.00
" 11	To filling 2 teeth for Mr Starr	2.00
	Mr Calvin Hatch Dr	
~~**Paid**~~	~~To filling 1 tooth~~	1.00
Paid	Miss Sarah McClin	2.00
24	Mr Abner Jackson Dr To filling 4 teeth	4.00
Paid		

−26−

Feb 26	Miss Bartlett To filling 1 tooth	1.00
Paid		
March 9	Mr Franklin Dibble Granby Dr	
Paid	To filling teeth	2.75
	"Mr Lorenzo Sexton D	
Paid	To filling 2 teeth for Wife	2.00
off ” 10	H.L. Champlin E.Hartford	.50
" 10	Miss Julia Wells (Windsor) Dr	
	To Inserting teeth	25.00
	Cr by Cash	11.00
		14.00
July 15	Cr by Cash	6.00
		8.00

	Miss Sheldon Dr	
off	To filling 5 teeth	5.00
Paid		

" 23	Miss Hamilton (Hatter) Dr	
off	To filling 2 teeth for Miss Pritchard	2.00
Paid		

24	Mr Richmond Dr (Richmond & Coleman)	
Paid	To filling 1 tooth	$1.00
off		

off	Mr J.E. Smith Dr	
Paid	To Operations on teeth for Mr Sexton	11.50
	" " " " " B.P.	2.00

–27–

April 1	Mr James B. Gilman Dr	
off	To filling teeth for Boy	$8.50
Paid		

April 4	Mr J.H. Goodwin Dr	
off	To ~~filling~~ Extracting	
Paid	1 tooth for Henry	.50

April 5	Samuel Goodrich Dr	
off	To filling 1 tooth	1.00
Paid		

" 18	Mr Burnham (Firm Case Tiffany & Co.) Dr	
	To Inserting 1 tooth for Wife	4.00

May 4	Mr Peter Stillman Dr	
off	To filling 3 teeth for Wife	3.00
Paid		

" 12	Mr Kendall (Crockery dealer) Dr	
off	To Operations on teeth for Wife	9.00
Paid		

16	Miss Maranda Barber (E. Windsor Dr	
	To filling 1 tooth	$1.00

19	Dr. D.D. Field Dr Hadam	
Paid	To filling 7 teeth for Son	7.00

–28–

Paid	Mr Pitkin (Jeweler) Dr	
	To Operations on teeth	3.12 1/2
	May 29Mr Calvin Pomeroy Suffield Dr	
Paid	To Operations on teeth	5.00
	To be paid the 29 Sept.	

" 31	Mr Boswell (Editor of Courant) Dr	
off	To filling 1 tooth for Boy	1.00
Paid	" Cleansing teeth	.50
		1.50

June 1.	Dr Comstock Dr	
off	To filling 7 teeth for daughter	$7.00

" 5	Miss Julia Spencer Dr	
Paid	To filling teeth	5.00

off	Mr Litchfield Livery Dr	
Paid	To Extracting 1 tooth for young Man	.50

13	Daniel M. Seymour Dr	
Paid	To filling 4 teeth for Daughter	4.00
	" Cleansing " " "	.75
	" " " " Wife	.75
	" Filling 2 " " "	2.00

–29–

19th	George Irving Dr	
	To Operations on teeth	$2.00

20	Mr Peck (Smith & Peck Dr	
off	To Extracting 1 tooth	.50
Paid		

Paid	Miss Spencer Suffield	2.00

24 off Paid	Mr Litchfield Dr To Extracting 1 tooth for Man	.50

off Paid	Mr Peck (S. & P.) Dr To filling teeth for girl " " 9 " with Gold for Wife " " 1 " " Sement	$10.00 9.00 .75 19.75

28 off Paid	Mr Clair (Lords Hill) Dr To filling 9 teeth @ $1 " " 1 Do @ $1.50 " Extracting 1 " .50	9.00 1.50 .50 $11.00

30 Paid off	Miss Mary Richmond Dr R. & Coleman To Extracting 1 tooth	.50

–30–

—	Mr Bartlett Dr To filling 1 tooth with sement " Extracting 1 " for Man	.75 .50 1.25

June 29 off Paid	Mr Jeremiah Hewlett Dr To filling 13 teeth for Wife	13.00

July 13 Paid	Mary Ann Simmons Dr To Extracting 1 tooth Enquire of Seth & Crocker	50,35

20 Paid	Mr Abner Jackson Dr To filling 1 tooth for Wife	1.00

20	Maria T. Porter Dr To filling 1 tooth	1.00

21 Paid	Mr W Goodwin (Goodwin & Dickerson) To filling teeth	$7.50

22 Paid	Mary E. GooldEast Granby	8.00

–31–

July 24	Gov. Ellsworth Dr	
off	To filling 3 teeth for Daughter	3.00
Paid		
25	W.H. Lee New Britain	
Paid	To filling 6 teeth	7.00
off		
25	Samuel Thomas	1.00
25	Mr Litchfield (Livery) Dr	
off	To Exrtracting 1 tooth for Mike	.25
Paid 26	" Extracting " " " Son	.50
27	Mr Richmond (R&C) Dr	
Paid	To filling 11 teeth for Mary	11.00
off	" Cleansing " " "	.50
Paid	Daniel Seymour Dr	
	To ~~filling~~ Cleansing teeth	
	for Mary S. Fuller	1.00
off	Mr A Janes Dr	
Paid	To operations on teeth for Daughter	1.00
	Young man at the *Retreat* Dr	
	To Operations on teeth	

–32–

Paid	Mr Elmore Dr	
	To Inserting 1 tooth for Wife	2.50
	" filling 1 " " "	1.00
August 1	Mr Hollister Dr	
Paid	To filling 2 teeth for Daughter	2.00
	" Extracting 1" " "	.50
		2.50
off	Peter Stillman	
Paid	filling with tin	.75

off	To Douglass (At Retreat) Dr	
Paid	To filling 8 teeth	8.00
	To Extracting ~~200~~	1.00
		9.00
Aug 11	J.G. Smith To	
Paid	filling 3 teeth for Mr Starr	3.00
14	Mr [?] Steel (Steel & Crocker) Dr	
Paid	To filling 1 tooth	1.00
15	Henry Humphrey Dr	
	To filling 4 teeth	5.00

–33–

off	Mr Loomis (Loomis & Parsons) Dr	
Paid	To Inserting and filling teeth for Lady	6.50
off	Miss Phelps Dr	
	To filling 4 teeth (D. Seymour)	4.00
Paid	Dr. Morton Dr	
	Gold	6.12 1/2
	H.L. Rider Notary	
Aug 24	Horace Stoughton Cr	
	By Load Chips	6.61
	" Honey	2.00
off	Mr Richmond (Richmond & Coleman)	
Paid	To filling 5 teeth for E.P.	$5.00
	G.P. Sperry Dr	
	To Extracting 1 tooth	.50
Dec.		
off	Gilbert Dr	
Paid	To filling 2 teeth for Son 1.50	3.00
	" " 9 " " " 1.00	9.00
	Cleansing	1.00
		13.00

–34–

Sept 1.	Miss Mary Porter Dr	
Paid	To filling 8 teeth	8.00
	To have 2 teeth inserted one week from Monday	
off	William Corming [?] Dr	
Paid	To Operations on teeth	11.50
Sept 5	William Havens Dr	
off	To Operations on teeth for Sister	5.50
Paid	Wethersfield	
10	Gov. Ellsworth Dr	
off	To filling 2 teeth for Daughter E	2.00
Paid		
	Mr Morton Dr	
Paid	To Solder	1.32
	To Spiral Springs	
Paid	Loomis & Thompson Dr	
off$	To filling 8 teeth for L. Parsons	8.00
Paid	J. Seymour Brown Dr	
	To Extracting teeth for yound Ladies	1.00
Paid	Dr Saltmarch [?] Dr	
	To Operations on teeth for Wife	7.00

(H.L. Rider Notary)

–35–

Paid	Mr Bartlett Dr	
	To Inserting teeth	$45.00
Paid	Mr Boswell (Courant) Dr	
off	To filling teeth or McCorck	1.00
Oct 10th	J.H. Goodwin Dr	
off	To filling 1 tooth for Miss Stanley	1.00
Paid		

13	Miss WhitteseyNewington Dr	
Paid	To filling 5 teeth	5.00
17	Mr Boswell Dr Editor	
off	To filling 1 tooth	1.00
Paid		
off	Mr Boardman Dr	
Paid	To filling 9 teeth with gold	9.00
	" " 1 " " Tin	.50
	Introduced by Charles Seymour	9.50
Nov 13	Mr Litchfield Dr	
Paid	To Extracting teeth for Wife	.75
off		
	Mary Wells Dr	
	Dr Saltmarsh's bill	13.50
	To Cash paid for Sundries	11.05
	" Cash " Mother [?]	12.00
	Paying Mr Stillmans bill for muff [?]	3.50

–36–

17	Miss Saunders Dr	
off	To filling 1 tooth	1.00
Paid		
18	Mr Jameson Dr	
Paid	To Inserting 1 tooth for Wife	3.00
19	Clerk at Woodruff	
Paid	To filling teeth	1.75
2	Miss Saunders Dr	
off	To filling 2 Cavities	2.00
Paid		
off	Mr Litchfield Dr	
Paid	To Extracting 1 tooth for Man	50.
off	Mr Henry Francis Dr (Town Clerk)	
	To filling teeth for Daughter	6.50

Paid	Mr S. Bartlett E.Windsor	
	To filling 10 teeth	10.00

A. Chapman Westfield
To have whole upper set of teeth
inserted 1 March principle[?]

–37–

27	John H. Goodwin Dr	
off	To filling 6 teeth	$6.00
Paid		

28	Mr Steel (S & C.) Dr	
	To filling 4 teeth for Wife	4.00
—	" Cleansing	1.00
		$5.00

Stephen Nelson   Dr
To filling 1 tooth for Daughter $1.00

–38–

[blank]

–39–

1844

Jan 1, 1844

Paid	Mr J.H. Goodwin Dr	
	To filling 12 teeth for James	12.00
	" Cleansing "	1.00
		13.00

Jan 5	Miss Maria Jones East Hartford	
Paid	To filling and inserting	7.50

Jan 7	Mr Stephen Nelson Dr Steel & Crocker	
	To filling 1 tooth for Daughter	1.00
Jan 7	Laura Case - with Daniel Pitkin E. Harford	

Paid	To Inserting 1 tooth		3.00

| 9 | Peter Stillman   Dr | | |
| Paid | To Extracting tooth for Daughter | | .25 |

16	John G. Smith Clerk Dr		
off	To filling 6 teeth for		
Paid	Horace Johnson		$6.00

Jan 22	Mr Loomis (Loomis & Thompson) Dr		
off	To filling 4 teeth with gold		4.00
Paid	" " 1 " " Tin		.75

–40–

1844

Barnes

| Feb 10 | Mr Joseph ~~Blodget~~   Windsor   Dr | | |
| Paid | To filling 4 teeth | | 4.00 |

| 13 | Pro. Abner Jackson   Dr | | |
| | To filling 1 tooth for Wife | | 1.00 |

Feb 20	Miss E.W. Hungerford Dr Wolcottville		
Paid	To Inserting 7 teeth on gold		47.00
	Cr by Cash		32.00
		Due	15.00

| "   20 | Mr Seth Clark   Dr | | |
| | To filling 2 teeth | | 2.00 |

" 21	Mr Joseph Church Dr		
off	To filling 9 teeth for Daughter S		9.00
Paid	" Cleansing " " " "		1.00
			10.00

| 23 | Gen Johnson   Dr | | |
| off | To Cleansing teeth for Emily | | 1.00 |

–41–

1844

Feb 26	Mr Joseph Church Dr	
Paid	To filling 7 teeth for Daughter Em	7.00
off		
26	Mr Hale Dr Glastonbury	
Paid	To filling 6 teeth	6.50
26	Mr E. Bartlett Dr Joiner [?]	
	To filling 1 toth with tin for Lady	.75
27	Ellery Hills Dr	
Paid	To Cleansing and extracting	1.00
28	Gen N. Johnson Dr	
off	To Filling 4 teeth for Daughter S	4.00
	" Filling 2 " " " L	2.00
March 4	Dr W.T.G. Morton Dr	
off	To Operations on teeth and instruction	
	in the art of Dentistry per agreement	$50.00
"	Mr Burnham (Case Tiffany & Co)	
Paid	To filling 4 teeth for Wife	4
off	cavities	

H.L. Rider Notary

–42–

1844		
March 6	Gen N Johnson	
off	To filling 1 tooth for Sarah	1.00
"	To filling 1 tooth for Laura	1.00
"	To filling 3 tooth for ~~Sarah~~ Emily	3.00
" March 9	Miss Francis Wadsworth Dr	
Paid	To filling 8 teeth	8.00
	Cr by Cash	2.50
	Paid	5.50

March 11 off	Gen N. Johnson Dr To filling 7 teeth for Elisa	7.00
March 12 Paid off	Mr John Goodwin Dr To filling 2 teeth for Henry	2.00
March 12 off	Gen N. Johnson Dr To filling 3 teeth for Wife	3.00
	Mr Edwin M. Roberts Dr	
Paid	To filling setting teeth for Mrs Roberts to be paid in a few weeks	10.00
March 15 off Paid	Mr A. Janes Dr To filling 9 teeth for Son " Cleansing " " "	9.00 1.00 10.00

—43—

March 16 off	Gen N. Johnson Dr To filling 8 teeth for Nathan	8.00
16th Paid	Peter Stillman Dr To filling 2 teeth for Wife	2.00
18 Paid	Dr Comstock Cr By Five Dollars	5.00
18 off Paid	Mr Saunders Dr To extracting 1 tooth for Daughter	.50
19 off Paid	Mr A Janes Dr To filling 3 teeth for Son " Cleansing " " " " Extracting 3 teeth	3.00 1.00 .75 4.75

Mr. Brinley   Dr
To filling teeth for Self & Sister

| Paid | Dr Comstock   Dr | |
| | To Extracting 1 tooth for Daughter | .50 |

–44–

1844

| March 23 | Gen N. Johnson   Dr | |
| off | To filling 6 teeth for Nathan | 6 |

29	Mr Saunders Dr	
Paid	To filling 2 teeth for Daughter	2.00
off		

April 3	Mr S.W. Goodrich Dr	
Paid	To filling 4 teeth for Daughter	4.00
off		
" 3	Mr Steel Dr	
	To filling 1 tooth for Wife	1.00

| " 6 | Mr Stephen Spencer   Dr | |
| Paid | To filling 2 teeth for Ambrose S | 2.00 |

| Paid | Mr Boswell   Courant   Dr | |
| off | To Extracting 1 tooth | .50 |

| " 19 | Miss Williams   (Wethersfield)   Dr | |
| Paid | To filling 4 teeth | 4.00 |

| Paid | Mr Boswell   (Courant)   Dr | |
| off | To filling 1 tooth | 1.00 |

–45–

April 22	Mr Adrian Janes Dr	
off	To filling 2 teeth for Miss Julia	2.00
Paid		

• 151 •

April 24	Mr Peter Stillman Dr	
	To Filling 1 Tooth for Wife	1.00
25	Dr Welch (Wethersfield) Dr	
	To filling [?] teeth for Daughter	2.50
April 26 off	Hariet E. Profit D	
	To ballance due on teeth	
	No 4 Chapel Street	$12.00
off Paid	Gov. Ellsworth Dr	
	To Filling 1 tooth for Daughter Hariet	1.00
	" " 1 large Do " " "	1.50
	" Extracting 1 tooth	.50
Paid	Dr Terry Dr	
	To Gold	$5.83
29 Paid off	B.W. Green Dr	
	To Extracting tooth for Daughter	.50

–46–

29 off	Gov Ellsworth Dr	
	~~To filling 1 tooth for daughter~~	1.00
	Cleansing teeth for Daughter E.	1.00
	Extracting 1 tooth " "	.50
May 3 Paid	John W. Thompson Dr	
	To filling 2 teeth	2.00
	Farmington	
Paid	Edward W. Wells Dr	
	To filling 2 teeth	2.00
4th	Dr Morton Dr	
	To Cash	$17.00
	To Gold foil used in filling teeth for self [?]	
	To Specimen work	7.00
	1/2 doz impression cases	

H.L. Rider Notary

	10	Gen Johnson Dr	
off		To Extracting 1 tooth for Harriet	.50
	10	Mr Stephen Spencer Dr	
Paid		To filling 5 teeth for Ambrose	5.00
	10	Mr E. Doane Dr	
Paid		To filling teeth	4.25
		N. Britain	

–47–

May 14		Mr Samuel W. Goodrich Dr	
Paid		To filling 1 tooth for Daughter	1.00
	15	" Extracting 1 " " "	.50
	16	Thomas Wales Dr	
		To Operations on teeth for Wife	1.50
	17	Dr. Morton Dr	
		To Specimen set of teeth	7.00
		2 teeth inserted for Specimen	3.00

H.L. Rider
notary

	20	Gen Johnson Dr	
off		To filling 1 tooth for Hariet	1.00
	18	Mr Loomis (Loomis & Thompson)	
Paid		To pulling 1 tooth for Samuel	.50
off			
	21	Gen N. Johnson Dr	
off		To filling 2 teeth for Hariet	2.00
		" Extracting 1 for Sarah	.50

H.L. Rider
Notary

Dr Morton Dr		
To Inserting teeth for Mrs Smith	16.00
" Difference in weight of gold	1.00
	17.00

–48-

1844

May 25 Pd	Mr Peter Stillman Dr To Extracting 1 tooth		.50
25 Paid	Elisabeth Coolidge Dr To Operations on teeth Sister of Mrs Ellery Hills Cr by Cash		22.50 $13.00
26 Paid off	Mr George Brinley Dr To filling tooth for Daughter at house		2.00
26	A. Hawley		
Paid		Farmington Dr To filling teeth for Daughter	5.75
27 Paid off	John Goodwins Foreman Dr To Inserting 1 tooth To Filling 1 "		3.00 1.00
	Dr Morton Cr By 14 teeth at 37 1/2		5.94
June 3 Paid	H.L. Rider Notary	Mr Edwin M. Roberts Dr To filling 1 tooth for Mrs R.	1.00

–49–

1844

June 3 Paid off	Mr George Brinley Dr To filling 1 tooth for Daughter at house	2.00
" 4 Paid off	Mr Saunders Dr To Filling 2 cavities in teeth for Daughter	2.00

	Pro. Jackson	
	To 1 Sheet of gold	.42
7	Mr Amon Hawley Dr	
Paid	To filling 10 teeth for Daughter	10.00
	Farmington	
9th	Daniel Seymour	
Paid	To Extracting 1 tooth for Daughter	.25
	Temporary tooth	
11	Mr Stebbins Dr	
Paid	To filling 4 teeth	4.00
	Dr W.T.G. Morton Dr	
	To Repairing teeth for Mrs Smith	2.00
19	Mr E P. Bartlett Joiner Dr	
	To Extracting 1 tooth for Sister	.50

H.L. Rider Notary

–50–

June 25	Timothy S. Whetmore New Britain	
	To have 5 teeth inserted on plate 6 weeks	
	from date price $20.00	
26	Mr Thomas Hender Dr	
Paid	To Cash	25.00
	" Cash paid to Mr Cunningham	2.87 1/2
26	Mr Steel (Jeweller) Dr	
Paid	To Extracting 1 tooth	.50
off		
28	Mr Tailor (Grocer) Dr	
Paid	To Filling 5 teeth for Wife	5.00
	" Extracting " "	.50
July 2	Anson Trion . Dr	
Paid	To filling 3 teeth for Lady	3.00

" 2	Dr Crofoot Dr	
Paid	To Cut	
Paid	Stephen R. Nelson	
Paid	Mr Brinley Dr	
off	To filling 14 teeth	14.00
	" " 1 tooth for Sister	1.00

–51–

July 12	Mr Camp Dr	
Paid	To operations on teeth for Wife	3.50
" 13	Miss Williams Wethersfield	
Paid	To filling 6 teeth	6.00
	" Cleansing	.50
" 15	Mr Pitkin Jeweller Dr	
Paid	To filling 2 teeth	3.00
" 24	Mr G. Brinley Dr	
Paid	To Cleansing teeth for Sister	1.00
off		
" 24	Mr Camp Dr	
Paid	To filling teeth for Wife	3.50
24	Lorenso Hamilton Dr	
Paid	To filling 2 teeth	2.00
off		
27	Mr Perkins (Lawyer) Dr	
Paid	To Operations on teeth for Wife	10.00
29	Dr. Butler Dr	
Paid	To H. Wells Dr	
	To filling 6 teeth	6.00

–52–

1844

July 29	Mrs Haskell Dr	
Paid	To Extracting 13 teeth for Daughter	5.00
off	At the Retreat	
Aug 13. ✕	Mr E.P. Bartlett (Joiner) Dr	
	To filling 5 teeth	
Paid	Mr Pa Potter Enfield firm Parsons & Potter	
	To filling 13 teeth	13.00
Aug 26	Lewis T Downs Dr (in College	
Paid	To filling 9 teeth	9.00
	" Extracting 1 "	.50
	" Cleansing teeth	1.00
		$10.50
" 27	James B. Gilman Dr	
Paid	To filling 7 teeth for Sister	7.00
off		
Aug 30	Mr J.H. Goodwin Dr	
Paid	To filling 3 teeth	3.00
off	" filling 1 large cavity with tin	.75

–53–

	Dr Morton Cr	
	By 1 set of teeth @ 37 1/2	5.25
Sept 2	Dr Morton Dr	
	To Inserting teeth for Mrs Phelps	$20.00
Paid	Rev Mr Nichols (South Glastonbury)	
	To filling 2 teeth for Young Lady	2.00
	" Cleansing " ' " '	1.00

H.L. Rider
Notary

Paid	N. or M. P. Seymour Dr	
	To filling 2 teeth @ 1.50	3.00
	" " 1 " @ 1.00	1.00
	To Cleansing	.50
		4.50

Sept 14	Mr Stephen R. Nelson Dr	
Paid	To filling 3 teeth for Daughter	3.00

" 15	B.W. Green Dr	
Paid off	To filling 1 tooth for Daughter	1.00

19	John W. Bull Dr	
Paid	To filling 2 teeth for Wife	3.00

–54–

Sept 20	Mr Lucien Hanks Dr	
Paid off	To Cleansing teeth for D	1.00

Sept 21	S.W. Goodrich Dr	
Paid off	To Extracting temporary tooth for Frederick	.25

" 21	B.W. Green Dr	
Paid off	To filling 1 tooth for Daughter	1.00

25	Mr J.H. Goodwin Dr	
Paid off	To Extracting 1 tooth for Wife	.50

26	Miss Mary Best Dr	
Paid	To Operations on teeth	7.50

Sept 30	Mr Lucien Hanks Dr	
Paid off	To Extracting 1 tooth for Daughter	.25

" 30	Mr J.H. Goodwin Dr	

Paid	To filling 2 teeth for Brother C.S.	2.00
offOct 11	" 1 " " " "	1.00
30th	H.R. Hills Dr	
Paid	To filling 2 teeth for Daughter	2.00

–55–

Oct 5	Mr Stephen R. Nelson Dr	
Paid	To filling 2 teeth for Miss Emily B	2.00
Oct 8	~~D.F. Robinson Dr~~	
	~~To filling 4 teeth for Boy~~	4.00
Oct 8	Mr Amon Hawley Dr	
Paid	To filling 4 teeth for Son	4.00
	" Cleansing " " "	1.00
	" Extracting 1 tooth	.50
		5.50
Oct 14	D.F. Robinson Dr	
off	To filling 1 tooth for Son	1.00
Paid	" " 1 Do " "	1.50
	" Cleansing teeth " "	1.00
" 18	Mr E. Hamilton Dr	
Paid	To filling 1 tooth	1.00
	" " 1 Do with tin	.50
19th	B W. Green Dr	
off	To filling 2 teeth for Daughter	2.00
Paid		
19	Mr Lucian Hanks Dr	
Paid	To Extracting permanent tooth for Daughter	.50
off		

–56–

1844

Oct 26	B.W. Green Dr	
off	To filling 2 teeth for Daughter	2.00
Paid		

	" 28	D.F. Robinson Dr	
Paid		To Extracting temporary tooth for Son	.50
off			
	" 29	Mr Kellogg Dr	
		To filling	100
	29	Noah A. Phelps Dr	
		To Extracting 1 tooth for Son	.50
Paid		Seth J. North New Britain Dr	
		To Inserting whole Set of teeth for Wife	$100.00

Nov 1.   Theodore Rogers   Rocky Hill   Dr
To filling 1 tooth for Wife
To have 12 teeth Inserted 2 months
from this date   Price @ [?]

	1	Isaac G. Allen Dr	
Paid		To filling 1 tooth for Lady	1.50
	1	Gen N. Johnson Dr	
off		To Extracting 1 tooth for Wife	.50

–57–

Nov 2.		Mr Burnham (Case Tiffany & CO) Dr	
Paid		To Extracting 1 tooth for Wife at house	.75
	" 2	E. Taylor Dr	
Paid		To Extracting temp tooth for Daughter	.25
	9th	Peter D. Stillman Dr	
		To Inserting 4 teeth on gold	10.00
	9th	Mr Camp Dr	
Paid		To filling 1 tooth for Wife	1.00

Mrs Rhoda Goodrich, Wethersfield

| Paid | Rev. Mr Spring   Dr | |
| | To Balance due for operations on teeth | .75 |

19	Mr Pascal Loomis Dr		
	To filling 11 teeth for Son		11.00
25	Mr Saunders Dr		
Paid	To Cleansing teeth for Daughter		.75.00
off			
Dec 2.	Mr Amon Hawley Dr		
Paid	To Operations on teeth for Daughter		7.00

–58–

Dec 6	Dr D. [?] Dodge Dr		
Paid	To Filling 1 tooth for Self		1.50
" 7	" Filling 4 teeth for Son		4.00
Dec 7th	Charles W. Everest Dr		
Paid	To filling 2 teeth		2.00
	" " 1 Do with tin		<u>.75</u>
			2.75
	Cr by Book		2.00
" 11th	Gov Ellsworth Dr		
off	To filling 3 teeth for Miss E		
Paid			
11	George W. Corning Dr		
	To Extracting tooth for Daughter		.50
Paid	Maria Jones East Hartford		
	To filling 2 teeth		2.00
Paid	Daniel Seymour Dr		
	To Extracting 1 tooth for Daughter		.25
Paid	Rev Mr Raimond Dr		
off	To filling 3 teeth for Wife		3.00
	" 2 visits at house		1.50

–59–

Dec 21st	C.A. Warner Dr New Britain	
Paid	To filling 9 teeth for Wife	$9.00

21	Dr A. Welch (Wethersfield) Dr	
	To filling 15 teeth for Son	
30th	To filling 3 teeth for Daughter	

30	~~To~~

31.	Gov Ellsworth Dr	
off	To Cleansing teeth for Wife	1.00
	" Filling 2 teeth " "	2.00

End of 1844

–60–

1845

Jan 6. 1845

	Mr Bartlett (Joiner) Dr	
	To Extracting tooth for Daughter	.25

" 7	Mr Cyprian Humphrey Dr	
Paid	To filling 2 teeth	2.00

11	Mr Ohoir [?] Stanley Dr New Britain	
Paid	To filling 11 teeth	

11	Samuel Goodrich Dr	
Paid	To filling 2 teeth for Son	2.00

Paid	William Goodwin Dr (Goodwin & Dickinson)	
	To filling 2 teeth	2.00

15	S.W. Goodrich Dr	
Paid	To filling 5 teeth for Daughter	5.00
	" Cleansing " " "	1.00

16	S.B. Hanks Dr	
Paid	To Cleansing teeth for Daughter	1.00

–61–

16	Daniel Seymour Dr	
Paid	To Filling 2 teeth for Wife	2.00
16	Mr Ambrose Spencer (At Humphrey Seyms & Co)	
Paid	To Filling 6 teeth	6.00
18	" " 2 "	2.00
17	Charles A. Warner Dr	
Paid	To Filling 17 teeth for Oliver Stanley per verbal order	17.00
17	Stephen R. Nelson Dr	
Paid	To Filling 1 tooth for Daughter	1.50
Feb 4	James Bartholemeu	3.00
Paid	Sister Hariet	2.00
" 6	J.O. Pitkin Dr	
Paid	To filling 1 tooth	1.50
" 7	Mr Ezra Clark Jr Dr	
Paid	To filling 11 teeth for Miss Sarah Colvin	11.00
17	James Noble Dr	
Paid	To ~~filling~~ Cleansing teeth for Son	1.00

H.L. Rider Notary

–62–

Paid	Mr Hills Dr	
	To filling 9 teeth for Wife	9.00
	To Extracting 1 " "	.50
	Mr Dayton (Mason) Dr	
	To filling 5 teeth	5.00
	" Extracting 1	

Paid Miss Eliza Ming   Dr
         To filling 6 teeth   (At Mr Browns Book Binder)

Paid Mr Howell   Dr   (At Mr Wright)
         To filling 9 teeth   9.00

–63–

θ Sept 10th   Mr Peter Stillman   Dr
Paid   To Filling 2 teeth   2.00

Sept 11   Mr Edward Parsons   Dr
          To Filling 1 tooth for Wife   1.50
          To Filling 1 Do   "   "   1.00
          " Extracting 1 Do   .50

Sept 12   Mr Stewart   Dr
          To filling 4 teeth for Daughter   4.00
          " Cleansing teeth   1.00
          " Extracting 1 tooth   .50

Sept 15   Mr Hull   (With Arault & Co)   Dr
Paid To Filling teeth   9.00
          " Cleansing "   1.00
          " Extracting "   .50
                                                              _____
                                                              10.50

16   L.H. Bacon   Dr
          To Extracting 1 Tooth   .50

–64–

Sept 16   Mr Edward Parsons   Dr
Paid To Filling 4 teeth for Wife   4.00
          " Filling 3   "   "   1.50   4.50
          " Cleansing teeth "   "   1.00
          " Extracting tooth   .50
                                                              _____
                                                              10.00

" 23	Miss Williams (Wethersfield)		
	To Filling 2 teeth		2.00
	" Cleansing teeth		1.00
	" 1 Box Powder		.25
			3.25
26	Mrs Perkins Dr		
	To Operations on teeth		2.50
Oct 9th	Mr P. Stillman Dr		
	To Extracting 1 tooth		.50
" 9th	Miss Saunders Dr		
	To Filling 1 tooth		1.00
"	" Cleansing teeth		.50

–65–

10th	James Standish Jr Dr Wethersfield		
	To Balance due on teeth		1.00
12th	H. Goodwin Dr		
Paid	To filling 1 tooth		1.00
	" Extracting 3 teeth		1.00
			2.00
Paid	Mr S.W. Goodrich Dr		
	To filling 1 tooth for Son		1.00
Paid	Gov Ellsworth Dr		
	To Cleansing teeth for Daughter		1.00
	" 2 Boxes Tooth Powder		.50
Nov. 5th	Dr Riggs Dr		
Paid	To Ballance Due on Act		6.71
April 1, 1844	Capt John Cole Dr		
	Do Ballance due on note		6.00

[Editor's note: Page 65 is the last page of accounts. The following two pages are numbered: "66 and 67" but nothing written thereon.

The remainder of the book, of an equal number of un-numbered pages, is blank with the exceptions as noted on the following pages.]

WELLS'S DAY BOOK

[Ten pages from the rear of this book, none of which are numbered the following appears:]

Gilding Solution
Take a little water add a tea spoon full
of Nitrate of Silver when dissolved add
Cyanuret of Potass until it becomes clear
Then immerse the plate and after
taking it out rinse it in water and wipe
it dry _____

Straw color - Lemon - Orange
Blue violet Black _____

Accllerating Mixture
To 1 Pt. Lime water mix 1/2 oz. Chloride
of Iodine - shake it well   then add
nearly 3/4oz of Bromine _____

Gold Solutions
To 1 dram of Chloride of Gold
add 7 drams of water
[On the following page appears:]

Solution for Gilding Pictures
Dissolve 1oz Hyposulphite of
soda in 2oz water in a retort
heating it with a lamp untill
boiling hot then turn it into a
tumbler and add 60 drops of gold

solution drop by drop stirring it
at the same time and let it stand
over night until cold and then
filter it into a pint bottle. Then
add water sufficient to make a
pint.

Sticking Paper
Gum Arabic and Fish
glue equal parts

Sealing Wax
venetian Turpentine and Gum
Shelac equal parts. Simmer
over a fire until amalgated

W. & W. H. Lewis
Mr Weston Cor Broadway, and
John St

Scoval No 6 Gold St

Langenharm & Beckers
New York

W. & T Langerham Exchange
Building   Philadelphia
keep German Instruments

Chloride gold	$20 oz
Hyposulphite Soda	1.50 to 3.00
Nitrate Silver chrystalized	1.00 oz
Chloride of Iodine	1.25 to 1.50
Bromine	2.00 oz
Rotten Stone	1.00 Bottle
Buck Skin	1.62 Small
Colors	1.25 Set
Pencils	12 1/2 cts each

[Editor's Note: The following appears on the second to last leaf of the book; and this page is numbered]

142

Box for Stove	1.42
Freight on Baggage from Farmington	.62 1/2
Fare from boat in Springfield	.12 1/2
Hotel board	3.00
Truckage	.12 1/2
Moving Baggage	12 1/2
Freight on Stove	1.75
Paid Boy	25
Pail	.25
Coal	5.75
Bed Clothes	6.50
Dr Jackson	40.00
Carpet	53.78
Stove pipe hole	2.50
Cash to Morton	10.00
Paid boy	1.25
Cash to Morton	3.00
Signs	3.75
Stove pipe	6.75
Floor Cloth	1.24
Cash	2.00

H.L. Rider Notary

[Editor's note: On the next to last leaf appears:]

Cash	6.00
Papers	1.00
"	.24
"	3.00
Oil Cloth	2.65
2 oz 83/4 dwt. gold at 87 1/2	40.76
3 leaves gold	1.20
200 pivot teeth	25.00
250 "	37.00
40 Double	5.00
Cash	10.00
Cash	65.00
Board at 33	1.75

[Editor's note: The following appears on the last leaf of the   Book:]

Notes deposited in the
Conn. River Bank for safe keeping

1 Note against John Olmsted & Co
Dated Jan 8th 1846 - amount $700.

1 Note against Robert Turnbull
Dated Jan 6. 1846. amount $550.

1 Note against W.T.G. Morton
Dated Aug 21. 1845 - amount $108

H.L. Rider
Notary

Appendix 1

Alphabetical Listing of Wells's Patients as Found in Day Book A with Dates of Billing and Notes for Whom Service was Rendered

With Town of Residence other than Hartford for the period
May 1841–November 1845

Name	Date(s) of Billing	Place of Residence
Isaac G. Allen (for lady)	11/1/44	
Mr J.W. Babcock	7/22/41	
Leonard Bacon	1/22/42	
L.H. Bacon	9/16/45	
Mr Frederick W. Barber	7/17/41	Farmington
Lewis Barber	6/16/41	
Miss Maranda Barber	5/16/43	East Windor
Mrs George Barnard	6/24/42	
Mr. Joseph Barnes	2/10/44	Windsor
James Bartholemeu for Sister Harriet	2/4/45	
Miss Mary Bartholemeu	5/22/42	
Miss Bartlett	2/26/43	
Mr. S. Bartlett	12/2/43	East Windsor
Mr. Bartlett	6/43; 9/43;	

Mr. Bartlett for daughter	1/6/45	
Mr. E. Bartlett	2/26/44	
Mr. E.P. Bartlett	6/19/44; 8/13/44	
Mr. Gilbert Beckwith	8/27/41	South Glastonbury
Miss Mary Best	9/26/44	
Mr. Bissell	6/10/42	East Windsor
Mr. Boardman	10/17/44	
Mr. Boswell	4/11/42; 10/17/43	
Mr. Boswell for McCorch	9/43; 4/6/44; 4/19/44	
Mr. J.L. Boswell	10/22/42; 11/28/42; 5/31/43	
Mr. Brinley and for sister	7/2/43	
Mr. George Brinley for daughter at house	5/26/44; 6/3/44	
Mr. George Brinley for sister	7/24/44	
J. Seymour Brown	2/25/42; 5/21/42	
Miss Rhoda Brown	6/10/41	
John W. Bull for wife	9/19/44	
Mr. Lucien Burleigh	9/16/41	Plainfield
Mr. Burnham	6/24/42; 4/18//43; 3/4/44	
Mr. Burnham for wife	11/2/44	
Dr. Butler	7/29/44	
Miss Butler	7/26/41	
Mr. Camp for wife	7/12/44; 11/9/44	
Laura Case	1/7/44	East Hartford
A. Chapman	12/2/43	Westfield, Ma
Irene Chapman	5/2/44	
Miss Lucy Chapman	1/2/42	
Silas Chapman	2/1/43	
H.L. Champlin	2/10/43	East Hartford
Hariet L. Charter	12/41	
Miss Cheney	7/15/41	
Clerk at Childs	12/8/41	
Mr. Joseph Church	2/21/44	
Mr. Joseph Church for daughter	2/26/44	
Silas F. Caldwin	10/17/41	
Mr. Clair	6/28/43	
Mr. Clark	4/6/42	
Mr. Ezra Clark Jr. for Sarah Calvin	2/7/45	
Seth Clark	2/20/44	

Capt. John Cole Ballance		
due on note	4/1/44	
A.B. Coleb	12/9/41	
Dr. Comstock	2/5/42; 7/16/42; 6/1/43	
Dr. Comstock for daughter	3/19/43	
Miss Cooley	10/16/41	
Elizabeth Coolidge	5/25/44	
George W. Corning for daughter	12/11/44	
William Corning	9/1/43	
Mr. Crocker	7/7/41; 9/11/41; 1/4/42;	
	6/7/42; 9/10/42	
Dr. Crofoot	7/2/44	
Mr. Crosby	1/21/43	
Miss Lois Curtis	7/24/41	
A. B. Cobb	12/9/41	Bridgewater, Ma.
Mr. Dayton	2/45	
Mr. Franklin Dibble	3/9/43	
Mr. Dimmick	6/10/42	
Mr. E. Doane	5/10/44	New Britain
Miss Maria Dodd	8/27/41	
Dr. Dodge for self & son	12/6/44	
Mrs. Donnel	7/11/41	
Douglass (at Retreat)	8/1/43	
Lewis T. Downs	5/26/44	
Mr. Franklin Dibble	3/9/42	Granby
Nathaniel H. Eggleston	8/23/42	
Governor Ellsworth for daughter	7/24/43	
Governor Ellsworth for daughter E	9/10/43; 4/29/44	
Governor Ellsworth for Hariet	4/20/44	
Governor Ellsworth for Miss E	12/1/44	
Governor Ellsworth for Wife	12/31/44	
Governor Ellsworth for daughter	10/2/45	
Mr. Elmore	11/23/42	
Julia Ann Eno	6/23/41	Rutland, Ma.
A. (?) Eno	7/12/42	Tarrifville
Miss Lucreta Ensign	10/16/41	
Charles W. Everett	12/7/44	
D.D. Field	5/19/43	Hadam
Stephen Field	12/3/42	New York
Mr. Henry Francis for daughter	12/2/43	

Adeline Fullr	11/11/42	
Miss Gaines	6/12/41	
Elisha Gilbert	9/17/42; 12/1/43	
Mr. James B. Gilman	4/1/43	
Mr. James B. Gilman for sister	8/7/44	
Mr. Gill	3/9/42	
Mr. Gladwin	12/15/41	
Mr. Elizur Goodrich	10/25/42	
Miss Jane Goodrich	6/10/42	
Mr. Samuel Goodrich	4/6/42; 1/10/43; 4/5/43	
S.W. Goodrich for daughter	4/3/44; 5/14/44; 1/15/45	
" Frederick	9/21/44	
" Son	1/11/45; 10/12/45	
William W. Goodrich	6/28/42	Wethersfield
Charles L. Goodwin	11/28/42	
Mr. James W. Goodwin	7/19/41	
John Goodwin's Foreman	5/27/44	
H. Goodwin	10/12/45	
Mr. John H. Goodwin	7/23/41; 8/10/41; 8/26/41; 11/21/41; 12/9/41; 3/29/42; 7/16/42; 9/2/42; 4/1/43; 10/10/43; 12/27/43	
For James	1/1/44	
For Henry	3/12/44; 8/30/44	
For Wife	9/25/44	
For Brother C.S.	9/30/44	
Mr. W. Goodwin	7/21/43	
William Goodwin	1/11/45	
Mary F. Goold	7/22/43	East Granby
B. W. Green	10/17/42	
For Daughter	4/29/44; 9/15/44; 9/21/44; 10/19/44; 10/20/44	
Isaac Haden	10/25/42	
Mr. Hale	2/26/44	Glastonbury
Miss Hamilton	7/23/43	
Mr. Hamilton	1/15/42	
Mr. E. Hamilton	10/18/44	
Lorenzo Hamilton	7/24/44	

Mr. Lucien Hanks	9/20/44	
Mr. Lucien Hanks for daughter	9/30/44; 10/19/44	
S. B. Hanks for daughter	1/16/45	
Samuel E. Hartwell	11/27/41	
Mrs. Haskell for daughter	7/29/44	
Mr. Calvin Hatch	8/21/41; 2/11/43	Farmington
William Havens	9/5/43	
A. Hawley for daughter	5/26/43; 6/7/44 12/2/44	Farmington
A. Hawley for son	10/8/44	
Thomas Hender	6/26/44	
Mr. Jeremiah Hewlett	6/29/43	
Mr. Elery Hills	6/24/41; 2/26/44	
Mr. Hills for wife	2/45	
H. R. Hills for daughter	10/30/44	
Miss Mary Ann Hill	6/7/41	
Miss Candance Holcomb	7/24/41	Simsbury
Mr. Hollister	8/1/43	
Mr. Howell	2/45	
Miss Elizabeth Hubbard	9/22/41	
Mr. William Hudson	7/11/41; 9/8/41; 9/5/42	
Mr. Humphrey	5/13/41	
Mr. Cyprian Humphrey	1/16/42; 1/6/45	
Willaim Humphrey	8/15/43	
Mr. Hull	9/15/45	
Mrs E.W. Hungerford	2/20/44	Wolcottville
Miss Irving	10/42	
George Irving	6/19/43	
Mrs. Lydia Irving for daughter	12/5/42; 12/6/42	
Mr. Abner Jackson	5/12/41; 2/24/43;	
for wife	2/13/44	
Pro. Jackson	6/4/44 Sheet of gold	
Mr. Jameson	11/18/43	
Gen. Johnson	2/23/44	
Gen N. Johnson for daughter	2/28/44	
for Sarah	3/6/44; 5/21/44	
for Laura	3/6/44	
for Emily	3/6/44	
for Elisa	3/11/44	
for Wife	3/12/44; 11/1/44	
for Nathan	3/16/44; 3/23/44	
for Harriet	5/10/44; 5/21/44	

Mr. A. Janes	7/27/43	
for Son	3/15/44; 3/19/44	
Miss Julia	4/22/44	
Miss Maria Jones	1/5/44; 12/11/44	East Hartford
Mr. William Jones	1/19/42	East Hartford
Mr. Kellogg	7/12/42; 10/29/44	
E. B. Kellogg	12/28/42	
Mr. Kelsey	12/11/42	
Mr. Kendall	5/12/43	
Mr. Joseph Langdon	9/29/42	
Mr. Litchfield	6/5/43; 6/24/43; 7/25/43; 11/13/43; 12/2/43	
W.H. Lee	7/25/43	New Britain
I. Henry Lloyd	5/21/41	
J.M. Loomis	6/28/42; 8/43; 1/2/44	Windsor
Mr. Loomis for Samuel	5/18/44	
Mr. Pascal Loomis for son	11/19/44	
Mr. Benning Mann	7/14/41; 9/7/42	
James R. Mershon	9/10/44	
Miss Sarah McClin	2/11/43	
Miss McHinney	5/15/41	
Mr. Mygott	9/22/41	
Dr. Morton	8/43; 5/3/44; 5/4/44; 5/21/44; 5/27/44; 9/2/44	
Mr. Morton	9/10/43	
Dr. W. T. G. Morton	3/4/44; 6/11/44	
Mr. Stephen Nelson	1/7/44	
for daughter	9/14/44; 1/17/45	
for Miss Emily	10/5/44	
Rev. Mr. Nichols for young lady	9/2/44	South Glastonbury
Mr. James Noble	7/15/41	
for son	2/17/45	
Seth J. North		
for wife	10/29/44	New Britain
Mr. Eben Parsons	6/9/41	Enfield
L. Parson	9/10/43	
Mr. Edward Parsons for wife	9/16/45	
Mr. Peck	6/20/43; 6/24/43	

Mr. Penfield	5/22/42	
Mr. Perkins for wife	7/27/44	
Mrs. Perkins	9/26/45	
Mrs. Phelps	6/23/41	
for Maria Phelps	4/6/42	
Miss Phelps	8/43	
G.W. Phelps	11/8/42	
Noah A. Phelps for son	10/29/44	
Mr. Ralph Pitkin	4/26/42; 5/43; 7/44	
J. O. Pitkin	2/6/45	
Mr. Calvin Pomroy	6/20/42; 5/29/43	Suffield
Marie T. Porter	6/20/43	
Miss Mary Porter	9/1/43	
Mr. Potter	8/13/44	
Charles Prentice	1/22/42	
Hariet E. Profit	4/26/44	
Mr. Raimond for wife	12/11/45	
Mr. Rathbone	2/10/42	
Mr. Edward Reed	5/24/41	
Mr. Richmond	9/22/41; 2/11/42; 12/16/42; 7/24/43; 7/27/43; 8/43	
Miss Mary Richmond	6/30/43	
Mr. John Riggs	5/14/41; 11/5/45	
Mr. Ritter	8/4/41	
Mr. David Ritter	1/3/41	
Mr. N. Ritter	1/15/42	
Mr. Horace Robbins	7/21/41	
Rev. Samuel Robbins	1/22/42	East Windsor Hill
Miss Roberts	6/26/41	
Mr. Edwin M. Roberts for Mrs. Roberts	3/12/44; 6/3/44	
Theadore Rogers for wife	11/1/44	Rocky Hill
D.F. Robinson for son	10/14/44; 10/28/44	
John Russel	5/20/41	
Henry Sage	7/9/41	New Britain
Miss Cornelia Savage	12/41	
Dr. Saltmarch	9/10/43	
Miss Saunders	11/17/43; 12/2/43; 10/9/45	

Mr. Saunders for daughter	3/18/43; 3/29/44; 6/4/44; 11/25/44	
Daniel M. Seymour	6/13/43; 7/27/43	
for daughter	6/9/44; 12/11/44	
for wife	1/16/45	
Harriet Seymour	7/26/42	
N. or M.P. Seymour	9/2/44	
Miss Sheldon	7/43	
Miss Ann Simmons	7/13/43	
Mr. Skinner	5/13/41	
Mr. Lorenzo Sexton	9/3/43	
Miss Phebe Smith	5/29/41	
J.G. Smith	9/30/42; 2/7/43; 8/11/43	
for Horace Jackson	1/16/43	
Mr. J.E. Smith	7/43	
William H. Snow	9/30/42	
Mr. Ambrose Spencer	1/16/45	
Miss Julia Spencer	6/5/43; 6/20/43	Suffield
Mr. Stephen Spencer for Ambrose	4/6/44; 5/10/44	
G.P. Sperry	8/24/43	
Miss Stebbins	6/23/42	
Mr. Stebbins	6/11/44	
Mr. Ohoir Stanley	1/11/45	New Britain
Mr. Steel	7/29/41; 5/22/42; 6/28/42; 8/14/43; 12/28/43; 6/28/44	
for wife	4/3/44	
Mr. Stewart for daughter	9/12/45	
Miss Lucy A. Stillman	4/26/42	
Miss I. Stillman	10/15/41	
Peter Stillman	10/22/42; 5/4/43; 8/1/43; 5/25/44 11/9/44; 9/10/45; 10/9/45	
for daughter	1/9/44	
for wife	3/16/43; 4/24/44	
Mr. Horace Stoughn	7/16/41; 8/24/43	
James Standish, Jr.	10/10/45	Wethersfield
Mr. Tailor for wife	6/28/44	
Mr. J.N. Talcott	6/11/41	
E. Taylor for daughter	11/2/44	
Dr. Terry	4/26/44	

Samuel Thomas	7/25/43	
Mr. Thompson	1/21/42	
John W. Thompson	8/3/44	Farmington
Anson Trion for lady	7/2/44	
Mr. Frederick Wales	2/9/42	
Dr. L. Wales	3/9/43	
Thomas Wales for wife	5/16/44	
Miss Francis Wadsworth	3/9/44	
C.A. Warner for wife	12/21/44	New Britain
for Oliver Stanley	1/17/45	
Mr. John Warren	8/29/41	
Mr. Henry Watson	3/2/42	East Windsor
James H. Webb	2/26/42	
Mr. Norman Webster	6/10/42; 11/11/42	East Hartford
C.P. Wells	10/11/41	
Miss Mary Wells	6/1/41	
Miss Julia Wells	3/10/43	Windsor
Edward W. Wells	5/3/44	
Horace Wells	7/27/41	Wethersfield
Roger Wells	11/8/42	Newington
Rogger Wells	11/26/41`	Newington
Dr. A. Welch for daughter	5/25/44; 12/21/44	
for son	12/21/44	Wethersfield
Timothy S. Whetstone	6/25/44	New Britain
Mr. Emery Wipple	9/8/41	East Hartford
P.B. Whitmore	8/12/41	
Mr. Whittlesey	9/17/42	
Miss Whittlesey	10/13/43	Newington
Miss Williams	4/19/44; 7/13/44; 9/23/45	Wethersfield

Appendix 2

Number of Entries in Wells's *Day Book A*
by Month for the Years 1841 through 1845
and Gross Sum Billed for Those Years

, *1841*
JAN FEB MAR APR MAY JUN JULY AUG SEPT OCT NOV DEC
8 10 17 10 9 5 3 7
, TOTAL SUM BILLED: $559.02
, *1842*
10 7 4 7 5 12 6 1 12 5 7 6
, TOTAL SUM BILLED: $458.95
, *1843*
4 7 7 4 7 12 13 13 10 4 12 0
, TOTAL SUM BILLED: $506.97
, *1844*
7 11 16 14 19 13 12 5 13 12 10 12
, TOTAL SUM BILLED: $758.00
, *1845*

11 8 0 0 0 0 0 0 0 7 6 1 0
, TOTAL SUM BILLED: $130.00

Appendix 3

The Entries in Wells's *Day Book A* which Pertain to W.T.G. Morton

All Entries Countersigned by "H.L. Rider, Notary", with Page of Entry and Status of Payment.

No.	Date of Entry	For		Page
1.	August 1843 Paid	Dr. Morton Dr Gold	6.12 1/2	33
2.	Sept. 10, 1843 Paid	Mr. Morton To Solder To Spiral Springs	1.32	34
3.	March 4, 1844	Dr. W.T.G. Morton Dr $50.00 To Operations on teeth and instruction in the art of Dentistry per agreement		41
4.	May 4, 1844	Dr Morton Dr To Cash $17.00 To Gold foil used in filling teeth for Self 7 ? To Specimen work 1/2 doz impression cases 7.00		46 46

5. May 17, 1844   Dr Morton   Dr
                     To Specimen set of teeth   7.00
                     2 teeth inserted for Specimen   3.00   47

6. May 21, 1844   Dr Morton   Dr
                     To Inserting teeth for Mrs Smith $16.00
                     To Difference in weight of gold   1.00
                                                       17.00   47

7. May 27, 1844   Dr Morton   Cr
                     By 14 teeth at 37 1/2   5.94   48

8. June 11, 1844   Dr W.T.G. Morton   Dr   2.00   49
                     To Repairing teeth for Mrs. Smith

9. Sept 2, 1844   Dr Morton   Cr
                     By 1 sett of teeth @ 37 1/2   5.25   53

                     Dr Morton   Dr
                     To Inserting teeth for Mrs Phelps $20.00

10.   Cash to Morton $10.00   142

11.   Note against W.T.G. Morton
                     Dated Aug. 21, 1845 - amount $108   on last
                                                                 leaf of
                                                                 book

4

The Shop On Main Street: Horace Wells's Hartford

Sarah H. Gordon

When Horace Wells left Hartford in December 1847, and sailed for France, his ties in Hartford put him at the very heart of that community, around which much of the history of this small city and its efforts on behalf of Wells can be understood. While he left his wife and small son at home on this journey, Wells had strong support from both family and friends, who were aware of his mission: to buy paintings in Paris for resale at profit in the United States, and to regain the health he had lost while trying to prevent rivals from claiming credit for the discovery of anesthesia. Although Wells had practiced dentistry in Hartford for only ten years when he left for Paris, his work and friendships extended far beyond the medical community: to his church, to many small businesses of the city, to its corporations, banks, and schools, and even to the fringes of the government of Hartford and Connecticut.

The commencement of these many ties dated earlier than 1836, the year Wells opened an office on Main Street in Hartford. While Horace Wells had not been born in Hartford, earlier generations of his family had lived in nearby Windsor. He had descended from the Wills family, whose members changed their name to Wells two generations before Horace Wells's birth.[1] He therefore had no direct relationship to the Wells family of Hartford, which included early Connecticut Governor Thomas Wells, and the newspaper editor and politician Gideon Welles.

His parents, Horace Wells and Betsy Heath, lived and married in Windsor. They then migrated to Hartford, Windsor County, Vermont, where Horace was born in 1815. Horace's brother Charles was born two years later, and his sister Mary in 1819.[2] In Vermont, the towns of Hartford, Norwich, and Pomfret are still known as the "Connecticut Towns," indicating that they were founded by Connecticut residents who had migrated north by way of the Connecticut River. The river formed a lifeline, connecting the Vermont towns to Hartford and to Long Island Sound. In the 1820s and 1830s, trade on the river commenced as soon as the ice broke in the spring, usually in March or April.[3] After Horace Wells's father died in 1829, his mother married Abiather Shaw, reputed to be a riverboat man on the Connecticut River. Shaw's large house in Westmoreland, New Hampshire, became home to Horace, and he became quite attached to his stepfamily, particularly to his stepbrother Abiather Lambert, whom Wells called Lambert, and his three stepsisters, Harriet, Betsy, and Susanna.[4]

Horace left Vermont in 1821 to attend school; he returned home for a time, and then, in 1834, he traveled to Boston where, at age nineteen, he began the apprenticeship training necessary to the practice of dentistry. While in Boston, Wells kept in touch with his parents by letter, and chastised them in fun for not writing to him. He made a similar plea to his brother Charles, and his stepsister Susan Shaw, whose letters did not come often enough. He told Susan she would like living in Boston, hinting playfully that she might join him there.[5]

Nevertheless, Wells moved to Hartford in 1836 and put an advertisement in the *Connecticut Courant* of April 4, indicating that his office could be found "in Main—street, nearly opposite the Connecticut Hotel, 2d door from State—street. . . ." (Illustration 13).[6] The exact address was 162 1/2 Main Street; his home address did not appear in the city directory of that year.

Illustration 13. Main Street, Hartford, in the 1890s, about fifty years after Horace Wells maintained his dental office there. Wells's office was located at 162 1/2 Main Street, the second door from State Street and the second door from the "Books" sign. Courtesy of the Historical Museum of Medicine and Dentistry, Hartford.

With the announcement that Wells put in the *Connecticut Courant* appeared an endorsement of his work from Mr. Joseph S. French, who wrote:

> This certifies that I the subscriber, a citizen of Hartford, employed Mr. Wells, while in Boston, in an operation on my teeth, and I am happy to say that it has answered my most sanguine expectations.[7]

Such endorsements were known as certificates, and were a standard means of promoting a new service or product. Joseph French was a baker, and was probably connected with the partnership of French & Wales, dealers in flour and grain. Whether his endorsement worked or not, the Main Street merchants of Hartford certainly contributed a large share of patients to Wells in the years to come.

In August, Wells wrote to his sister Mary, who by then had also left home and was attending school in Ipswich, Massachusetts. "How are you? Where have you been this long time? Why have you not written me before?" While Mary had been tardy in contacting him, Horace wrote that their brother Charles, then at school in Nashua, New Hampshire, had travelled to Hartford to visit with his newly settled brother.[8] Also, Wells told his sister cheerfully, he had joined the church, in response to the religious stirring we now call the Second Great Awakening, and to assuage his isolation in a new community. This was the Center or First Congregational Church of Hartford, located at 124 Main Street, only a block south of Wells's office.[9]

As the offshoot of Thomas Hooker's original meeting house of the 1630s, the Center Church membership included the descendants of Hooker and other founding families of the Hartford Colony.[10] Among the parishioners whom we know Horace Wells met were William W. Ellsworth, a former Congressman and Governor of Connecticut when Wells joined the Church; Thomas Day, a long—time benefactor of the city and its institutions; and, a few years later, Joseph Church, a Main Street merchant, father of artist Frederick E. Church, and descendant of Richard Church, who had travelled through the wilderness to Hartford with Thomas Hooker in 1636. Catharine and Harriet Beecher, who had recently left Litchfield,

Connecticut, and Tapping Reeve, founder of the Litchfield Law School, were also members of this church.[11]

Despite Wells's efforts to take hold in Hartford, restlessness had seized him by November. When he wrote to his stepfather that month, he spoke of possibly travelling to Boston to see Harriet (he was alluding probably to his stepsister), and expressed a wish to "continue in the pubishing business,"[12] but he said nothing of his daily work in dentistry. Also, his wish for more company emerged again as he told his parents that he had spent Thanksgiving without family, and that he had not heard from them since he had last seen them.

In April of 1837, a year after the opening of his dental office, he wrote to his sister Mary, who had by then returned to Westmoreland, but again made no reference to his dental career. He commenced by chiding her, "You say you won't write me because I don't write to you," and he invited her to come to Hartford to attend Miss Draper's Seminary. He also suggested, still in a somewhat jesting mood, that Lambert, Charles, Elizabeth (probably Betsy), Susan and his parents should all come to Hartford.[13]

In the same letter, however, Wells revealed something that his family must have already known: that he did in fact have friends in Hartford. He had mentioned a friend named Henry Humphrey in an 1836 letter to his sister: "Henry Humphrey has gone to Boston."[14] Clearly, he wrote about someone whom Mary also knew of, or knew personally. Less than a year later, in his letter of 1837 to his sister, he again referred to Henry Humphrey: "Henry is well and dispensing pills as fast as ever, he has moved and is close now by me I told him . . . if he would take a tour into the country with me we would happen along through We[s]tmoreland."[15]

Henry Humphrey, a pharmacist, was one of Wells's earliest and closest associates in Hartford. Horace's report that "he is close by me now" refers to the fact that Humphrey ran a pharmacy at 178 Main Street, just a few doors from Wells's office, in partnership with Charles P. Wells, a relative of Governor Thomas Wells and of Gideon Welles, but not of Horace. Wells & Humphrey offered customers "a full and well selected assortment of genuine Drugs and Medicines, Chemical Preparations, Food for the Sick, Wines, &c."[16]

That Henry Humphrey knew Wells's family is confirmed by

Wells's references to Frances Humphrey, probably Henry's sister or perhaps daughter, as a correspondent of Mary Wells. Horace informed Mary in the April 1837 letter that he saw Frances frequently and had heard that she had received a letter from sister Mary Wells, "just before she had given you a real scolding for not writing or answering her letters." Frances attended school at Miss Draper's Seminary, located on Trumbull Street, only a block west of Main Street. Horace hoped Mary would join her there. Mary did not come to Hartford to stay, or to attend the Seminary. But the relationship between Frances Humphrey and Mary was clearly a warm one.

Contact with the Humphreys eased Wells's feelings of isolation somewhat, although he still reported to his sister that

> All the family I have is 3 canary birds and one French Linnet which sings sweetly. I have now a splendid accordian and when I commence playing the birds commence singing.[17]

He also wrote that he had been ill, but had recovered. Mention of his illnesses recurred in Horace's letters throughout the remainder of his life. The exact nature of his health problems is not known, but they do not appear to have been life threatening.

The Center Church soon remedied Wells's lack of family in Hartford. Two years before he had joined, Elizabeth Wales, daughter of merchant Nathaniel Wales and East Windsor native Sally Hender, had become a member of the Church. One of her brothers, Joseph Wales, also belonged to the Church, as did her uncle, Thomas Hender.[18] In early 1838, Wells asked Miss Wales permission to become better acquainted with her. Four months later, Reverend Joel Hawes, minister of Center Church, married them.

Wells's sister Mary came to Hartford for the wedding. At this time, Mary had returned to school in Ipswich, and indicated in her correspondence that Lambert, her stepbrother, had become a superintendent of schools, though it is not known where. She wrote in a letter to her mother that about thirty guests had attended the wedding, and that Henry Humphrey was the groom's man. At the wedding she also met Henry Wells, a cousin she had not previously known, who worked in a Hartford store. She reported her satisfaction with Horace's new wife—"I like her much"—but she inquired in a tone reminiscent of Horace, "Why did not Charles come to the wedding?

We expected him; and where is Elizabeth too?"[19] We also do not know why his parents were not there.

When Wells and his wife returned from their honeymoon, Horace wrote to his parents expressing his happiness.

> It was next to a miracle that I chanced to find a friend so well suited in every respect to be my partner for life—I am enjoying myself right well, making money fast enough, and good friends to spend my leisure with . . .[20]

After that, extant family correspondence indicates, he wrote less often to his family, and it is necessary to turn to other sources for information about his life. The Hartford city directory informs us that the couple boarded at 117 Main Street, near Mulberry Street, two blocks south of Wells's office. The house belonged to Thomas Hender, Elizabeth's fifty—four—year—old uncle. Also sharing the house was Francis Birge, a partner in F. & M. Birge & Co., a drygoods store located at 205 Main. Finally, Alfred P. Warner, a cordwainer (shoemaker), operated his business "over 117 Main." He lived, however, on Ellery Street.[21]

A study of the immediate neighbors on Main Street reflects the same pattern of businesses and residences, with more individual businessmen and craftsmen than partnerships like that of Wells & Humphrey a few blocks further north. Many of the people in this neighborhood would have business or personal relationships with the Wells over the next few years. Francis Parsons, an attorney, had offices at 111 Main. Parsons, forty-three years old in 1838, who had graduated from Yale, and studied law, worked for Hartford as city attorney. He later became a judge of Hartford County Court. In 1845, Wells turned to Parsons to help resolve a dispute he had with Colonel Thomas Roberts over the invention of a shower bath.[22] Edward Parsons, Francis's cousin, also a friend of the Wells's and a member of the Center Church, ran a bookstore, Brown & Parsons, a few blocks north.[23] Pinckney W. Ellsworth, M.D., a prominent physician and son of the governor, who later supported Wells in his claim as the discoverer of anesthesia, had an office at 122 1/2 Main Street.[24] Finally, William Pease, a music teacher at 134 Main, was related to Persis Pease, one of Wells's aunts who lived in Windsor.[25]

Other immediate neighbors included James Doolittle, a fruit seller at 118 Main; Darius Stone, who ran a shoestore at 112 Main; Daniel Phelps, who made umbrellas; and Mary Hinsdale, who ran a boarding house at 129 Main. Humphrey, Seyms & Company, a drygoods store, was one of the few partnerships in this neighborhood, located at 124 Main Street. Also, a man named Lester Pasco, clearly not from one of the founding families, ran a provision store at 126 Main.[26]

The entire Main Street district was small, the street being less than a mile in length. It extended on a north-to-south axis, paralleling the Connecticut River, which was less than four blocks to the east. The most important cross streets in a business sense were Asylum and State, two east-to-west streets which met at Main. Wells's office stood right at this intersection, approximately opposite the State House, as well as the Connecticut Hotel.

Main Street supported any number of merchants in partnership or working alone, specializing in everything from drygoods to shoes, books, and jewelry.[27] From the time the ice broke on the Connecticut River in the spring until the following winter, the shops on Main Street advertised imported goods which came up the river from New York or directly from European ports. For example, the jewelry firm of Steele & Crocker, at 195 Main Street, posted the following advertisement on the front page of the *Connecticut Courant* in April 1841:

STEELE & CROCKER have just received a new assortment of Watches, Jewelry, silver plated and Britannia Ware; gilt, alabaster and ebony French clocks, which they offer as low as the lowest.[28]

The wholesalers, who tended to congregate in shops to the east of Main Street nearer the wharves on the river, also depended on the river trade:

FLOUR—1500 bbls. Genesee, Ohio and Michigan superfine Flour, fresh ground, just received and for sale by
RICHMOND & COLEMAN, foot State St.[29]

Elizabeth Wales Wells's brother, Joseph, also participated in Hartford's flour and grain trade as a partner in the firm of French & Wales.[30]

Hartford boasted a small number of corporations at this time,

most notably insurance companies, including Aetna and the Protection Fire Marine Insurance Companies, both of which had headquarters just off Main Street, and included many members of the
Main Street businesses on their boards of directors.[31] The older
families, with help from the merchants, also supported a number of
non-profit institutions: the American Asylum for the Deaf & Dumb;
the Retreat for the Insane, which became the present Institute for
Living; and Washington College, which changed its name to Trinity
College in the mid-1840s. The Young Men's Institute, forerunner of
the Hartford Public Library, was founded in 1838, and Wells became
a member in 1843. And in 1842, the Wadsworth Atheneum opened
its small gallery of paintings to the public.[32] It was the first public
museum in the United States.

Main Street was home as well as office for many families. The
pattern of living on or close to Main, or operating a business at a
residence was not peculiar either to Wells or to his immediate neighbors. Henry Humphrey lived on Main, about five blocks north of
his pharmacy, and for a time fitted out his residence as a branch of
his pharmacy. Unfortunately, Humphrey disappeared from the city
directory about 1841, which makes it difficult to trace him, and his
business reverted to Leonard Welles shortly thereafter.[33]

Harriet and Nancy Humphrey, two unmarried relatives of
Henry's, who taught school, lived on Trumbull near Miss Draper's
Seminary, but by 1843 had moved into 289 Main, where Humphrey
had opened his second drug store. A widow, Lucy Humphrey, also
moved in there, but she was not Henry's widow. These addresses
were within half a mile of each other and clearly both Wells and
Humphrey, and probably also Harriet and Nancy Humphrey, could
walk to work, as could most of those in business on Main Street.[34]

Like the Wells's and Humphrey's, other Hartford families frequently lived in a succession of different residences, and frequently
within walking distance of Main, at least during the decade extending from 1837 to 1847. Wells himself changed his residential address
once, and relocated his office to 8 Asylum in 1841. Upon discovering
that 8 Asylum Street was Flavia Anderson's boarding house, the
historian may be tempted to put Wells on the margins of polite
society. In fact, it was Flavia who had trouble. Her boarding house
moved every year but one fron 1838 to 1844.[35] Though sources

conflict, Wells is also recorded as having offices at 14 Asylum Street and 180 1/2 Main Street during the remaining years of his practice.[36]

Another acquaintance of both Wells and his wife, Joseph Church, had a jewelry business on Main Street throughout the decade, but the business changed hands during that period, though Church remained an influential and highly respected member of the community.[37] Jospeh Church lived at 28 Trumbull, next door to Miss Draper's Seminary, and worked in a shop which in 1838 was at 206 Main Street, a block north of Wells's dental office.[38] Church's twelve-year-old son Frederick E. Church probably lived with him or near him until he left for New York in 1844 to study painting with Thomas Cole.[39]

Church's shop was assumed in 1842 by the partnership of Wells & Strong, who remained at the same address, employing Joseph Church to work for them.[40] His business reputation was such that Elizabeth Wells still referred to the shop as Mr. Church's some years later.[41] Church's influence extended beyond Main Street, to the Aetna Insurance Company, where he served as a board member. Church also served on the board of the Connecticut River Bank, likewise located on State, near the corner of Main.[42] The bank was a great boon to investors in trade up and down the Connecticut River.

By 1838, Wells had established a way of life which centered around his marriage to Elizabeth Wales, his dental practice, the merchants' shops on Main Street, and the Center Church, all within less than a quarter of a mile radius of each other, and of the State House opposite his office. In 1838, a small book Wells had compiled, *An Essay on Teeth*, was produced by Case, Tiffany & Company, on Trumbull Street, a printing shop located one block west of Wells's office. In publishing this work, Wells joined the ranks of a generation of dentists who were struggling to emerge from low work status and establish their profession on a solid scientific foundation.[43]

In 1839, Elizabeth gave birth to the couple's only child, Charles Thomas Wells, on August 26. Nevertheless, a year after the birth of his son, Wells had again become sick, to the extent that he could not continue his dental practice. The *Connecticut Courant*, with offices a few doors north of Wells' office, published the following announcement, beginning on November 9, 1840:

DENTISTS

H. Wells, Dentist, having resolved to remove from Hartford to a warmer climate, in consequence of ill health, has left his business to Drs. Cuyler and Crofoot, to whom he would cheerfully refer his friends as fully worth of his confidence.[44]

Vernon Cuyler, also a member of the Center Church,[45] set up an official partnership with Evelyn Crofoot a month after Wells's announcement appeared. They did not stray far from the fold:

Cuyler and Crofoot have this day entered into copartnership, for the practice of Dental Surgery, and may be consulted at their rooms over 132 Main Street, 2d building north of the Centre Church. Hartford, December 5, 1840.[46]

Wells changed his plans at least twice before he reestablished himself in Hartford. On February 13, the announcement in the *Courant* continued to "cheerfully refer friends" to Cuyler & Crofoot, but concluded "Dr. Wells has removed to Boston." While this latter announcement bore the date of the previous December, it did not appear until February.[47]

In the first half of 1841, Wells announced his intention to resume the practice of dentistry in Hartford, and surviving records clearly indicate that he treated patients during the month of May.[48] But that announcement immediately vanished from the ensuing issues of the *Courant*, being succeeded by a new announcement, dated June 12, which read as follows:

TEETH. TEETH

H. Wells, DENTIST, having resumed his professional business in Hartford, after an absence of six months, is now prepared to execute all operations in the line of his profession in the best manner, at his new operating rooms, No. 8 Asylum st.[49]

Wells's new office was only a few paces distant from his previous office at the corner of Main and Asylum. Had Wells's family left Hartford with him during his illness? Probably not, since the baby was less than two years old, and living with his mother and great uncle. But it is impossible to be certain. Did Wells really go south and then on to Boston? No evidence to the contrary can be found. Did a six-month absence from Hartford destroy his business? It emphatically did not. During this hiatus in practice, he had met with a young student named Linus P. Brockett, who graduated from the Yale Medical College three years later and would write over fifty books in addition to having a medical career in Hartford. Wells shared with him the idea that dental surgery without pain might be possible. This is the earliest record of Wells's thinking on this subject.[50]

When Wells recommenced his practice, he began to keep a day book listing his credit transactions, that is, patients he treated who deferred payment. An examination of this book shows how quickly his business expanded after his return. Furthermore, the names which appear in this record clearly demonstrate why he addressed his patients as "friends" in his newspaper announcements, rather than treating them as an anonymous public. Those acquaintances of his who were patients could not possibly be distinguished from the members of the Center Church, the proprietors and employees of the shops on Main Street, or his own extended family.[51]

The first name entered in Wells's day book, on May 13, 1841, was the familiar one of Henry Humphrey, who had disappeared from the city directory but not, apparently, from Hartford, for his name reappeared in August of 1843. In 1841 Wells also treated a Miss Grimes, introduced to him by an old friend, Frances Humphrey. Business acquaintances, with shops on or near Main, patronized Wells's office, including Charles P. Wells, Humphrey's former partner in the pharmacy next door, and John Boswell, editor of the *Courant*, whose print shop and editorial offices were just north of Pratt Street on Main. In 1841, Wells also treated Mr. Crocker, a partner in the jewelry store of Steele & Crocker, across the street from "Mr Churchs" [sic] store; Mr. Steele; and Mr. Hills, an employee of Whiting, Rising & Company, a shoestore on State Street. Members of his own family who made appointments with him included his sister Mary, in 1841, and his wife's relations Frederick and Dr. Lemuel Wales, in 1842.

Aside from the business community and a few members of his family, Wells treated a large number of women and children, many of whom were related to members of the business community. Almost a third of his credit customers in 1841 were women, and many of these were single. This pattern continued in the following years.

In January, 1842, Mr. Crocker paid the bill for his niece to receive treatment from Wells. Mr. Richmond, of the Richmond & Coleman flour store on State Street, brought his sons in for treatment, and paid their bills. Mr. Burnham, of Case, Tiffany & Company, the shop that printed Wells's *An Essay on Teeth,* paid Wells to treat his wife. In 1842, almost half of Wells's credit customers were women.

A number of men asked Wells to treat their wives or daughters in their homes. Mr. Steele asked this favor in May of 1842; a Mr. George Brinley had his daughter treated at home in 1844; and Mr. Burnham had Wells come to his home to treat his wife. Wells also took his instruments out the the Hartford Retreat for the Insane to treat patients. The Retreat was located half-a-mile south and west of Wells's office on Asylum Street.[52] Also during the period 1841–1844, Wells tutored a number of young men who were training to become dentists: William T. G. Morton, who latered claimed credit as the discoverer of anesthesia, and reportedly also John Riggs and Charles A. Kingsbury, later a founder of the Philadelphia Dental College.[53]

In 1843, Wells's practice widened to include more members of the Center Church, and the government. William Ellsworth sent his daughter to Wells for treatment. His son Pinckney Ellsworth joined the Center Church in this same year. Joseph Church, since 1841 a member of Center Church as well as the Main Street business community, sent his daughter to Wells in 1844. Henry Francis, Town Clerk of the City of Hartford, also sent his daughter to Horace Wells for dentistry.

One possible clue to the influx of more influential families to Wells's office may be ascribed to the fact that he had built a house for himself and his family on Lord's Hill, out of the center of Hartford. In summer, 1842, he wrote to his mother

> My house is almost done, we think of moving in about 10 days. We think it is the most convenient house in all creation beside its being the prettiest, and odd as all outdoors. The cost of the whole including land fences and all will be $4000. I shall not be able to pay for the whole as the expense of house-keeping articles I find will cost me almost enough to build a small house therefore I wish you would make some special effort to assist me.[54]

In moving away from the center of town and building his own house, Wells was clearly moving up in his world, as well as away from Main Street. He joined those who could afford houses on the outskirts of the downtown area, including Governor Ellsworth. He noted in the same letter to his mother, however, that he would have to ride his horse into town every morning, rather than walking to work.

Wells's move clearly did not entirely change his business, however, and many of his customers continued to come from his old neighborhood at 117 Main. Mr. Litchfield, from the family firm of J.G. & U. Litchfield at 115 Main, was a patient in June of 1843, as was his wife. In the following year, Wells treated his wife's uncle Thomas Hender, still at 117 Main, and Mr. Ambrose Spencer, an employee of Humphrey Seym & Company at 124 Main. Despite the growth in numbers and status of his customers, very few of Wells's credit customers fell outside the range of his acquaintance. Among those patients who came from out of town, a number were kin; and while he may have treated individuals who were strangers to him, clearly he did not extend credit to them.

What direction Wells's practice might have taken after this cannot be guessed. The consequences of his teaching and his experiments with the use of nitrous oxide as an anesthetic virtually determined his actions for the remaining three years of his life. In an effort to exploit a new invention, a gold solder for teeth, Wells started a business in Boston with his dental student Thomas Morton, accompanying him there in October 1843, and forming a partnership which lasted only a short time. Apparently the business brought little return, in sales or in recognition. He had returned to Hartford by mid-November.[55]

Wells's parents and siblings began to renew their correspondence with him shortly after this period of time; but Wells found less time to keep up his end of the correspondence. To his mother and sisters he wrote:

You must excuse me for not answering your letters before, for you know I am no letter writer, but I have come to the conclusion that if I do not write you will strike me from your list . . .[56]

An issue on which Wells remained silent was his relationship with his wife. Elizabeth may have remained in Hartford during his absence in 1841, and she did stay behind while he went to Boston with Morton in 1843. By 1844, Elizabeth had a liver ailment and was was under the care of Dr. David Dodge, a resident of Pearl Street, with an office on Asylum. Nevertheless, Wells left town more frequently during the next two years, with no word of complaint from his wife. She supported the long absences with apparent good cheer, in spite of words of sympathy from some of their friends.[57]

Immediately after the evening of December 10, 1844, when Wells observed Samuel Cooley's obliviousness to pain while under the influence of nitrous oxide, also known as laughing gas, Wells, Cooley and another dentist, John Riggs, confirmed the use of nitrous oxide as a successful anesthetic for dental purposes. They met the next day in Wells's office, where Riggs removed one of Wells's teeth while the latter was under the influence of nitrous oxide. Wells, excited by the discovery, made plans to demonstrate it at Harvard in January, 1845. Morton helped make the arrangements for this demonstration. But when it failed, the patient crying out in pain, Wells returned to Hartford feeling deeply shamed, while his health and ability to work began to suffer.

From that time on, Wells's professional and personal life became increasingly uprooted. Only a few weeks after his return from Boston, on February 5, Wells advertised his cottage on Lord's Hill for rent, at a very low rate. He stated as his reason his desire to "give up housekeeping." He also gave up his regular dental practice to John Riggs, citing ill health. He then involved himself in a succession of projects other than his dentistry.[58]

In April and May, he put together a series of theatrical exhibitions of natural history and ornathology, both subjects having reportedly been hobbies of his in the past; witness the Linnets he spoke of to his sister Mary. But family letters indicate that this and other schemes failed to steady him.[59]

In the summer of 1845, an outpouring of correspondence among members of the Wells family clearly indicates that they saw Horace as being in a state of turmoil. City directories locate Horace at 117 Main Street during 1845, 1846, and 1847, the address of Elizabeth's uncle Thomas Hender, and it seems a reasonable conclusion that she and Charles lived there also. Nevertheless Wells's restlessness continued. In a June 17 letter to Mary Wells, his mother quoted him describing himself as "neither sick nor well & . . . at present a loafer, . . . uneasy as a fish out of water."

She went on to quote his wife as saying:

> Dr. Taft says there is nothing to hinder H. doing well if he will take medicine & attend to him self. He has examined his lungs & says they are not diseased but weak, but they do not tell whether his has a cough or pain in his side. if H. goes to the sea shores I think it will terminate soon whether his lungs are effected or not.

She concluded, "they do not write whether E. was going with Horace or not. but they both spoke of coming here."[60] During this time, Dr. Pinckney Ellsworth is reported to have been "living in the same house with Dr. Wells;" whether they lived at 117 Main or at Dr. Ellsworth's house isn't known.[61] Wells also continued to experiment with anesthesia intermittently.

Despite a temporary renewal of his dental practice in September at 14 Asylum Street, Wells continued to seek success in another field, or with another invention. He focussed his attention on an automatic shower bath which he had patented. Unfortunately he got into a legal dispute almost immediately, with a Colonel Thomas Roberts who also claimed rights to the patent. After obtaining legal help from his old neighbor Francis Parsons, Wells entered into a partnership with Roberts, and set about travelling the region to find customers.[62]

In April, 1846, Wells's mother once again wrote to his sister, now married, to say that she planned to go to Hartford: "I feel as though I must see Horace." By May, however, Horace had come to her, but the visit did not reassure her. Once again she wrote, this time to her daughter's new husband, a sea captain named John Cole:

> [Horace] has been studying out some new invention for showering and has sent on for a patant [sic] he is going largely into the business he came up to Hinsdale to made a contract for showering bath. he thinks he is now on his way to fortune, but I think he is building castles in the air which will soon burst. but I can do nothing but leave him in the hand of God.[63]

In November of the same year, 1846, Wells's world came even further undone. His former student Morton, who had helped him arrange the demontration of nitrous oxide the previous year, contacted Wells with the news that he, Morton, had patented an anesthetic compound for use by dentists and was trying to sell the rights to its use. While Morton used an ether compound rather than nitrous oxide, Wells had stated on more than one occasion that he had not patented anesthesia because he felt that it should be free to all who needed it.[64] Furthermore, Morton claimed all the credit and all the remuneration for the discovery of anesthesia.[65]

Wells thereafter sold out his shower bath business to his partner and tried to focus his own attention on establishing a claim to his earlier discovery. By December 7, he had written a statement of his claim which was published in the new daily *Hartford Courant* two days later. But at the end of the month, in his somewhat scattered fashion, he left for Paris, saying at different times that he went for his health, that he wished to buy European paintings for resale in the United States, and, according to other accounts, that he wished to establish his claim to anesthesia in Paris. Once again, another Hartford dentist, this time John B. Terry, advertised his services in lieu of Wells's.[66]

Shortly after his departure, his wife Elizabeth wrote to him. Most of the letter kept him apprised of developments in the "gas war," a phrase she invented to describe the rivalry with Morton which had become public. But she also alluded to a visit she had made to one of the shops on Main Street, the jewelry store of Joseph Church, located across the street from Horace's first office, and only a few yards from his newest and last office, at 180 1/2 Main. "I called yesterday at Mr. Churchs and unexpectedly met Frederick [Church]." She wrote:

> "He has sold his large painting. The Emmigration [sic] of Hooker to our Institute for $130 and is now painting for Dr. Beresford. He leaves this week for N.Y."[67]

The news that Frederick Church had sold one of his paintings had relevance for Horace, who also hoped to make money selling paintings, purchased in Europe.

Church, then twenty years old, was about to return to New York, where he had been working with Thomas Cole, the English painter who had helped form the Hudson River School of painting.[68] The "Institute" was the Young Men's Institute, but the painting is now in the Wadsworth Atheneum, named for the family of Hartford founders and merchants who had prospered from the trade coming across their wharf on the city waterfront. The painting Elizabeth referred to, now entitled "Hooker and Company, Journey Through the Wilderness from Plymouth to Hartford in 1636," memorializes the journey made by Thomas Hooker who in 1636 walked west with his congregation and founded Hartford.[69]

Church may well have met Cole through the efforts of Daniel Wadsworth, whose purchases of Cole's paintings were among the first for the Atheneum, when it opened in 1842.[70] Wells's interest in purchasing paintings may also have been related to the opening of the Atheneum. In any event, Church, like many eminent Hartford citizens, respected Wells and never forgot him. Though he lived in New York for much of his adult life, in 1872 he corresponded with the editor of the *Hartford Courant* regarding the design of a memorial statue to Wells.[71]

A number of family friends called on Elizabeth after her husband's departure, out of concern over the "gas war" which filled the press. She wrote in her letter that she had "plenty of calls from my friends brimful of sympathy and a long one from Mrs. Buer" (probably Buel) who offered much advice that Elizabeth passed on to Horace about being careful not to get robbed in foreign cities or cheated by interpreters. Mrs. Ellsworth, the wife of Pinckney Ellsworth, promised Elizabeth "the reading of the medical papers" regarding the anesthesia battle. And finally, Dr. Terry, the most recent substitute in Wells's dental practice, dropped by and was "quite kind and attentive." When Terry departed, he left behind "two papers from Joe" (probably Joseph Wales, Elizabeth's brother).[72]

Wells returned home in mid—March, 1847, to find that the gas battle still raging, pitting Hartford against Boston. He rejoined the fight despite the fact that his health and life continued to unravel under the stress. While his wife admired the paintings he had brought back from Europe, and helped old neighbors Edward Parsons and Humphrey, Seyms & Company assemble a shipment of clothing for famine-ridden Ireland, Wells busily engaged in writing letters and a pamphlet supporting his claim.[73] The pamphlet, *History of the Discovery of the Application of Nitrous Oxide Gas, Ether, and other Vapors, to Surgical Operations,* was published in 1847 by J. Gaylord Wells, one of his former patients. [74]

No evidence exists that Wells attended to his dental business again, at least on a regular basis, although he continued to experiment with the use of anesthesia in surgery. By late 1847, he had moved to New York, without much planning and without his family, to further his work with anesthesia. And although he made trips back to Hartford intermittently, it was in New York that he finally took his own life on January 23, 1848, while under the influence of chloroform, another anesthetic. His body was returned to Hartford, and a funeral service took place at 117 Main Street, Thomas Hender's house, before it was interred in the Old North Burying Ground, four days after his death.[75]

Among Hartford court documents may be found a record of Wells's estate, of which Edward W. Parsons, the bookseller, was appointed administrator. The estate record includes a list of all Wells's outstanding business transactions at the time of his death. In this short list, familiar names and projects are mentioned for the last time. Amounts were paid on small debts due to John L. Boswell, editor of the *Courant;* to Joseph Wales, Elizabeth's brother; and to E.W.P., without much doubt Edward W. Parsons. Among Wells's assets were $400 in the Fire & Marine Bank; and money owed to him by Morton, Pinckney Ellsworth, John Riggs and David Dodge, his wife's doctor. Finally, "J.S.H." owed him ten dollars for two pictures, perhaps paintings.[76] The only "J.S.H." in the Hartford city directory of that time was J.S. Hewlitt, an importer of foreign teas and fruits at 132 Main Street.[77]

At the time of Wells's death in 1848, Main Street had already begun to lose many of the landmarks familiar to him. Small shops continued to predominate, but gone were many of the merchant partnerships whose members he had treated as a dentist. The jewelry firm of Steele & Crocker had dissolved, and so had the jewelry partnership across the street, Welles & Strong. Leonard T. Welles, one of the distinguished local Wells line, who had learned his trade from Joseph Church, continued in the jewelry business without a partner until his retirement in 1875.[78] At the time of his death, Leonard Welles's obituary in the *Hartford Courant* reflected the closeness of family and community ties, both within Hartford and beyond its immediate borders, which had characterized Horace Wells's experience. It reads, "his store was a favorite rendezvous for Glastonbury people and for his many warm friends there." Also like the dentist, Leonard Welles had moved from Asylum Street to the area of Lord's Hill, and his funeral service took place at his house, at 766 Asylum Avenue.[79]

While the Case, Tiffany & Company print shop remained, it faced new competition from J. Gaylord Wells, who had published a city directory as well as Horace Wells's history of anesthesia. Other businessmen persevered. John Boswell continued to publish the *Hartford Courant* from his Main Street offices. Humphrey, Seyms & Company, the provision store which aided the victims of the Irish famine, also stayed in business. Edward Parson's firm of Brown & Parsons also survived the rapid turnover of local businesses.[80] Samuel A. Cooley, the young pharmacist's assistant whose experience with laughing gas provoked Wells's first experiment with anesthesia, turned to photography and opened a "Dauguerrian Room" on Main Street in 1848, but it remained open for less than a year.[81]

The other members of Wells's family outlived him by decades. Horace's mother did not die until 1879, at the age of ninety. His brother Charles lived until 1884. Thomas Hender, Elizabeth's uncle stayed for a time at 117 Main Street, but Elizabeth moved out a few years after Horace's death, and relocated a number of times before her death in 1889. William Ellsworth died in 1868; Joseph Church survived until the mid—1870s.[82]

As the face of Main Street changed, a number of residents, some family or friends of the Wells and some less close to them personally, worked to vindicate Wells's claim to his discovery, and to create a permanent memorial in Hartford to Wells's life and work. In 1867, his friend Dr. Pinckney Ellsworth contributed to the final edition of Truman Smith's *An Examination of the Origin of Modern Anesthesia* a section entitled "The Life of Horace Wells, M.D.," one of the very first accounts written about the dentist's life.[83] In 1870, the citizens of Hartford began preparations to erect a monument from the people of Hartford, for Horace Wells.[84]

By this time, a new circle of accomplished men and women had emerged in the city, composed of many descendents of earlier generations, but once again including gifted newcomers as well. The Nook Farm Enclave, for example, which included Mark Twain and Charles Dudley Warner, neither born locally, had in it also Harriet Beecher Stowe, who had attended Center Church in 1836, and later Warner's brother's wife, a descendent of Hooker. Nook Farm itself stood on land still owned by the Hooker family.[85]

Charles Dudley Warner, editor of the *Hartford Courant* after 1867, coordinated publicity for the monument. In April, 1872, he received a note from Frederick Church, by then living on his estate known as Olana, on the Hudson River north of West Point. Church's note, apparently unsolicited, read:

> Dr. Wells has conferred great honor upon Hartford. It is therefore fitting that Hartford should show her appreciation of it—by erecting a statue to his memory. We hope that the result many prove artistically equal to the occasion.
>
> The base should be simple and of noble proportions. Would it not be well to have this designed as to leave one or more sunken panels to be filled here after if not now with bronze bas releivos [sic] illustrative of the important service rendered to mankind by Dr. Wells's great and very original discovery? It is capable of highly artistic treatment.
>
> Please pardon the liberality I have taken in writing to you on this subject.
>
> Yours sincerely
Frederick E. Church[86]

The committee of dentists chosen to petition the city and state for permission and funds to erect the statue included the familiar names of John Riggs, who had joined Wells in his first experiment with anesthesia, and Evelyn Crofoot, one of the dentists who cared for Wells's patients during his absence from Hartford.[87] The committee chose Truman H. Bartlett, a locally known sculptor, and had his creation cast in Paris. Bartlett elected not to follow Church's suggestion, but rather made the base of the statue plain, with engraved lettering. Occupying its present position in Bushnell Park since July

22, 1875, the statue stands just within view of Center Church, and the Wadsworth Atheneum.[88]

In 1894, on the fiftieth anniversary of Wells's discovery, a group of dentists put a bronze tablet at the old familiar intersection of Main and Asylum, marking the location where Wells's historic discovery took place. This plaque also still remains, only a few blocks north of the Center Church.[89] Finally, in 1903, Center Church itself memorialized Wells and his wife Elizabeth with a stained glass window dedicated on Easter Sunday. Part of the text on the window proclaims that

> Mercy and Truth Are Met Together. Righteousness and Peace Have Kissed Each Other. Neither Shall There be Any More Pain For the Former Things Are Passed Away.[90]

APPENDIX I

Below are the complete citations of the Hartford city directories for the years 1838–1851, listed chronologically.

Gardner's Hartford City Directory for 1838. Hartford: Case, Tiffany & Co., 1838.

Gardner's Hartford City Directory for 1839. Hartford: Case, Tiffany & Co., 1839.

Gardner's Hartford City Directory for 1840. Hartford: Case, Tiffany & Co., 1840.

Bolles, Isaac N. comp. and ed. *New Directory and Guide Book for the City of Hartford for 1843.* Hartford: C. Martinson, 1841.

Gardner's Hartford City Directory for 1841. Hartford: Elihu Geer, 1841.

Bolles, Isaac N. comp. and ed. *Directory and Guide Book for the City of Hartford for 1842.* Hartford: Courier Office, 1842.

Geer's Hartford City Directory for 1842. Hartford: Elihu Geer, 1842.

Bolles, Isaac, N. comp. and pub. *New Directory and Guide Book for the City of Hartford for 1843.* Hartford: Courier Office, 1843.

Geer's Hartford City Directory for 1843. Hartford: Elihu Geer, 1843.

Bolles, Isaac, N. comp. and pub. *Directory and Guidebook for the City of Hartford 1844.* Hartford, 1844.

Geer's Hartford City Directory for 1844. Hartford: Elihu Geer, 1844.

Bolles, Isaac N. *Directory and Guidebook for the City of Hartford, 1845.* Hartford, 1845.

Geer's Hartford City Directoy for 1845. Hartford: Elihu Geer, 1845.

Bolles, Isaac N. comp. and ed. *Directory and Guidebook for the City of Hartford for 1846.* Hartford: Courier Office, 1846.

Geer's Hartford City Directory for 1846. Hartford: Elihu Geer, 1846.

Bolles, Isaac N. comp. and pub. *Directory and Guide Book for the City of Hartford for 1847.* Hartford: 1847.

Geer's Hartford City Directory for 1847. Hartford: Elihu Geer, 1847.

Geer's Hartford City Directory for 1848. Hartford: Elihu Geer, 1848.

Geer's Hartford City Directoy for 1849. Hartford: Elihu Geer, 1849.

Geer's Hartford City Directory for 1850. Hartford: Elihu Geer, 1850

Geer's Hartford City Directory for 1851. Hartford: Elihu Geer, 1851.

APPENDIX II

Below are the street addresses given in *Gardner's Hartford City Directory for 1838* for each street which crosses Main Street in the area of Horace Well's homes and offices. The list shown here puts the streets in order from north to south. Gardner's original list put the streets in alphabetical order. These streets appear on Illustrations 14 and 15, following, which focus on Main Street and its shops.[91]

Morgan	263 Main
Talcott	253 Main
Church	244 Main
Temple	223 Main
Pratt	214 Main
Kingsley	203 Main
State	191 Main
Asylum	184 Main
Pearl	158 Main
Central Row	147 Main
Grove	127 Main
Nichols	122 Main
Wadsworth	111 Main
Mulberry	116 Main

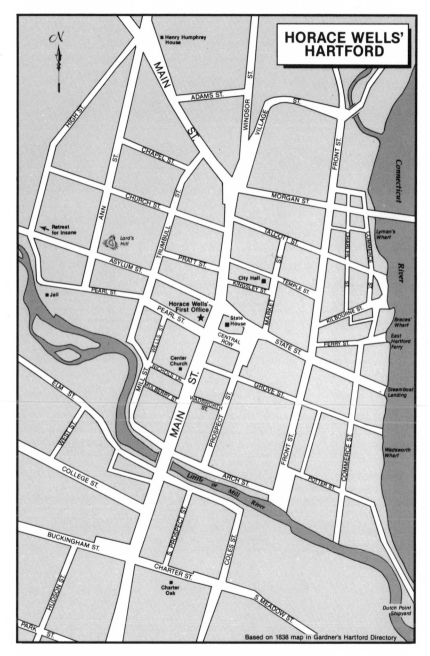

Illustration 14. Map of Horace Wells's Hartford

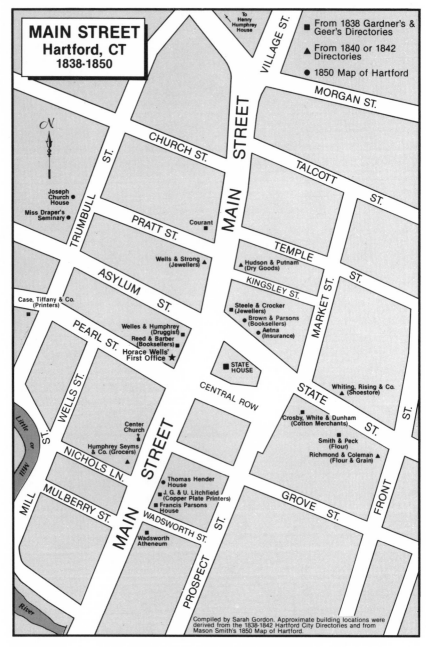

Illustration 15. Map of Main Street, Hartford, 1839–1850

NOTES

1. Henry R. Stiles, *The History of Ancient Windsor* (Somersworth, N.H., New Hampshire Publishing, 1976), 784–787.
2. Ibid.
3. Personal communication from the Curator of the Hartford, Vermont Historical Society; *Connecticut Courant,* 1841. In general, settlement followed the Connecticut River north from Hartford, after the founding of that colony in 1636.
4. Westmoreland, Vermont, "First Town Record Book," 423.
5. Horace Wells to Susan Shaw, Boston, November 21, 1835, in W. Harry Archer, "Life and Letters of Horace Wells, Discoverer of Anesthesia, Chronologically Arranged," *Journal of the American College of Dentists* 11, no. 2 (June 1944): 88; hereafter referred to as Archer.
6. Archer, 89.
7. Archer, 89.
8. Horace Wells to Mary Wells, Hartford, August 29, 1836, Archer, 89—90.
9. Center Church, Hartford, "Records." The church of most seventeenth century New England towns also had governmental powers. The descendents of a number of these early families, such as William Ellsworth, not only remained in the same church, but still sought and held governmental positions in the nineteenth century.
10. Ellsworth Strong Grant and Marian Hepburn Grant, *The City of Hartford, 1784–1988* (Hartford, Connecticut Historical Society, 1986), 169.
11. Center Church, Hartford, "Records." It was in that same year, 1836, that Harriet Beecher married Calvin Ellis Stowe, a clergyman and seminary professor who managed her literary activity. The Beechers, who came from the Hartford area, migrated to Litchfield where they lived during the second decade of the nineteenth century, at which time Litchfield had a reputation as an intellectual mecca. Harriet and Catharine Beecher attended Miss Pierce's Female Academy there, and Tapping Reeve founded and ran the Litchfield Law School. The coming of the railroad, which bypassed Litchfield, marked the beginnig of the town's decline, and the gain by Hartford of many former inhabitants of Litchfield, including John Brace, the nephew of Sarah Pierce, as well as Tapping Reeve and the Beechers.
12. Horace Wells to Abiather Shaw, Jr., Hartford, November 25, 1836, Archer, 90–91. While the exact meaning of Wells's phrase is not clear, Hartford had a very active publishing trade, which involved all phases

of publication, from writing, to printing and publishing, to book-selling. Wells's friend John Boswell, the editor of the *Connecticut Courant*, and then the newer *Hartford Courant*, had his printing press on the first floor of a building at 214 Main Street, at the corner of Pratt, and his editorial offices on the second floor. Hartford also supported a number of bookstores, including Reed & Barber as well as Brown & Parsons. Brown, of the latter firm, worked as a book-binder too, according to the Hartford city directories.

13. Horace Wells to Mary Wells, Hartford, April 29, 1837, Archer, 91–92.
14. Horace Wells to Mary Wells, Hartford, August 29, 1836, Archer, 90.
15. Horace Wells to Mary Wells, Hartford, April 29, 1837, Archer, 91–92.
16. *Connecticut Courant*, April 24, 1841, 3. The front page of the weekly *Courant* was devoted almost exclusively to advertisements, placed there routinely by Hartford businesses, to let the public know what new wares had come into stock. Also placed here were announcements of the forming and dissolution of business partnerships, and the opening of new stores. The other three pages of the paper contained the national, state and local news, boat and train schedules, and reports of crime and disasters, and births, marriages and deaths.
17. Horace Wells to Mary Wells, Hartford, April 29, 1837, Archer, 91–92. Charles Thomas Wells, the son of Horace, described his father as "a good deal of a naturalist. . . . I liked to be with him . . . for he had . . . cases of butterflies and stuffed birds, and other things that inter-ested me." Charles' statement is quoted in Archer, 204.
18. Center Church, Hartford, "Records;" Russell Donald Ramette, *The Wales Family of Dorchester, Massachusetts* ([West Hartford, Conn.] 1979), no. 107.
19. Mary Wells to Mrs. Abiather Shaw, Hartford, July 9, 1838, Archer, 96–97. Archer indicates on page 159 that Mary Wells taught at Ipswich Academy after she completed her studies there. It appears from the full context of her letter to her mother that in 1838 she was still a student.
20. Horace Wells to Abiather Shaw, Jr., Hartford, September 21, 1838, Archer, 97–98.
21. Hartford City Directories, 1838–1851. The Hartford directories through 1860 can be found listed in Dorothea N. Spears's *Bibliography of American Directories Through 1860* (Worcester, Mass., American Antiquarian Society, 1961), 141–150, with a census of copies located. Runs, including annuals after 1860, can be found in the Library of the Connecticut Historical Society and The Connecticut

State Library, both in Hartford. See Appendix I to this article for a complete list of citations of the Hartford directories used in this article.

22. Henry Parsons, *Parsons Family; Descendents of Cornet Joseph Parsons, Springfield 1636—Northampton, 1655* (New York, Frank Allaben Geneological Company, 1912), 169; Archer, 113.

23. Henry Parsons, *Parsons Family*, 240; Hartford city directories, 1838–1851.

24. Donna Holt Siemiatkoski, *The Ancestors and Descendents of Chief Justice Oliver Ellsworth and His Wife Abigail Wolcott, and the Story of Elmwood, Their Homestead* (Baltimore, Gateway Press, 1992); Hartford city directory, 1840.

25. Henry R. Stiles, *The History of Ancient Windsor*, 784–787; Hartford city directory, 1840.

26. Hartford city directory, 1840.

27. *Connecticut Courant*, January through June, 1841, 1.

28. *Connecticut Courant*, April 17, 1841, 1.

29. *Connecticut Courant*, June 26, 1841, 1.

30. "Joseph Wales," obituary, Mary Morris Scrapbook, Connecticut Historical Society, Vol. 19, 101. The Mary Morris Scrapbook, a collection of obituaries of Hartford citizens for the year 1877 to 1923, is in the holdings of the Connecticut Historical Society Library.

31. Hartford city directories, 1838–1851.

32. Eugene R. Gaddis, "Foremost Upon This Continent: A History of the Wadsworth Atheneum," in Linda Ayres, ed. *"The Spirit of Genius": Art at the Wadsworth Atheneum* (New York: Hudson Hills Press, 1992) 11.

33. Hartford city directories, 1838–1851.

34. Ibid.

35. Ibid.

36. Ibid. There are records of five street addresses for Horace Wells's dental practice, but it is not entirely clear how long he stayed at each address. It is fairly clear that he stayed at his first address, 162 1/2 Main, from 1836 to 1840; and at 8 Asylum from 1841 to 1844. After this date his whereabouts are more difficult to trace. It appears that he had offices at 14 Asylum, 180 Main, and 180 1/2 Main, in that order, but the Hartford city directories and documents in Archer conflict as to the dates.

37. Hartford city directories, 1838–1851.

38. Ibid.

39. Theodore E. Stebbins, *Close Observation, Selected Oil Sketches by*

Frederic E. Church (Washington, Smithsonian Institution Press, 1978), 13; In *Geer's Hartford City Directory for 1848*, Frederick Church, then twenty-two, was listed as boarding with his father. The year, 1848, corresponds to the time the younger Church was said to have completed his studies in New York with artist Thomas Cole.

40. Hartford city directories, 1838–1851; Elizabeth Wales Wells to Horace Wells, December 27, 1846; Archer, 123–124.

41. Elizabeth Wales Wells to Horace Wells, December 27, 1846, Archer, 123–124.

42. Hartford city directories, 1838—1851.

43. Horace Wells, *An Essay on Teeth; Comprising a Brief Description of Their Formation, Diseases, and Proper Treatment* (Hartford, Printed for the Author by Case, Tiffany & Co., 1838).

44. *Connecticut Courant,* January 1, 1841, 4. Wells's announcement appeared in the *Courant* on a regular basis until Wells replaced it with a new one in February.

45. Center Church, Hartford, "Records."

46. *Connecticut Courant,* January 1, 1841, 4. Like Wells, Cuyler and Crofoot ran their announcment in numerous successive issues of the *Courant.*

47. *Connecticut Courant,* February 13, 1841, 4.

48. Connecticut Courant, April 17, 1841, 1; Horace Wells, "Day Book A," Historical Museum of Medicine and Dentistry, Hartford Medical Society, Transcription in Leonard F. Menczer, "Horace Wells 'Day Book A," pp. 122; Center Church, Hartford, "Records;" Hartford city directories, 1838–1851. All information on Horace Wells's patients is drawn from these three sources.

49. *Connecticut Courant,* June 19, 1841, 4.

50. Brockett testified in 1852 that early in the spring of 1840, during the time that Brockett was attending medical lectures at Yale, Wells had extracted one of Brockett's molar teeth, which caused him much pain. Calling at Wells's office some time in the summer following, he found Wells engaged in some experient, which led to a conversation between Wells and Brockett respecting nitrous oxide gas. At the end of their conversation, Wells remarked that he believed that a man might be made so drunk by this gas or by some similar agent that dental and other operations might be performed upon him without any sensation of pain. Brockett's testimony appeared in United States Senate, *An Examination of the Questions of Anaesthesia, on the Memorial of Charles Thomas Wells* (Washington 1853), 11–12, compiled by Tru-

man Smith, and in the 1858, 1859, and 1867 editions of this work which Smith reissued under the same title, with himself listed as author. *Appletons' Cyclopaedia of American Biography,* edited by James Grant Wilson and John Fisk, (New York, D. Appleton and Company, 1887), provides a brief biography of Linus Pierpont Brockett (v. 1, p. 382). This relates that after obtaining the M.D. degree from Yale in 1843, Brockett practiced medicine for several years and then devoted himself to literary pursuits in Hartford, editing and writing for religious papers, encyclopedias and magazines. In addition to editing several magazines at different times, Brockett compiled and published nearly fifty distinct works on geography, biography, history, religion and social and literary subjects.

51. Horace Wells, "Day Book A;" Center Church, Hartford, "Records;" Hartford city directories, 1838–1851.

52. Hartford city directory, 1838.

53. Archer, 99.

54. Horace Wells to Betsy Wells Shaw, Hartford, June 26, 1842, Archer, 99–100.

55. Archer, 101–103. Archer quotes Wells as writing that "'I—assisted in establishing him [Morton] in the city of Boston.'"

56. Horace Wells to Betsy Wells Shaw and his sisters, Hartford, July 6, 1844, Archer, 105–106.

57. Elizabeth Wells to Horace Wells, Hartford, December 27, 1846, Archer, 123–125.

58. *Hartford Courant,* April 7, 1845, 3. The notices appear in Archer, 110.

59. The "Wells Panorama of Nature" entertainment is discussed in Archer, 111. See footnote 18 for Wells's son's comments on his father's interest in nature.

60. Betsy Wells Shaw to Mary Wells, Westmoreland, June 17, 1845, Archer 111–112.

61. Archer, 112.

62. Archer, 113. Archer discusses Wells's shower bath invention on pp. 113 and 119 of his "Life and Letters of Horace Wells," and reprints Wells's patent application on pp. 195–197. Charles Thomas Wells, Horace's son, helped place this interest in the context of his father's life some years later when he wrote that "He studied much; was observant and interested in whatever of discovery and invention took place in those days. . . . He had inventive faculties of a high order, and had invented some of the instruments he used in his prac-

tice and some household appliances only for personal use, which have since come into general use." This statement is quoted in Archer, 204.

63. Betsy Wells Shaw to John Cole, Westmoreland, May 4, 1846, Archer, 114–115.
64. Archer, 108–109.
65. Archer, 113.
66. Archer, 122.
67. Elizabeth Wales Wells to Horace Wells, Hartford, December 27, 1846, Archer, 123–125.
68. Theodore E. Stebbins, *Close Observation,* 13.
69. Personal communication from the Librarian of the Wadsworth Atheneum.
70. Ellsworth Strong Grant and Marian Hepburn Grant, *The City of Hartford,* 11.
71. Frederick Edwin Church to Charles Dudley Warner, April 8, 1872, Olana State Historic Site Archives, Hudson, New York.
72. Elizabeth Wales Wells to Horace Wells, Hartford, December 27, 1846; Archer, 123–125.
73. Elizabeth Wales Wells to Joseph Wales, [Hartford], April 27, 1847; Archer, 129.
74. Horace Wells, *History of the Discovery of the Application of Nitrous Oxide Gas, Ether, and Other Vapors, to Surgical Operations* (Hartford, J. Gaylord Wells, 1847).
75. Archer, 141.
76. Court of Probate of the District of Hartford, Connecticut, "Commissioner's Report on Horace Wells Estate," submitted and accepted by the Court, December 21, 1850.
77. Hartford city directory, 1848.
78. Hartford city directories, 1848–1875.
79. *Hartford Courant,* September 12, 1876.
80. Information on these individuals is derived from the Hartford city directories of the period 1838–1851.
81. Hartford city directory, 1848. Information on Samuel Cooley is based on research completed by Judith Ellen Johnson, Librarian and Genealogist at the Connecticut Historical Society Library. Her work indicates that Samuel Cooley, born in 1821, was a clerk in Hartford's largest drug store at the time he volunteered to try the laughing gas on December 10, 1844. He claimed both to have assisted in the discovery of anesthesia and to have conferred with Horace Wells with respect to the two of them going into partnership and manufacturing it. After trying his hand at daguerreotypy in 1848, he had a succession

of jobs: clerk, druggist, railroad station master, U.S. mail route agent and railroad conductor before returing to daguerreotypy and photography. He is listed in Hartford city directories with the above occupational descriptions. He then reappears in the directories through 1870 with the description "state arsenal armorer" station master, painter, reporter and chemist through 1898–99, with only his sister Mary A. Cooley appearing thereafter. In 1855, Cooley held the rank of Colonel, First Regiment, First Brigade of the Connecticut Militia, for which reason he was sometimes referred to as "Col. Cooley." Cooley died May 15, 1900, and is buried in the Old North Cemetary, Hartford.

82. Hartford city directories, 1851–1875; Siemiatoski, *The Ancestors and Descendents of Chief Justice Oliver Ellsworth*. Elizabeth Wales Wells continued to live at 117 Main Street until about 1851 or 1852; she then boarded at 26 Pearl Street from 1853 until 1855; she lived at 76 Trumbull Street from 1856 until 1861; at 24 Temple Street from 1861 until 1873; and at 17 Spring Street from 1874 until her death in 1889.

83. Pinckney Webster Ellsworth, "The Life of Horace Wells, M.D.," in Truman Smith, *An Inquiry of the Origin of Modern Anaesthesia* (Hartford, Brown and Gross, 1867),

84. Archer, 174–175.

85. Kenneth R. Andrews, *Nook Farm: Mark Twain's Hartford Circle* (Cambridge, Harvard University Press, 1950), 3–4.

86. Frederick Edwin Church to Charles Dudley Warner, April 8, 1872.

87. Archer, 200.

88. Archer, 174–175.

89. Ibid., 178–179. The tablet itself is pictured on p. 179.

90. Center Church, Hartford. "Records;" the memorial window to Wells and his wife is pictured on p. 186 of Archer's "Life and Letters of Horace Wells."

91. The two maps of Hartford, one of the city, and one focused on Main Street and its shops, were based on a map in *Gardner's Hartford City Directory for 1838*, frontispiece. The locations of buildings are approximate and derived from *Gardner's Directory*, as well as directories for 1840 and 1842. Also consulted was a 1850 map of Hartford, published by Mason & , which is in the collection of the Connecticut Historical Society Library.

5

"I Sleep To Awaken:"
An Appreciation Of
Elizabeth Wales Wells

Richard J. Wolfe

A considerable amount of information has been put on the record concerning the life and achievements of Horace Wells, but little has been written about his wife Elizabeth. A loving and affectionate wife and mother, Elizabeth has remained in the background of a landscape that has been illuminated mainly by the brillance of the man whose bride she became at age twenty and widow at age thirty. Nonetheless, having played an important role in nearly a third of Horace's life, she is deserving of closer notice.

Thanks to the efforts of W. Harry Archer in locating and preserving Wells family correspondence, and the controversy which arose over the claims for the discovery of anesthesia and the campaign that was waged on her husband's behalf, there is actually more information available on Elizabeth than would appear at first glance, although it lies scattered about that landscape. We will now assemble the bits and pieces of information on Elizabeth that are recorded in

Archer's "Life and Letters of Horace Wells," in the literature of the so-called "ether controversy," and in other sources. Their bringing-together will reveal a fine, intelligent woman who possessed a charming personality and an inner strength which enabled her to weather the circumstances of her husband's tragic death and continue the fight for recognition of his claim. The evidence will also show that Horace chose wisely when selecting Elizabeth to be his wife.

We learn from genealogical, family and burial records that Elizabeth was born at Hartford on April 8, 1818, the seventh of nine children of Nathaniel Wales and Sally Hender, and their only daughter. According to Russell D. Ramette, the family genealogist,[1] the Wales family originated in Yorkshire, England; it transferred to America in the person of Nathaniel Wales (1582–1661), a weaver, who emigrated with his family in 1635 on the ship *James* and settled initially at Dorchester, Massachusetts, and later at Boston. He and his wife Susanna had three sons, the last one, Nathaniel (1623–1662), born in England before the family's emigration, being the originator of the line whence Elizabeth sprang. His son, also called Nathaniel (1650–1718), formed the third generation; Nathaniel's son Joseph (1697–1767), the fourth; and Lemuel (1742–1786), the twelfth of fourteen children of Joseph and Hannah Allen Wales, made up the fifth generation of the Wales family in America. Their first child, Nathaniel, who began the sixth generation, was Elizabeth's father.

Nathaniel Wales was born probably at Randolph, Massachusetts, on August 8, 1776, and he died at Hartford on March 25, 1835, at age fifty-nine. His branch of the Wales family had farmed at Braintree and Randolph for several generations. According to Ramette, Nathaniel left home at an early age, having been denied his desire to study for the ministry, and wandered down to Connecticut, where he engaged in boot and shoe manufacturing for his livlihood. In 1805, he married Sally Hender at East Windsor. Sally, whose parents were raised at Windsor and Middletown, had been born in East Windsor on July 26, 1779; and she died at Hartford on January 5, 1825, at age forty-six, when Elizabeth was seven years old. There is an unexplainable discrepancy between the actual date of her death and the date "December 27, 1821," which appears on her headstone in Old North Cemetery in Hartford, where she and Nathaniel are buried.[2] However, the Wales family Bible,[3] Ramette's genealogy, and other sources clearly establish her birth and death dates. On January 3, 1827, Nathaniel married Betsy Hosmer (1789–1874), who assumedly raised Elizabeth and the other Wales siblings to adulthood.

Among the few letters of Elizabeth that have survived is a curious one concerning her family's genealogy. Included in the Wells family papers which Dr. Archer collected and partially published in his documentary biography of Horace Wells is an undated letter Elizabeth wrote about 1873, when she was approximately fifty-five years old. Archer did not print or otherwise refer to it; at its top is penned in an unidentified hand, "written about 1873." Addressed from Hartford to "Dear J.," probably to her younger brother Joseph, it is signed "E. Wells."[4] (Joseph is the only one of Elizabeth's brothers who figures directly in Horace Wells's story; he was born the eighth child of Nathaniel and Sally on November 20, 1820, and he died at East Orange, New Jersey, on March 25, 1893.)[5]

Elizabeth reported that she had just had a talk with Tom (undoubtedly her brother Thomas, the oldest child in the Wales family, who had been born in 1808), and that Henry (probably Tom's son, and her nephew), while visiting the Windham post office, had encountered an elderly gentleman who identified himself as a relative and then asked what place Henry came from. When Henry answered "East Hartford," the old man told him that his grandfather's name was Nathaniel Wales and that he could tell Henry the names of his whole family. "So he did," Elizabeth wrote, "even to one daughter who married Dr. H. Wells."

Elizabeth reported in her letter that the old man then proceeded to tell Henry that the Wales family came from two brothers, Nathaniel and William, who came over from Scotland and settled in old Windsor. He said that there were several great grandfathers by the name of Nathaniel Wales whose graves are there, including a large family monument to one Nath. Wales with the many offices he held and his high standing in olden times. One of the family went to Massachusetts, the old man informed Henry, and he told him about that branch of the family also. Elizabeth related that Tom later visited the monument and learned about the other members of the family, including inlaws named "Lugden," who told him that the family never had any people of bad character in it. "I am not surprised at this family history," Elizabeth continued, "as I always knew that our father was altho not one of the rich ones of this world, was a man of fine mind and our ancestry the best of the land in olden times."

The detailed and documented record in Ramette's genealogy of the Wales family clearly shows the old man was confusing Henry's line with another of the family in America. This other line descended from the weaver Nathaniel Wale's son Timothy (born 1616; died 1690, probably at Milton, Massachusetts), whose son Nathaniel (born about 1661; died 1744) moved to Windham about 1716, where he attained wealth and rank. It was his monument that the old gentleman was referring to, and it was his descendants who populated the graveyard which Tom visited.

We knew nothing about Elizabeth's upbringing and schooling; however, her well-written letters are indicative of a good education for her times, probably at the available free or common school. The next time we encounter Elizabeth, she is a twenty-year-old maiden who had caught the eye of Horace Wells. The ancestors of Horace were among the earliest settlers of Windsor, Connecticut. His grandparents were Captain Hezekiah Wells and Sarah Trumbull. His father married Miss Betsy Heath of Warehouse Point, Connecticut, and they afterwards moved up the Connecticut River to Hartford, Windsor County, Vermont, where Horace was born. Therefore, it was not completely coincidental that, after studying dentistry in Boston for two years, Horace elected to establish his practice in Hartford, Connecticut, in 1836, where his activity, intelligence, inventiveness and mechanical skills soon placed him at the head of his profession.[6] His enounter with Elizabeth, Sarah Gordon has informed us, came about at the Center Church in Hartford, which Elizabeth joined about 1834 and which Horace became a member of two years later (see page 187). On March 5, 1838, he mailed the following letter to her:

Hartford, March 5th

Miss Wales:

It is with no little diffidence that I take my pen in hand to address you at this time, and to ask one or two questions for which I may be charged with presumption; the purpose, however, has not been formed without due consideration. We are comparatively strangers, and for that reason I at first resolved in this communication to ask you only one, viz. Would it be in accordance with your wishes to become more familiarly acquainted with me? Here I intended to sign my name, but there are reasons which have induced me to ask one more question and abide the consequences.

Whatever the answer may be, you must excuse me for being so explicit.

Are there circumstances which preclude the possibility of this proposed acquaintance ever resulting in a more intimate connexion than that of brother and sister in Christ? Now, Elizabeth, you doubtless understand the import of this, and I shall expect a candid answer.

If I have been premature in the last query, it remains for you to forgive.

Truly yours,
H. Wells

N.B. It would be well to add the word Dentist, with the super scription of your letter as there is another of my name.[7]

Elizabeth did not waste any time replying to Horace's frank inquiry, for she answered him on the very next day:

Hartford, March 6th

Dr. Wells,
    Sir,
        with no small surprise I received your communication of the 5th and felt it to be my duty to confide in my Aunt who has ever manifested the highest interest in my welfare. She wishes me to act agreeable to my judgment as her only wish is for my happiness, with the hope that the intercourse may be commenced and continued in such a manner that should it hereafter terminate it may still exist as brother & sister in Christ without injured feelings to either.

I am therefore prepared to say in answer to your first question it being direct that to cultivate a farther acquaintance with you would be agreeable to my wishes, if the confession is too full pardon it. If I comprehend your second question it is one which involves our temporal happiness. You will not expect me to say much upon that subject at this time. I will only add that had I seen any insurmountable obstacle to the second I should not have been so explicit in answering the first.

Yours
E. Wales[8]

That the relationship began and blossomed is proved by another letter in the correspondence which Archer collected and published. This was sent by Horace's sister Mary to their mother, who was now Mrs. Abiather Shaw, Jr., living in Westmoreland, New Hampshire. Written at Hartford on July 9, 1838, about four months after the initial exchange of correspondence between Horace and Elizabeth, Mary's letter reported the events of her brother's wedding. Mary opened her letter by asking her mother,

Can you imagine what has been the business of the day with us here? Yes, I feel as if you had thought much of us, for I take it for granted that you know this is Horace's wedding day—but perhaps you are surprised to find you daughter is here, but 'tis even so; you may be surprised to know that I could leave my school; but I found I could on so important an occasion as this—funny was it not that brother should strike up such a sudden match? However, I believe it is a very good one. I have become acquainted with this new sister and like her very much; she is not handsome, but good looking and a very pleasant lady, and withal I believe she is a Christian. To such a one was our Horace united in holy matrimony this morning at seven o'clock, and should I tell the bride's maid, it was a near relative of yours, [i.e. Mary] and the groom's man was H Humphrey; the time passed off pleasantly among the circle of friends about thirty in number, till about eight, when the carriage stopped at the door and in stepped the bride and the bridegroom, with *attendants* of two. Stoped at Weathersfield and took some refreshments, then Horace and lady took their carriage which had previously sent down, and we turned ourselves back toward Hartford . . . They have gone to Guilford to spend about a week on the seashore.[9]

On September 21, a little more than ten weeks later, Horace wrote to his parents, Betsy and Abiather Shaw, affirming his choice of a wife:

I have been married 11 or 12 weeks and with this short experience in the marriage state I can truly say that I have bettered my condition. It was next to a miracle that I chanced to find a friend so well suited in every respect to be my partner for   life—I am now enjoying myself right well, making money fast enough, and good friends to spend my leisure time with, week before last, I made $100. clear of all expenses—last week I went to New York with my wife to attend a wedding party for her brother we have just got back, and feel rather worse for the wear, going down we were caught in a gale which took off both smoke pipes of the boat, and detained us for one day to repair at New Haven. Coming up as luck would have it the boat ran aground and detained us another day.

After inquiring about his brother Charles, Horace asked his parents:

> Have you collected more money for me? If so you may put it into the savings bank at Keene untill [sic] I send for it—next Spring I some think of building in the vicinity of Hartford and have my horse to ride in every morning which will give me more exercise which I find to be necessary.
>
> I cannot write more until I hear from you. Wife sends much love and wishes to see you very much— by the way I think you would be much pleased with her, come and see.[10]

Archer has reproduced on page 157 of his "Life and Letters of Horace Wells" miniature oil portraits on ivory of Horace and Elizabeth which were painted by an unknown artist probably in 1839. These miniatures, now in the Smithsonian Institution, are reproduced elsewhere in this compilation (Illustration 30). They show the twenty- four or twenty-five year old Horace in something of a Napoleonic pose, while Elizabeth, younger but more serious, points to the paper on the desk at the foot of her picture. Horace appears handsome and proud, and perhaps carefree. Elizabeth seems a bit gawky, showing a long nose and a rather awkward neck, with her hair combed straight back in the manner she wore it throughout her life. While not handsome, as Mary commented, she nonetheless displays a solidarity and straightforwardness which permeates her letters. On August 26, 1839, a little over a year after their marriage, a son was born to the couple, the only child they would have. They named him Charles, after Horace's brother who as then studying at the Jefferson Medical College in Philadelphia, from which he would graduate the following year; his middle name, Thomas, may have been chosen to honor Elizabeth's oldest brother, twelve years her senior, who passed his life at East Hartford, where he died in 1878. For the next six years or so, Elizabeth seems to have lived the life of contented housewife and mother, her day-to-day existence being probably little different from other married women of that day, centered around home and husband and family relationships, her happiness and equanimity marred only by occasional family illnesses or squabbles or Horace's absence from home on business. Some of her and the Wells's doings are recorded in the few family letters that remain from that period. For example, on June 26, 1842, in a letter he sent to his mother, Horace reported that

> My house is almost done, we think of moving in about 10 days. We think it is the most convenient house in all creation beside it being the prettiest, and odd as all out doors. The cost of the whole including land fences and all will be but $4000. I shall not be able to pay for the whole as the expense for house keeping articles I find will cost me almost enough to build a small house therefore I wish you would make some special effort to assist me, if you cannot do it now please send it as soon as you can. You have no idea how pleasant it is, at the house the prospect is so fine, I have planted a great number of trees and all of them doing well. I wish you and Mary would come down and see us.[11]

Horace was referring to the house he was building on Lord's Hill, out of the center of Hartford, and the evidence indicates that he was now asking his mother for a loan, which was made and later repaid in part from his estate. It is likely a guess that a silhouette which Wells cut, showing himself on a porch in a rural setting (Illustration 26) was made about this time, and depicts him standing proudly on the porch of his new home viewing the rustic scene around him. After discussing family matters, he added, as a proud father would, a paragraph about his now three-year-old son:

> Our Charley talks and is more interesting than ever. I will give you an example of his intellectual powers—the other day when it was raining he saw a bird on the tree he says "Mother poor bird gets cold and cough." We asked him the other day if he was a little boy. He says "No!" "Young man"—

Horace concluded his letter with the comment that "we are gogging along after the same old sort."

In 1843, the partnership which Horace had set up with W. T. G. Morton in Boston for the manufacture of dental plates incorporating his newly invented method of soldering with gold necessitated his absence from home. Writing to Elizabeth from Boston on October 28, he apologized for having rushed off without saying good-bye to her and Charley. "I expected as a matter of course I should have time to come down to 'Aunt Bays' to bid you and all others good bye, but the time was past before I was aware of it." After relating the details of setting up the business, Horace concluded:

> I shall probably remain here about 2 weeks longer and I wish you to write to me as soon as you receive this and inform me of your health and how Charley comes on and all others. Write often say every other day. You don't know how much I prize letters when I am absent from home.[12]

"Aunt Bay" or "Baa" or "Ba," as she is alternatively referred to in family letters, appears to have been the name the Wales children gave to their new mother, Betsy Hosmer, following their father's remarriage in 1827. It would seem that Elizabeth and Charley were visiting with her during Horace's absence.

On July 6, 1844, five months and a few days before he made his momentous discovery, Horace wrote to his mother and sisters (Mary and his step-sisters) telling them about his and Elizabeth's health, but devoting the greater part of his letter to the break-up of his partnership with Morton that is referred to more fully in the account of his "Day Book A." As to the former, he related that

> In the first place I am in the enjoyment of good health, animal magnetism to the contrary. Notwithstanding—yesterday a magnetised lady examined my system and pronounced my lungs alightly affected I think it must be *very slightly* indeed—however, she placed her finger upon my side and said that I had at times a slight pain which was really true, however, her verdict does not alarm me in the least. She's examined Elizabeth also and pronounced her liver a little affected and what was remarkable she described every painful feeling to which she is subject, and pointed out the locality correctly—her statement in regard to Elizabeth agrees perfectly with the Dr's opinion—not Dr. Saltmash—but Dr. Dodge. The lady's name is Mrs. Powers, who is undoubtedly the best magnetic subject in the United States. No one would think her asleep to hear her converse when under the magnetic influence; yesterday, when in this state she gave us a lecture on Light.
>
> I believe it would be impossible for any clergyman in this city, to

discourse on that subject as she did, using the most elegant language I ever heard. She dwelt on the analagy [sic] of the natural and spiritual light.[13]

Horace's mention of Mrs. Powers suggests interesting possibilities. Could he have visited her for purposes other than seeking reassurance about his and Elizabeth's health—an interest in investigating the possiblity of using mesmerism and hypnotism for diminishing pain during dental operations, for instance? Two English physicians, John Elliotson and James Braid, were investigating this very possibility in the early 1840s with regard to surgery,[14] and the later testimony of Elizabeth, which we shall review shortly, indicates that Horace was doing so as well. Also, the above letter and another one which Horace's mother wrote to his sister Mary about eleven months later, on June 17, 1845, to be specific, leads to the conclusion that Horace may have suffered from an underlying health problem which affected his lungs. Betsy Shaw then told Mary Wells that

> Dr. Taft says there is nothing to hinder H. doing well if he will take medicine & attend to him self. He has examined his lungs & says they are not diseased but weak. but they do not tell whether he has a cough or not or pain in the side. If H. goes to the sea shores I think it will terminate soon whether his lungs are affected or not.[15]

The events of December 10 and 11, 1844 were to have an unforeseen and dramatic effect on Elizabeth's life; they would result in unhappiness and tragedy as they unfolded in the next three years and to lonliness for the remainder of her life. A great deal has been written about the episode that took place on December 10 when she and Horace attended Gardner Colton's nitrous oxide demonstration, but no attention seems to have been paid to Elizabeth's account of that evening or its aftermath. Yet, her remembrance was published in 1853 when Truman Smith gathered together statements of Wells's friends and associates and other documentary evidence in support of the claim he entered in Congress on behalf of her son Charles for recognition of his father's discovery and renumeration for it; and it reappeared in reissues of the 1853 Memorial of Charles T. Wells which Smith published in various altered forms under his own name in 1858, 1859 and 1867.

After identifying herself and recounting the events of her marriage,

Elizabeth declared, when speaking of her husband and his dental practice, that

> He had a large, extensive and lucrative practice, which he pursued for several years, until he was obliged to abandon it on account of ill health. He possessed an inquiring mind, and was of the habit of making experiments, particularly on subjects that had a bearing on his profession. For some months previous to the delivery of a course of chemical lectures by Mr. G. Q. Colton, in the city of Hartford, December, 1844, Dr. Wells had turned his attention to the discovery of some means of rendering the human system insensible to pain under dental and surgical operations, and made several experiments in mesmerism with reference to that object.[16]

Elizabeth's reference to Horace's interest in mesmerism brings to mind his visit to Mrs. Powers only five months previously. As for the events of December 10, 1844, Elizabeth continued:

> Towards the close of Mr. Colton's course of lectures, I went with my husband to witness an exhibition of the effects of inhaling nitrous oxyd, or laughing gas. It was in the evening, at Union Hall, in this city. My husband and several others took the gas in my presence, the effect of which on the parties occasioned much amusement to those present. When we came out of the lecture to return home, I reproached my husband for taking the gas and making himself rediculous before a public assembly. He replied to me that he thought it might be used in extracting teeth, and in surgical operations, so as to prevent pain; and he said he meant to try the experiment on himself the next day. And accordingly, he took the gas and had his tooth extracted the next day, and declared that he did not experience any pain. It was a wisdom tooth, and had troubled him a considerable length of time.

Elizabeth related in this deposition that Horace began to use gas in extracting teeth and continued to do so from time to time down to the day of his death. He seemed to take a profound interest in this subject, she related, and was incessantly engaged in extracting teeth with this agency, and in trying experiments on himself and others for many months after his discovery. "He would lie awake nights, and often abruptly leave his meals to hasten to his office. At length excitement and other causes in this connection undermined his health, and he was obliged to give over his profession for a time." She told that in the winter of 1844–1845, and repeatedly thereafter, she had made bags of India rubber cloth for her husband to use in administering nitrous oxide and often observed him employing them in his profession.[17]

In the aftermath of his unsuccessful trail with nitrous oxide in Boston in late January of 1845, Horace became sick and depressed and, as Elizabeth expressed it, "gave over his profession" for the next seven months. There can be no doubt that this experience had a traumatizing effect on the otherwise ebullient and confident dentist. He was not the same self-assured person after that event that he had been before. His depression or whatever indisposition he suffered from may perhaps be ascribed to the fact that this was the first time that the usually successful and inventive dentist had met defeat, and he did not know how to cope with it, turning away from dentistry and its constant reminder of defeat; indeed, he seems to have developed an aversion to dentistry, and attempted to support himself by other pursuits instead: first, his panorama of nature, then his shower bath, and finally his speculation in the sale of French paintings, practicing only a little dentistry inbetween. When looking at the matter in greater detail, one can detect signs of fear of defeat in Horace's initial letter to Elizabeth, which was almost a preproposal of marriage; he seems to have needed to be assured of success before commencing the relationship.

Wells's volatility and proneness to flit from one interest to another have been commented on by a number of people, but such actions mainly followed rather than preceeded the events of January 1845. In spite of the fact that, as an inventive and creative person, he always had a number of irons in the fire that required his attention or presence elsewhere from time to time, his actions before 1845 were relatively stable, as his day book and other evidence show (interruptions caused by health problems excepted), when compared with those that followed the Boston trial. Thereafter, as I have noted before and emphasize now, he appears to have wanted to avoid dentistry, and he never really got back to it again in a permanent and enduring way. There is also the possibility—indeed, liklihood—that his incapacitation was exacerbated by his continued self-experimentation with chemical agents such as nitrous oxide, ether, and later, chloroform.

Nonetheless, there were some happy moments during this trying time. In a letter written to her daughter Mary on May 30, 1846, Horace's mother described one of them, which occurred during a visit she made to Horace and Elizabeth in Hartford. Following her arrival, she related, "Horace got a carriage and took Elizabeth Charley & myself & we all went out to West Hartford to make a call on Uncle and had a very pleasant call."[18] On September 20, after Horace had resumed his dental practice, Elizabeth wrote a short letter to her brother Joseph in which she discussed family friends and local doings. The second half of Elizabeth's letter contained a note from Horace about his resumption of practice: "I have taken my old office for the practice of Dentistry again, how long I shall continue at it is very uncertain." He also talked about joining the "Odd Fellows," adding that "this extra touch of oddity will do me no harm," and finally referring to the shower bath he had invented.[19]

And on November 9 following, Elizabeth reported, when writing to Horace's mother, that

> Horace has turned dentist and it seems like old times to have him home again. His health is good and he boasts that he weighs more than he ever did We had a very pleasant visit from Charles. I introduced him to several young ladies, but they did not suit him. The one I wished him to see lives in Bridgeport. I know he could not resist her.
>
> My Charley is getting to be a great boy. He attends school and learns quite fast.

She concluded by referring to trouble she was having with her eyes, saying, "I have suffered considerably the last week and have done little but knit. They trouble me as they did six years since." Once more Horace added a note. This related that his $10,000 speculation with the shower bath had not turned out well. He had made only half that sum back, had not been granted his patent, and was getting ready to start for New York and Boston to close up his business in those cities.[20]

On December 24, we now know, Horace sailed for Europe—by his own account, "just for a little recreation," although Elizabeth would state in a deposition collected and printed by Truman Smith in 1853 that "one object of his visit was to publish his discovery."[21] Elizabeth must have sent numerous letters to Horace during his two month absence from home, but only one has survived. Writing on December 27, 1846, a week after his departure, she informed Horace that she had received his two letters and recounted all of the events that had transpired since he left Hartford, devoting much of her communication to their son Charles. Continuing her letter on the following day, she began:

> How do you do this evening! I wish you would answer me, I imagine I could hear you . . . Do you know it is just one week since you left us, Charley cannot realize you being away so far . . . Now Horace I wish you would be punctual and write as often as possible. Don't think me foolish. Your letters will do me more good than you are aware. Even writing this has done me much good.

Archer, in publishing this letter,[22] commented that Elizabeth added on the back page, which was folded and sealed underneath, thus forming the envelope, the note, "I wish I could get inside and come to you, don't you?"

There exists no information on Elizabeth's reaction to her husband's tragic death, which occurred on January 23, 1848, about ten months after his return from Europe. These months must have proved a trying time for her, despite the euphoria which followed his safe return, for Horace was absent from home much of the time and had begun to behave strangly under the influence of nitrous oxide, ether and especially chloroform, which he began experimenting with soon after the annoucement of the discoverry of its anesthetizing powers by James Young Simpson in November of 1847. In the long suicide note he wrote to the New York *Journal of Commerce,* in which he explained the events leading up to his final act, and his reasons for it and his remorse, he addressed only a few lines to Elizabeth:

> To My Dear Wife
> I feel that I am fast becoming a deranged man, or I would desist from this act. I can not live and keep my reason, and on this account God will forgive the deed. I can say no more.
> Farewell. H.[23]

He did, however, express regrets about what his action would do to her:

> Oh! my dear wife and child, whom I leave destitute of the means of support—I would still live and work for you, but I cannot—for were I to live on, I would become a maniac. I feel that I am but little better

than one already. The instrument of my destruction was obtained when the officer who had me in charge kindly permitted me to go to my room yesterday.

And, addressing a note to Mr. Dwyer of the Weston Hotel, he requested that "I wish he would take my watch and present it to my dear wife . . . I wish you and Mr. Barber [also of the Weston Hotel] would go immediately to Hartford, and reveal this misfortune to my wife in the most . . . unobjectionable manner possible."

It is impossible to know whether Wells was referring to the pen-knife and razor or the empty vial labelled "Chloroform" that was found beside his body when he referred to the instrument of his destruction that the unwitting jailer permitted him to conceal and remove from his room. That his experimentation with chloroform was leading him down a disastrous path is affirmed by the evidence. I have already mentioned in another article here (see page 48) that some of his friends supposed that he was somewhat deranged when he left Hartford, and that his mind had been greatly excited for some time previously. Further evidence of his perturbed state of mind is afforded by a little noticed editorial concerning his suicide that appeared in the *New York Dental Recorder* on February 1, 1848, nine days after his death. This reported the details of his death, pointing out that "the full effects of chloroform when taken in an over-dose, are not yet well understood." When recounting the details of Wells's arrest, the editorial reported that

> The statement of the lady with whom he was boarding on Chambers street, shows that his whole system must have been thoroughly saturated with chloroform, for she asserts that on entering the room where he was distilling it, the atmosphere was so completely impregnated with it, that she could not remain. She also states that there was something strange in the appearance and conversation of Mr. Wells for several days previously.

The editorial ended by pointing out that when used properly, chloroform was capable of preventing and alleviating an immense amount of pain and human suffering; but if the depraved desires and appetites for excitement and exhiliration shall cause it to take the place of alcohol or opium as a habitual stimulant, it will prove a curse to the human race. "Mr. Wells admits that for several days he frequently inhaled it for its pleasurable exhiliration," and the editor admonished others to take warning of the effects it had produced on him and avoid taking it except in cases of absolute necessity. That Wells had become addicted to chloroform cannot, I believe, be doubted; and the import of this article, and other evidence, raises the possibility that he may have been poisoned by it.[24]

Despite Horace's wish that he be buried in a pauper's grave in New York, his body was returned to Hartford where, on January 27, at half past two o'clock, it was interred in the Old North Burying Ground. Shortly before burial, as is described in greater detail elsewhere (pages 262–263), Elizabeth gave John Riggs permission to make an impression of her husband's face in death. As Archer points out, in the legal proceedings which followed, Horace's estate was declared insolvent, and his office furniture, dental tools, and even household furniture were sold at auction to satisfy the demands of creditors, leaving Elizabeth dependent for her and Charles's livlihood on her own meager resources and initiative (doing handwork, such as sewing) and upon the good will of family and friends.[25]

Archer reprints a partial inventory of Wells's estate—listing only his office furniture and dental tools—from the records of the Probate Court and says nothing about the other details of administrating and closing out the estate. However, a little more information on this matter was provided in an article published by Ralph W. Edwards, Assistant Professor of Oral Surgery at the University of Kansas Medical Center, in 1951. Edward's article is mainly concerned with reporting the gift to the Medical Center's History of Medicine Library of a promissory note signed by Wells, which had emanated from his son Charles, and four letters from Charles himself.[26] However, he also printed the inventory and account of Wells's estate in full, and, in discussing the details of the promissory note, touched on a number of puzzling questions concerning Wells's financial embarassment at the time of his death. Edwards notes that the effects listed on the inventory, with a total appraised value of $270.77, were disposed of at public auction and the proceeds assigned to the administrator, E. W. Parsons; furthermore, that it took a long time for the estate to be settled and the Commissioner's Report of it to be finally accepted by the Court of Probate on December 21, 1850, nearly three years after Wells's death.

Among the claims against the estate were four promissory notes which Wells executed to his mother between May 8, 1841 and May 1, 1842, the note that Edwards was writing about being one of them. Representing money borrowed from the mother to construct Wells's house or cottage on Lord's Hill, these constituted by far the largest claim against the estate, for only on the first of these had Wells made any repayment. (Nowhere in the record of Wells's estate is the Lord's Hill property mentioned; one can only conclude that it was disposed of prior to his death.) From the information provided in the Commissioner's Report, it appears that Wells's liabilities amounted to nearly twice the total of his assets. As a result, the court allowed payment of claims at only fifty-five percent of full value and granted Elizabeth almost nothing—less than $10!

While Wells's office records and other evidence (including Elizabeth's own testimony) indicate that Wells had been a successful practitioner and had had an excellent income, the changes in his life brought about by his discovery of anesthesia and especially by the disappointment of his unsuccessful trial in Boston resulted in a reversal of his good fortune. His health having suffered as a result of the Boston debacle, his life literally fell apart and he was unable or was unwilling to practice dentistry thereafter and was without the significant income which his practice had provided. Furthermore, in attempts to obtain income in other ways, he dissipated most of his savings in a number of ventures which did not prove successful: his "panorama of nature," the shower bath, and the picture speculation, which involved the expense of a two-month European trip; and, with his involvement in the controversy with his former student and partner Morton over the discovery of anesthesia, and his self-experimentation with anesthetic agents, he neglected his personal affairs.

The first part of Elizabeth's life was over at age thirty, and she would now commence the second part, a span of forty-one years, as a widow. A large part of her existence would now be devoted—for the next twenty five years or more—to promoting her husband's claim to priority in the discovery of anesthesia. It is well known that Morton, after revealing that the disguised preparation he had been using in the trials at the Massachusetts General Hospital in Boston in October 1846 was in reality sulfuric ether, pinned his hopes on receiving financial remuneration for the introduction of anesthesia on a cash award of $100,000 from Congress. There was a precedent for such an expectation. Edward Jenner had, in 1806, been awarded the sum of £20,000—the equivalent of $10,000 in American dollars—by the House of Commons for his discovery that vaccination with cowpox matter established immunity against smallpox, probably the most dreaded infection ever unleashed upon mankind. (Recent research has established, however, that this award may have come about, in part at least, due to Jenner's connection with many powerful figures at the royal court.)[27] Morton's petition to Congress in the first months of 1849 immediately embroiled him in a bitter controversy with the Boston physician and chemist Charles T. Jackson, who also claimed priority in the discovery.

It was in the background of these events, and probably as a reaction to them, that in 1850 Isaac Toucey, then a member of the Connecticut state senate, published a small pamphlet entitled *Discovery by the Late Dr. Horace Wells, of the Applicability of Nitrous Oxyd Gas, Sulphuric Ether and Other Vapors, in Surgical Operations, Nearly Two Years Before the Patented Discovery of Drs. Charles T. Jackson and W. T. G. Morton.* This attempted to prove that Wells was the discoverer, and not Morton or Jackson. Toucey was undoubtedly enlisted to come to Horace's defense by Elizabeth, who had little means to pursue such a course of action on her own. While this pamphlet was published anonymously, we are told in another article here (page 315) how Dr. Archer came across its manuscript in the Connecticut Historical Society and, through handwriting analysis, proved Toucey to be its author. Previously, its authorship had been attributed to Elizabeth's brother Joseph Wales who, upon publication of a second edition in 1852, wrote a brief introductory note for it.[28]

Truman Smith, in the introduction to the 1858 edition of his *An Examination of the Question of Anesthesia*, relates how, while sitting in Congress as a senator from Connecticut, he watched the events of the Morton-Jackson dispute unfold.[29] Morton's petition, praying for remuneration as the discoverer of "Etherization," had been referred to a committee in the House of Representatives, while a petition by Dr. Jackson, setting forth his claim, had also been referred to the same committee. Smith tells that he took no interest in the inquiry, which was mainly concerned with the controversy between Morton and Jackson; his aim was to push Wells's claim on behalf of the widow and young son, who were in destitute circumstances with no resources to assert the claim on their own or to repudiate the claims of the others. Smith felt assured that, should the claim of either Morton or Jackson be recognized by the House committee and sanctioned by the House, he could, by a statement of the case of Wells, defeat the measure in the Senate.

Contrary to his expectation, however, and much to his surprise, the House committee made no report. Instead of bringing a bill before the House, those on the committee who were friendly to Morton tacked Morton's claim onto a general appropriation bill towards the end of the 1852 session, attempting to push it through unnoticed in that way. However, the ruse was discovered and, due to Smith's efforts, and with the help of Toucey and others, the proposed amendment was defeated. This extinguished Morton's hopes for the time being. But fearing that further efforts might be made on Morton's behalf in the following session of Congress, Smith and the friends of Elizabeth introduced into Congress a petition on behalf of her son, Charles, asking for a gratuity in consideration of the discovery by his father of the employment of anesthetic agents in surgical operations. The petition was put together by Smith and his staff. In order to document Horace's claim, Smith and Mrs. Wells's friends collected the necessary testimony and evidence requisite to proving their case. Numerous despositions were taken, including those of Elizabeth referred to before, and, as was described previously, the complete statement, entitled *An Examination of the Question of Anaesthesia,* was presented to Congress in early 1853 and referred to a select committee of the Senate, of which Isaac P. Walker was chairman.

That committee soon arrived at the conclusion that the question of priority would only be settled in a satisfactory manner by referring it to the judicial tribunals of the country. However, the amendment to refer the matter to the Circuit Court of the Northern District of New York, which passed the Senate, was rejected when the bill was sent to the House for concurrence, and the bill finally lost. As a result, the controversy over the discovery of anesthesia bogged down for a number of years into a series of petty intrigues and squabbles between Morton and Jackson.

In 1856, ten years after the surgical trials with ether at the Massachusetts General Hospital and the success and acclaim he had derived from them, Morton now found himself beset with legal and pecuniary difficulties, being besieged, as the late Henry Viets put it,[30] on all sides by duns, writs and constables. He had ruined his health and his occupation and had dissapated his fortune in an attempt to justify his position as the major claimant in what has since become familiarly known as the "ether controversy." Some of his Boston friends, who were soon supported by the medical professions of New York and Philadelphia, now began to plan a "national testimonial" on Morton's behalf. The 1849 petition to Congress was gotten out, meetings were held at various points, and new appeals to the public were issued. Finally, work was commenced on a comprehensive account of the background of the ether discovery from Morton's point of view, which Nathan P. Rice, M.D., a twenty-nine year old New York practitioner, was chosen to write. The result of Rice's efforts, carried on in close collaboration with Morton at a very fast pace, was a book issued in early 1859 under the title *Trials of a Public Benefactor*.[31]

It was probably as a reaction to these events that Truman Smith in 1858 dusted off the memorial he had presented to Congress in 1853 on Charles's behalf and, with some reorganizing, rewriting and the addition of new material, issued it in book form, and under his own name, but with the same title, *An Examination of the Question of Anaesthesia*.[32] And in the following year, he reissued this work with an appendix containing material which had to do with more recent events growing out of Morton's "national testimonial."[33] This new material included, for example, recent statements of Valentine Mott and Willard Parker, New York surgeons who earlier had made depositions favoring Wells's priority, but lately had been persuaded to come over to Morton's side. Some copies contained a tipped-in endorsement by Elizabeth's brother Joseph, who listed his address at 170 William Street in New York City and described himself as a near relative and representative of the late Horace Wells. And, in direct response to the Morton testimonial, Smith on December 22, 1858, penned a long pro-Wells article which was published in the New York *Journal of Commerce* under the title "Anaesthesia! The Greatest Discovery of the Age! Who Is Entitled to the Credit of It?", to which he appended the subtitle, "Let Those Read Who Desire to Know the Truth."[34]

In 1860, there appeared yet another pamphlet championing Horace Wells as the discoverer of anesthesia. Published anonymously under the title *Dr. Wells, the Discoverer of Anesthesia,* it contained two frontispieces: the first was a portrait of Horace, the first to be published, the other being a two-page lithographic copy of a letter Elizabeth had written to an unidentified correspondent, which is quoted in full below. The composition and publication of this work may have been timed to coincide with the meeting of the American Medical Association in New Haven on June 5–7 of that year. There is reason to believe that Truman Smith was the author of this polemic as well, for it is written in his style, and it issued from the press of the same person who had printed both the 1858 and 1859 editions of Smith's *An Examination of the Question of Anaesthesia,* J. A. Gray of New York City, where Smith maintained a legal office; furthermore, the portrait of Wells in this work would be reemployed by Smith when reissuing his *An Examination of the Question of Anaesthesia* for the last time in 1867, although in retouched form. If Smith did compose it, we can only speculate that he may have thought it counterproductive to issue still another pro-Wells statement under his name and thus chose to remain anonymous.

That Elizabeth was actively engaged in promoting her husband's cause, and was soliciting the help of others in her effort, is affirmed by her frontispiece letter, which reads:

Hartford April 1860

Sir,

As the widow of Dr. Horace Wells I beg leave to address you. The discovery which my husband made and which has so largely benefitted mankind has been to his family only a source of bitter misfortune. The experiments which he constantly made upon himself terminated fatally and he died in fear and dispair that the fame due him would not be accorded after his death.

The only inheritance which Horace Wells has left is the reputation he has earned as a benefactor of mankind and my highest ambition is to leave this unquestioned before the world.

Although it may now be too late to do anything but justice to my husband's memory I pray that at least this should be accomplished.

To this end let me beg you to give some attention to the evidence which will be forwarded to you. It has been prepared by the friends of a helpless woman whose duty it is to redeem the memory of a good man and rescue the credit of his discovery from the grasp of men who presuming upon his sensitive nature and afterwards upon my helpless widowhood have laid claim to a discovery which I know belongs to my husband alone.

Yours respectfully
Elizabeth Wells

At the time Elizabeth penned this letter, tense events were taking place which would explode into open rebellion and calls to arms a year later. When war did break out in April of 1861, following the siege of Fort Sumpter, legislators would turn their attention away from anesthesia to more current and pressing matters. Nonetheless, the battle over who had discovered anesthesia continued to rage, although at a slower and more subdued pace. In 1861, Charles T. Jackson issued his only large publication dealing with anesthesia, a book of 134 pages bearing the title *A Manual of Etherization.* [35] Jackson was correct when he modestly stated that his work was not meant to compete with more extended and elaborate treatises on this subject by others, for it offered no new information, but was intended mainly as a means of keeping his claim alive during the national emergency.

And in this troubled time Morton made another attempt to gain compensation for the introduction of anesthesia into general surgical practice, basing his argument now on its current value in military surgery. In early 1863, he petitioned Congress once more for compensation, and since his claim now had reference to military matters, his petition was referred to the Senate's Committee on Military Affairs and the Militia.[36] But once more Jackson jumped in to oppose him; and, despite the fact that in the following year the Morton Testimonial Association made another appeal to Congress on Morton's behalf, issuing a sixty-seven page pamphlet containing many testimonials of military surgeons,[37] the Civil War ended with no decision made on this matter. This would be the last appeal that Morton would make to the federal government for compensation, although he would continue to wage his battle for recognition whenever and as best he could.

In 1867, Truman Smith issued still another edition of his *Examination of the Question of Anaesthesia,* the last that would appear.[38] Rewritten in more descriptive and more organized and enlarged form, and retitled, it contained as a frontispiece the same portrait of Wells that appeared in the 1860 *Dr. Wells, the Discoverer of Anaesthesia* pamphlet, although the portrait now appeared in more finished form, and it included a brief biography of Wells by his friend and former associate Pinckney W. Ellsworth. There exists in the Connecticut Historical Society in Hartford a file of twelve letters of Smith's dealing with the publication of this last edition. They were written by Smith from his office in New York to Brown and Gross in Hartford, who published the book; and they show that the work was put together and printed in the space of a few months, for the letters date between January 4 and March 12, 1867. In his letter of January 8, Smith related, when sending off his manuscript, that "The plate containing the likeness of Dr. Wells will be forwarded at the same time." The letters also contain the information that Gardner Colton had arranged for pay for 500 copies and wanted them delivered by March 10, for he intended to soon sail for Europe to attend the general exhibition in Paris and presumably would distribute them there. The last significant piece of information in this correspondence is Smith's mention that he had "seen Mr. Joseph Wales a brother of Mrs. Horace Wells and we had a consultation on the subject of obtaining a circulation of 'Modern Anaesthesia' in this city."

Truman Smith provided constant support to Elizabeth and Charles for nearly two decades following Horace's death. Charles, when reminiscing about his father during the memorial services held at Philadelphia in 1894 to mark the semicentennial of Wells's discovery,[39] would not fail to acknowledge his assistance. "I wish at this time," he said,

> to pay a grateful tribute to the Hon. Truman Smith, United States Senator from Connecticut, to whom we owe much. Other claims coming before Congress, upon investigation, he became convinced of the justice of that of Horace Wells, became his defender and champion, ever after giving his time and pen freely to his cause and defeating attempts by others for recognition and appropriation of money.

On July 16, 1868, William Thomas Green Morton died in New York City, after having collapsed from heat stroke while riding through Central Park with his wife on the previous day.[40] And five years later, in 1873, his rival litigant in the ether controversy, Charles T. Jackson, suffered an acute maniacal attack when he stumbled upon Morton's tomb and epitaph in Mount Auburn Cemetary in Cambridge, Massachusetts: "W. T. G. Morton, Inventor and Revealer of Anesthetic Inhalation." His eccentric personality long tortured by frustrations arising out of the controversy, Jackson finally lost his reason and passed his last years at the McLean Asylum in nearby Charlestown, where he died in 1880. Thus, as beneficial as the introduction of painless surgery has proved to be to mankind, it was equally tragic for the principal characters who participated in the event. Nonetheless, with the passing of Morton the controversy over the identity of the discoverer of anesthesia did not entirely abate, nor did Elizabeth's interest in gaining recognition for her husband lessen.

When publishing, in 1941, an article entitled "Historical Notes on Horace Wells,"[41] Max E. Soifer (who identified himself as Librarian of the Hartford Dental Society) pointed out another gesture Elizabeth made on Horace's behalf. The incident that precipitated it was a speech made during ceremonies held at Edinburgh in October 1869 honoring Sir James Young Simpson, who in the fall of 1847 had introduced chloroform as an anesthetic. When awarding Simpson the honor of the freedom of the city, the Lord Provost in his speech referred to Simpson's discovery of this use of chloroform as "the greatest of all discoveries in modern times."

When a copy of the *Edinburgh Daily Review* containing an account of these ceremonies reached Jacob Bigelow in Boston, he sat down and wrote Simpson a strong rebuttal. Bigelow, who had participated with his son in the events of October and November 1846 leading up to the public proving of ether as a viable anesthetic, was plainly irritatd by the Lord Provost's remarks; he felt that Simpson had taken too much credit for himself and had failed to credit Boston as the place where the final step in introducing anesthesia into surgery had taken place. Bigelow published his letter to Simpson in the November 25, 1869 issue of *The Boston Medical and Surgical Journal*, which provoked Simpson to publish a reply in the London

Medical Times and Gazette on January 22 of the following year,[42] and he then sent a copy of that issue to Bigelow. In his reply to Bigelow, Simpson pointed out that although Bigelow implied that Morton was the "first man" of "sufficient courage" to breathe vapor in order to produce a state of anesthesia, in 1844, two years before Morton had made his ultimate experiment in 1846, Dr. Marcy of Hartford had excised a tumor from the arm of a man who had been rendered insensible by the vapor of sulfuric ether and, by that same early date Horace Wells had extracted teeth from a dozen or more patients rendered insensible by inhaling nitrous oxide gas, according to Humphry Davy's earlier suggestion.

As Dr. Soifer points out in his "Historical Notes on Horace Wells," when Elizabeth saw Simpson's account, she felt compelled to write on March 3, 1870, the following letter to him, thanking Simpson for his recognition of her husband's contribution to medical science:

> I have had the pleasure of receiving a copy of your historical letter on the introduction of Anesthetics in Dentistry and Surgery in America, from the Medical Times and Gazette, January 22nd, 1870, addressed by mail to the Editor of the chief newspaper in this city, and handed by him to me.
>
> It is needless to say that I am greatly grateful that from so distinguished an authority, the honor of this great discovery is unhesitatingly accorded to my late husband, Dr. Wells. Personally intelligent of the facts of this discovery, I have never lost faith in the belief that despite misrepresentation, the final opinion, both at home and abroad, would reach a unanimous decision in favor of Dr. Wells. It was all he sought and after twenty-six years of waiting, I begin to believe that the desired conclusions are at hand.
>
> Will you please accept a small volume giving some intelligence upon the matter of possible importance to you, which I addressed to you by mail.
>
> Thanking you for your considerable kindness, I remain,
>
> > Yours respectfully,
> > Elizabeth Wells.[43]

Although Dr. Soifer did not cite the location of Elizabeth's letter, he did reproduce it in facsimile, together with a contemporary photograph of her (Illustration 16), the fourth image of Elizabeth which

Illustration 16. Photograph of Elizabeth Wales Wells in mid-life. Reproduced from Max E. Soifer's "Historical Notes on Horace Wells" where it was noted that the original was in 1941 in the possession of Mrs. A. W. Cole, the widow of the son of Horace Wells's sister, Mary Wells Cole. The original is at present unlocated. Courtesy of the *Bulletin of the History of Medicine*, Baltimore.

we know about at this time. Soifer located the original picture in the possession of Mrs. A. W. Cole, the widow of the son of Horace's sister Mary, but its present location is unknown. It shows Elizabeth at about age fifty, posed in profile beside a chair. It seems a certainty that the volume Elizabeth talked about sending to Simpson was a copy of Truman Smith's 1858 *An Examination of the Question of Anaesthesia*. Included in the Horace Wells's collection of books emanating from his and the family's library (discussed in my "brief for Horace Wells," note 62) is a copy of this work inscribed by Smith to Simpson on March 10, 1870, "at the request of the widow of Horace Wells, Discoverer of Anaesthesia." Either the volume was never sent, or it was returned following Simpson's death, which occurred about two months later.

The dispute between Bigelow and Simpson did not end with the publication of Simpson's January 22 article. Bigelow sent his rebuttal, and additional replies and rebuttals followed. The Bigelow-Simpson controversy has been the subject of a recent study by Walter J. Friedlander,[44] and it need not concern us greatly here. However, Dr. Friedlander did not locate or cite all of the correspondence that appeared in print, of which one letter is of particular importance and requires further consideration. The piece of correspondence which Dr. Friedlander apparently did not find—at least, he did not discuss or otherwise refer to it—was published in *The Journal of the Gynaecological Society of Boston in 1870.*[45]

Simpson was friendly with Horatio R. Storer, one of the *Journal's* editors and a leading Boston gynecologist. Indeed, after graduating from medical school in 1853, Storer had spent two years abroad, during one of which he was assistant in private practice to Simpson in Edinburgh. It may have been this association which made Storer displeasing to the Bigelows, who blocked his entrance into several Boston medical societies, for about 1853 Simpson had written an article on "Anaesthesia" for the *Encyclopaedia Britannica* in which he had been far from liberal in his allusions to Morton and Boston and had written almost entirely about his own discovery.[46] As the episode unfolded, Simpson sent his views on Bigelow's letters to Storer, who, being unfriendly to Bigelow and feeling that Bigelow had been ill-advised in allowing his initial letter to be printed and thus bring this unpleasant affair into the open, published Simpson's letters in the Society's *Journal*. The letter—Simpson's final word on the subject—which was most important in expressing Simpson's views on Horace Wells was received too late to be included in the May 1870 number of the *Journal*, having arrived after that issue had gone to press; but it was immediately published as a supplement to that issue, as its prefatory note explained, "in accordance with Prof. Simpson's desire that it should appear in this country before its publication in Europe, and through the medium of the Gynaecological Society."

In writing this last communication to Bigelow—he died prior to or at about the time it came into print, having dictated it on his final sickbed—Simpson summed up the whole matter in great detail. In fact, his published letter extended to nineteen closely printed pages, in which he took off the proverbial "gloves" and went at Bigelow with bare fists. In the second part of his letter Simpson discussed the "Earliest Anaesthetic Operations in America, and Their Connection with Hartford and Boston," berating Bigelow for insinuating that the medical world should be content with using only sulfuric ether, and it alone. He pointed out that the Boston obstetrician Walter Channing had reported that Bigelow himself had used chloroform in midwifery, and that Bigelow's son had used nitrous oxide when performing a mastectomy and that nitrous oxide was then being employed successfully in Paris, London and elsewhere in tooth extraction.

Simpson argued that nearly two years before Morton drew a tooth from the head of Eben Frost in September 1846, that same operation had been successfully performed at Hartford on December 11, 1844, "the anaesthetic inhaled not being sulphuric ether, but nitrous oxide gas, and the patient being Dr. Wells himself, to whose mind the idea had suggested itself previously." Next, Simpson recounted the early history of nitrous oxide anesthesia, as reported by Wells, Riggs and others, and then alluded to the mistrial of the gas at the exhibition by Wells in Boston the following January. Simpson then referred to a statement Bigelow had made in one of his letters to him, namely, that Humphry Davy must be exonerated from all practical knowledge of anesthetic inhalation, otherwise, in Bigelow's words, "he is chargeable with all the tortures of amputation and lithotomy which have taken place since he made the discovery and concealed it."

After pointing out that Bigelow had used the same wild and irrelevant argument against Dr. Jackson, forgetting that Jackson's and Davy's profession was that of chemist and not surgeon, Simpson observed:

But now mark what subsequently occurs. An American dentist works out to its practical results the suggestion published in England half a century before by Sir Humphrey [sic] Davy, and which you seem to wish to efface from anaesthetic records; and he travels a long distance to place an important result before the Medical School at Boston, and some surgeons at the Massachusetts General Hospital. There is a slip in the single experiment allowed him. He is spurned and hooted away. In doing this the Medical School of Boston thus delays the whole subject of artificial surgical anaesthesia for a couple of years. Was not the Medical School of Boston then, in your violent language, "charge-able with the continuance of operative tortures," for that period, much more than Sir Humphrey Davy? Did not your school stamp out—and thus prevent for two years—the "most beneficent discovery," to use your own grandiloquent words, "which has blessed humanity since the primeval days of paradise"? I am using here not my language and logic, but yours.

Simpson related that there was sufficient evidence that Dr. Wells and Marcy debated the question whether sulfuric ether would not be an agent preferable to nitrous oxide, but that Marcy thought nitrous oxide safer and the pleasanter of the two, and also more easy to inhale. "I found that no busy obstetric practitioner," Simpson declared, "could extensively employ sulphuric ether without inevi-tably carrying about with him, and upon his clothes, an odor so disagreeable to many patients and other houses, as to make his presence there aught but desirable." He also pointed out that Bigelow's son, when first reporting the inhalation of sulfuric ether in surgery, remarked on its similarity to nitrous oxide. "But," Simpson then observed,

the step from *using* nitrous oxide to using sulphuric ether was great and momentous in its results. Dr. Morton, who, as his friend and old partner, assisted at Dr. Wells' experiment at Boston, no doubt knew all the results obtained at Hartford, where he twice visited Wells after 1844; and he evidently, betimes, got the speculation into his mind that sulphuric ether might prove successful. From a different line of observation, Professor Charles Jackson was led to the entertainment of the same *speculation*. Assisted, apparently, by one of two hints from Dr. Jackson regarding the pure quality of the ether, or, possibly, its easiest mode of exhibition, Dr. Morton *verified* the speculation on the 30th September, 1846, by operating on Eben Frost, and fixed that date as an era of science.

We have no idea whether or not Elizabeth read these last words of Simpson's; but if she did, probably the only word sufficient to express her happiness in the fullfillment of her goal would be "extatic."

As Max Soifer has pointed out, in the five year period that followed Elizabeth was privileged to observe other successes. In 1871, the medical and dental professions of England commenced a "Horace Wells Testimonial Fund" to raise money for the benefit of his widow and son, and in 1873 made a joint resolution crediting her husband with not only the introduction of nitrous oxide anesthesia but for giving impetus to the study of anesthesia which led to the introduction of ether, chloroform and other agents for accomplishing this objective; and, in 1875, the citizens of Hartford and Connecticut and the dentists of the United States erected a statue of Wells on the east side of Bushnell Park in downtown Hartford, which stands today as the city's proudest moment in medicine.

Probably in connection with raising money for this monument, a public program was held at Steinway Hall in New York on May 21, 1873, at which a number of distinquished speakers discussed the subject of anesthesia, focusing on Horace Wells's discovery of it, and the whole proceedings were the subject of a lengthy report in the *New York Times* on the following day.[47] The first speaker was the distinguished gynecological surgeon J. Marion Sims, who discussed the history of anesthesia in general but devoted most of his talk to Wells's initial experiment leading to his discovery. He was followed by Professor Robert O. Doremus, the toxicologist and inventor, who reviewed the chemisty of nitrous oxide. Then the leading New York surgeon Frank H. Hamilton discussed the importance of anesthesia to surgery and also credited Wells with its discovery. The evening concluded after the Rev. Henry Ward Beecher pronounced a benediction. While the *Times* said nothing about Elizabeth's presence at these proceedings, a subsequent report in the *British Journal of*

Illustration 17. Charles Thomas Wells in later life, reproduced from W. Harry Archer's "Life and Letters of Horace Wells."

Dental Science, when reprinting a large part of the discussion of the evening, related that she was present and also reported that the intention of the program was to start a fund for her benefit.[48]

Elizabeth spent her last years in a period of calm and content, her quest for recognition of her husband as the discoverer of anesthesia having, in her mind, been successfully concluded. We know of only one other letter of hers which has survived from these years, in addition to the genealogical one referred to earlier. Also undated, it was written perhaps at about the time of the other, or possibly a bit later. Addressed to her niece May, it talks of family, of her visit to friends or relatives in the Hudson River valley, and of her caring for her plants and home.[49] Elizabeth died at her home at 17 Spring Street in Hartford on Monday, July 17, 1889, at age seventy-one. Three days later, her body was interred alongside that of her husband is in the Old North Burying Ground. She was, like Horace, a deeply spiritual person, finding consolation and hope in her religion. During the services conducted at her funeral, the Rev. Walker of the Center Church, which she had attended for more than thirty-five years, eulogized her as "a gentle, humble-hearted, Christian woman."[50]

Charles Thomas Wells, the only child of Elizabeth and Horace, early assumed the chair of head of the household at 17 Spring Street, where he lived with his mother. As W. Harry Archer has related,[51] Charles never married. He worked as a clerk for the Aetna Life Insurance Company for many years, helping to keep up the home and providing some of the comforts Elizabeth enjoyed in later life. But, as a later article he informs us (see page 309), at about age thirty-four his health broke down and his eyesight had deteriorated from overwork. He was said to have been a kindly man of sterling principles, yet modest and shunning publicity. About five feet six inches tall but well set up, he walked with a military bearing which earned him the respectful title of "Major," an effect that was heightened by his moustache, long side whiskers, and serious mien (Illustration 17). He was interested in collecting rare books, china and antiques, which were sold at auction following his death on June 8, 1909, this occurring in his seventy-first year of life and twenty years after that of his mother. With his death, the line begun by Horace and Elizabeth quickly came to an end.

One of Charles's last accomplishments was to arrange for the final interment of his parents, as well as his own. On May 18, 1908, their bodies were disinterred from Old North and reburied in Cedar Hill Cemetary, a more spacious and pleasanter garden-type of cemetary opened in 1859, where he would be buried alongside them a year later. Charles also had a large granite monument erected on the plot, along with appropriate grave markers. On the face of the monument, he had affixed a bronze tablet showing an angel administering anesthesia, and below it was engraved the words "There Shall Be No Pain." And, at either end of the monument he had affixed a three-dimensional figure of a woman, presumably representing an angel. On its right side, was engraved the phrase "I Sleep to Awaken," and on the left, the words "I Awaken to Glory."[52]

NOTES

1. Russell Donald Ramette, *The Wales Family of Dorchester, Massachusetts.* ([West Hartford, Conn.] 1979). This compilation was produced through typescript and xerography.
2. Leonard F. Menczer, "Wells' Death and Hartford Burial Sites," *Connecticut State Dental Association Journal* 66, no. 2 (Fall 1990): 20–22.
3. Nathaniel and Sally Wales acquird a copy of *The New Testament of Our Lord and Saviour Jesus Christ* that had been published at Walpole, New Hampshire, by Anson Whipple in 1815 and into its front endpapers entered the names and birth dates of all of their children. It was subsequently owned by Elizabeth Wales Wells and her son Charles T. Wells, who apparently made death and other entries from time to time. Following Charles's death in 1909, it was sold at public auction along with other of his effects, and its present whereabouts are unknown. The title-page and preliminary leaves containing the family genealogy are, however, preserved in copies in the Connecticut State Library in Hartford.
4. Elizabeth Wales Wells to "Dear J." (probably Joseph Wales), undated, but described by an unknown hand as "written about 1873." W. Harry Archer collection of Wells Family correspondence.
5. Joseph Wales, about seventeen months Elizabeth's junior, seems to have been the member of the family to whom she was most closely allied. He spent his earlier years at Hartford, where he was in the

employ of the old firm of R. B. & W. A. Ward, and was afterwards in the flour and grain trade under the name of French and Wales. In 1850, he moved to New York. He left a family of four children.

6. These few facts about Horace Wells's ancestry are taken from Charles J. Wells, "Horace Wells", *Current Researches in Anesthesia & Analgesia* 14, no 4 (July-August 1935): 176–189; no. 5 (September-October 1935): 216–224.

7. Horace Wells's surviving daybook, discussed by Dr. Menczer elsewhere in this compilation, shows that on July 27, 1841, he billed one Horace Wells of Weathersfield for various dental services noted there.

8. Both Horace's letter to Elizabeth, and her reply, were published by W. Harry Archer, "Life and Letters of Horace Wells, Discoverer of Anesthesia, Chronologically Arranged with an Appendix," *Journal of the American College of Dentistry* 11, no. 2 (June 1944): 83–210. These letters appear on pp. 93–94.

9. W. Harry Archer, "Life and Letters of Horace Wells," 96–97.

10. Ibid., 97–98.

11. Ibid., 99–100.

12. Ibid., 101–102.

13. Ibid., 105–106.

14. These and other early experiments with mesmerism and hypnotism for producing anesthesia are discussed in John F. Fulton and Madeline E. Stanton, *The Centennial of Surgical Anesthesia; an Annotated Catalogue of Books and Pamphlets Bearing on the Early History of Surgical Anesthesia, Exhibited at the Yale Medical Library October 1946* (New York, Henry Schuman, 1946), 15–20.

15. W. Harry Archer, "Life and Letters of Horace Wells," 111–112.

16. United States Senate, *An Examination of the Question of Anaesthesia, on the Memorial of Charles Thomas Wells, Referred to a Select Committee of the Senate of the United States, of Which Hon. Isaac P. Walker Is Chairman* ([Washington 1853]), 14.

17. Ibid., 19–20.

18. W. Harry Archer, "Life and Letters of Horace Wells," 115.

19. Ibid., 115–116.

20. Ibid., 118–119.

21. United States Senate, *An Examination of the Question of Anaesthesia, on the Memorial of Charles T. Wells,* 20.

22. W. Harry Archer, "Life and Letters of Horace Wells," 123–125.

23. Ibid., 137–139.

24. "Suicide," *New York Dental Recorder* 2, no. 5 (February 1, 1848): 99–100. In view of the above reference to Wells's continual inhalation

of chloroform, the question arises whether he may not have suffered from acute chloroform poisoning in his final days, a condition which only became apparent to physicians about fifty years after his death. One has only to read in his suicide letter the long account he made of the events leading up to his imprisonment and suicide to find justification in this possibility. For example, Wells related, when recounting what influenced him to commit the act which led to his arrest, that he had been in the constant practice of inhaling chloroform during the previous week for the exhilarating effect it produced; and, three days before his death, had lost all consciousness before removing the inhalor from his mouth, not being cognizant of how long it remained there and coming out of the stupor in an exhilarated state exceeding anything he had ever experienced before. His euphoria led him to commit the act resulting in his imprisonment, an act he had morally condemmed a day or so earlier when less influenced by chloroform. Chloroform is now recognized as one of the most potent liver poisons known. Chloroform poisoning, and the resultant pathology, is discussed and documented in S. S. Lichtman's *Diseases of the Liver, Gallbladder and Bile Ducts* (Philadelphia, Lea & Febiger, 1942), 111–112, 391–393. According to Lichtman, the toxic effect of chloroform on the liver began to be recognized in the 1890's, and in 1911 the Dutch neurologist Louis J. J. Muskens was able to show in animals under chloroform narcosis that one third died in the next twenty-four to one hundred and twenty hours with liver degeneration. It became recognized that the inhalation of chloroform produces necrosis of the the hepatic cells in the center of each lobule of the liver, with fatty degeneration resulting and death in extreme cases or under constant use. George Hoyt Whipple, who won the Nobel Prize in medicine in 1934 for his studies of the effect of diet on anemia, conducted many experiments and published a number of papers on the pernicious effect of chloroform on the liver, and he frequently demonstrated this reaction to his students in pathology at the University of Rochester, where he also served as Dean of the School of Medicine and Dentistry from 1921. I wish to thank Dr. Erling Johansen, currently Dean of Tufts University's School of Dental Medicine, for pointing out to me the pernicious effect of chloroform on the liver. Dr. Johansen trained at the University of Rochester in the late 1940s, and, while earning a Ph.D. degree in pathology, in addition to his dental degree, studied with Dr. Whipple, who demonstrated to his students the deleterious effect of chloroform on the liver.

25. W. Harry Archer, "Life and Letters of Horace Wells," 142–143.

26. Ralph W. Edwards, "Horace Wells, Dentist; a Further Contribution to His Life," *Journal, American College of Dentists* 18 (1950–1951): 91–103.

27. See Paul Saunders, *Edward Jenner, the Cheltenham Years,. Being a Chronicle of the Vaccination Campaign* (Hanover, New Hampshire, University Press of New England, 1982).

28. [Isaac Toucey], *Discovery by the Late Dr. Horace Wells, of the Applicability of Nitrous Oxyd Gas, Sulphuric Ether and Other Vapours, in Surgical Operations, Nearly Two Years. Before the Patented Discovery of Drs. Charles T. Jackson and W. T. G. Morton* (Hartford, Case, Tiffany & Co., 1850). A second edition would issue from the press of Elihu Geer, stationer and steam printer of Hartford, in 1852, to which Joseph Wales contributed a prefatory statement, for which reason he was for some time thought to be its author. Born in 1796, Toucey died at Hartford in 1869. He served as representative from Connecticut in Congress; as that state's attorney general; in 1848 and 1849 as Attorney General of the United States (also acting for part of this time as Secretary of State); and U.S. Senator from Connecticut from 1852 to 1857. During Buchanan's presidency, Toucey held the post of Secretary of the Navy, afterwards returning to the practice of law in Hartford.

29. Truman Smith, *An Examination of the Question of Anaesthesia, Arising on the Memorial of Charles T. Wells, Presented to the United States Senate, Second Session, Thirty-second Congress, and Referred to a Select Committee, of Which the Hon. Isaac P. Walker Is Chairman. Prepared for the Information of Said Committee. By the Hon. Truman Smith, U.S. Senator from Connecticut* (New York, John A. Gray, Printer, 1858). This matter is discussed on pages [iii]-viii.

30. Henry R. Viets, "Nathan P. Rice and His *Trials of a Public. Benefactor,* New York, 1859," *Bulletin of the History of Medicine* 22, no. 2 (July 1946): 232–243.

31. Nathan P. Rice, *Trials of a Public Benefactor, As Illustrated in the Discovery of Etherization* (New York, Pudney & Russell, 1859).

32. See Note 29.

33. Truman Smith, *An Examination of the Question of Anaesthesia, Arising on the Memorial of Charles Thomas Wells, Presented to the United States Senate, Second Session, Thirty-second Congress, and Referred to a Select Committee of Which the Hon. Isaac P. Walker is Chairman* (New York, John A. Gray, Printer, 1859).

34. Truman Smith, "Anaesthesia! The Greatest Discovery of the Age! Who

Is Entitled to the Credit of It? Let Those Read Who Desire. To Know the Truth," *Journal of Commerce*, N.Y., December 22, 1858. This was also issued as a separate pamphlet.

35. Charles T. Jackson, *A Manual of Etherization: Containing Directions for the Employment of Ether, Chloroform, and Other Anaesthetic Agents, by Inhalation, in Surgical Operations, Intended for Military and Naval Surgeons, and All Who May be Exposed to Surgical Operations; with Instructions for the Preparation of Ether and Chloroform, and for Testing Them for Impurities. Comprising, Also, a Brief History of the Discovery of Anaesthesia* (Boston, Published for the Author by J. B. Mansfield, 1861).

36. Two reports were ordered printed by the Senate's Committee on Military Affairs and the Militia on February 14, 1863 respecting Morton's petition for compensation. These are listed as Senate, 37th Congress, 3d Session, Rep. Com. No. 89.

37. *A Representation to Congress by the Morton Testimonial Association, Covering a Portion of the New and Recently Received Petitions, Memorials, Resolutions, & Letters from a Large Number of the American Medical Association, Scientific Societies, Professors and Surgeons of the Principal Colleges and Hospitals, Surgeons, Officers and Wounded Soldiers of the Federal Army and Navy. Submitted to the 38th Congress, and Printed for the Use of Its Members* (N.p., 1864).

38. Truman Smith, *An Inquiry into the Origin of Modern Anaesthesia*. (Hartford, Brown and Gross, 1867). Its pages [7]-13 contain a "Life of Horace Wells," by P. W. Ellsworth.

39. *Discovery of Anesthesia by Dr. Horace Wells. Memorial Services at the Fiftieth Anniversary* (Philadelphia, Patterson & White Company, 1900), 99. This celebration was organized and sponsored by the Odontological Society of Pennsylvania.

40. According to information solicited in 1967 from the Health Services Administration of the City of New York, the official cause of Morton's death was, according to the findings of the coroner's jury, "coup de soleil," or sunstroke. Since his death occurred on July 15, 1868, in midsummer, during a major heat wave attended by many deaths, such a finding would be an obvious conclusion for a jury to make. There is no record of an autopsy having been performed. This information on the cause of Morton's death is contained in a letter written by Carl L. Erhardt, Director, Health Intelligence Statistics, to Mr. Bruce H. Lamphrey, Committee on Research for the town of Charleton, Mas-

sachusetts, the place of Morton's birth, dated 5 January 1967, of which a copy is in the author's files, it having been given to him by Dr. Leroy D. Vandam of Boston. In the September-October 1957 issue of the journal *Anesthesiology*, volume 18, pp. 785–786, had appeared an editorial by Dr. Albert M. Bletcher of New York, entitled "A Ride Through Central Park," suggesting this possibility.

41. Max E. Soifer, "Historical Notes on Horace Wells," *Bulletin of the History of Medicine* 9, no. 1 (January 1941): 101–112.

42. Jacob Bigelow, "Anaesthetic Inhalation," *The Boston Medical and Surgical Journal* 80 (November 25, 1869): 295–296; Sir J. Y. Simpson, "Historical Letter on the Introduction of Anaesthetics in Dentistry and Surgery in America, and on Their First Employment in Midwifery in Great Britain," *The Medical Times and Gazette* 1870, v. 1, 90–91.

43. Elizabeth's letter is printed on pp. 103 and 106 of Dr. Soifer's article, cited above, and reproduced in facsimile on p. 105. While he was mute as to where he found it, we may presume that it was preserved among Simpson's papers, assumedly at the University of Edinburgh.

44. Walter J. Friedlander, "The Bigelow-Simpson Controversy: Still Another Early Argument over the Discovery of Anesthesia," *Anesthesia History Association Newsletter* 11, no. 4 (October 1993): 10–15.

45. James Y. Simpson, "A Reply to Dr. Jacob Biegelow's Second Letter," Supplement to the May number of the *Journal of the Gynaecological Society of Boston* 2 (May 1870): 1–19. Previous correspondence from Dr. Simpson on this matter had appeared in issues of the *Journal* from February into May of that year.

46. Simpson's article was written for the eighth edition of the *Encyclopaedia Britannica* edited by T. S. Trail and issued at Edinburgh by A. and C. Black in twenty-two volumes between 1853 and 1860, with an American edition appearing at Boston under the imprint of Little, Brown and Company at the same time.

47. "Anesthesia Its History, Chemistry, and Practice—Addresses. by Famous Medicists—Experiments by Professor Doremus," *The New York Times*, May 22, 1873, p. 8, columns 1–3.

48. "The Late Horace Wells," *British Journal of Dental Science* 16 (July 1873): 333–339.

49. Elizabeth Wales Wells to an unidentified correspondent addressed only as "May," probably a niece. This undated letter, written about 1873 or after, is preserved in photostat form in the W. Harry Archer collection of Wells Family correspondence.

50. The services were reported in the *Hartford Courant* the day after her

burial. Her obituary had appeared in the *Springfield Republican* on Tuesday, July 18, the day following her death.

51. W. Harry Archer, "Life and Letters of Horace Wells," 161.

52. As is noted elsewhere (page 395), the monument was vandalized in the 1979–1980 period and the two angels were stolen; in 1992, they were replaced with low-relief reproductions.

6

"Genius, The Result Of Original Mental Superiority:" John M. Riggs And Horace Wells

David A. Chernin

"He is gifted with genius who knoweth much by natural talent."
Ralph Waldo Emerson[1]

Prior to the eighteenth century, Robert Nisbet has recently pointed out,[2] the word "genius" meant mostly a special talent or skill. "But," he has observed, "that meaning has for two centuries been buried in large measure by another which the word then took on: a person of greatness who achieves solely through the 'genius' that is endowed in him by God or nature." Nisbet attributes two influences in bringing about the altered meaning of the word: the Philosophes in France and the Romantics in Germany.

> The former, in their running warfare with church, university, and other institutions of the old regime, saw themselves as minds of almost

unprecedented brilliance, capable of every achievement from running governments to writing encyclopedias. Moreover, in their judgment, history has essentially been made by "geniuses" such as themselves: those of the ancient world, the Renaissance . . . the Age of Science, and now in the Enlightenment.

At the time when Voltaire and the other philosophers were twisting the word, Nisbet continues,

> The Romantics in Germany seized upon it for special application to themselves and to others of Germanic descent. In the same way that the Romantics found a special genius in their racial ancestry, they found individuals in the past of towering intellect and spiritual being who had helped form and then express the Germanic soul or consciousness. These could be generals or poets, statesmen or painters, religious leaders or dramatists. Each was a "genius" because he had been formed of special clay and from this inner majesty issued forth the great works which characterized his life.

Such was the concept of genius into which John Riggs was born.

John Riggs, the fifth child of seven and the first of three sons of John and Mary (Beecher) Riggs, was born in Seymour, Connecticut, on October 25, 1811.[3] His parents, both born at Oxford, Connecticut, were well-to-do farmers of Revolutionary stock. Until the age of twenty-one, he spent his time on his father's farm in Derby, where he became skillful in designing and making tools needed to accomplish his duties. During this time, he developed a fascination with building stone walls, dams and irrigation systems. His early education was confined to attendance at the local district school.

At age twenty-one, his appreciation of farm work began to waver and he entered the blacksmith trade. However, a desire for "mental culture" enticed him to pursue a course of instruction and study at Washington (now Trinity) College in Hartford. In 1835, at the age of twenty-three, he entered as a sophomore with the intention of becoming an Episcopal clergyman. The expenses incurred for his college years were defrayed by his employment as a blacksmith and by teaching in local district schools. His education at Washington, the college's statement of its course of study and instruction tells us,[4] included, in addition to the usual classical subjects emphasized at that time (Horace, Cicero, Juvenal, and Tacitus), courses in mathematics, logic, mechanics, moral philosophy, theology, political economy and speaking and constitutional law, as well as lectures and demonstrations on optics, astronomy and chemistry in his senior year. John Riggs had been given no middle name at birth, but while in college he began to add "M" as his middle initial, and no one knew why. While he was home on a visit, his father said to him, "I see you write your name with an 'M': what does that stand for?" "Mankey," replied young Riggs, but he never explained why.[5]

Riggs was characterized by all who knew him as a man of marked individuality. He was described by one associate as an independent thinker who was fearless in expressing his views on all matters, and he always had views.[6] At his commencement exercises at Washington College on August 3, 1837, two events occurred which provide us with insights into the independent character and personality of John M. Riggs. First, he delivered an oration entitled "Genius, the Result of Original Mental Superiority." Unfortunately, the text of his oration has become lost or has not come to light. The second event at the commencement was his response to the Rev. Nathaniel S. Wheaton's baccalaureate sermon on "The Trinity." Upon the completion of the bishop's discourse, Riggs advanced and greeted him by saying, "I believe in one God, and one God only: I do not believe in three, and I'll be (damned) if I will preach it."[7] He switched to the Unitarian Church thereafter and attended it throughout his life.

Upon receiving the A.B. degree in 1837, Riggs, now twenty-six years old, began teaching school. He became the principal of the Brown School formerly known as the Stone School, and now the first district school of Hartford, continuing in this position for the next two school term years. According to one biographer, still desiring to better his condition, he took a partial course at the Jefferson Medical College in Philadelphia and then turned his attention to dentistry, which he studied with Horace Wells, beginning practice about 1840;[8] another source merely states that he commenced his studies in dental surgery soon after his graduation from Trinity;[9] while a third, James McManus, who entered dental practice in Hartford eight years after Wells's death and knew Riggs well, states that Riggs trained with Wells.[10] Other than the above statements, we have no direct evidence—from Riggs or Wells themselves—that John Riggs studied dentistry with Horace Wells.

Although such an idea is purely speculative, it is conceivable that Riggs could have noticed the advertisement which Wells ran in the *Connecticut Courant* on October 28, 1837, and on a weekly basis thereafter until 1840,

> H. Wells would inform his friends and the public generally that he has invented a set of instruments for filling teeth, which by their construction entirely supersede those in common use,

and, intrigued by and curious about such a claim, in light of his mechanical bent, went to see these newly constructed instruments; or, as we know from Wells's "Day Book A," he may have gone to Wells to obtain his professional services, as he did in 1841, and, during their association, Wells could have influenced him to pursue a career in dentistry. Wells could also have advised or made arrangements for Riggs to receive a basic medical education at Jefferson, where Wells's brother was attending lectures and from which Charles would graduate in 1840. Upon his return to Hartford, Riggs then presumably apprenticed in the office of Horace Wells. In 1843, Riggs established an office with Dr. C. Kirkland, and by 1844 had opened his own office across the hall from Wells.

The remaining four years of his relationship with Wells confirmed a conclusion that Riggs, the older of the two, had earlier reached, namely that Wells was a genius. Riggs greatly admired Wells and became his friend and confident. Sharing adjoining treatment rooms at 180 1/2 Main Street, the two men were often together to discuss cases and ideas. It was with Riggs that Wells stayed up late into the night of December 10, 1844 (Riggs would later state), discussing the possibility of preventing suffering during tooth extraction and surgery by means of the gas Wells had just experienced and the reactions of which he had just observed at the Colton Laughing Gas Frolics. It was Riggs upon whom Wells would depend to go forward with his newly formed idea that nitrous oxide presented a means to cause unconsciousness of pain during dental and surgical procedures. The success that was achieved on December 11 was repeated both by

Wells and Riggs on patients during the weeks that followed; they found the gas to be safe and reliable.

Riggs never wavered in his support of Wells and his admission that Wells was the discoverer of anesthesia, and he never claimed part of the honor for its discovery; his loyalty to Wells in the sad events that followed in the wake of the successful ether trials two years later was unswerving. His participation with Wells in that first experiment was scarcely less dangerous than the role assumed by Wells himself. While the former risked his life when attempting the unknown, Riggs risked the charge of being a party to Wells's death had it occurred.

Let us now review the accounts in Riggs's own words of the events that brought about the discovery of anesthesia. His depositions on the subject appeared in both the volume of evidence collected by Truman Smith and published by Congress in 1853, as well as in the several editions of it Smith reprinted independently afterwards, and in the appendix pertaining to Wells that concluded the volume of statements entered on Morton's behalf that was also printed by Congress that same year. Furthermore, Riggs gave additional testimony under oath and under court examination on this matter and a transcript of his testimony appears in the later volume also. Finally, we will read what Riggs wrote about this episode approximately twenty-seven and forty years afterwards. His descriptions of the events of December 10 and 11, 1844 are, next to those of Wells himself, the most direct accounts we have. Riggs stated, when making the deposition published by Smith in 1853, that

> I settled in Hartford as a surgeon-dentist in the fall of 1842, but I resided here for two years before that, engaged in teaching and studying dentistry . . . I was intimately acquainted with the late Dr. H. Wells, who occupied an office immediately adjoining my own, and I was in the habit of daily and familiar intercourse with him. We were particular friends.[11]

Riggs then recounted the events leading up to the discovery, telling about the lecture Colton delivered in Hartford in December of 1844, on which occasion he demonstrated the strange behavior brought about through the inhalation of nitrous oxide gas:

On the evening of the 10th of said December, Dr. Wells came into my office after Mr. Colton's lecture, and said that he and others had taken the above gas; and remarked that one of the persons had injured himself, and stated, after recovering from the effects of the gas, that he did not know at the time that he had suffered such injury. Dr. Wells then said: "He did not feel it; why cannot the gas be used in extracting teeth?"

Riggs went on to describe a long discussion that ensued between Wells and himself, the result of which was that Wells decided to try to have a bothersome tooth extracted while under the influence of the gas on the following day. "He would take the gas and have the tooth extracted, if I would perform the operation." Riggs agreed to do this on the following day, telling Wells that it would be fair to commence the experiment upon themselves.

Accordingly, the next morning Dr. Wells came with Mr. Colton and his bag of gas to his, Dr. Wells's office, and called me in. There were present, besides Dr. Wells and myself, Mr. Colton, Mr. Samuel A. Cooley and some others, whose names I cannot now recall. Dr. Wells, after seating himself in the operating-chair, took the bag and inhaled the gas, and after he had been brought sufficiently under its influence, he threw back his head, and I extracted the tooth.[12] It was a large molar tooth, in the upper jaw, such as is sometimes called a "wisdom tooth." It required great force to extract it. Dr. Wells did not manifest any sensibility to pain. He remained under the influence of the gas some time after, and immediately upon recovering from it, he swung his hands and exclaimed: *"A new era of tooth-pulling!"* He remarked he did not feel any pain from the operation.

Riggs repeated some of the above facts in other depositions which are printed in the volume of statements supporting Morton's claim that was published the same year, but for the most part his various depositions there are concerned with the use of the gas during extractions he performed in the weeks and months following the discovery.[13] In 1872, Riggs was asked by Drs. Hasbrouck and Howland of New York City to relate to them the facts of the discovery. In a long letter which he wrote in longhand on September 17, he repeated many of the facts we have just read, and there is no need to allude to them further here.[14] However, three paragraphs toward the end of Riggs's letter are particularly significant and worthy of mention, for they impart some of the original flavor of this momentous discovery. "Mr. Colton, Cooley and the two others stood by the open door, ready to run out if Wells jumped up from the chair and made any hostile demonstrations," Riggs related in the first of these paragraphs. "You may ask, 'why did he not get up?' Simply because he could not. Our agreement the night previous was to push the administration to a point hitherto unknown."

Riggs continued to tell Drs. Hasbrouck and Howland what he remembered about the events of that day:

> We knew not whether death or success confronted us. It was a *terra incognita* we were bound to explore—the result is known to the world. No one but Wells and myself *knew* to what point the inhalation was to be carried—the result was painfully problematical to us but the great law of Nature, hitherto unknown, was kind to us and a grand discovery was born into the world.

And in his third paragraph, he added, modestly,

> Now, Gentlemen, do not understand me as claiming *joint-discovery* with Dr. Wells. The great idea or inspiration was his—that we elaborated it together is honor enough for me.

Towards the end of his life, Riggs was persuaded to publish his remberance of the event yet one more time. In early 1885, B. H. Catching, Editor of the *Southern Dental Journal,* aware that Riggs, the most important living witness of the first administration of anesthesia, would soon pass away, wrote to Riggs and asked him to give him the facts of the discovery so that he could hand them down to posterity as indisputable evidence that to the dental profession belonged this great discovery. Riggs's response to Catching was published in the *Southern Dental Journal* in August 1885 under the title "The Discovery of Anaesthesea. As Told by the Only Living Witness, Dr. John M. Riggs, of Hartford, Connecticut."[15] For the last time perhaps, Riggs recalled the facts of that event:

> At the close of the exhibition (by Colton), Dr. Wells came to my office, and we there canvassed till near midnight the whole subject, as to its safety, and the degree of inhalation. As we had resolved to push the inhalation much farther than for a mere exhibition for fun, we naturally looked for a patient upon whom to make the trial, but the

chances of the death of said patient confronting us, Dr. Wells volunteered to be the patient, and to make the trial upon himself, charging me to stand by and care for him.

On the following morning, as per agreement, Riggs related, Wells came to his office and took a seat in his operating chair.

> I examined the tooth, and he took the bag in his own hands and inhaled the gas; as he lost control of the muscles of his arms, his elbows slipped off the arms of the chair, dragging the gastube from his mouth; his head dropped back on the head-rest, and I slipped the forceps on the tooth (a left superior molar) and extracted it.

No one administered the gas to Wells, Riggs stated; he assumed sole responsibility of the act. Several witnesses, he remembered, including G. Q. Colton, the maker of the gas, and Samuel Cooley, observed the events from positions near the door.

"We were so elated by the success of this experiment," Riggs had earlier deposed,[16] "that we immediately turned our attention to the extraction of teeth by means of this agent, and continued to devote ourselves to this subject for several weeks, almost exclusively." In his 1885 *Southern Dental Journal* statement, Riggs would recall that "From that time onward Dr. Wells and myself gave the gas and extracted teeth, as patients presented themselves. All would not take it; there was great fear that it would cause death." Riggs also noted that only two physicians of Hartford—young men—approved of the administration of the gas or took any interest in its discovery; these performed several painless operations under the influence of the gas, with Wells administering it himself. In the interval that followed the unsuccessful trial in Boston, however, Wells ceased practicing dentistry for a while and turned his attention to matters outside his profession, carrying on dentistry only sporadically afterwards.

When making some observations on Riggs's life in 1887, shortly after Riggs's death, George A. Mills, who had known Riggs since 1865, recounted an incident concerning Riggs that had been little known.[17] Several days after Wells's death, while his body was lying in a receiving tomb in Hartford's Old North Burying Ground awaiting burial, it occurred to Riggs that possibly the time would come when his discovery would be honored by the profession in some fitting memorial. He therefore requested permission of the widow to go to the tomb and make a mask mould of Wells's face. In the early

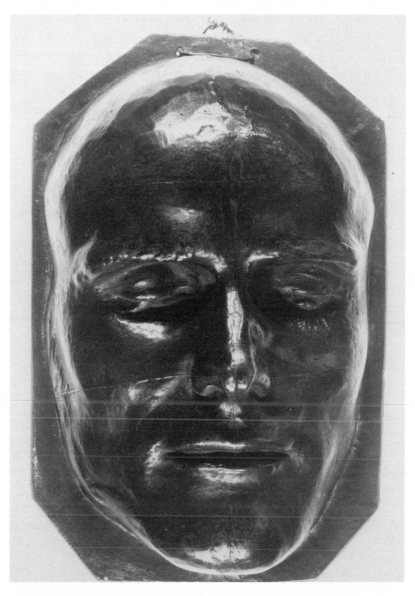

Illustration 18. Bronze casting of a plaster death mask of Horace Wells, made by John Riggs on January 27, 1848, the day of Wells's burial. The mask was employed by Truman Bartlett in authenticating Wells's face for his 1875 statue of Wells, at which time the bronze casting was probably made, and the casting was donated by Bartlett to the Boston Medical Library in 1887. Courtesy of the Boston Medical Library in The Francis A. Countway Library of Medicine.

hours of Wednesday, January 27, 1848, the day of Wells's burial, John Riggs made a mixture of stone and water and carefully prepared the face of Horace Wells for a plaster impression. "This he laid away as a hidden treasure," Mills reported, "to serve its purpose as the future might decide. Dr. Riggs had, even before his commencement of professional life, evinced no small degree of skill as a sculptor . . . and how this talent served him, the face now moulded in bronze will testify, as it was designed from the original cast" (Illustration 18). Mills was, of course, referring to the statue which Truman Bartlett created in 1873 and 1874 and which was erected in Hartford's Bushnell park in the following year, for which Riggs's death mask would be used to help authenticate Wells's facial appearance.

In the first half of the 1840s Riggs developed a surgical technique for treating a disease known to the dental profession today as Pyorrhoea Alveolaris, but which was usually referred to in Riggs's time as "scurvy of the gums." Up to the time of Riggs, Arthur Merritt has pointed out,[18] practically all treatment was of a palliative nature, mainly the application to the gums of a drug such as tincture of myrrh, or the use of astringent mouth washes. When the teeth became so loose as to be troublesome, they were extracted. What set Riggs apart from his contemporaries, Merritt points out, was his insistence that this disease could be cured and that its treatment was not therapeutic, but surgical, that is, it should be treated through the use of instruments. Riggs did not surgically remove the gum tissues or make use of modern operations employed in peridontia. His treatment consisted of subginival curettage, crude as compared with the same operation today, but the same in principal except that he emphasized curettement of the alveolar process. He performed this operation with six instruments of his own devising. Thus, Riggs is credited by Merritt with making the first important contribution to the foundation of modern periodontology.

As Koch relates,[19] Riggs's treatment eventually attracted such attention that his name was given to the disease, and it came to be called as it is today, "Riggs' disease." Rigg's opinion that the etiology of the disease, regarded at the time as a premature wasting of the alveolar edge, would prove to have a likeness to caries, was later confirmed. His treatment with small instruments required remarkable skill and deftness of touch, sometimes down to the extreme points of the roots of the teeth, removing the cause of the trouble. When the cause was removed, he allowed nature to do the rest. Regarding the delicate skill which the dentist was called upon to exercise, Riggs later would say, "At the present day, we need the nicest manipulation. The dentist . . . must have his eyesight at the ends of his fingers."[20]

Riggs waited for a full twenty years before, when, fortified by experience, he made known his methods and his success to the dental profession; nonetheless, many dentists were for a long time skeptical as to the correctness of his ideas. Riggs began exhibiting his method at clinics from the mid-1860s on, and, in 1875, following his election to the American Academy of Dental Surgery in New York City, read a paper embodying his views on the pathology and treatment of this disorder. This paper, published in the *Pennsylvania Journal of the Dental Sciences,*[21] is now regarded as a classic contribution to medicine. Aside from his few statements regarding the origin of anesthesia, it was the only article that Riggs ever published under his name.

The poor reception that Horace Wells received in Boston in 1845 and the deleterious effect that it had on Wells's mental and physical health was not lost on Riggs. Regarding his own original contribution to curing the second most common scourge affecting mankind's oral health, he would thus wait for more than two decades before making known his accurate findings and correct treatment modality.

A personal account of one of Riggs's patients undergoing treatment for "Riggs' disease" survives in the form of an unpublished manuscript by no less a personage than Mark Twain. Titled "Happy Memories of the Dental Chair," this account is preserved among the Mark Twain Papers in the Library of the University of California at Berkeley and was the subject of an article by Dr. Sheldon Baumrind in 1973.[22] Twain, who probably underwent treatment by Riggs in the 1870s, reported that Riggs's method was to dig up under the gums with his instruments and carve and scrape all the dead bone away, down to the living bone, so that the gums would return to their place, attach themselves to the living bone, and become healthy again.

Riggs offered his patient the option of chloroform analgesia, prompting Twain to remark:

The chloroform created a radical change; it made everything comfortable and pleasant. The pains were about as sharp as they had been before, but they seemed to be impersonal pains; pains that belonged to the community in general, including me but not me particularly, not me any more than the others. So, I did not care for them any longer; I do not care for a pain unless I can have it all to myself.

Twain's account provides an unusual and interesting description of a periodontal operation by a leading nineteenth century dentist. He reported the outcome of his treatment by Riggs as follows:

I was in the chair a good part of two days—nine hours the first day and five the next—and came out of it with my thirty-two teeth as polished and ship-shape and raw as if they had been taken out of their sockets and filed. It was a good job, and quickly and skillfully done; but if I opened my mouth and drew a cold breath it woke up my attention like pouring ice water down my back. I could not touch anything to my teeth for several days, they were so supersensitive. But after that they became as tough as iron, and a thorough comfort. If by some blessed accident my conscience could catch the Riggs' disease, I know what I could do with it.

Riggs's motto was, "The dentist's duty is not to see how many teeth he can fill, but how many he can save from decay."[23] He was an advocate of what was termed by some in his day as "oral gardening."[24] He preached the rule of the general hygiene of the mouth (the same as Horace Wells did), and was referred to by one of his adherents as the "original father of hygienic care of the mouth."[25] As has been pointed out, however, he was not a contributor to dental and surgical periodicals and seems to have had an aversion to writing, preferring to work with his hands and demonstrate manually instead. George Mills, when memorializing Riggs in 1887, would characterize him as

Truly a type of the old-school practice, and he tenaciously held to it throughout his professional life. His practice in general might justly be termed radically conservative, as opposed to the radical idealist. To the dental student of the present day, the methods of preparing a cavity and placing gold within it that were the common practice in Dr. Riggs' day, would seem crude indeed. The principle of condensing gold, and the form of the instrument used, would prove, on close examination, to be the same as those now coming largely into favor, viz., lateral and rotary pressure.[26]

In 1866, Riggs was appointed to a committee by the Connecticut State Dental Association with reference to establishing a dental department at Yale College, an idea that was strongly and successfully opposed by the Connecticut Medical Society. (Whereupon Harvard was able to achieve that objective.) And in 1870, he was appointed along with James McManus and others to a committee to present to the General Assembly of Connecticut, on behalf of the Connecticut State Dental Association, a proposal for the erection of a bronze statue honoring the memory of Horace Wells. Riggs lectured and demonstrated his methods before a number of dental schools, including the newly founded dental department of Harvard University. His voice was often heard in debate at dental meetings, and in 1881 he went to Europe to participate in the Seventh International Medical Congress at London, giving clinical lectures and demonstrations to that body on the prophylactic treatment of the gums and teeth.

Riggs's individuality, proneness to original thinking, and preference to "go it alone" are reflected in a letter which Dr. C. T. Stockwell of Springfield wrote to B. H. Catching in 1886 congratulating him for publishing an obituary of Riggs in the *Southern Dental Journal* and enclosing a letter Riggs had written to Stockwell a year earlier. Catching saw fit to publish both of these in his journal.[27] In his letter to Catching, Stockwell voiced the following sentiments about Riggs:

> Dr. Riggs was a modest man—one that did not push himself to the front. He did not contend for a prominent place personally. He devoted himself persistently, for a long series of years, to the development of a truth, which, as he says, he "mined from the bed-rock;" and when, in his judgment, he had found and proven the truth, he gave it fully and frankly, although modestly, to the profession. He was always ready to meet opposition with *demonstration*. Like the famous Pasteur, he considered words, or argument, of minor importance. So sure was he of his ground, that he never hesitated to appeal to actual demonstration; and, like Pasteur's, his opponents learned to dislike that kind of argument. But he was more than a dentist: he was a *man* . . . he was to the dental, what Goethe was to the poetical, world. In his work, thought, philosophy, independence of character, and stand-

ards of acting and living, he was in advance of his time, and consequently met with the social treatment that such men always encounter.

Catching then printed the letter which Stockwell had enclosed with his own, sent by Riggs to Stockwell on May 12, 1885, about six months prior to Riggs's death. Riggs had declined to speak at a meeting in Worcester, telling Stockwell,

> I feel that the profession has outgrown or outstripped me, in its progress, and that it only remains for me to perfect the methods long since given to it, and which never had much interest or weight in its deliberations. Whatever I gave, was mined, by the hardest work, from the bed-rock, through years of enthusiastic occupation. But the doubt— the *feeling* the *controversy* engendered as to the value of the products (to say nothing of their originality) thus produced, has convinced me that my province is to quietly work out my own methods and leave their estimation to another age, to approve or condemn.

Riggs then told Stockwell that the question of "Bread and butter" intimately concerns most men and that the pecuniary view often seems most paramount to all others in life and the benefits conferred on the world only subsidiary. "Wealth," he philosophized, "reinforces moderate abilities, and often dominates the opinions of men of genius; so that men of large wealth, with no other ability except to accumulate money, dictate affairs of state, and rule in social circles." That inestimable quality, "genius," it is obvious, had never left his mind.

Riggs was no less independent in his views on dental education. After he had listened to a debate on improving dental education at the sixth annual meeting of the American Dental Association, held in Boston on July 31, 1866, and specifically, after hearing a proposal made that dental students should attend regular courses at a dental college, Riggs asked for permission to have the floor and delivered his rebuke.[28] After pointing out that attendance at Oxford or Cambridge was deemed essential in the past to be considered learned, he predicted that "That day is past."

> In this country we have imitations of those colleges. They are barely imitations. It is like going into a railroad depot in Boston, paying for your ticket, getting into the sleeping car, and into a musty bed, going to sleep and waking up at the end of the journey without any more

information than you had when you got in. In these colleges you run the ruts of thought that everybody else has been in.

After pointing out that dentistry has heretofore been an exception to that rule, for which reason it has seen much improvement, Riggs proclaimed that

I never wish to see dental colleges bearing the same relation to the profession, that the present literary institutions do to the intelligence and learning of the people. These are mere machines that grind men out, and give them a title to teach theology or practice medicine or law . . . they introduce a chronic mode of thought, the man follows it up through life, and we seldom hear of any new discovery or invention from any of these men. But when you take a man who has on his hands the scar of the plough-handle or of some mechanical art, you will find that it is from these sources you get native talent . . . I hope never to see the time come when the profession shall be diverted and drawn into any particular worn channels of education in college, to the exclusion of a proper education. The man must educate himself. He must apply himself to books, to thought, and to his laboratory, working out his ideas in one branch or another.

Toward the end of his commentary, Riggs urged, "let us reform the old idea of colleges. Let us have a practical thing. Let us teach them self-education, self-discipline, and to regard the colleges as a mere help; then we shall find discovery after discovery from our profession."

Riggs was a man of marked personal appearance, which was enhanced by his later years by a striking gray beard (Illustration 19). He never married. He was strictly a professional man. Possessing little business ability, he was very careless in keeping his accounts. According to Koch, it was said of him, "He would work hard all day and perhaps make a note of his operations in an old gold-foil book and then lose the book. Business reverses a few years before his death depleted his possessions, which were at one time considerable."[29] In politics, Riggs was a Whig, and is said by Koch to have been among the men of Hartford who were foremost in the movement which led to the formation of the Republican party. He held anti-slavery views and was a vigorous Abolitionist and advocate of human rights and freedom in the widest sense.

Illustration 19. John M. Riggs in later life. Courtesy of the Historical Museum of Medicine and Dentistry, Hartford.

Nearly forty years after commencing practice as a surgeon-dentist in Hartford, John M. Riggs died at his rooms in the Cheney Building on the evening of November 11, 1885. He had suffered an acute bronchial attack in the spring of that year, but had convalesced to the point that he had been able to resume his practice. However, in October, while attending the one hundred and fortieth anniversary of the Governor's Foot Guard, to which organization he had been a long-time member, he caught cold and his condition rapidly turned to acute bronchitis, finally progressing to pneumonia. His funeral services were attended by a number of members of his profession, who paid tribute to his memory and work.[30] As did others, Dr. C. S. Hurlbut of Springfield credited Riggs with an attribute which had intrigued Riggs in early life and which he possibly shared with Horace Wells: genius. Said Dr. Hurlbut:

> Dr. Riggs was a genius. A genius has some quality that prevents him from being perfectly symmetrical in his formation, according to the popular idea, but he was one of those men who wrote history. He has more than a national reputation. He does not belong to Hartford, but to the whole world, not a city or State of the country but what his name is known and respected; and more, his name and fame has reached England and Europe. Hurlbut concluded by professing that "I loved him for his thorough integrity. He was truthful. He desired truth; he sought it, and all his works and operations were stamped with it—pure gold."

The services for John Riggs concluded with the terse statement, "His body was cremated in the Le Moyne furnace."

Notes

1. Ralph Waldo Emerson, "Quotation and Originality," *Letters and Social Aims*, in the *Centennary Edition, The Complete Works of Ralph Waldo Emerson* (Boston, Houghton, Mifflin and Company, 1904), v. 8, p. 203.
2. Robert Nisbet, "Sociology: Genius," *The Wilson Quarterly*, Special Issue, 1982, 98–107.
3. The most complete account of John Riggs's life appears in Charles R. E. Koch, *History of Dental Surgery* (Chicago, National Art Publishing

Company, 1909), v. 2, pp. 345–352. The information there is based upon interviews with Riggs's nephews and with dentists, such as Drs. James and Charles McManus, with whom he was long associated. Other accounts are: "Obituary, Dr. John M. Riggs," *The Southern Dental Journal* 4, no. 11 (December 1885): 475–481; George A. Mills, "Some Observations from the Life of the Late Dr. John M. Riggs, of Hartford, Conn.; Abstract of Paper Read before the Connecticut Valley Dental Society at Their Annual Meeting Held at Holyoke, Mass., October 14th and 15th, " *The Independent Practitioner* 8, no. 3 (March 1887): 129–133; and "Dr. John M. Riggs," *Western Dental Journal* 1, no. 4 (April 1887): {145}-146,which is, for the most part, an abstract of the Mills obituary. An interesting discussion of him also appears on pp. 10–13 of Arthur H Merritt's "The Historical Background of Periodontology," *The Journal of Periodontology* 10, no. 1 (January 1939): 7–25.

4. Washington College, *Statement of the Course of Study and Instruction Pursued at Washington College, Hartford, Connecticut; with a Catalogueof the Officers and Students. January, 1835* (Hartford, Printed by P. Canfield, 1835).

5. Charles R. E. Koch, *History of Dental Surgery,* 345, is the source of information. There is no acceptable explanation of the term as voiced by Riggs. *The Oxford English Dictionary* (1933 ed., reprinted 1961) defines the term, under Manco, v. 6, p. 109, as a shortened form of Calamanco, which *Webster's New International Dictionary of the English Language* defines as a European woolen fabric of satin weave and plain or striped design, imitating camel's-hair cloth, or a garment of the same stuff, or something suggestive of calamanco, as a wood and plaster building. It is possible that the word reported by Koch could have contained a typographical error, being printed, for example, "mankey" instead of "mankeen" which recorded later than the synonymous uses of *mankine,* or Mankind, possibly its original form. Or the term may have been bestowed upon him by his classmates with respect to its connotation associated with animals that attack humans.

6. "Obituary, Dr. John M. Riggs," *The Southern Dental Journal,* 477.

7. Charles R. E. Koch, *History of Dental Surgery,* v. 2, pp. 345–346.

8. Ibid., 347

9. "Obituary, Dr. John M. Riggs," *The Southern Dental Journal,* 476.

10. James McManus, *Notes on the History of Anesthesia . . . Early Records of Dentists in Connecticut* (Hartford, Clark and Smith, 1896), 81; W. Harry Archer, "Life and Letters of Horace Wells, Discoverer of Anesthesia, chronologically arranged, with an Appen-

dix," *Journal of the American College of Dentists,* 11, no. 2 (June 1944): 99, counts Riggs and C. A. Kingsbury among Wells's students.

11. United State Senate, *An Examination of the Question of Anaesthesia, on the Memorial of Charles Thomas Wells, Referred to a Select Committee of the Senate of the United States, of Which Hon. Isaac P. Walker is Chairman* (Washington 1853), 14–15. As noted, Rigg's deposition was reprinted by Smith in the editions of this work which he published in enlarged form under his own name in 1858, 1859 and 1867.

12. In 1870, the *Dental Register,* published in Cincinnati, printed an anonymous article entitled "Anaesthesia in Surgery.— Who Discovered It?" (Volume 24, pp. 166–170). This article, written obviously by someone of Hartford, went over the familiar facts of the discovery, and it need concern us no further, except to add that it contained a number of inaccuracies and even errors of fact. However, it brought a response from Gardner Q. Colton, who read it and agreed with the writer that honor of the discovery belonged to Wells. Colton noted, however, that he had administered the gas, and that Riggs drew Wells's tooth. "The statement (in the foregoing anonymous article) that 'Dr. Wells took the pipe of the gas-bag in his mouth, and it was kept there till his hands fell lifeless and his head drooped,' is slightly incorrect, as Dr. Wells did not touch the 'pipe' with his hands, neither did his hands fall lifeless or his head droop. I used but a small bag, such as would ordinarily produce inhalation." G. Q. Colton, "Anaesthesia," *Dental Register* 24, no. 6 (June 1870): 264–266.

13. United States Senate, *Statements, Supported by Evidence, of Wm. T. G. Morton, M.D. and His Claim to the Discovery of the Anaesthetic Properties of Ether* (Washington 1853), Appendix, 9–105.

14. Riggs's letter to Drs. Hasbrouck and Howland is printed in full in Arthur H. Merritt, "The Historical Background of Periodontology," 13, together with facsimiles of its four pages and the envelope containing it.

15. Riggs's letter appeared in volume 4, no. 7, August 1885, of *The Southern Dental Journal,* pp. 281–283. Catching would explain the background of the publication of Riggs's letter on p. 306 of the same journal. At that time, Riggs was not the only living witness; Colton and Cooley were still very much alive and would outlive Riggs for about another decade and a half.

16. United States Senate, *An Examination of the Question of Anaesthesia, on the Memorial of Charles Thomas Wells,* 17.

17. George A. Mills, "Some Observations from the Life of the Late Dr. John M. Riggs, of Hartford, Conn.," 130.
18. Arthur H. Merritt, "The Historical Background of Periodontology," 10.
19. Charles R. E. Koch, *History of Dental Surgery,* v. 2, p. 347.
20. Riggs's comment appears in a section titled "Reflex Nervous Disorders from Dental Irritation," published in *The Dental Register* 30, no. 3 (March 1876): 133–137. This consists of discussion of a paper on that subject by Dr. A. L. Carroll which appeared in the previous January's issue of the *Register.* The discussion, between several dentists, centered around the delicate skill which the dentist is called upon to exercise, and the unsuitability of some men to do it naturally.
21. John M. Riggs, "Suppurative Inflammation of the Gums, and Absorption of the Gums and Alveolar Process," *Pennsylvania Journal of Dental Science* 3, no. 3 (March 1876): 99–104. This is entry 3685 in *Morton's Medical Bibliography; an Annotated Check-List of Texts Illustrating the History of Medicine (Garrison and Morton),* edited by Jeremy Norman (5th ed., [London] Scholar Press [1991]).
22. Sheldon Baumrind, "Mark Twain Visits the Dentist," *Bulletin of the History of Dentistry* 21, no. 1 (June 1973): [25]-30.
23. Charles R. E. Koch, *History of Dental Surgery,* v. 2, p. 349.
24. George A. Mills, "Some Observations on the Life of the Late Dr. John M. Riggs, of Hartford, Conn.," 131.
25. Charles R. E. Koch, *History of Dental Surgery,* v. 2, p. 348.
26. George A. Mills, "Some Observations on the Life of the Late Dr. John M. Riggs, of Hartford, Conn.," 131
27. Stockwell's letter to Catching, dated January 3, 1886, and Riggs's letter to Stockwell, dated May 12, 1885, are published under the heading "Correspondence" in *The Southern Dental Journal* 5, no. 1 (February 1886): 31–33.
28. The proceedings of the sixth annual meeting of the American Dental Association, and Riggs's remarks at its session on dental education, are recorded in the *Transactions of the American Dental Association,* fifth and sixth annual meetings, published conjointly in 1868, pp. 501–504.
29. Charles R. E. Koch, *History of Dental Surgery,* v. 2, p. 350.
30. "The Funeral in His Honor by Professional Friends" is printed at the conclusion of the "Obituary, Dr. John M. Riggs, *The Southern Dental Journal,* 477–481.

7

Christopher Starr Brewster: American Dentist In Paris And Patron Of Horace Wells

Jacques Fouré

The name of Christopher Starr Brewster crops up in biographical works on Horace Wells and Thomas W. Evans, fellow American dentists who had connections with Paris. Brewster was probably the first native American to practice dentistry in Paris, where he obtained a fair share of success, fame and fortune. But references to him even in the literature on Wells and Evans are vague; he comes across only as a shadowy figure, referred to mostly by his last name; or, when his first Christian name is given, it is often cited incorrectly as "Cyrus." We will now reconstruct—for the first time, in detail—the background and activities of this extraordinary man and see why he is deserving of the fame and fortune he achieved. And we will also see how he strove to advance dentistry in general and Horace Wells in particular.

Brewster was born to Seabury Brewster and Fanny Starr Baker at Norwich, Connecticut, on June 27, 1799. His parents, both of Norwich, had been married on February 1, 1798. Seabury had been married twice before and had one son by his first wife and three by his second; he would have still another son, also called Seabury, in 1806.[1] Christopher was proud to carry his mother's family name; in fact, so proud, that he usually signed his name C. Starr Brewster, which accounts for an occasional misinterpretation of the "C" for "Cyrus." The record of his death seventy-one years later, however, would bear the name Christopher Starr Brewster.

Seabury Brewster had been born at Kingston, in Plymouth County, Massachusetts, in 1754, and he died at age ninety-three at Norwich in 1847. He was the sixth in descent from Elder William Brewster, one of the Pilgrims who emigrated on the *Mayflower* and landed at Plymouth in 1620. Christopher's forebear, Benjamin Brewster, came to Norwich in 1669 and was recorded as one of the twenty-five freeman of the town.[2]

We know nothing of Christopher's early years or of his professional training, save information provided in a brief biographical sketch in the *Norwich Courier*, which mentions that he was a "self made man, having had none but the ordinary advantages of education, and neither wealth nor professional patronage to smooth his way upward."[3] He seems to have been endowed with an adventurous spirit, for when twenty-one, with no capital and only a set of instruments, in the use of which he was his own instructor, he commenced the practice of dentistry, traveling northward into Canada. He began to practice first in Montreal in the summer of 1820; in the fall, he moved on to Quebec, where he remained until the spring of 1821, when he returned to the United States. After residing some time at New Orleans, he next visited the West Indies. Upon his return to the United States, he traveled through most of the southern cities, gaining skill and reputation at every step, until he established himself finally at Charleston, where he stood for some years at the head of his profession.[4]

Brewster's apprenticeship travels, during which daily practice and observation contributed to his knowledge, brings to mind the peripatetic Greek physicians of antiquity, who always moved about seeking to perfect their art. To this end, Brewster is said to have enrolled in the Medical College of South Carolina and received a doctor's diploma.[5] In spite of the fame and success he enjoyed during an almost ten year stay at Charleston, he decided to move on, relinquishing his practice to a brilliant young dentist, Benjamin Adolph Rodriguez (1815–1871), who was to become one of the most prominent Jewish leaders in the medical and dental professions of nineteenth century America.[6]

Encouraged by his success and the extensive practice he had acquired in Charleston, Brewster selected London as the field of his future labors. However, he found it difficult to practice alone and therefore tried to go into partnership with some of the most eminent members of the dental profession of that city. Not succeeding in finding a suitable partner, he decided to go on to Paris, a city offering all of the advantages he sought.[7] He subsequently established himself at 11 rue de la Paix, in the heart of the business district, a stone's throw from the fashionable Place Vendôme.

Brewster soon made a name for himself in Paris. His skill, conscientiousness and discretion brought him numerous and wealthy patients. When Brewster arrived in Paris in 1834, the level of dentistry in France had struck a low ebb. While France had attained leadership in the field of dentistry in the wake of Pierre Fauchard, who in 1728 had published the first scientific account of that field,[8] the picture had long since changed. The reason for this decline dated to the French Revolution, and exactly to August 4, 1789, when the National Assembly decreed that all privileges would be abolished, thus eliminating all professional schools. All diplomas and licenses were abolished, including that of "dental expert." Afterwards, anyone was free to offer dental care. It can be said, with regard to dentistry in France, that the nineteenth century was a near vacuum in which, by and large, incompetence and charletanism characterized practice.

Christopher Brewster thus came to France at an opportune time. He was able to satisfy the requirements of an opulent clientele. Although he published little, he seems to have been appreciated for his skills, and, by his work, he made important contributions to French dentistry. He particularly excelled in "plugging" and "regulating." His fillings with gold foil impressed the French. Indeed, although gold fillings were known in France and had been described in the works of Fauchard and Bourdet,[9] the technique was used less extensively than that of filling with lead and tin, which discolored the teeth. Throughout his career, Brewster would have the gold he used sent over from America, where better gold leaf for dental use was manufactured than that made by European producers.

That Brewster and his work were appreciated by the French practitioners is evident by an article in praise of him in the first number of *L'Art Dentaire,* the first French dental publication that was issued in the nineteenth century in an attempt to restore the standing of the profession.[10] The only publication by Brewster that we have been able to find appeared in the November 1840 issue of the *La Lancette Francaise,* a medical-surgical publication better known by its subtitle *Gazette des Hôpitaux,* on the "Abnormal Development of the Anterior Part of the Superior Maxillary with the Retraction of the Upper Lip."[11] Walter Hoffmann-Axthelm, in his history of dentistry,[12] says about Brewster:

> An American dentist working in Paris recommended the spiral spring as the first elastic means of treatment in 1840. Unfortunately, this was only a vague description with no illustrations. With a gold palate plate which carried a system of spiral springs he was able in less than three months to close a severely open bite with a distal position through a progressive and constant pulling on the crooked teeth towards an approximately normal position.

During the critical period of restoring the prestige of the French profession, Brewster manifested his support of his French colleagues by joining the dental society when it was organized in 1846.[13]

If Brewster's income during his first year in Paris (1834) was not encouraging, his perseverance and skill, together with his conservative approach to dental care rather than the expediency of extractions—which was the general practice—soon brought him numerous distinguished patients. Thus it was that in 1839 the Royal Family of France sought his care. Louis Philippe (1773–1850), King from 1830 to 1848, was treated by Brewster. It has been said that the King rewarded him with the Cross of the Legion of Honor; however, there is no record of this award and distinction in the National Archives or in the Chancellery of the Legion of Honor. On the other hand, we have found in the archives of the King's household mention of two other dentists, one, Bousquet, from 1836 until his death in 1840, and the other, Dudet, in 1847, both on the payroll at 2,400 Francs per annum. We can surmise from this that the King and the Royal Family were treated on a strictly private basis. Brewster was soon called to many European courts. In 1842, he was summoned by the Imperial Family of Russia to Saint Petersburg and afterwards was made Knight of the Order of Saint Stanislas and named Honorary Dentist to His Majesty the Emperor of Russia.[14]

One of Brewster's famous patients, Prosper Mérimee (1803–1870), author of *Carmen, Colombo*, etc., and Minister of Public Education, in one of his numerous letters in 1846 to a certain Jenny Dacquin, said:

> I am displeased that you have so little courage. One should never wait for pain when teeth are concerned, and it is because one does not dare go to the dentist that one invites abominable pain. Do go and see Brewster or any other sooner than later. If you wish I shall go with you and will hold you if necessary. Believe me, he is the most skillful man and is, among other things, conservative in nature.[15]

Mérimee was not sparing in praise of Brewster. The Minister was a great friend of the Montijo family and carried on a voluminous correspondence with the Comtesse Montijo, the mother of Eugenie, the future Empress. It was more than probable that Mérimee was responsible for sending Eugenie to Brewster for dental care; and later, when Thomas Evans had taken over Brewster's practice and Louis Napolean had replaced Louis Philippe, Louis, then Emperor Napoleon III (1852–1870), met Eugenie in the waiting room, and later made her his bride.[16]

Brewster's practice became so extensive that he considered talking on an associate. In 1847, he asked his friend and physician Dr. John Y. Clark to be on the look-out in the United States for a likely capable associate. While attending the annual exhibit at the Franklin Institute in Philadelphia, Dr. Clark was impressed by the work of Thomas W. Evans who had received the first Premium for his demonstration of filling teeth with gold foil; Clark immediately put Evans in touch with Brewster and an agreement was soon concluded between the two dentists which provided for the newcomer to take over the entire practice upon Brewster's retirement in 1851.[17] Evans went on to establish a world-wide reputation in his profession, accumulated a fortune, and also became friend and confident of most of the royal families of Europe. Following the defeat of the French army at the Battle of Sedan on the first day of September 1870, and the subsequent revolution and the end of the Second Empire, Evans made plans for the escape into exile of Empress Eugenie and personally escorted her to safety across the Channel in England.

In February 1847, Brewster had the opportunity to meet and befriend Horace Wells, who, by some accounts, had come to Paris to purchase paintings for resale in the United States; by others, to present his claims as the discoverer of anesthesia; while still others have held that Wells' intention was to do both. However, Horace's exact objective in going to Paris has remained a matter of conjecture. In rendering his own account of his journey, we shall soon see, Wells claimed that he intended not to mention his discovery while in France, and he said nothing about the purchase of pictures there, although we know that he did bring many back to America for resale. Finally, in a letter which he wrote to William T. G. Morton on March 21, 1847—this was reprinted in the Appendix to the volume presented to Congress in support of Morton's claim, as proof that Wells had visited Paris on the speculation of paintings alone— Brewster stated that Wells's visit had no connection with the discovery.[18]

Morton had, on December 18, 1846, sent a letter to Brewster together with the apparatus he had invented for inhaling ether. We may presume that, having heard that Charles T. Jackson had recently sent a letter to the French Académie des Sciences claiming the discovery of anesthesia as his, Morton looked around for a contact in Paris to support his claim before the Académie and oppose Jackson's and learned of Brewster, a fellow American dentist practicing there.

When replying, Brewster informed Morton that the discovery and use of the apparatus was first communicated to him in December by an American medical student upon whom Brewster had made an unsuccessful experiment with the apparatus, although his later attempts to use it did succeed. Brewster told Morton that the discovery of performing operations in surgery without giving pain was being regarded in Paris as the greatest event in medical science, save for

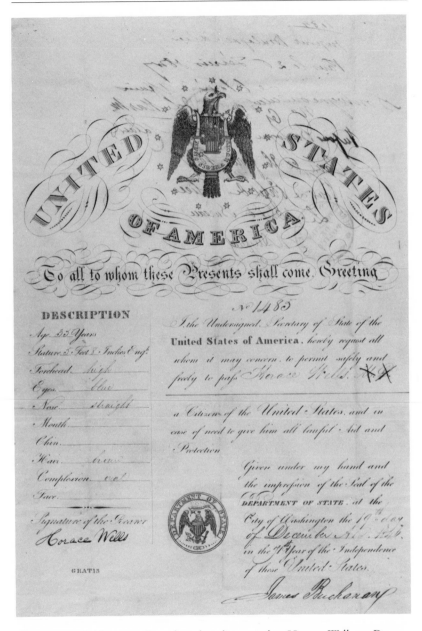

Illustration 20. Passport (greatly reduced) granted to Horace Wells on December 19, 1847. Courtesy of the Historical Museum of Medicine and Dentistry, Hartford.

the discovery of vaccination as a prevention against smallpox. "I am often appealed to by persons here as to who is the true discoverer," Brewster went on to say. "By the statement of some of the Boston dentists one would think that Dr. Jackson deserves the credit. Then by a letter published in your Boston Medical and Surgical Journal, from Dr. Ellsworth, it seems that all the credit is due to Dr. Horace Wells." After reporting that Dr. Marcy of New York, in the *Journal of Commerce*, gives all of the credit to Wells,[19] Brewster told Morton that

> Dr. Wells has been here. I have freely conversed with him, and I am disposed to believe him the true original discoverer who first practiced surgical operations (extractions of teeth) without pain. Dr. W's visit to Europe had no connection with this discovery, and it was only after I had seen the letters of Ellsworth and Marcy, that I prevailed upon him to present his claim to the Academy of Sciences, the Academy of Medicine and the Parisian Medical Society. If his statements are susceptible of proof, he will unquestionably be considered the discoverer.

A letter of Brewster's which the same source printed immediately afterwards[20] shows that Morton did not accept Brewster's support of Wells as final, but still hoping to make him an ally, sent him a letter written by his supporter Dr. Edward Warren on February 27, 1847. In his reply, Brewster thanked Morton "for thinking of me," then related that accident had thrown him into the acquaintance of Wells, but he added parenthetically, "(yet I ought not to say accident for I sought it)," being prompted to do so, he added, from a high sense of justice. He continued:

> I had seen Drs. Ellsworth's and Marcy's letter, and sent to Dr. or Mr. Wells, begging him to call on me. I then told him, 'are you the true man.' His answers, his manner, convinced me that he was.

Not content with supporting Wells in his correspondence with Morton, Brewster on March 1, 1847 sent a letter to the *New York Journal of Commerce* which the *Boston Transcript* reprinted on March 20.[21] (This was partly printed in Morton's volume of evidence to prove that Well's intention when visiting Paris was not to claim credit for the discovery of anesthesia.)[22] Brewster began his letter to the *Journal of Commerce* by observing that "The all-absorbing topic

of conversation in the saloons of Paris, and the all engrossing discussions in the learned and scientific societies here, as most of Europe
is 'our American discovery' of performing surgical operations without pain." Noting that many individuals are trying to claim the merit
of the discovery, but have not succeeded, he reported that

> I have seen, in your paper on the 30th December last, a letter from
> Dr. Marcy, which gives the whole honor to Dr. Horace Wells, dentist
> of Hartford. I have also seen in the 6th January, Dr. Jackson's reply,
> and the rejoinder of Dr. Marcy, in the 8th. In the 'Boston Medical and
> Surgical Journal' I see a letter[23] which gives the discovery to Dr. Wells.
> These are things I hope you will settle fairly on your side of the water,
> and let "Caesar have the things that are Caesar's."

Brewster then reported that Dr. Wells had for the last days been
in Paris, and had presented his claim to the discovery to both the
Académie des Sciences and the Académie de Médecine, which have
taken it under consideration.[24] And he had also been before the
Parisian Medical Society where he had described the history, progress and final result of his discovery. "I was present," Brewster
related; "the society were of opinion, that if Dr. Wells brought forth
proofs that he had performed extractions of teeth in 1845 without
pain, then he would be entitled to the merit of being the discoverer."
He continued: "Imagine to yourselves, Messrs. Editors, a man to
have made this *more than brilliant discovery* visiting Europe without
bringing with him the proofs." He concluded his lengthy letter by
stating, "As an American, I feel proud that this discovery originated
in my native land, and regret that any efforts should have been made
to rob the rightful discoverer of his just due."

Brewster entreated Wells to go home and send him the necessary
documents; consequently, upon his return to Hartford, Wells set
about writing up an account of his discovery in the form of a
pamphlet which he published on March 30, 1847 under the title,
*History of the Discovery of the Application of Nitrous Oxide Gas,
Ether, and Other Vapours, to Surgical Operations;* and he sent
copies of it to Brewster at No. 11, rue de la Paix in Paris to be
presented to the medical and scientific societies of Europe. Before
leaving France on the previous February 27 for a week in England

prior to sailing from Liverpool on March 4, Wells wrote out a brief Memoir relating the incidents of his discovery, which was read to the Academy of Sciences on March 8, while he was en route home. A copy of Wells's Memoir has been obtained from the archives of the Académie des Sciences and is now published for the first time as an Appendix here, both in facsimile and transcribed form. It is obvious that Wells's employed this and the Academy of Medicine letter as an outline or draft for the pamphlet which he probably began writing during his return voyage and completed and published shortly after his arrival home.

Brewster apparently was diligent in approaching the societies on Horace's behalf. The following letter, written eleven days before Horace's death and received by Elizabeth following it, was published in the 1858 edition of Truman Smith's *An Examination of the Question of Anesthesia:*

Paris, January 12th, 1848

My Dear Wells:

I have just returned from a meeting of the 'Parisian Medical Society,' where they have voted that 'to Horace Wells, of Hartford, United States of America, is due all the honors of having first discovered and successfully applied the uses of vapors or gases, whereby surgical operations could be performed without pain.'

They have done even more, for they have elected you an honorary member of the Society.

This was the third evening that the Society had deliberated upon the subject. On the two previous occasions Mr. Warren, the agent of Morton, was present, and endeavored to show that to his client were due the honors; but he, having completely failed, did not attend the last meeting.

The use of the ether took the place of the nitrous oxyd gas, but chloroform has supplanted both; yet the first person who first discovered and performed surgical operations without pain was Horace Wells, and to the last day of time must suffering humanity bless his name.

Your diploma and the vote of the P. M. S, shall be forwarded to you. In the interim, you may use this letter as you please.

Believe me ever truly yours,

Brewster.[25]

Furthermore, the *New York Dental Recorder* in April 1848 mentioned that Wells had also been awarded a premium of 25,000 francs for his discovery.[26] However, as Elizabeth would later relate:

> From letters of my husband, French newspapers, English medical journals, letters of C. S. Brewster, and H. J. Bennett, editor of the London Lancet, I was informed of my husband's flattering reception, and happy termination of a long discussion before the Academy of Medicine in his favor, the strenuous exertions of Drs. Jackson and Morton to the contrary notwithstanding. A letter from C. S. Brewster, dentist in Paris, was received by my husband, announcing that the society had conferred on him the degree of M.D., and that the diploma would be forwarded by the next steamer. The occurrence of the revolution of 1848, which broke out at this critical moment, caused either that it should be forgotten or lost.[27]

There exists among the Wells family letters, which W. Harry Archer collected, a long letter that Horace wrote to his mother and sister Mary on March 28, 1847, informing them of his recent European trip, which he had kept secret from them, and describing its events. For some unexplained reason, Dr. Archer did not see fit to publish this communication of Horace's; because of its importance, it is printed here (for the first time) in its entirety as Appendix 2.[28] After relating that he sailed for England on December 24, 1846, "just for a little recreation," and landed in Liverpool after a rough but "not very long" passage of twenty-four days,[29] he devoted its first third to an account of his visit to England.

His account of his stay in England ended with a description of a meeting of Parliament during which the Queen, with Prince Albert and a royal escort, proceeded from Buckingham Palace to the House of Lords to address Parliament in person from the throne. Upon this occasion, Horace was able to get a "standee" position near the entrance of the palace; and on the following day, he managed to get a look at the crown which was being deposited in the jewel-room of the Tower, provoking him to comment: "This crown which was worn on this occasion cost five millions of dollars—look on this picture and then look on that which shows us starving millions who are subjects of her Majesty—it is truly a painful contrast."

After seeing the principal sights of London, Horace proceeded to Paris by way of Havre. He reported:

I like Paris much; the spacious grounds planted with magnificent trees in the city, thronged with a people who seem to be intent on enjoyment, conspire to make the visitors feel happy in spite of himself. Although I had no intentions of having anything to say about ether or gas which has made so much noise of late, yet when it was known that I was in Paris, I was politely told that I was a *great* man!! for my name had gone before me. You are aware that Drs. Jackson and Morton have been claiming a discovery that properly belongs to me. Dr. Jackson it seems had sent out letters to Europe claiming the discovery, he therefore was first known there—but soon after an article which was published in the Boston Medical Journal which gave me credit of it was republished there—by the way you cannot conceive what excitement there is in Europe on this subject—indeed it is the topic of the day and is admitted by all to be the most important discovery of the age, and they are desirous of knowing who is the discoverer and it is rumored that whoever substantiates his claim to priority is to receive a pension from the French government. Well, after it was known that I was in Paris I was invited to address the various Scientific Academies upon the subject—which I did—and not only this, several gentlemen wearing the Royal Ribbon interested themselves in my behalf and are now electioneering for me with a right good will. I was invited to parties, soiries [sic], balls and dinners constantly for the last 10 days of my residence in Paris; indeed balls and parties embracing the aristocracy of Paris were given in my honor—in short I was quite a Lion, having horses and equipage second only to that of the King placed at my command. I also had the offer of becoming dentist to his Majesty Louis Philip.

After pointing out that Dr. Jackson had influential friends in France also, and that he would do his best to establish his own claim, although, he added, "it is not impossible that he may out general me," Horace reported that he was now gathering his own evidence, taking affidavits, and the like, which would go out by way of the next steamer. "Mr. Bennett, editor of the New York Herald," Horace related, "is now in Europe and I see that he has written home a letter which is going the newspaper rounds.

> He states that I am to return to Europe this spring— this is the first news I have of it for I have no idea of returning. I understand that a petition has been presented to Congress in refference [sic] to furnishing this gas to the Army in Mexico and to remunerate the discoverer in

the sum of $100,000. When it was stated that Jackson and Morton were the men, the member (Mr. Dixon) from Connecticut rose and stated that Drs. Jackson and Morton were not the discoverers but this honor belonged to Dr. Horace Wells of Connecticut. Congress appointed a committee to enquire into the matter and I have just received a letter from that committee requesting me to furnish them with the evidence of my priority of discovery, as they have been informed that it properly belonged to me.

In view of Brewster's successful practice in Paris, his membership in the scientific societies, his prestige among the noble and wealthy, and his connection to the innermost chambers of the court, it cannot be denied that much of the success that Wells encountered in France was due to Brewster's belief in him and his support and efforts on his behalf. Once convinced that Wells was the true discoverer of anesthesia, Brewster left no stone unturned to help him gain credit for his discovery, which he emphasized by underlining in the letter quoted before as a *more than brilliant discovery*. And undoubtedly to Brewster is due partial credit for the fact that Wells has been accepted in France as the discoverer to the exclusion of all others.

Although Thomas Evans arrived in Paris in November 1847, too late to meet Horace Wells personally, he undoubtedly accepted Brewster's view as to the true discoverer of anesthesia, for it was Evans who was instrumental in introducing nitrous oxide as a general anesthetic in dentistry in both France and England. Henry Rainey, Evan's biographer, describes how, at a World's Fair held in Paris in 1867, Evans arranged for an exhibit from the United States as a contribution to the exposition. Evans was informed of the work of Gardner Q. Colton in the use of nitrous oxide as an anesthetic. After investigating, he decided that nitrous oxide should be made part of the exhibit and arranged for Colton to go to Paris with his equipment. At the close of the exhibition in the fall of 1867, Evans invited Colton to remain in his office during the winter, at which time nitrous oxide was administered to over 1,000 patients. Convinced that nitrous oxide deserved wider publicity, Evans accompanied Colton to London in 1868 and demonstrated the administration of the gas for painless extraction of teeth before many physicians and dentists. Despite much initial opposition, as a result of Evans's efforts, nitrous oxide finally came to be recommended as a safe general anesthetic for use by the dental profession.[30]

Brewster was peripherally involved in the so-called "amalgam controversy" which broke out in the late 1840s, and he is referred to in several articles or letters published in the *New York Dental Recorder* in 1848 and 1849.[31] Many dentists—most notably, Dr. E. Parmly of London—felt that it was dangerous to fill teeth with amalgam, a combination of silver and quicksilver, because they feared that it became oxidized in the form of black oxide of mercury. The matter became exacerbated in 1847 when an American named Ames was reported to have died some time after having had his teeth filled with amalgam, and those opposing amalgam saw it as the cause of his death. In actuality, however, no such death occurred.

Brewster, along with some of the leading dentists of Europe and America, held that amalgam was a proper filling material in cases where the cavity is so situated as to make it inconvenient to pack it densely with gold or other foil. In the war of words which followed, Brewster's name appeared a number of times in the *Recorder* among those opting for amalgam under these certain circumstances. And, in an article in the *Recorder* in June 1849 there appeared a letter of Thomas Evans, who was now working with Brewster, in which he claimed to have successfully used an amalgam of his own invention, which was composed of pure tin, cadmium in small quantities, and mercury. The latter was employed in more or less quantities as might be required to make the substance more or less plastic. Evans claimed that his composition retained its color perfectly, prevented the recurrence of caries, and became sufficiently hard to withstand the friction of mastication.

Brewster made several trips to England and during one of his many visits there married Anna Maria Bennett, a native of Leeds, in London on June 8, 1848. She was to give him three children; the first, Louis Seabury James, born a year after their marriage, was to bear the name Louis at the insistence of King Louis Phillippe. Having settled Thomas Evans into his lucrative practice and having himself acquired a considerable fortune, Brewster decided to retire from the duties of professional life and enjoy his family. His long residence in Paris had made the country, the people, and the mode of living so congenial that he decided to remain in France. For a number of years

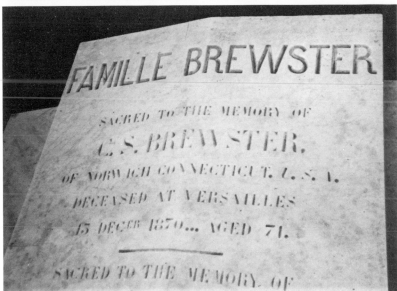

Illustration 21. The author at the grave of Christopher Starr Brewster in Notre Dame Cemetery in Versailles in 1991. The photographs were taken by the author's wife.

the Brewster family occupied a mansion at 26 rue Montaigne (presently rue Jean Mermoz) in an elegant quarter of the city near the Champs Elysées, but in 1857 Brewster decided to move to a more rural area, probably for the sake of his young children who were then: Louis, nine years old, Henri, seven, and Marie, two.[32]

The Brewsters acquired a beautiful and spacious house in Versailles, only twenty-two kilometers from Paris. Versailles was a small, quiet provincial town, enjoying the remains of the splendor imparted to it by the kings and the royal courts in the seventeenth and eighteenth centuries. Brewster liked the broad, tree-lined avenues, easily accessible from Paris, where he could occasionally, as fancy suited him, return to see his friends. However, his happy family life and his last days were darkened by political events and war.

The downfall of Napoleon III and the defeat of the French armies in the east were to bring the Prussians to the gates of Paris, which was to endure a long and painful siege. Versailles was occupied by the Prussian General Staff and became the site of the headquarters of Emperor Wilhelm. Brewster and his family had to undergo, along with other residents of France, many privations, and when Versailles became the Imperial Headquarters of the Prussian army, he had twelve German officers billeted with him and a corresponding number of rank and file occupying his best apartments.

It was under these tragic circumstances that Christopher Starr Brewster died of "ramollissement," which would probably imply a stroke, on December 15, 1870. He was buried at Notre Dame Cemetery in Versailles where his grave can still be viewed today (Illustration 21). He left a considerable estate of over a million French Francs to his wife and three children. Anna Maria survived him by only three years, dying in Vienna in 1875 during an epidemic of cholera. His descendants still tend his grave.

NOTES

1 Norwich, Connecticut. *Vital Records of Norwich, 1659–1848* (Hartford, Society of Colonial Wars in the State of Connecticut, 1913).
2. Francis M. Caulkins, *History of Norwich* (Norwich, Pequot Press, 1976).
3. A biography of Brewster in the *American Journal of the Dental Sciences* 3 (1848): 149, reportedly deriving this information from an otherwise unidentified sketch in the *Norwich Courier,* does not cite when that sketch appeared.
4. Milton B. Asbell, "Vignettes in Dental History: Benjamin Adolph Rodriguez, 1815–1871," *The Alpha Omegan* 42, no. 2 (June 1948): 85–87.
5. This information comes from a biographical article on Brewster, "Biographie. Le Docteur Brewster," published in *L'Art Dentaire* 1, no. 1 (January 1857): 26–28. However, Brewster's name is not listed among the graduates of the Medical College of South Carolina from its founding in 1824 through 1838 in Joseph I. Waring's *A History of Medicine in South Carolina, 1825–1900* ([Columbia] South Carolina Medical Association, 1967), 351–353. But, as Dr. Waring points out, the minutes of the Medical Society of South Carolina, upon which he based these lists, are incomplete, there being, for example, no official entry of graduates of the College in 1832.
6. Milton B. Asbell, "Vignettes in Dental History: Benjamin Adolph Rodriguez, 1815–1871."
7. "Obituary Dr. Christopher Starr Brewster," *British Journal of Dental Science* 14 (January 1871): 42–43.
8. Pierre Fauchard, *Le Chirurgien Dentiste, ou Traité des Dents* (Paris, J. Mariette, 1728), 2 v.
9. Etienne Bourdet (1722–1789), who became royal dentist to Kings Louis XV and Louis XVI, published several works on dentistry, of which his *Operations sur les Dents* (Paris 1754) is best known and most important.
10. "Biographie. Le Docteur Brewster." *L'Art Dentaire.*
11. C. S. Brewster, "Dévelopment Abnormal de la Portion Antérieure de l'Os Maxillaire Supérieur. Obliquité Considérable et Proéminence des Dents Incisives de Cet Os. Guérison Après Deux Mois de Traitement," *La Lancette Francaise. Gazette des Hôpitaux* no. 135, tome 2, 2d serie (November 14, 1840): 538–539.
12. Walter Hoffman-Axthelm, *History of Dentistry* (Chicago, Quintessence Publishing Company, 1981).

13. Henri Morgenstern, *La Guerre des Dentistes en France en 1846*, thesis, École Pratique des Hautes Études (Paris 1990).

14. "Biographie. Le Docteur Brewster," *L'Art Dentaire*.

15. Prosper Mérimée, *Correspondence Générale, Etablié et Annotée par Maurice Parturier avec la Collaboration de Pierre et Jean Mallion* (Paris, Le Divan, 1941–1964), v. 4, January 19, 1846.

16. Henry Rainey, *Dr. Thomas W. Evans, American Dentist to European Royalty* (Philadelphia, Printed at the Evons Company, 1964), 24. See also, Milton B. Asbell, "The French Connection," *Health Affairs* 15 (Spring 1978): 17–19; and Anthony D. Branch, "American Dentist in Paris, Dr. Thomas W. Evans," doctoral dissertation, University of California at Santa Barbara, 1971.

17. Henry Rainey, *Dr. Thomas Evans, American Dentist to European Royalty.*

18. United States Senate, *Statements, Supported by Evidence, of Wm. T. G. Morton, M. D. on His Claim to the Discovery of the Anaesthetic Properties of Ether* (Washington 1853), Appendix, 130.

19. Brewster was referring to a letter which P. W. Ellsworth had published in the *Boston Medical and Surgical Journal* under the title, "The Discoverer of the Effects of Sulphuric Ether," on December 9, 1846 (v. 35, no. 20, pp. 397–398; and to C. C. Marcy's article, "Sulphuric Ether, &c., in Surgical Operations," published in the New York *Journal of Commerce* on December 30, 1846, and a second communication, replying to an answer to his article by Charles T. Jackson, which appeared in the *Journal of Commerce* on January 8, 1847. Marcy's first article was reprinted on pp. 113–115 of the Appendix of United States Senate, *Statements, Supported by Evidence, of Wm. T. G. Morton*, and his second on pp. 116–118 of the same work.

20. United States Senate, *Statements, Supported by Evidence, of Wm. T. G. Morton*, Appendix, 130–131.

21. Brewster's entire March 1, 1847 letter to the New York *Journal of Commerce* is printed in W. Harry Archer's "Life and Letters of Horace Wells," 127–128.

22. United States Senate, *Statements, Supported by Evidence, of Wm. T. G. Morton*, Appendix, 110.

23. Brewster was referring here to Ellsworth's communication cited in Note 19.

24. Wells's letter to the Academy of Medicine was published in its *Bulletin* in late February, *Bulletin de l'Académie Royale de Médecine* 23 (February 1847): 396–396; an English translation appeared in the *Souvenir* volume issued by the Wellcome Foundation in 1930 to honor Henry Hickman, the English surgeon who, in the 1820s, had experi-

mented on animals using carbon dioxide as a means of rendering them insensible during surgery, The Wellcome Historical Museum, *Souvenir Henry Hickman Centenary Exhibition, 54, Wigmore Street, London* . . . (London, Wellcome Foundation, 1930).

25. Truman Smith, *An Examination of the Question of Anaesthesia, Arising on the Memorial of Charles Thomas Wells* (New York, John A. Gray, printer, 1858), 105–106. Brewster's letter did not appear in the 1853 memorial for Charles T. Wells, upon which Smith based his 1858 edition.

26. This appears on p. 153 of a two-part article which was published under the title "Etherization and Chloroform" in the *New York Dental Recorder* 2, nos. 7–8 (April-May 1848): 130–134, 151–154.

27. United States Senate, *An Examination of the Question of Anaesthesia, on the Memorial of Charles T. Wells, Referred to a Select Committee of the Senate of the United States, of Which Hon. Isaac P. Walker is Chairman* ([Washington, 1853]), 20. The Revolution of 1848 broke out first in France, on February 22, 1848, and quickly led to to abdication of Louis Philippe.

28. The original Wells's family letters and papers which W. Harry Archer collected cannot be traced at this time; however, photostatic copies and transcriptions of them are now in The Francis A. Countway Library of Medicine in Boston, including the letter referred to here and published in Appendix 2.

29. Contact with the Public Relations Office of the Cunard Line in New York has established that in 1840 four transatlantic vessels were placed in operation for the purpose of providing weekly mail service between Paris, London, and New York. The vessels made eight and a half knots per hour and took two weeks in crossing (two were always passing each other in opposite directions one week out of port). Thus, since Wells left America on December 25, 1846, Christmas Eve, we can feel fairly assured that he landed at Liverpool on or about January 7, 1847. He undoubtedly should have written "14" and not "24" when reporting his "not very long" journey to Liverpool.

30. Henry Rainey, *Dr. Thomas W. Evans, Americaan Dentist to European Royalty,* 17–18.

31. The articles appearing in the *New York Dental Recorder* on the amalgam controversy in 1848 and 1849 are too numerous to cite individually. Letters or articles were printed in the majority of issues printed in volumes two and three between January 1848 and September 1849.

32. Department des Yvelines-90 5278, archives, no. 191.

APPENDIX 1

The "Memoir" of Horace Wells
Presented to the Académie des Sciences on March 8, 1847
From the archives of the Academy

8 Mar 1847

To the Academy of Sciences

Gentlemen

With your permission
I will make a few suggestions respecting the use of stimulant gasses or vapour as a means of rendering the system insensible to pain during the performance of surgical operations, trusting you will pardon me for presuming to address so enlightened a body upon this important subject when it shall appear that I have been the humble instrument of first introducing this subject to public notice. Reasoning from analogy I was led to believe that surgical operations might be performed without pain by the fact that an individual when much excited from ordinary causes may receive severe wounds without manifesting the least pain; as for instance the man who is engaged in combat may have a limb severed from his body after which he testifies that it was attended with little or no pain at the time; and so with the man who is intoxicated with spiritous liquor may be treated severely without manifesting pain, and his frame seems in this state more tenacious of life than under ordinary circumstances. By these facts I was led to enquire if the same effect would not follow by the inhalation of some exhilarating gas or vapour, the effects of which would pass off immediately leaving the system none the worse for its use. After inhaling nitrous oxide gas and the vapour of sulphuric ether I became satisfied that both were identical in their effects—first exhilarating, then acting as a powerful sedative, and both when taken to excess producing a kind of paralyzing effect. I resolved to submit to the operation of having a tooth extracted under the influence of one of these stimulants

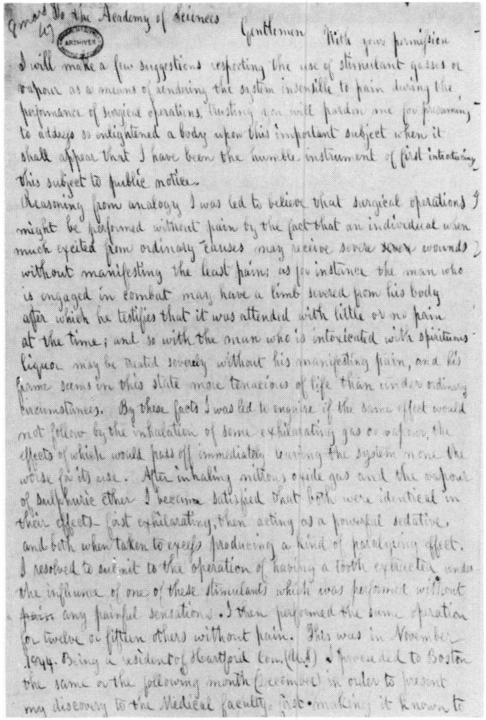

Illustration 22. Pages one and three of the holograph "Memoir" by Wells that was read before the Académie des Sciences, Paris, on March 8, 1847. Courtesy of the Académie des Sciences, Paris.

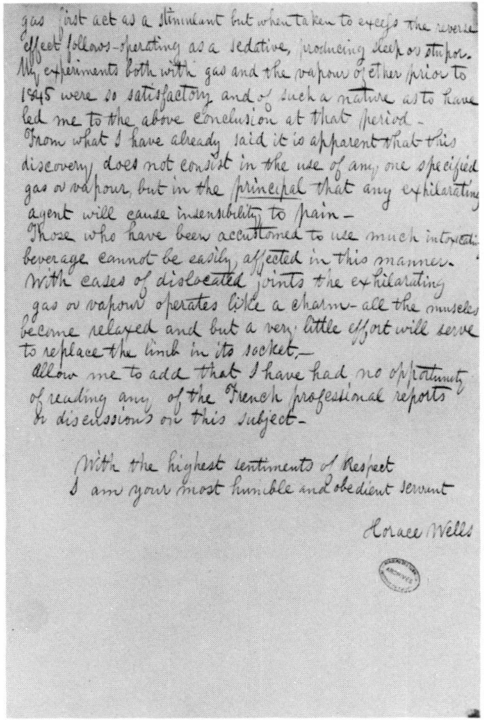

which was performed without any painful sensations. I then performed the same operation for twelve or fifteen others without pain. This was in November 1844. Being a resident of Hartford Con. (U.S.) I proceeded to Boston the same or the following month (December) in order to present my discovery to the Medical faculty, first making it known to Drs. Warren and Hayward of the Massachusetts General Hospital and to Drs. Jackson and Morton. By invitation of Dr. Warren I addressed his class upon the subject of producing insensibility to pain by inhalation of stimulants, endeavoring to establish the theory which had become in my own mind a matter of fact viz. that excitement caused by any means and carried to excess would produce a nervous insensibility; as evidence of the truth of my theory I instanced the man who is intoxicated with liquor or excited by anger or fear. The Medical class whom [sic] I addressed were apparently very skeptical on this subject, and the first experiment in the presence failing by reason of the gas apparatus being removed too soon, no one was inclined to assist me in further operations. The excitement of this adverse adventure immediately caused an illness from which I did not recover for many months. From this cause and for that reason I did not wish to incur the responsibility of performing many operations by the aid of this new agent without the cooperation of the Medical faculty whom my efforts had failed to enlist in its behalf - my experiments have been somewhat limited. However prior to Feb 1845 I performed the operation of extracting teeth for more than twenty five patients without causing pain - giving the preference to the nitrous oxide gas as it was more agreeable to inhale than the vapour of ether. Having seen both the gas and vapour administered to more than two hundred persons I am fully convinced that their effects on the nervous system are identical, provided they are properly prepared—the ether being rectified—and the nitrous oxide—after the nitrate of amonia has been converted into gas remaining in the same vessel with a body of water for one or two hours, that the nitric acid may be absorbed, which would otherwise prove detrimental. When thus prepared both the vapour of ether and nitrous oxide gas first act as a stimulant but when taken to excess the reverse effect follows—operating as a sedative, producing sleep or stupor. My experiments both with gas and the vapour of ether prior to 1845 were so satisfactory and of such a nature as to have led me to the above conclusion at that period. From what I have already said it is apparent that this discovery does not consist in the use of any one specified gas or vapour, but in the *principal* that any exhilarating agent will cause insensibility to pain. Those who have been accustomed to use much intoxicating beverage cannot be easily affected in this manner. With cases of dislocated joints the exhilarating gas or vapour operates like a charm—all the muscles become relaxed and but a very little effort will serve to replace the limb in its socket. Allow me to add that I have had no opportunity of reading any of the French professional reports or discoveries on this subject.

With the highest sentiments of Respect
I am your most humble and obedient servant
Horace Wells

APPENDIX 2

Letter Written by Horace Wells to "Dear Mother & Sister M.,"
following His Return from Europe. Previously unpublished,
It was found among the W. Harry Archer Collection of
Wells family letters and papers.

Hartford, March 28, 1847

Dear Mother and Sister M.

You have undoubtedly thought strange that I have not written before, for a long time has elapsed since you have heard direct from me. I will now proceed to tell the whole secret. In your letter to Elisabeth a short time since you ask if I have taken wings and flown away. In answer to this I say yes and at the time that letter was written I was flying over Europe as fast as rail road cars could carry me. Don't be alarmed for I am safe in America again. On the 24th of Dec. last just for a little recreation, I sailed for Liverpool with the intention of visiting London and Paris, which object has been accomplished. I have just returned with better health than I have enjoyed for years before, having seen so much to interest and instruct. I had a rough passage out but not a very long one being 24 days to Liverpool—this place is remarkable for nothing, except its magnificent docks, as you are aware that its commercial business is perhaps second to none in the world— from thence I proceeded to London at the rate of some 40 miles an hour. I arrived there the day before the meeting of Parliament, and I had the pleasure of seeing one of the most splendid sights ever beheld by mortal eyes. I mean so far as it is in the power of man to create splendour—This was on the occasion of the meeting of Parliament when the Queen proceeds from Buckingham Pallace to the House of Lords to address Parliament in person from the throne. I succeeded in getting a good "standee" near the entrance of the Pallace and had a fine view of Queen Victoria and Prince Albert, also the whole of the Royal escort. The Queen looked very much like the portraits we see of her and is much prettier than I had supposed from hear say. The horses and entire equipage exceeded anything I had ever imagined to exist. The following day I had a near-view of the crown which was deposited in the jewel room of the Tower, this crown which was worn on this occasion cost five millions of dollars—look on this picture and then look on that which shews us starving millions who are subjects of her Majesty—it is truly a painful contrast. After visiting the principal sights of London I proceeded to Paris by way of Havre. I like Paris much; the spacious grounds planted with magnificent trees in the city, thronged with a people who seem to be intent on enjoyment, conspire to make the visitors feel happy in spite of himself. Although I had no intentions of having anything to say about ether or gas which has made so much noise of late, yet when it was known that I was in Paris, I was politely told that I was a *great* man!! for my name had gone before me. You are aware that Drs. Jackson and Morton have been claiming a discovery which properly belongs to me. Dr. Jackson it seems had sent out letters to Europe claiming the discovery, he therefore was first known there—but soon after an article which was published in the Boston Medical Journal which gave me the credit of it was republished there—by the way you cannot conceive what excitement there is in Europe on this subject—indeed it is the topic of the day and is admitted by all to be the most important discovery of the age, and they are desirous of knowing who is the discoverer and it is rumored that whoever substantiates his claim to priority is to receive a pension from the French government. Well after it was known that I was in Paris I was invited to address the various Scientific Academies upon the subject—which I did—and not only this, several gentlemen wearing the Royal Ribbon interested themselves in my behalf and are now electioneering for me with a right good will. I was invited to parties, soiries, balls and dinners constantly for the last 10 days of my residence in Paris; indeed balls and parties embracing the Aristocracy of Paris were given in honor of me—in short I was quite a Lion, having horses and equipage second only to that of the King placed at my command. I also had the offer of becoming dentist to his Majesty Louis Philip, King of France—Dr. Jackson has influential friends in France also and he will do his best to establish his claim to this discovery although he really has no right in justice to this honor yet it is not impossible but he may out-general me. I am now getting my evidence, taking affidavits &c which will go out by the next steamer. Mr. Bennet editor of the New York Herald is now in Europe and I see that he has written home a letter which is going the newspaper rounds. He states that I am to return to Europe this Spring— this is the first news I have had of it for I have no idea of returning. I understand that a petition has been presented to Congress in refference to furnishing this gas to the Army in Mexico and to remunerate the discoverer in the sum of $100,000. When it was stated that Jackson and Morton were the men, the member (Mr. Dixon) from Connecticut rose and stated that Drs. Jackson and Morton were not the discoverers but this honor belonged to Dr. Horace Wells of Connecticut. Congress appointed a committee to enquire into the matter and I have just received a letter from that committee requesting me to furnish them with the evidence of my priority of discovery, as they have been informed that it properly belonged to me. As my sheet is full I must close. Please to let Mary see this letter and tell her it is for herself as much as for you. I do not write her a separate letter for it is impossible for me to surmise where she is at present as she is about moving. Remember me to all.

Your affec. son
Horace.

Dear Mother.
   You will doubtless be surprised at this letter and also think it strange we should be silent on such a voyage. I have wished many times during Horaces absence that you knew about it but Horace felt it would be so short an absence it would be best to keep it a secret till his return as he knew you would feel anxious concerning him. He has returned safe and perfectly well, our friends say they hardly know him he is so fleshy. He has also become quite a distinguished man and Hartford citizens are quite proud of him. I hear it rumored he will be a rich man and I am sure he is entitled to it. Your letters have been truely welcome, the last one aboit [sic] the time H - arrived. I felt anxious to hear from Capt. Cole and am glad to hear he is recovering. You may expect a small pamphlet concerning the gas which Horace is having printed in a few days. Remember to all and please write soon and congratulate us.

Yours,
Elizabeth

Dear grand Mother
   I have received your kind letter and in answer Would say that I am quite Well and hope you are enjoying the same blessing.
Charles Wells

8

Recognition From Britain: The Horace Wells Testimonial Fund, 1871–1873

J. A. W. Wildsmith

W hatever the merits, absolute or relative, of the claims of Crawford Long or Horace Wells to have been the first to employ inhalational anaesthesia, its development was, like all scientific advances, the culmination of the studies and observations of many individuals. If Priestly had not isolated nitrous oxide, Davy could not have studied its effects and Colton would not have had anything to demonstrate so Wells would hardly have been able to take his definative step forward. In addition, nothing succeeds like an idea whose time has come and it is clear in retrospect that "anaesthesia" was just waiting to be discovered by the middle third of the nineteenth century, although, it is also evident that, until Wells came on the scene, it was hard pressed to find a "discoverer" in the complete sense of that word.

For "that discovery" two components were required: an appreciation of the concept and benefit of obtunding pain during surgery, together with the availability of effective agents for that purpose. At times throughout history many had sought ways of producing insensibility, but observations of relevance were not made by those with the necessary interest. Similarly, those with the interest were unaware of the effects of suitable agents. Wells deserves his recognition because he connected observation with concept, performed an experiment (on himself first!) *and* tried to tell the world about it without thought of financial gain.

Sadly for Wells, he had not quite perfected his method of administration and perhaps the time was not quite right when he went to Boston. In spite of the dismissive response he received, he continued to administer nitrous oxide for dental and surgical procedures, but he practiced dentistry only intermittently and devoted his time to other matters. It is arguable, likely even, that this lack of career resolve and failure to pursue his discovery more actively were early features of the depressive illness that ultimately lead him to take his own life.

After Morton had successfully demonstrated ether, Wells became obsessed (not without justification) with showing that he was at least the originator of the process of inhalational anaesthesia. Morton not only denied Wells any scientific credit, but did so almost certainly as part of his attempt to patent his discovery for financial gain. His squalid treatment of Wells will taint Morton's reputation for evermore.

Because Wells' fateful demonstration in Boston was treated as being a failure, no word of anaesthesia by inhalation spread across the Atlantic until Morton followed in Wells' footsteps, but with another chemical agent and with infinitely more success. Ether was embraced rapidly in Britain, notably by Simpson, who not only advocated its use by arguing the cause against religious objections, but also sought better agents and soon discovered the anaesthetic effects of chloroform.

However, not even Simpson (who, when he later heard of Wells, clearly acknowledged his primacy) made any attempt to look at nitrous oxide, even though its analgesic actions had been described so clearly by Humphry Davy in Britain at the turn of the nineteenth century. This is all the more surprising, given that "laughing gas parties" were as well known as "ether frolics." Once again, no connection was made between observation and requirement, and word had to come from the United States, although in this instance by way of France. In 1848 (after a personal visit the previous year) Wells was credited with the discovery of anaesthesia by inhalation by the French Academy, then considered to be the most important medical forum in the world, but he died without knowing this result. The campaign for his recognition obviously faltered. C. S. Brewster, an American dentist working in Paris sent word of the French recognition and provides a later link in this story because in 1847, the same year as Wells' visit to Paris, he was joined in practice by another American, C. W. Evans, the man who would introduce nitrous oxide into Britain in 1868.

After the events of 1844 in Hartford, Colton continued with his demonstrations. Then, in 1849, following his brother Walter's appointment as Civil Governor of California, Gardner sailed around Cape Horn to join him in San Francisco and quickly became caught up in the events of the Gold Rush of that year. He practiced medicine, prospected for gold, and ran a ferry boat and a hospital, finally involving himself in land speculation and leaving California a rich man. After losing much of his fortune in an unwise investment in Syracuse, New York, he returned to his lectures and laughing gas demonstrations for a living. [1] Meanwhile, nitrous oxide anesthesia had fallen into disuse following Wells' death.

In 1863, after lecturing on nitrous oxide at New Haven, Colton was asked by the wealthy patient of a dentist with whom he was then in contact if he would give her gas rather than chloroform for extraction of a number of her teeth, since the dentist had been unwilling to administer chloroform to her. This was done, and local dentists were so impressed that they began to use nitrous oxide regularly because it was clearly superior to the volatile agents for brief dental procedures. Colton moved to New York, formed his Dental Institute, and by 1871 could claim to have used nitrous oxide on more than 51,000 patients. In his writings and speeches, however, he always added mention of Wells and his experiments, being quite clear in ascribing credit to Wells for originating this use of nitrous oxide.

In 1867, Colton demonstrated his methods at the Paris Exhibition and introduced Evans to the use of nitrous oxide. The following year, Evans visited Britain and gave demonstrations at the London Dental Hospital and Moorfields Eye Hospital. Despite the fact that initial reactions were mixed, use of the gas spread widely in dentistry, helped by visits from Colton himself in 1868 and 1871.

When staying a few days in London in 1871, while on his way from Europe to America, Colton spent many hours in the company of Charles James Fox, one of the leading dental surgeons of the day, editor of *The British Journal of Dental Science* (in the pages of which most of this story is recorded), and an early enthusiast of nitrous oxide. During one of their numerous conversations, Fox asked Colton if anything had been done in America on behalf of the widow and son of Wells, who, he had heard from Colton during a visit to Britain three years previously, were, if not in absolute poverty, still not in comfortable circumstances. "To my surprise," Fox wrote in an editorial in *The British Journal of Dental Science* in September 1871,[2] "I learnt that they were still unprovided for, and that the lady had to support herself almost entirely by the work of her hands."

Fox felt that it was not right that the widow of a man to whom so many people were indebted for relief of their pain should be in anything approaching want, and especially since so many of his brother dentists had increased their incomes owing to Wells' first efforts. As a result, he conceived the idea of raising a public subscription on behalf of Mrs. Wells and her son, and a committee was soon formed, with John Erichsen, an eminent surgeon, as chairman. Fox and another dentist, Edwin Sercombe, shared the duties of secretary, while the treasurers were Joseph J. Clover and F. Woodhouse Braine. The latter two are particularly important because they were two of the three first full-time physician-anaesthetists in Britain.

Others on the committee included a number of workers (from all over Britain) who had taken up nitrous oxide enthusiastically, as well as very eminent members of the medical and dental professions at large. These included Elizabeth Garrett Anderson, F. Le Gros Clark, Sir William Ferguson, Joseph (later Lord) Lister, Sir James Paget and T. Spencer Wells. Thus the project was given splendid support. Fox had reasoned that amidst the hundreds of thousands who were more or less indebted to the gas throughout England and America, there would be no difficulty in raising a sufficient sum to provide a small annuity for Mrs. Wells and her son during their lifetime. Afterwards, the capital might be devoted to some objective which would perpetuate the memory of Wells himself. In view of the widow's straightened circumstances, it seemed a cruel mockery to Fox to erect a statue to Wells, as he had heard suggested, while those dear to him were in comparative want. In his editorial, Fox suggested that every dental practitioner who had profited by the gas devote a little time to bringing the matter before his patients, "when they are in that happy state of mind that prompts them often to say, 'I would pay double rather than suffer the pain without the gas'."

"Let the practitioners contribute their mite, too," Fox wrote, "if they will," but above all, he urged, let them contribute a little time to spread the idea of a subscription to provide Mrs. Wells with an annuity. "I have had the assurance of Dr. Colton," he said,

> that he, for one, will not only contribute handsomely to such a fund, but will use his best endeavours to urge the cause in America. We in England have raised a statue to Davy, who needed no more; let us now exert ourselves so that Mrs. Wells shall no longer have to say, as she does, that "that which has been a boon to the world has been to me and my family an unspeakable evil;" for it is unhappily too true that Horace Wells first *realised* that nitrous oxide would give absolute immunity from pain in extractions, was so led away in the study of this and other anaesthetics, that his practice, and finally his reason, suffered fatally and led to his untimely end.

In its November 1871 issue, *The British Journal of Dental Science* republished a notice that had appeared in the medical journal *Lancet* the previous October 7 concerning the movement that Fox had initiated to equip the widow of Horce Wells, "the originator of modern anaesthesia," with an annuity. "It is only natural," the *Lancet* notice stated,

> that the Dental profession, whose members have now, after a quarter of century's disuse, returned to the daily employment of the original anaesthetic, nitrous oxide, should have had their attention directed to the original discoverer of the use of the gas for Dental purposes. Wells was undoubtedly the first to put in practice the suggestion of Sir Humphrey [sic] Davy that nitrous oxide might be employed as an anaesthetic, and it was after attending an exhibition of the effects of

the "laughing gas" on December 18th [sic], 1844, that he formed an opinion respecting its anaesthetic uses.[3]

Over the next two years *The British Journal of Dental Science* printed letters from contributors—dentists, surgeons and patients alike—which they sent in along with their offerings to the fund. It also published lists of subscribers and the amounts of their donations during the life of the campaign. In its January 1872 issue, the Journal published an extract from the *Canada Journal of Dental Science* fully supporting the action then going on in England to assist Mrs. Wells. [4] "The reputation and the glory of the discovery of anaesthesia," the Canadian editors avowed, "undoubtedly belongs to the Dental Profession collectively, and to the late Horace Wells, of Hartford, Conn., individually. The recent death of Sir James Young Simpson revived the discussion as to priority of claim; but the facts stand on record that the claims of Dr. Wells were confirmed by Sir James Simpson himself, in the very last article he wrote."

The Canadian journal referred to a series of resolutions passed at a meeting of the Dental Society at Hartford in April 1870, which had been referred to its editors. The Hartford dentists had voted to raise funds to erect a monument to the memory of Dr. Wells and were looking for support. Now the Canadian editors stated their reasons for not publishing the resolutions at the time they were referred. Having become aware that Wells' widow was in poor circumstances, being obliged to earn her living by her own hands and entirely supporting herself and her son since her husband's death, they stated their lack of sympathy or the erection of a monument while she was still in need; and they reported that they had written to the committee in Hartford, offering to give any assistance toward providing an annuity for Mrs. Wells as the first consideration. "We are glad," the Canadian article concluded, "to learn that Mr. Fox, editor of the 'British Journal of Dental Science' has made a similar appeal to the Dentists of England, and we trust that the Hartford Committee will so change their action as to first secure comfort for Mrs. Wells, and then the monument; otherwise any such erection would stand as a memorial of a mistaken enthusiasm, and a reproach on the humanity of the profession." The protestations of the Canadians notwithstanding, the idea of a monument to Wells in Hartford did go forward to a successful conclusion.

Subscribers and subscriptions to the Wells fund continued to be listed in the pages of *The British Journal of Dental Science* throughout 1872. However, in its second issue in 1873, the committee announced that it had fixed upon March 25 as the last date for receiving subscriptions, regretting that the amount collected had not exceeded much over £100 and hoping that before the closing of the subscription efforts would be made to make the sum a more substantial evidence to Mrs. Wells of appreciation of the benefits conferred upon humanity by the labours of her husband. "We fear the limitation of the subscription to one guinea has had the effect of checking much liberality; but as it *so* limited, let each one who has already subscribed endeavour to persuade at least two or three others to send their guineas." [5] In the March issue the committee published a more formal announcement, expressing the same views, and urging its readers not to content themselves with sending one guinea only. [6]

Upon the closing of the subscription, those individuals who had initiated and conducted it met and passed the following resolution:

At a meeting held 25th March 1873

at 6 Cavendish Place, London W:
It was resolved that the sum of Money subscribed by several Members of the Medical and Dental Profession and others in England, be forwarded to Mrs. H. Wells, as a slight testimony to the merits of her late husband Horace Wells (of Hartford, Connecticut, U.S.) to whom the world is indebted, not only for the introduction of Nitrous Oxide as an Anaesthetic but also for giving that impetus to the study of Anaesthesia which has resulted in the introduction of ether, chloroform and various other agents for effecting that object.
Signed on behalf of the Committee

John Eric Erichsen		Chairman
Joseph J. Clover	)	Treasurers
F. Woodhouse Braine	)	
Charles James Fox	)	Secretaries
Edwin Sercombe	)	

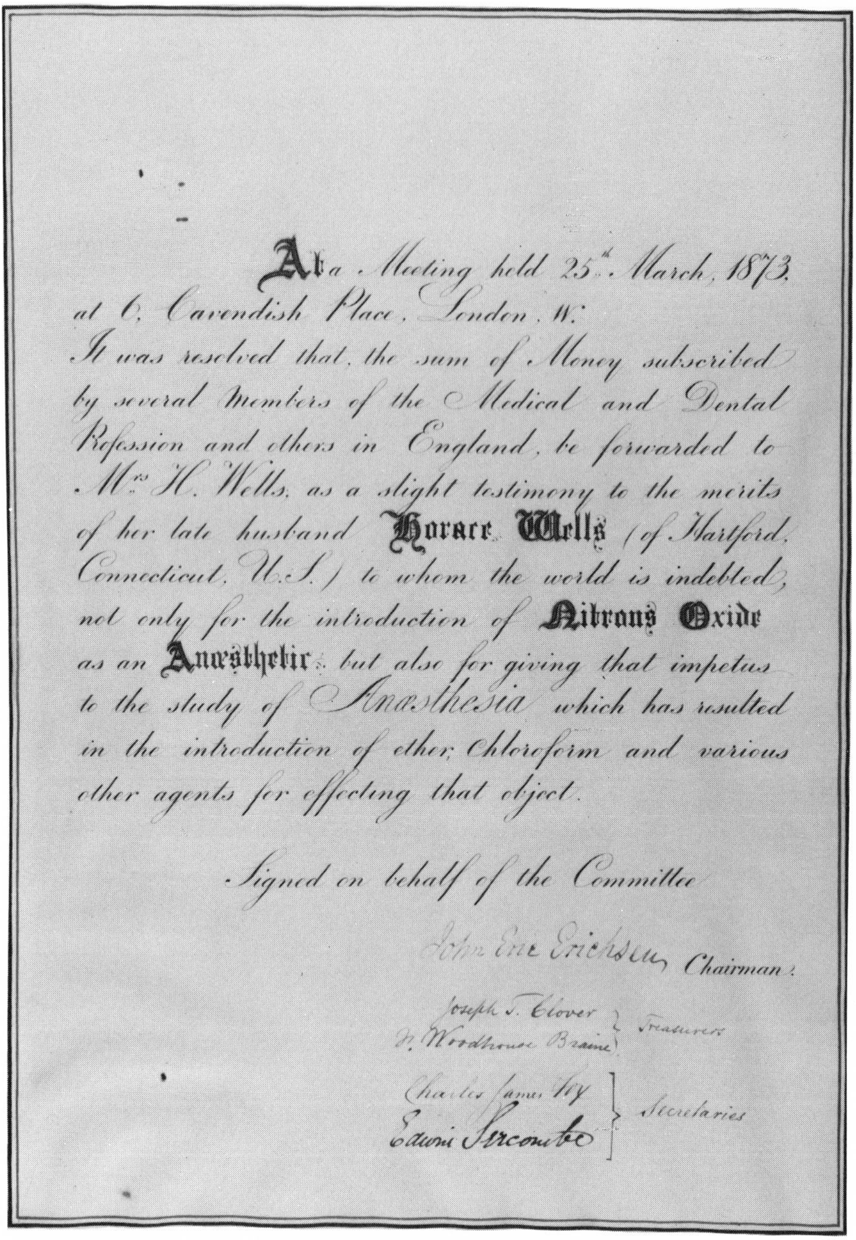

At a Meeting held 25th March, 1873, at 6, Cavendish Place, London. W.

It was resolved that, the sum of Money subscribed by several Members of the Medical and Dental Profession and others in England, be forwarded to Mrs H. Wells, as a slight testimony to the merits of her late husband **Horace Wells** *(of Hartford, Connecticut, U.S.) to whom the world is indebted, not only for the introduction of* **Nitrous Oxide** *as an* **Anæsthetic** *but also for giving that impetus to the study of* **Anæsthesia** *which has resulted in the introduction of ether, Chloroform and various other agents for effecting that object.*

Signed on behalf of the Committee

John Eric Erichsen, Chairman

Joseph T. Clover
W. Woodhouse Braine } Treasurers

Charles James Fox
Edwin Larcombe } Secretaries

Illustration 23. Resolution of the medical and dental professions of Britain, 1871, awarding Wells credit for the discovery of anesthesia. Courtesy of the Historical Museum of Medicine and Dentistry, Hartford.

The subscription proved to be a disappointment to those who conceived and promoted it, for a total of only £149 was collected over the two year period. This sum was forwarded to Elizabeth Wells, along with the vellum certificate (now in the possession of the Historical Museum of Medicine and Dentistry in Hartford) that is shown in the accompanying illustration.

There are a number of reasons why more money was not collected. Although *The British Journal of Dental Science* gave a great deal of publicity and support to this project, the response from other journals and the public was miserly, perhaps reflecting the lack of interest in, and use of, nitrous oxide outside of dentistry at the time. The size of the collection may also have been influenced adversely by an unfortunate conjunction: the report of the first death in Britain during nitrous oxide inhalation, this occurring in January 1873 and attracting significant publicity.[7]

Later in 1873 Fox's journal published a postscript to this episode in the form of an article entitled "The Late Horace Wells." This related that the editors of *The British Journal of Dental Science* had been favoured by a visit from Mr. Charles T. Wells, the only son of Horace. The article continued:

> We regret to find that his visit to Europe is, by the advice of his medical friends, owing to serious ill-health arising from overwork, and threatened injury to his sight. He has expressed himself most warmly in appreciation of the efforts that have been made in this country towards the recognition and establishment of his father's claims, and the raising of a testimonial fund for the benefit of his mother, Mrs. Wells; and although this has unhappily resulted in so small an offering he expresses himself not the less grateful for the moral support which this testimonial will afford him and his friends in supporting his father's cause in the United States. His weak health compels him to avoid all excitement, and he has, therefore, preferred complete retirement during his short stay in London, which he leaves in a day or two for Paris, at the request of the American Committee, to view and report upon a statue of his father now preparing there for erection in Hartford, Connecticut. [8]

The final word on this matter appeared in the second issue of *The British Journal of Dental Science* in 1874, in the form of a letter to the Editor from F. Woodhouse Braine, one of the treasurers of the subscription fund. Relating that he was now attempting to augment the small sum collected, he appealed to the thousands who had escaped much suffering by having painless operations performed under the influence of nitrous oxide gas to help according to their means. He also reported, regretfully, that the son of Horace Wells, who presently held the post of clerk in an insurance office, was suffering from rapidly failing vision, the result of having overtaxed his eyes at night while endeavouring by extra work to support his widowed mother and his father's aged sister out of his own slender means.

In conclusion, it must be pointed out that the effort made in Britain in the 1871–1873 period to raise a subscription for Elizabeth and Charles Wells constituted an acknowledgement of Horace Wells' original contribution to anesthesia by a group that included some of the most eminent dental and medical practitioners of that time and place. Their efforts provided true recognition from the "old world" of the man who, more than any other, deserves the credit for discovering inhalational anaesthesia. Sadly, he himself did not enjoy the satisfaction or glory of recognition as his reward, and surely there is no truer subject than Wells for Shakespeare's philosophical insight:

Oh the fierce wretchedness that glory brings us.

NOTES

1. The most complete account of Gardner Quincy Colton's fascinating and event-filled life is a recent article by Gary B. Smith and Nicholas P. Hirsch, "Gardner Quincy Colton: Pioneer of Nitrous Oxide Anes-thesia," *Anesthesia and Analgesia; Journal of the International Anesthesia Research Society* 72, no. 3 (March 1991): 382–391.
2. Charles James Fox, "The Late Horace Wells," *The British Journal of Dental Science* 14 (September 1871): 415–417.
3. "The Case of Mrs. Horace Wells," *The British Journal of Dental Science* 14 (November 1871): 555–558; "Horace Wells," *The Lancet* (October 7, 1871): 518–519.
4. "Horace Wells Testimonial Fund," *The British Journal of Dental Science* 15 (January 1872): 40–44; "The Late Horace Wells," *The Canada Journal of Dental Science* 3, no. 11 (September 1871): 351–

352. This article was signed "B," for its coeditor W. George Beers, of Montreal.

5. "Wells Testimonial Fund," *The British Journal of Dental Science* 16 (February 1873): 94.

6. This untitled notice appeared on pp. 114–115 of v. 16 of *The British Journal of Dental Science.*

7. The article reporting the death from nitrous oxide during tooth extraction appeared on pp. 65–68 of v. 16 of *The British Journal of Dental Science* and was discussed in issues appearing in February and March.

8. "The Late Horace Wells," *The British Journal of Dental Science* 16 (July 1873): 333–339.

9. F. Woodhouse Braine, "The Horace Wells Fund," *The British Journal of Dental Science* (17 February 1874): 92.

9

W. Harry Archer, D.D.S. Biographer Of Horace Wells

C. Richard Bennett

Had it not been for the pioneering efforts of W. Harry Archer, the world would be far less knowledgeable today about the life of Horace Wells. While Archer made the teaching and practice of oral surgery and dental anesthesia his lifelong vocation, he made research into the life and times of Horace Wells his lifelong avocation. As a result of Archer's efforts, Howard R. Raper would write in his "epic of anesthesia," *Man Against Pain*[1], "Thanks mainly to the published work of W. Harry Archer, more of a reliable nature is known about the life and personality of Horace Wells than any other discoverer." This statement remains essentially as true in 1994, the year of the sesquicentennial of Horace Well's discovery, as it did at the time of its centennial celebration fifty years earlier.

Although he contributed significantly to the development of oral surgery in this country, the improvement of dental anesthesia also remained a major concern for Dr. Archer throughout his career. To

Archer, anesthesia was synonymous with Horace Wells. It is appropriate therefore, in a work intended to recelebrate the discovery of surgical anesthesia by Wells in 1844, to devote a few pages to his biographer, W. Harry Archer, and to pay tribute to him as well.

W. Harry Archer was born on March 6, 1905 in Ambridge, Pennsylvania, a steel town on the Ohio River sixteen miles from Pittsburgh. He attended schools in Ambridge as well as in neighboring Zelienople, to which the Archer family later moved. After graduation from Zelienople High School, Archer won an appointment to the United States Navel Academy, expecting to train in his father's profession, engineering. Archer met the physical requirements of the Academy in all but one aspect. Due to prior loss of two teeth, his application was marked "deficient teeth" and his appointment was denied. He was unable to obtain a waiver in time for entrance that Fall because the congressman who had appointed him was then traveling in the far East and could not be reached. Giving up the idea of engineering as a career, Archer reasoned that if the loss of two teeth was serious enough to keep someone out the Navel Academy, dentistry would be an important and worthwhile career.

After attending the University of Pittsburgh, he graduated from its dental school in 1927. It was during his first two years as a dental student that Archer developed a special interest in anesthesia, an interest that continued throughout his professional life. Learning almost immediately after entrance that no dental school in Pennsylvania and very few schools in the United States taught the use of anesthesia, he voluntarily took up the study of both general and local anesthesia. The young student and some classmates would inject ink into cadavers that they were dissecting. Then, as the dissection reached the area of the nerve they were attempting to "anesthetize", observance for presence of ink would determine the "success" or "failure" of the nerve block.

During those days he spent every possible spare moment in the office of a leading exodontist who would allow him to observe the administration of nitrous oxide and oxygen anesthesia while assisting at surgery. His roommate at the time, a part-time teacher at the dental school, also permitted him, from his sophomore year on, to extract teeth from patients under anesthesia on Sundays. "My patients," Archer later recalled, "were the ushers, porters, cleaning women, ticket takers, etc. who worked for me at Loews Aldine [Theater] where I was working my way through dental school."[2] By the time Archer was a junior dental student, he was an "authority" on anesthesia, and his first published article, "Technique for Producing Local Anesthesia in the Mandible", appeared in the May 1926 issue of *Dental Rays*.

While attempting to read everything that he could on the subject of anesthesia, Archer also learned about the controversy that had arisen concerning credit for its discovery and set out to determine which of the claimants had actually been responsible for it. After reviewing all literature available on the subject, Archer concluded that Horace Wells was the person most deserving of credit. Thus begun a life-long love affair with the early history of anesthesia in general and Horace Wells in particular. Harry's wife, Billie, who shared Archer's interest in and enthusiasm for Wells, recently remarked: "Horace Wells became his hero."

Harry Archer spent the time between his teaching duties and dental practice collecting books and other materials on the history of anesthesia and Horace Wells. He also began to collect early anesthesia machinery and apparatus, including many syringes and other devices, until he had accumulated what he felt was the largest and most complete collection of anesthesia instruments in the world. For many years, his collection was housed in the Dental Library and Museum of the School of Dentistry, University of Pittsburgh. However, due to physical changes that subsequntly took place during the reconstruction of the school, Archer would relate in 1970, "We finally had to close our anesthesia museum and I gave our collection to the Smithsonian Institute in Washington."

Mrs. Archer has related how she and her husband took trips to and around New England in search of information on Wells while gathering printed literature on the introduction and history of anesthesia. During one trip, she recalled, they visited Well's birth house in Hartford, Vermont. It was found to be not only intact, but in approximately the same condition it had been in when Horace Wells was born there in 1815. The owners of the house at the time of the Archer's visit were very friendly and courteous, allowing them to investigate the interior of the house as well as the grounds around it. Their searches led to the discovery of original letters of Horace

Wells and his family that had remained in a cupboard over the years. These letters, as well as ivory miniatures of Wells and his wife Elizabeth and other memorabilia that were uncovered, were brought back to Pittsburgh to form the core of Archer's Horace Wells collection and to serve as sources for the biography that would be written later.

In all, Archer would publish more than twenty articles on Horace Wells, William T. G. Morton, and the history of anesthesia. One such publication serves an example of his persistence in reconstructing the personal history of Wells. In an article published in *Dental Rays* in March 1939,[3] Archer discussed an anonymous pamphlet that had been published at Hartford in 1850 under the lengthy title, *Discovery by the late Dr. Horace Wells of the Applicability of Nitrous Oxide Gas, Sulphuric Ether and Other Vapors in Surgical Operations, Nearly two Years before the Patented Discovery of Drs. Charles T. Jackson and W. T. G. Morton.* Until Archer arrived on the scene, authorship of this work, which he described as "one of the most powerfully written pamphlets in existence presenting Horace Wells's case as the true discoverer of anesthesia," had been attributed by the Library of Congress to Joseph Wales, the brother of Horace's wife Elizabeth.

Archer described how he discovered the true identity of the author of this work while visiting the Connecticut Historical Society to investigate its collection relating to the discovery to anesthesia. He noticed on a large manila envelope in a collection of materials that had come from Charles T. Wells, Horace and Elizabeth's only child, a manuscript notation said to be in the handwriting of Charles: "Charles T. Wells Ms. of Pamphlet of Isaac Toucey." And inside was the holograph of the printed pamphlet!

Archer went on to tell how, by comparing the handwriting of the manuscript with a copy of a letter written by Toucey in 1848 to the poetess Lydia Sigourney while Toucey was Attorney General of the United States, and by submitting photostats of both documents to hand writing experts, he proved that the anonymous pamphlet had actually been written by Toucey. Toucey served in the United States House of Representatives between 1835 and 1839 and as Governor of Connecticut in 1846. The *Dental Rays* article also reported the discovery by Archer in the Passport Division of the Department of

State of an heretofore unknown letter which Wells wrote to the Hon. James Dixon, Congressman from Connecticut, on December 28, 1846, asking Dixon to obtain a passport for Well's proposed trip to France.

Archer's major contribution to the history of anesthesia and to the lore of Horace Wells came in 1944, at the time of the centennial of Well's discovery of nitrous oxide anesthesia. In 1942, Archer had been appointed a member of the Horace Wells Centenary Committee of the American Dental Association as well as the Chairman of the Society's History Committee. He used these offices and the occasion to write and publish his "Life and Letters of Horace Wells, Discoverer of Anesthesia, Chronologically Arranged, with an Appendix."

This work, the only serious biography of Wells published to date, remains the major source document of Well's life and career in dentistry and anesthesia. It was published in the *Journal of the American College of Dentists* in June 1944 and was subsequently issued in monographic form. Archer printed in this work (in many cases for the first time) almost every important letter and document relating to Horace Wells's life and career, including many of the family letters he had uncovered at Hartford, Vermont, more than a decade earlier.

Had it not been for Archer's enthusiasm and persistence, original manuscript materials relating to Horace Wells might remain unknown or might have been lost forever. Posterity could have been denied knowledge of information about a large part of Wells' private life and about his efforts in popularizing the use of anesthesia. In addition, the charming courtship letters which Horace and Elizabeth exchanged in 1838, as well as family correspondence detailing other personal matters, would otherwise be unknown. Thanks to Archer, this important information is now safely "on the record."

After Archer's graduation in dentistry in 1927, he found that the chief of the Exodontia Department at Pitt was opposed to the use of general anesthesia, and Archer's attempts to persuade him to introduce these new techniques into the teaching program were unsuccessful. However, when the chief resigned in 1929 to head a new department, Archer was free to complete a postgraduate course in nitrous oxide anesthesia presented by Dr. E. I. McKesson of

Toledo, Ohio. He subsequently taught at the University of Pittsburgh the first course in general anesthesia to be offered in an American dental school. Archer would boast that:

> It was a *good course*. As a matter of fact, during World War II, because of the scarcity of anesthetists, we were asked to supply the hospitals in our health center with dental students to give anesthetics at nights and on weekends. Our students were the only ones who had any training in anesthesia. The medical students had none. So we selected our best seniors, gave them more training than we would ordinarily give our students and for over five years our students gave anesthesia in our hospitals. I am proud to say that we did not have a *single fatality*.

For twenty years after graduation, W. Harry Archer taught oral surgery and anesthesia at the University of Pittsburgh. He was active on local and national levels in maintaining and elevating the status of dentists in various professional organizations and hospitals. He founded the first Department of Hospital Dentistry at Magee Hospital in 1936 in Pittsburgh, Pennsylvania.

One of the offices Archer held was Chairman of the Executive Committee of the Eastern Society of Anesthetists, the largest anesthesia society in the United States at the time. Membership was ninety percent physicians and only five percent dentists. Archer was the first dentist to hold such an office. In addition, he was made a Fellow of the International Congress of Anesthetists. He lectured before many anesthesia societies and published books on oral surgery, dental anesthesia and on anesthesia in oral surgery, as well as sixty articles on a variety of clinical and basic research projects. His two textbooks were translated into fourteen languages and served as models for standard oral surgery and anesthesia procedures in many dental schools in America and parts of Europe.

In 1946, Archer was appointed Professor of Oral Surgery and Anesthesia, as well as Chairman of the Department of Oral Surgery at the University of Pittsburgh Dental School, having worked his way up the ranks from his original 1927 appointment as Demonstrator in the Department of Exodontia Anesthesia.

In 1948, while serving as head of the Department of Oral Surgery

Illustration 24. W. Harry Archer, photographed in his University of Pittsburgh dental school office, about 1970. The portrait of Horace Wells, which he commissioned Verona Kiralfy to paint, appears in the background. Courtesy of Mrs. W. Harry Archer.

and Anesthesia in the School of Dentistry at Pittsburgh, Archer had a student who showed great promise in anesthesiology. Realizing that no individual could be equally capable and knowledgeable as both an anesthetist and an oral surgeon, Archer made arrangements for the student to undertake graduate study and training in anesthesia. He also convinced the administration of the school that anesthesiology was important enough to be afforded departmental status with a full professor as chairman. Subsequently, he recommended that student, Dr. Leonard M. Monheim, be appointed to this position, thus establishing the first separate department of anesthesiology in any dental school in the world. Monheim's success allowed Archer to later remark that "My faith in this man has been more than vindicated."

Harry Archer continued as Professor and Chairman of the Department of Oral Surgery at Pitt until 1970, when he became University Professor. In 1975, he was awarded the title and status of University Professor Emeritus. Previously, in 1968, a new oral surgery clinic had been dedicated at the school in his name. Until his death on April 21, 1980, Archer remained active in his associations with the University of Pittsburgh's School of Dental Medicine by spending many of his idle hours working with the materials he had accumulated on Horace Wells and the history of anesthesia. During this time, he amused himself by assembling two large scrapbooks of pictures of early anesthesia machinery, devices, and portraits of major and pioneering personalities in the field.

W. Harry Archer was a teacher throughout his adult life. A lesson he can still teach us after death is the importance of having heroes and role models. His hero, Horace Wells, set a standard and an ideal that Archer pursued, and achieved, in living a successful and useful life. Like Wells, the world is a better place for his having been among us.

Notes

1. Howard Ripley Raper, *Man Against Pain, the Epic of Anesthesia*, (New York, Prentice Hall, Inc., 1945), 161. Dr. Raper was an authority on dental x-ray technique.

2. Information on Archer's life and career, including many quotations here, derives mainly from a six-page letter he wrote to Dr. Daniel F. Lynch of Washington, D.C., on January 5, 1970. In this he reported, at Dr. Lynch's request, his activities that were directly related to anesthesia. Copies of this letter and his Curriculum Vitae are in Dr. Archer files. Other information was obtained from conversations with Mrs. Archer or are based upon my recollections and on the recollections of colleagues at the University of Pittsburgh's School of Dental Medicine, many of whom were trained by Archer.

3. W. Harry Archer, "Historical Notes on Horace Wells; Authorship of Old Pamphlet Claiming Wells the Discoverer of Anesthesia Established," *Dental Rays* 14, no. 3 (March 1939): 71–77. This thirty-eight page pamphlet was published by Case, Tiffany & Co.

10

The Charles Noel Flagg Posthumous Portrait Of Horace Wells: An Examination Of Its Documentation And Sources And Of The Iconography Of Horace Wells

Richard J. Wolfe and Leroy D. Vandam

About fifty years after Horace Wells's death, the eminent Hartford artist Charles Noel Flagg painted his portrait (Illustration 25) after a daguerreotype and full length silhouette, both of which, the artist reported, Wells had made himself. Upon the occasion of the presentation by Flagg of this portrait to the Wadsworth Atheneum in 1899, the *Hartford Courant* of November 25 published the following news item:

> In presenting his portrait of Dr. Horace Wells, the discoverer of anesthesia, Mr. Flagg wrote as follows:
>
> The Rev. Francis Goodwin,
>   President of the Wadsworth Atheneum.
>
> Dear Sir—I take pleasure in presenting to the Wadsworth Atheneum, through you and your associate trustees, a portrait of the late Dr. Horace Wells, painted by me and actuated from the first stroke of the brush by the hope that in the place for which I have destined it, it might make friends for one of the most unfortunate and greatest men who ever lived. The head was painted from a daguerreotype which Dr. Wells took of himself when experimenting with the process, shortly after its invention by Daguerre. The pose was suggested by a silhouette by Dr. Wells, now in the possession of his son, Mr. Charles Wells. In the cut and color of the costume I have been guided by my father's description of what he and Dr. Wells wore at the time when they were contemporary and intimate friends. I am prompted to give this picture to the Atheneum by a profound regard for the man who was able through his genius to prove his life for mankind by the greatest gift ever bestowed by a human being under his fellows. I am further prompted by a desire to co-operate in the small way possible to me in the effort of the trustees of the Atheneum to make its picture gallery more interesting to the people of Hartford.
>
>
>
> I am, dear sirs,
> Yours with great respect
> Charles Noel Flagg[1]
>
>

This study will discuss the Flagg portrait and its sources and will describe all of the important paintings, photographs and other artistic renderings of Horace Wells that are known to be extant or of which can be traced at this time. It will exclude, however, modern copies of portraits of Wells as well as sculptures and three-dimensional recreations of Wells' face and figure, since these are either discussed elsewhere in this work or are derived from some of the original materials that will be reviewed. Let us now look at Charles Noel Flagg and the circumstances which led him to recreate on canvas the best known portrait of the man who, in the eyes of many, is credited with the discovery of surgical anesthesia.

Illustration 25. Life-size portrait of Horace Wells painted by Charles Noel Flagg and presented by him to the Wadsworth Atheneum in 1899. This oil on canvas measures 57 x 43 inches. It is now on extended loan to The Hartford Medical and Dental Society's Historical Museum of Medicine and Dentistry. Courtesy of the Wadsworth Atheneum, Hartford.

Charles Noel Flagg derived his middle name from the fact that he had been born on Christmas day, at Brooklyn Heights, New York, in 1848, into a family of professional artists. Two uncles, George Whiting Flagg and Henry Collins Flagg, were a genre and portrait painter, and a marine, animal painter and caricaturist, respectively. Charles's half brother, Montague Flagg, was also an artist, while all of the Flaggs were related to Charles's half great-uncle, Washington Alston, the well-known portrait, historical, religious and allegorical painter. Charles's father, Jared Bradley Flagg (born 1820), was an artist also, having taken up the study of painting after his graduation from Washington (now Trinity) College. Following a period of instruction with his brother George, Jared worked as a portrait painter in Hartford between 1840 and 1849; in the latter year, he began the study of theology and was ordained a priest in the Episcopal Church in 1854. While serving as Rector of the Grace Episcopal Church in Brooklyn, Jared became disenchanted with parish work and in 1863 moved the family to New Haven to resume his art career.[2]

This branch of the Flagg family, one genealogical source informs us, was only distantly related to a well-known family of Boston dentists of that name, having come down through different lines from a common seventeenth-century ancestor. The first dentist of the Boston line, Josiah Foster Flagg (1764–1816?), was long known as the "Boston dentist" because he was almost the only person in that locale who devoted his whole attention to dentistry. One of his sons, also named Josiah Foster Flagg (1789–1853), was a dentist, anatomical illustrator, and an inventor of surgical apparatus.[3] Another son, Dr. J.F.B. Flagg, practiced dentistry in Philadelphia and in 1851 wrote the first American textbook on anesthesia.[4] Horace Wells may have been apprenticed to the younger Josiah Foster Flagg or to Dr. Nathan Cooley Keep, with whom the younger Flagg was associated in the manufacture of mineral teeth, as well as to other dentists in the Boston area.[5]

After an apprenticeship in his father's studio, at age twenty, Charles Noel Flagg moved to Hartford. In 1872, upon the advice of Horace Bushnell, one of America's foremost clergymen and educators, Charles, along with several members of his family, went to Paris to study with Jacquesson de la Chevreuse, the famous pupil of Ingres who had founded the "French School of Painting." After two years,

Flagg returned to New York where he married Ellen Fannie Earle. In 1877, following the birth of their first child—there were to be four more, with one dying in infancy—the couple returned to Paris. The Flaggs came back to America in 1882, settling in Eastchester, New York. Charles commuted to New York City where he maintained a studio in association with his half-brother Montague and taught at the National Academy of Design.

In 1887, the Flagg family settled permanently in Hartford. There Flagg established the Flagg Night School for Men which was incorporated with the Connecticut League of Art Students in 1895. Along with Robert B. Brandegee, he also formed the Society of Hartford Artists which in 1893 arranged with the Reverend Francis Goodwin, President of the Wadsworth Atheneum, to hold an exhibit in the newly opened wing of that institution. Flagg exhibited every year at the National Academy of Design and, as a result of a prize award, earned the distinction of "A.N.A." after his name. While remaining active as a portraitist and painter, Flagg formed other artistic groups, became Chairman of the Committee on Civic Centers and Public Buildings, and was largely responsible for the preservation of the Old State House in Hartford, a Charles Bullfinch structure. The Committee also arranged for the restoration and disposition of a portrait of George Washington painted by Gilbert Stuart for the State of Carolina which is now displayed in the museum of the Connecticut State Library. (Its acceptance was refused by the North Carolina authorities because Washington was not pictured in uniform.) At the height of his professional career and to the dismay of the community, Charles Noel Flagg died suddenly of "heart failure" on 10 November 1916 at the age of sixty-eight.

Flagg is known to have painted 150 portraits and fifty-four other paintings, still-lifes, and studies.[6] While most of the portraits depict Hartford and Connecticut notables, there are some subjects of more than local interest. James Wales Ball, originally from Vermont but later of St. Paul Minnesota, bore the maiden name of Horace Wells's wife. Samuel Langhorne Clemens, Mark Twain, had his portrait done in 1890. This portrait is now owned by New York City's Metropolitan Museum and is considered to be one of Flagg's most important works. Another important portrait was that of Charles Dudley Warner, a close friend of Clemens, Editor of the *Hartford*

Illustration 26. Original silhouette of Horace Wells, presumed to have been made by him, with his authentic signature mounted at the base of its outside mat. The original measures $10\,^1/_8$ x 8." The gift of Dr. John Bockstoce to the Boston Medical Library, 1985. Courtesy of the Boston Medical Library in The Francis A. Countway Library of Medicine.

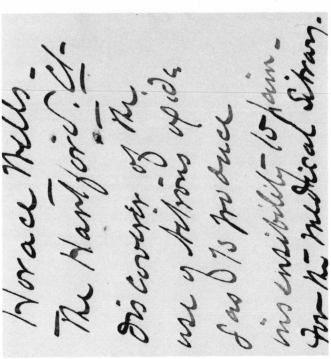

Illustrations 27. Right: Tintype portrait of Horace Wells, copied from an original daguerreotype reportedly made by him ca. 1840. It measures 3 1/4 x 2 3/4". The oval impression was made by a gilt mounting covering it so that only its center appears in its daguerreotype-style case. Left: Note, in the hand of Truman Howe Bartlett, pinned into the inside lid of the case. Courtesy of the Boston Medical Library in The Francis Medical Library of Medicine.

Courant, and widely known in his day as a subtle humorist and the author of many charming sketches and books. Junius Spencer Morgan, founder of one of the world's greatest banking houses, was portrayed posthumously in 1898. Brigadier General Joseph Warren Revere, grandson of Paul Revere, sat for his portrait in 1912. Flagg painted a copy of Gilbert Stuart's original portrait of John Trumbull, the New England artist who depicted more than 250 people and events of the American Revolution. He also completed a portrait of Gideon Welles, a notable Connecticut son who served as Secretary of the Navy in President Lincoln's cabinet during the Civil War.

Flagg's posthumous portrait of Horace Wells, the subject of this essay, was commissioned by Charles T. Wells, Horace Wells's only child. It was reproduced by W. Harry Archer as the frontispiece of his "Life and Letters of Horace Wells, Discoverer of Anesthesia, Chronologically Arranged," the only extensive and serious biographical treatment of Wells that has been undertaken. As Flagg noted in his presentation letter to the Wadsworth Atheneum, he based Wells's features and pose upon a daguerreotype and a silhouette (presumably, a full-length or three-quarter length silhouette), both of which were executed by Wells himself. Although neither of these sources were known when Dr. Archer published his biography of Wells in 1944, the situation has since changed.

The Boston Medical Library in The Francis A. Countway Library of Medicine of Harvard University was recently given a full length silhouette of Wells (Illustration 26) which, in all likelihood, was one of Flagg's original sources. And in the Library's picture collection is a recently discovered tintype (Illustration 27) which undoubtedly is a copy of the daguerreotype upon which the portrait was based. This is the only photographic image of Wells that is now known. The silhouette is reported to have been in the possession of the Wells family, but the provenance of the tintype could not initially be traced. A manuscript note (Illustration 27), pinned into the lid of the later nineteenth-century embossed, gutta-percha or composition case in which the tintype is mounted, merely records, "Horace Wells, the Hartford Ct. discoverer of the use of nitrous oxide gas to produce insensibility to pain. For the Medical Library."

The authenticity of this as a tintype and not a daguerreotype has been verified by several experts on the history of photography. This copy of the original Wells's daguerreotype was thought to have been made between 1856, when the tintype (originally called a melaino-type or a ferrotype) was introduced, and the 1870s or 1880s, when the popularity of the tintype began to wane. And more than one may have been made. The tintype presented to the Boston Medical Library was mounted in the usual small, squarish, embossed case that was commonly employed for holding tintypes, so that they could be safely and conveniently carried in the coat pocket or purse. However, since such cases were modeled after earlier daguerreotype cases, which tended to be larger and oblong in shape, confusion might arise in the mind of anyone not versed in nineteenth-century photography as to whether the Wells's image was a tintype or a daguerreotype.

This image, however, was reproduced on tin and not on copper and has the usual features of a tintype, although it was lacquered over to protect it, giving it some of the glossy, mirror-like appearance of a daguerreotype.[7] On the back of a piece of lining paper, which was discovered when the portrait was removed from its case and its inner mounting to verify the medium and allow it to be photographed, is written in pencil, "Dr. Horace Wells of Hartford Ct." The present whereabouts of Wells's original daguerreotype is not known at this time.

For two or three years after its discovery, the origin of the tintype and the identity of its donor remained unknown. However, the donor was subsequently identified as Truman Howe Bartlett, the sculptor of the statue of Wells that in 1875 was erected in Hartford's Bushnell Park. In 1887, Bartlett gave to the Boston Medical Library a bronze death mask of Wells, which he had employed in creating the face on his statue, together with a copy of the 1867 edition of Truman Smith's *An Enquiry into the Origin of Modern Anaesthesia*, a work which will figure significantly in this study. Onto the free endpaper of the book he had penned the note:

From T. H. Bartlett
June 1887.
The death mask of Horace Wells was taken three weeks after death by John M. Riggs, dentist, of Hartford, Conn.
The state of Conn., & the city of Hartford, erected a bronze statue of Wells in Bushnell Park, in that city in 1875.[8]

It would appear that Riggs loaned the original death mask that he had made of Wells, a fact previously unknown,[9] or a casting of it[10], to Bartlett about 1873 or 1874 to help the latter authenticate his statue. And because Bartlett's handwriting in the Smith volume exactly matches the hand that wrote the note pinned into the tintype case, it would be reasonable to assume that the tintype was copied from the original daguerreotype at about the same time and for the same purpose, and that it, too, was probably given to the library along with the mask and Smith book, or shortly afterwards.[11]

There is little doubt about the verisimilitude of the likeness in the tintype and its striking resemblance to the still-youthful and handsome face in Flagg's portrait. The posture of the figure in his three quarter length painting is also that of the full length silhouette in Illustration 26 (making allowances for the transposition from a lateral to a frontal view and the possibility that the image was reversed in order to accommodate the direction and angle of the original daguerreotype that Flagg employed). In both the silhouette and Flagg's painting, we can see that one leg is slightly forward and partly flexed, the other straightened to support the torso, one arm not quite akimbo on the hip.

Other identical or near identical features appearing in Flagg's picture and in the silhouette and tintype include the rounded head and bob coiffure typical in those times; Wells's somewhat sensuous face, with more than a hint of a double chin; the cravat knotted above a high stiff collar; and the broad, probably velvet lapels of a three quarter Prince Albert coat. In his presentation letter Flagg informed us that he had followed his father's description of Wells's dress. Jared Flagg had attended Trinity College and had remained in Hartford during Wells's residence there and, hence, could describe Wells's attire to his son. Jared Flagg died in 1899, at about the same time that his son was completing Wells's portrait.

Thus, the silhouette now in the Boston Medical Library's collections appears to be the silhouette which, Flagg stated, was cut by Wells himself. And the signature mounted on the bottom of the mat bordering the silhouette—both the frame and mat are modern, indicating reframing in recent times—is an authentic autograph of Horace Wells. However, it is obvious from the remnants of letters above and below that it had been cut from a letter or document. It could have been placed there in recent times, or it may have been re-mounted at the time of the reframing, having been removed from an earlier, or even the original matting.[12]

We have found no evidence that the silhouette was done by any-one other than Wells, nor have we been able to attribute it to any known artisan of that era. However, with its sepia wash or pencil background, it appears to be in the style of the best known and most prolific artisan working in that medium in America at the time, the French silhouettist Auguste Edouart. It was Edouart's custom to have simple scenes lithographed onto paper, or sometimes to have artists sketch them in simple ink-wash grounds, over which the silhouette was later pasted. This gave the black silhouette a richer and more picture-like quality.

Auguste Edouart came to America in 1840 and remained here for nearly a decade, touring parts of New England, the Eastern Sea-board, and the South in search of patrons. He went as far north as Brattleboro, Vermont and as far south as New Orleans. He was particularly fond of Saratoga Springs, where he spent five summers cutting silhouettes of wealthy vacationers and their entourages who flocked there to drink the medicinal waters and attend the famous thoroughbred races. It was Edouart's custom to insert a duplicate copy of the silhouette he had cut into an album or pattern book which he retained, and one of his American albums has survived intact, as has a list of subjects who sat for him between 1839 and 1845 when he was actively pursuing his art in the United States.[13] This sole surviving American album was recently published in fac-simile by its owner, Andrew Oliver, in a volume entitled *Auguste Edouart's Silhouettes of Eminent Americans, 1839–1844*.[14]

There is no reference to Horace Wells or any indication that Edouart ever worked in Hartford in the "Complete List of 3,800 Silhouette Portraits of American Citizens Taken Between 1839–1849 by August [sic] Edouart During His Tour of the United States," which makes an appendix to the Oliver book.[15] Furthermore, the Wells silhouette appears somewhat crude when compared with the facsimiles in the Oliver publication, and it lacks the embellishments so characteristic of the French master. Edouart cut miniature objects such as eyeglasses and walking canes, and often buttons or a collar

Illustration 28. Reproductions of two silhouettes, no. 133, John Ross, left, and no. 112, Robert Gould Shaw, right, from Andrew Oliver's *Auguste Edouart's Silhouette of Eminent Americans, 1839–1844.* These show his most typical styles in poses similar to the silhouette of Horace Wells in Figure 2. Courtesy of the University Press of Virginia.

are shown through minute cutouts or a slit in the silhouette through which the underlying white background appears. Many of his creations are also highlighted by silver pen strokes outlining hair style, the contours of arms and legs, military braid, sheen on lapels, and many other external features (Illustration 28). In fact, such additions are almost the signature of Auguste Edouart.

It seems possible that Wells may have seen the works of the French artist during sojourns to Boston in the 1841–1844 period and imitated them. The background of the Wells silhouette—the outline of what appears to be the porch of a cottage or rural home, with a lake and hills in the background—is reminiscent of an Edouart silhouette. Edouart was in Boston between October 1841 and June 1842 and cut silhouettes of hundreds of prominent citizens as well as eminent visitors. It was Edouart's custom to sign the copies he sold and to write the name and title or occupation of the subject and the date of the sitting onto them. However, no such markings appear on the Wells silhouette.

There is additional evidence that the nearly full-length silhouette presented to the Boston Medical Library in 1985 originated in the Wells family. Its donor, Dr. John Bockstoce of South Dartmouth, Massachusetts, referred us to his mother when asked for details about its history and provenance. Mrs. Clifton Bockstoce (née Elizabeth Roberts) subsequently informed us that she had inherited the silhouette from her grandfather, Henry Roberts (1853–1926), who had been Governor of Connecticut in 1905–1907. His parents, born in the early 1830's, had been lifelong friends of the Wells family. Undoubtedly, it was with Charles T. Wells, Horace Wells's son, and perhaps with Horace Wells's widow, but not with Horace Wells himself, that the Roberts family had been friendly. Mrs. Bockstoce reported that the silhouette had been given to either her great-grandfather or grandfather by a member of the Wells family.[16] Since it apparently was used by Charles N. Flagg in 1898 or 1899 in composing his portrait of Horace Wells, it can be assumed that Governor Roberts acquired it from Charles Wells sometime afterwards. Flagg later—in 1906—painted a portrait of Henry Roberts which now hangs in the Connecticut State Library Museum.

Indeed, additional evidence concerning the silhouette's origin has recently come to light. During a trip to the Historical Museum of

Medicine in Dentistry, its Curator, Dr. Leonard F. Menczer, drew our attention to a little-known portrait of Horace Wells's widow, Elizabeth Wales Wells, which now hangs in the dental office of Dr. Philip S. Moran of West Hartford (Illustration 34).[17] We also found hanging in Dr. Moran's office an engraved portrait of Horace Wells by H. B. Hall which has an undated, two-page letter affixed to the back of its frame. This letter, which contains information about Charles T. Wells's relationship with Governor Roberts and his wife, was written to Dr. Charles E. Barrett, the Governor's dentist, by Mrs. Roberts who was presenting him with the Hall engraving (which she incorrectly presumed to be a photograph because a legend at its base states that it had been copied from an original photograph).

> Dear Dr. Barrett—
> I hope that this little sketch will answer the purpose for which you wanted it. So far as I *know* (and I handled *every* thing that Charles T. Wells possessed) there isn't another photograph of Horace Wells existing, with the exception of one like yours, in the book in the Historical Soc. giving a sketch of the proceedings against Dr. Morton's claims.[18] If you haven't seen that book I think it would be of great interest to you. I have labeled the gift of the photograph from Mr. Roberts, as I thought he would like to be the *donor,* owing to his fondness for *you.*
>
> Very Sincerely,
> Carolyn Roberts

At the top of the second page of her letter she wrote briefly about Horace Wells's experimentation with anesthesia and about his subsequent death. She concluded:

> This photograph was given to Dr. Charles E. Barrett, by his patient, Gov. Henry Roberts who obtained it from Horace Wells's son, the late Charles T. Wells.

It is obvious from the tone of her letter that Mr. Robert was writing after the Governor's death in 1926.[19]

Contemporary dental directories indicate that Dr. Barrett practiced dentistry in Hartford from at least the mid 1890s (when the directories began) until the 1930s and possibly later. In 1921 he was joined in practice by his son, Charles E. Barrett Jr., who inherited his father's practice and his collection of Wells memorabilia. Dr. Moran practiced with the younger Dr. Barrett and acquired these materials when assuming Barrett's practice.

Mrs. Robert's letter adds additional support to the belief that the silhouette originated in the Wells family. She states that she handled *everything* that Charles T. Wells possessed, indicating close friendship with him and suggesting involvement in the disposal of Charles's estate, which appears to have included the full-length silhouette of Horace Wells used by Flagg for his painting of Wells. Thus, available evidence tends to confirm C. N. Flagg's assertion that both the silhouette and the daguerreotype from which our tintype was copied had their origins with Horace Wells himself.

All of the portraiture of Horace Wells known to him was reproduced by W. Harry Archer when he published his "Life and Letters of Horace Wells" study in 1944. In addition to the Flagg portrait, which he placed at the front of his article, and the death mask, which he placed in the Appendix, Archer reproduced the steel engraving by H. B. Hall based on an original photograph of Wells (Illustration 29); an unsigned oil portrait of him that hung in his son Charles's home until the latter's death in 1909 (Illustration 31); and more recent portraits, one completed by Verona Kiralfy (about 1940) and another by James McManus (painted probably in the 1920s). Archer's article also illustrates miniature oil paintings on ivory of Dr. Wells and his wife (Illustration 30) and a silhouette of Horace Wells's bust (Illustration 32).

The steel engraving made by H. B. Hall in the 1860s is the most frequently encountered image of Horace Wells. It, too, was based on a photograph of Wells, though assumedly a different one than the daguerreotype available to Flagg, because in it Wells's pose and features are different. The steel engraving is additionally interesting because two other oil portraits of Wells illustrated by Archer—those painted by Kiralfy and McManus—appear to have been based on it. A third portrait, the one owned by Wells's son, may also have been based on the Hall engraving, although it might have been based directly on the original photograph used by Hall. The pose and features in these three are nearly identical. And it would not be unreasonable to suppose that the photograph upon which the Hall

Horace Wells

The value of a safe anaesthetic agent, which can be used without anticipation of danger by the patient, is a great boon to suffering humanity.

J. M. CARNOCHAN, M. D.,
Surgeon-in-Chief to the State Emigrant's Hospital, N. Y., etc., etc.

" Let full and ample justice be done to that noble genius which first conceived the grand idea which has been the basis of all the experiments and the father of all the discoveries. To the spirit of Dr. HORACE WELLS belongs the honor of having given to suffering humanity the greatest boon ever received from science."

C. H. HAYWOOD,
Formerly House Surgeon of the Mass. General Hospital.

No one, I think, who has taken pains to examine the evidence on the subject, can doubt that the honor of the discovery belongs to the late Dr. HORACE WELLS, of Hartford, Conn.

DR. G. Q. COLTON,
Colton Dental Association.

AN INQUIRY
INTO THE
"ORIGIN OF MODERN ANAESTHESIA,"
By Hon. TRUMAN SMITH.
FOR SALE HERE.

Illustration 29. Advertisement for the Honorable Truman Smith's *An Inquiry into the Origin of Modern Anaesthesia*, published at Hartford in 1867 in defense of Horace Wells' claim to priority for the discovery of anesthesia. It reproduces a steel engraving of Wells made by H. B. Hall of New York. The same portrait also appeared as the frontispiece of Smith's book, where the engraving is signed "Engd. by H. B. Hall, from a Photograph." Courtesy of the Boston Medical Library in The Francis A. Countway Library of Medicine.

Illustration 30. Miniature oil portraits on ivory of Horace Wells (left) and his wife, Elizabeth Wales Wells (right), painted about 1839, shortly after their marriage. These were presented by W. Harry Archer to the Smithsonian Institution, and are now republished with the permission of Mrs. W. Harry Archer and the Smithsonian Institution.

Illustration 31. The portrait of Horace Wells that hung in his son Charles's home until Charles's death in 1909. Its present location is unknown. It appears to have been copied by an unidentified artist in the latter nineteenth century (possibly by Charles T. Wells himself) after the steel engraving by H. B. Hall reproduced in Illustration 29, or after the original photograph upon which the Hall engraving is based. Reproduced from W. H. Archer's "Life and Letters of Horace Wells."

Illustration 32. Silhouette of Horace Wells, made by an unidentified artisan, with Wells's authentic signature mounted at its base. Courtesy of the Historical Museum of Medicine and Dentistry where it now hangs.

engraving was based was another daguerreotype made by Wells himself.

The Hall engraving first appeared as the frontispiece to an 1860 anonymous publication entitled *Dr. Wells, the Discoverer of Anaesthesia*, which summed up evidence supporting Horace Well's priority to the discovery,[20] but there appeared no reference here as to who had engraved it; Wells's signature was reproduced beneath it, and it was accompanied by a lithographed facsimile of a letter of Elizabeth Wells that is discussed in the profile on her (pages 236–237). The plate was re-employed in touched up and more finished form, giving it something of a photographic appearance, in the 1867 edition of Truman Smith's *An Examination of the Question of Anaesthesia,*[21] and on an advertisement for that work (Illustration 29); and it also reappeared in the 1870 reissue of the *Dr. Wells, the Discoverer of Anaesthesia* pamphlet (but now without Elizabeth's letter).[22] In the Smith publication, and in the 1870 reissue, the caption "Engd. by H. B. Hall from a Photograph" appears beneath, indicating who had produced it.

In the article on Elizabeth Wells, it has been noted that while corresponding with his publisher, when preparing the final 1867 edition of his *An Examination of the Question of Anaesthesia,* Smith informed the publisher that he would be sending on the plate, which begs the assumption that he was author of the other work as well. Notwithstanding, it is somewhat ironic that in 1858 Henry Bryan Hall[23] also engraved two plates depicting W. T. G. Morton administering ether, which were published in Nathan P. Rice's *Trials of a Public Benefactor,* a work supporting Morton's claim to the discovery of painless surgery.[24]

The miniatures of the youthful Wells and his wife (Illustration 30) undoubtedly were made soon after their marriage in 1838. Archer attributes the painting of these to the year 1839.[25] They are naive pieces, possibly the products of an itinerant artist of moderate talent. They are noteworthy, nonetheless, because the portrait of Wells is the earliest known likeness of him and the only painting of him we know of that was done from life. However, the image of Wells on this miniature is not nearly so vivid or so representative of the man as is that in the tintype, which remains the only photographic representation of Wells from life. Dr. Archer owned these two miniatures at the time he published his "Life and Letters" study, but he afterwards donated them to the Smithsonian Institution.

The unsigned portrait of Wells which hung in his son Charles's home (Illustration 31) seems to be a copy made either from the Hall engraving or from a photograph upon which the Hall engraving was based.[26] (More likely it was the former, and it could even have been made from the very copy that Carolyn Roberts presented to Dr. Barrett.) Charles Wells loaned or bequeathed this painting to his cousin Arthur Wells Cole, the son of Horace Wells's sister who died at Chicago in 1900. By the time that Archer published his 1944 study of Horace Wells, the painting was in the possession of the widow of Arthur Wells Cole. An interesting aspect of this painting, which we will shortly suggest, is that it could have been painted by Charles T. Wells himself.

Both the Kiralfy and McManus portraits appear to have been based upon the Hall engraving. The McManus portrait was painted probably in the 1920s, possibly at the instigation of the artist's uncle, Dr. James McManus, who was Dental Commissioner of Connecticut and owner of Horace Wells's "Day Book," which is discussed in another article in this collection.[27] It now hangs in the Historical Museum of Medicine and Dentistry in Hartford. The Kiralfy portrait, painted about 1940, was commissioned to be part of the collection of Wells's letters and memorabilia established by Dr. Archer at the School of Dentistry at the University of Pittsburgh.[28] Unfortunately, that collection has since been scattered and the whereabouts of Kiralfy's portrait, and many of the documents and memorabilia relating to Horace Wells which Dr. Archer assembled, are presently unknown.[29] (Part of this portrait is, however, visible in the photograph of Dr. Archer that appears as Illustration 24.)

Finally, Archer reproduces a silhouette of Horace Wells's bust made by an unknown artist (Illustration 32).[30] He provides no information about its making or provenance, merely locating it in "the Walter R. Steiner Medical Library, Hartford Conn." This small, delicate and most interesting depiction of Horace Wells now hangs in the Historical Museum of Medicine and Dentistry in Hartford. Cut from a lighter colored paper than that used for the full-length silhouette discussed earlier, this rendering shows such features as hair and parts of clothing accented in darker tones by means of

Illustration 33. Oil portrait of Horace Wells located at the Historical Museum of Medicine and Dentistry, Hartford. The portrait is unsigned and undated, but may have been painted in Wells's lifetime, possibly by Charles Hine. Courtesy of the Historical Museum of Medicine and Dentistry.

Illustration 34. Oil portrait of Elizabeth Wales Wells, the wife of Horace Wells, by an unknown artist, possibly Jared Flagg or Charles Hine. This portrait now hangs in the dental office of Dr. Philip S. Moran of West Hartford, Connecticut. Originating in the Wells family, it passed to Dr. Moran through Henry Roberts, former Governor of Connecticut, and Dr. Charles E. Barrett, Governor Roberts's dentist, and through Dr. Barrett's son, Dr. Charles E. Barrett, Jr., to its present owner. Courtesy of Dr. Philip S. Moran, West Hartford, Connecticut.

pencil or brush; a bit of white shows beneath the cravat, and there are also white strokes in the hair. Once more, we see a reflection of Edouart's style in a silhouette of Horace Wells. The likeness, like the full-length silhouette, contains Wells's holographic signature mounted at its base. It is a fine, delicate work with qualities reminiscent of a photograph. One is tempted to speculate whether it, too, could have been cut by Horace Wells himself, perhaps using a daguerreotype as its model.[31]

During our visit to the Historical Museum of Medicine and Dentistry we were surprised to find yet another oil portrait of Horace Wells (Illustration 33), one that we had not been aware of previously, and one which had not been reproduced before. Although this portrait appeared to be unsigned, and there was no identification of its subject, it obviously depicted Horace Wells. It is a fine likeness and a delicate and highly artistic representation as well, in fact, the most sensitive depiction of Wells that we know of. Both the painting and its frame seem to date to about the middle of the nineteenth century, or slightly after. One is left with the impression that it was probably painted from life or posthumously by a professional artist who had known Horace Wells personally, for it is fresher, less stiff, and depicts a more youthful and a more placid and contented Horace Wells than do other oil portraits of him. There is a breath of life about it. Although there is some similarity between it and the Hall steel engraving, the hair is bushier in the portrait and there are other variances.

When we encountered this portrait initially, we found it hanging high up on the wall of a room that had little natural light. As a result, it appeared, upon close inspection, to bear no signature or identification of its maker. More recently, during a visit to Hartford, the primary author viewed the picture in a different location and light and thought he detected the initials "C.H." in its lower right hand corner, a matter which could not be verified subsequently through photography, for the picture is dark and in need of cleaning.

Subsequent research on local and area artists turned up two individuals with these initials: Chester Harding (1792–1866), a notable portrait painter of Northampton, Massachusetts, and Charles Hine (1827–1871), who actually did paint for a while in Hartford. After further research and consultation with museum curators, it appeared unlikely that Harding painted this portrait. However, such research indicated that it was indeed possible that Hine could have. Hine, like Jared Flagg, began the study of art (in 1842, at age fifteen) with George Whiting Flagg and afterwards continued to study with Jared Flagg until about 1844.[32] Definitive assignment of this portrait to Charles Hine, however, or to any other artist for that matter, will have to await the results of further investigation, and, for the time being, Hine's connection with it remains merely a possibility.

The unsigned oil portrait of Horace's wife, Elizabeth (Illustration 34), which we found hanging in the dental office of Dr. Moran in West Hartford, was reputed to have been painted by Charles T. Wells. Dr. Moran informed us that when he had acquired this painting, it had been accompanied by a "paper" documenting this fact. However, he could not locate this document during our visit, and his subsequent searches have not turned it up. The portrait of Mrs. Wells is a striking one, with fine, vivid coloring, despite the fact that it is badly in need of cleaning and restoration. It appears to be the work of a professional artist and not of an amateur, as Charles Wells was. Although we will soon show that Charles did, indeed, paint portraits, his ability and technique was not up to that displayed in the Elizabeth Wells portrait, which is an exceptional one. We have submitted photographs of this picture to a number of museum curators, and all agree that it was painted by a professional, and one of them has ventured the guess (as we had) that it could have been painted by Jared Flagg or Charles Hine.[33] Judging from Elizabeth's appearance and age in this portrait, it seems likely that it was painted before 1846, when she was in her late twenties, and the picture of her husband, which we have attributed to the hand of Charles Hine, could have been painted contemporarily. In fact, it seems likely that, like the miniatures on ivory, the two could have been painted at about the same time and perhaps by the same artist.

One other portrait of Horace Wells remains to be considered. This oil painting (Illustration 35) hangs in the foyer of the Harvard School of Dental Medicine. Records at Harvard's Fogg Art Museum identify this as a portrait of Horace Wells and indicate that it was presented to Harvard University in 1927 by Dr. Charles P. Briggs, whose brother Dr. E. C. Briggs had intended it to go to the Harvard Dental School.[34] Since this portrait seems to show a man older than

Illustration 35. Oil portrait of Horace Wells, which now hangs in the lobby of the Harvard School of Dental Medicine. The monogram "CTW" appearing in its lower left hand corner and shown in enlarged form above, represents the initials of Charles T. Wells, Horace Wells' son, who undoubtedly painted it. The above photographs were taken before the picture was recently restored. Courtesy of the Harvard School of Dental Medicine.

Wells was at the time of his death, and because features in it appear different from other pictures of him, initially we were somewhat doubtful about it being a likeness of Wells. However, subsequent viewing and details which later came to our attention overcame our initial skepticism and convinced us that it does indeed depict Horace Wells. Furthermore, evidence exists which indicates that it had actually been painted by Charles T. Wells.

Registration records at the Fogg Museum recorded that the artist was unknown, but that the initials "CW" or "CIW" had been detected on a monogram in the lower left hand corner of the painting (Illustration 35). The C appears above the W, with a line, making up the letter I (or more likely T), crossing them.[35] As these are the initials of Charles T. Wells, it seems reasonable to conclude, in light of the evidence provided by Dr. Moran, that he was the artist who created this work. The hands in the portrait are somewhat crudely and amateurishly painted, indicating a limited ability on the part of the artist, although overall the portrait is fairly well done.[36]

Another interesting aspect of this picture is that it was painted over the unfinished portrait of a woman (Illustration 36), who we believe to be Elizabeth Wales Wells. The underpainting was discovered when the portrait was x-rayed many years ago.[37] The female face is situated to the left and slightly above the area of the canvas where Horace's hands appear in figure 11, and it faces in the opposite direction, looking towards Horace's face. Thus, the artist initially painted Elizabeth in the area of the canvas opposite to where he eventually overpainted Dr. Wells.

The painting beneath not only shows the face of a woman, but it displays many of the features of Elizabeth Wales Wells evident in Illustrations 30, 34, and especially 36: the large, bovine, deep-set eyes, the fleshy, sensuous lips, the long curving nose which dips under at its base and protrudes at the outer nostrils, the curve of the eyebrows. Only the hairline appears slightly different, although it, too, is similar. The face painted in Illustration 36 has been "recaptured" through the medium of x-ray, which does not provide coloration and requires the interpretation of shadows. But it does seem to tell enough.

We now have a comprehensive record of the portraiture of Horace Wells; furthermore, we possess direct evidence of the involvement of

Illustration 36. Photograph of an x-ray of the portrait of a woman, appearing to be Elizabeth Wales Wells, found beneath the portrait of Horace Wells probably painted by the son, Charles T. Wells. Courtesy of the Harvard School of Dental Medicine and the Fogg Art Museum of Harvard University.

both him and his son in creating it. And the recently discovered (or more accurately, rediscovered) tintype and the full-length silhouette, both of which can be attributed to Wells's own making, are important additions to the iconography of the man, as are the portraits of Wells and his wife in Illustrations 33 and 34. In addition to giving us, through the tintype, the best image *from life* of this seminal contributor to the advancement of surgery, they provide a picture to the sensitivity, artistry, and inventiveness of the person who is still looked upon by many, in and outside of Hartford, as the true discoverer of surgical anesthesia.

Notes

1. Flagg's letter is reprinted on the verso of a reproduction of his painting of Horace Wells that serves as the frontispiece to W. Harry Archer's "Life and Letters of Horace Wells, Discoverer of Anesthesia, Chronologically Arranged, with an Appendix," *Journal of the American College of Dentists* 2, no. 2 (June 1944): 81–210. This long article, which constitutes the best biography of Wells to date, was also issued as a separate pamphlet.

2. Information on Charles Noel Flagg derives mainly from an article on him that accompanies an exhibition of his and his family's work at the Connecticut Historical Society in 1975: Helen D. Perkins, "Charles Noel Flagg, A.N.A., 1848–1916," *Connecticut Historical Society Bulletin,* 40 (1975): 97–140. The major part of Perkin's article is devoted to a checklist of C. N. Flagg's paintings. Some data on Flagg and his family had been provided at the time of an earlier exhibition of their works, *Paintings by the Flagg Family,* issued by the Wadsworth Atheneum for the exhibition of 2 February–1 March 1944. Information of Jared Flagg and the other Flaggs also derives from George C. Groce and David H. Wallace, *The New-York Historical Society's Dictionary of Artists in America. 1564–1860* (New Haven, Yale University Press [1957]), 230.

3. The best source of Flagg family genealogy is Norman Gershom Flagg and Lucius C. S. Flagg, *Family Records of the Descendants of Gershom Flagg (born 1730) of Lancaster, Massachusetts, with Other Genealogical Records of the Flagg Family Descended from Thomas Flegg of Watertown, Mass. and Including the Flegg Lineage in England* ([Quincy, Ill.] 1907). The American Flaggs were descended from

Lieut. Gershom Flagg (born Watertown, Mass., 1641; slain by Indians at Lamprey River, New Hampshire, 1690), the son of Thomas Flegg who had emigrated from England to Massachusetts in the 1630's. The line through which the painter Charles Noel Flagg descended was founded by John Flagg (born 1673) of Boston, the third son of Lieut. Gershom Flagg, and Henry Collins Flagg (born 1724), of Charleston, South Carolina. John Flagg's descendants had wandered south to Rhode Island, Connecticut, and South Carolina. It was from the South Carolina branch that the painter Washington Alston descended, as did the grandfather of Charles Noel Flagg, Henry Collins Flagg, Jr., who practiced law in Charleston and in New Haven, Connecticut. The Flagg family of dentists descended from the eldest of Lieut. Gershom Flagg's sons, also named Gershom (born 1669). The second Gershom Flagg had a son, also named Gershom, whose son Josiah (born 1737) of Boston was known as Col. Josiah Flagg because he had been an officer of the Rhode Island line in the Revolution. His son Josiah was the "Boston dentist." The latter, who was also a musician, later practiced dentistry in Providence, Rhode Island.

4. J. F. B. Flagg, *Ether and Chloroform: Their Employment in Surgery, Dentistry, Midwifery, Therapeutics, Etc.* (Philadelphia, Lindsay and Blakiston, 1851). Flagg, who used only his initials on his publications, listed himself on the title-page here as "Member of the Rhode Island Medical Society." According to an unpublished "Catalogue of the Rhode Island Medical Society, 1812–1916" (of which a xeroxed copy is in the Rare Books Department of the Countway Library), "John Foster Brewster Flagg" was admitted to membership in 1840, moved to Philadelphia in 1842, and died in 1872 at the age of sixty-eight (which would date his birth to about 1804). Charles R. E. Koch's *History of Dental Surgery,* v. 2, p. 14) reports that John F. Brewster Flagg (Brewster was the maiden name of his mother, Eliza, who appears to have been "the Boston dentist's" second wife) was the inventor of the lateral vacuum cavity for dentures and was the first professor of anatomy and physiology at the old Philadelphia College of Dental Surgery which later reorganized as the Pennsylvania College of Dental Surgery. Forty-five years ago excerpts from the diary of John B. F. Flagg's son, Josiah Foster Flagg (died 1903), were published. (He had been named after his Boston uncle.) Josiah Foster Flagg's diary records his experiences as a forty-niner in search of his fortune following his graduation from Jefferson Medical College and before attending the Philadelphia College of Dental Surgery and entering the profession that his family had followed for several generations, ac-

cording to N[icholas] W[ainwright], "A Philadelphia Forty-Niner," *Pennsylvania Magazine of History and Biography* 70 (1946): 390–422. Attempts to link a pioneering anesthetist of this century, Paluel J. Flagg (1886–1970), who was born in Yonkers, New York, and practiced in many hospitals in New York City and its environs, to this line of dentists have proved unsuccessful.

5. The city directories of Boston for the years 1834–36 listed only four individuals designated as "dentist" or "surgeon-dentist" with whom Wells could have studied: T. W. Parsons, J. F. Flagg, N. C. Keep, and D. Harwood. Keep had built up a wide reputation for proficiency in mechanical dentistry, and since Horace Wells's parents were able to give their children the best, it might well be that Wells was apprenticed to Keep. Keep is alleged to have been the first in America to administer ether in an obstetrical case at the unattended delivery of Fanny Longfellow in 1847. (Charles B. Pittinger, "The Anesthetization of Fanny Longfellow for Childbirth on April 7, 1847," *Anesthesia and Analgesia* 66, 1987: 368–69). In 1868 Keep became the first Dean of the newly organized Dental School of Harvard University, as well as its Professor of Mechanical Dentistry. An argument against Wells's having studied with Josiah Foster Flagg can be based on evidence in the United States House of Representatives, *Report to the House of Representatives of the United States of America, Vindicating the Rights of Charles T. Jackson to the Discovery of the Anaesthetic Effect of Ether Vapor, and Disproving the Claims of W. T. G. Morton to That Discovery* (Boston, Printed by Authority of the Minority Committee [1852]), which lists (p. 50) Josiah F. Flagg among a group of physicians and others who signed a petition supporting Jackson's claim. While Flagg was known to oppose Morton's claim because Morton had initially withheld the identity of his preparation, hoping to patent and profit from it, one might suppose that he would have been inclined to support Wells's claim instead of Jackson's had Wells studied with him in the 1834 period.

6. Helen D. Perkins, "Charles Noel Flagg, A. N. A., 1848–1916."

7. Tintypes were often mounted in paper envelopes with a cutout through which the picture could be seen. Also, special albums for holding them were introduced. The tintype was particularly popular during the Civil War because it was rugged and could be sent through mails easily and safely. Tintypes came to be mounted in cases similar to daguerreotype cases but smaller and of lighter construction. During the Civil War many tintype operators followed the armies and made small fortunes recording the faces of soldiers in the field. Although

the demand for daguerreotype cases had practically ceased, with the coming of the war the manufacturing of such cases took on new life. In the summer of 1862, one stockhouse received an order for 3,000 gross of these cases from one operator alone. See Robert Taft, *Photography and the American Scene: a Social History, 1839–1889* (New York, Macmillan Co., 1938; Dover Publications, Inc. [1946]), 160–62.

8. Bartlett's note was discovered accidentally after the volume containing it was recataloged recently. A Boston Medical Library Association bookplate mounted on the pastedown endpaper indicates that this copy was received (that is, was accessioned) on July 15, 1887, the gift of T. H. Bartlett, Esq. Truman Howe Bartlett (1835–1921), who studied sculpture under Fremier in Paris, for nearly a quarter of a century held the appointment as Lecturer on Modeling (Sculpture) at the Massachusetts Institute of Technology. His sculpture of Horace Wells is reproduced on p. 175 of the Archer study, with accompanying description on pp. 174 and 176, and as Illustration 37 here. Bartlett was a student or protégé of the art anatomist and sculptor Dr. William Rimmer. Three years after Rimmer's death, he published a full length biography of the man. Truman Howe Bartlett, *The Art Life of William Rimmer, Sculptor, Painter, and Physician* (Boston, James R. Osgood and Co., 1882; 2nd ed., Houghton Mifflin and Co., 1890). The Boston Medical Library possesses among a collection of Rimmer's drawings, manuscript notebooks and other materials which his daughter Caroline donated earlier in this century a scrapbook containing drawings copied after illustrations that Rimmer had made on the blackboard during his lectures on art anatomy. These were recorded on paper by Bartlett and the illustrator and architect Hammatt Billings and mounted within. Bartlett's son, Paul Wayland Bartlett, a student of Auguste Rodin, achieved a national reputation as a sculptor.

9. When illustrating the bronze death mask on p. 190 of his study of Horace Wells, Archer related that the date on which the mask was made or by whom was unknown. He further noted that the authorities of the Boston Medical Library could find no reference to its acquisition, specifying only that it had been in the Library for a great many years. The Library's Director, James F. Ballard, remembered only that it had hung in a building that the Library had previously occupied before 1904 and supposed that the Library had acquired it sometime before 1892. We now know the full facts of the matter, and, as is noted elsewhere in this book, that John Riggs made the mask *three days,* and not three weeks after Wells's death. The combined "Twelfth and Thirteenth Annual Reports" of the Boston Medical Library for

the years ending October, 1888 contain in a section of "Special Donations" the entry, "Mr. F. [sic] H. Bartlett. Bronze death-mask of Dr. Horace Wells of Hartford Ct."

10. Bartlett presented this bronze casting to the Library two years after Dr. Rigg's death in 1885. We do not know whether Riggs or Bartlett arranged for the casting. The casting could have been made in America, from a plaster mold that Riggs had made some time after Wells's death. Being versed in the mechanical arts and in molding metal in his dental practice, it is possible that Riggs made the casting himself. It is also possible that he (or Bartlett) had the work done at a nearby foundry. A foundry at Chicopee, Massachusetts, located about twenty-five miles north of Hartford, began making castings of sculptures in the 1860 decade, being among the first in America to do so. More likely, however, the casting was made in France about 1873 when Bartlett's statue of Wells was being cast in Paris.

11. Wells's countenance on Bartlett's statue closely resembles the casting of the original mask that Riggs made. This fact, and the fact that Bartlett had the casting in his possession, indicate that Bartlett employed Riggs's original mask for authenticating the face on his Wells statue. And since the mask shows Wells's face only, and because Bartlett had the tintype in his possession also, it would be a likely conclusion that he (or Charles Wells) had Wells's original daguerreotype copied so that the sculptor could faithfully reproduce the details of Wells's hair, eyes, and other features.

12. We removed the silhouette from its frame in order to photograph it and to determine if any identification had been added to its back. We found several unintelligible pencil notes of arithmetic symbols at the top, possibly relating to its earlier framing. Across the bottom is written in an early, unidentified hand, "Profile of Horace Wells."

13. It was Edouart's custom to have the subject sign the face of the copy of the silhouette that he retained in an album, and on the front or back he wrote the names and biographical data of his sitters in case he might be asked to make additional copies. Some of these signatures and descriptions can be seen in the album cited in the following note.

14. Andrew Oliver, *Auguste Edouart's Silhouettes of Eminent Americans, 1839–1844* (Charlottesville, Va., Published for the National Portrait Gallery, Smithsonian Institution, by the University Press of Virginia [1977]).

15. While Edouart remained in the United States until 1849, he did not cut silhouettes after 1844 or 1845. In his introduction to the Oliver book, A. Hyatt Major speculates that Edouart may have spent the

end of the 1840s in New York, possibly supporting himself by giving French lessons as he had done earlier in England.

16. Personal communication from Mrs. Clifton Bockstoce of Bloomfield, Connecticut to Richard J. Wolfe, 13 August 1990.

17. We are greatly indebted to Dr. Leonard F. Menczer for his assistance in the preparation of this paper. His wide knowledge of Wells and of his milieu were important in giving us leads for additional research and for correcting errors that we made. He was also most helpful in drawing relevant materials to our attention.

18. Mrs. Roberts was undoubtedly referring to Truman Smith's *An Inquiry into the Origin of Modern Anaesthesia*, cited in note 21, which contains a frontispiece portrait of Horace Wells engraved after a photograph of him. It was a copy of this engraving that we found hanging in Dr. Moran's office.

19. A telephone call to Mrs. Bockstoce confirmed our strong suspicion that Carolyn Roberts, the writer of the letter, was the Governor's widow. In 1881, Roberts married Carrie E. Smith of New York. Mrs. Bockstoce related that her grandmother never liked her given name and used the name Carolyn instead. She also informed us that Carolyn Roberts lived until 1944 or 1945. Nonetheless, it seems a reasonable conclusion that she probably wrote this letter and made this gift within a few years of her husband's death, and perhaps closely following upon it.

20. *Dr. Wells, The Discoverer of Anaesthesia* (New York, J. A. Gray, Printer and Stereotyper, 1860).

21. Truman Smith, *An Inquiry into the Origin of Modern Anaesthesia* (Hartford, Brown and Gross, 1867). Smith, we know, championed Wells's cause in Congress in the 1850s and 1860s after the hearings were initiated to investigate the various claims for the discovery of anesthesia and award compensation for it. Smith published several works in support of Wells's claim. His 1867 *Inquiry*, which had appeared initially as a Congressional Study in 1853 and as a book under Smith's name in 1858 and 1859, was his final word on the subject.

22. *Dr. Wells, the Discoverer of Anaesthesia,* (Hartford, Case, Lockwood and Brainard, printer, 1870).

23. Henry Bryan Hall, an English engraver, and his son, Henry Bryan Hall, Jr. migrated to New York and established a very extensive business as engravers and publishers or portraits in the 1850s.

24. Nathan P. Rice, *Trials of a Public Benefactor, as Illustrated in the Discovery of Etherization* (New York: Pudney & Russell, 1859). This book has a frontispiece portrait of W. T. G. Morton, a plate depicting

Morton administering ether in his dental office prepatory to the operation which demonstrated the anesthetic powers of ether in surgery, and another plate showing Morton making the first public demonstration of etherization. In the earlier copies of the edition, there is also a lithographic reproduction of medals Morton received from the Institut National de France and the Académie Royale des Sciences.

25. W. Harry Archer, "Life and Letters of Horace Wells," 157.

26. Ibid., 154.

27. Archer reproduced the McManus portrait on p. 169 of his "Life and Letters of Horace Wells." James Goodwin McManus was born at Hartford in 1882. He was a pupil of Charles Noel Flagg, Montage Flagg, Robert B. Brandagee, and other local artists.

28. Verona Arnold Kiralfy was born in New York City in 1893. Her artistic career was passed mostly in the Pittsburgh area.

29. The original letters and documents pertaining to Horace Wells, which Dr. Archer collected and used when writing his biographical treatment of Wells, were, along with transcriptions of them and other Wells-related materials, presented to the University of Pittsburgh's School of Dental Medicine. Unfortunately, during a subsequent renovation of the School's quarters, they were misplaced, and the present whereabouts of part of the collection, including the original letters and documents, are unknown at this time. Part of Dr. Archer's files which have been located have recently been donated by Mrs. Archer to the Boston Medical Library in the Countway Library.

30. W. Harry Archer, "Life and Letters of Horace Wells," 168.

31. This "painted" silhouette of Wells measures only three and a half inches in height. As is the case with his full-length silhouette, Wells's signature appears on a separate slip of paper mounted at its base. Characteristics of this silhouette suggest that it may have been based on a photograph. It could date from the 1840s or afterwards, by which time daguerreotypy and photography were beginning to replace the silhouette as the popular form of image making. From the 1840s on, there were still many amateur silhouettists at work, but only professionals of lesser talent (Edouart excepted; his arrival brought about something of a rebirth of this art in America). The outstanding artisans who had worked in this medium in America at the end of the eighteenth century and during the first three decades of the nineteenth—the golden era—had either passed away or were doing other things. Those professionals still at work were "the lesser lights," observed Alice Van Leer Carrick, *Shades of Our Ancestors; American Profiles and Profilists* (Boston, Little, Brown and Co., 1928).

32. The only information on Charles Hine that I could find appears in

George C. Croce and David H. Wallace's *The New-York Historical Society's Dictionary of Artists in America,* p. 318. According to this source, Hine, after study in Hartford with Jared Flagg and two years of painting in Derby, Connecticut, returned to New Haven in 1846 and remained there for the next decade, before moving to New York City. His work with Flagg dated probably to the years 1842–1844, during which time this picture could have been painted from life. At the time that Hine studied with Flagg, Wells and Flagg were neighbors (see p. 386).

33. Elizabeth R. McClintock to Richard J. Wolfe, June 13, 1994, authors' files. Ms. McClintock is Assistant Curator of American Paintings, Sculpture and Drawings at the Wadsworth Atheneum.

34. Edward Cornelius Briggs received his D.M.D. degree from Harvard in 1878 and the M.D. degree two years later. He was a member of the Harvard dental faculty until 1915, when he became emeritus. He died in 1926.

35. Louise Ambler, formerly Curator of the Harvard University Portrait Collection, provided background information on the acquisition of this portrait and informed us about the monogram in the lower left hand corner of the painting.

36. We applied to Elizabeth R. McClintock of the Wadsworth Atheneum to learn if any information on Charles T. Wells as a painter existed in the Hartford area. Ms. McClintock, who kindly furnished us with a print of the Flagg portrait of Horace Wells for reproduction here and was helpful in other ways, reported that she could not locate information on Charles in any known source on Hartford and Connecticut artists; furthermore, there was no record of any work by him in an exhibition. Charles seems to have restricted his activities to family portraiture. His monogram on the painting in the Harvard School of Dental Medicine indicates that he sometimes signed his work. The monogram is hardly visible, being in an area almost covered by the frame; one needs the assistance of a flashlight to see it. There is, among the Wells family papers collected by W. Harry Archer, a letter written by Charles T. Wells to "Dear Uncle," possibly Joseph Wales, from Hartford on September 19, 1852. It consists of four pages, two of them designated "Friday morn," and two "Friday evening." It is the usual chatty letter that one would expect of a twelve or thirteen year old boy, with news of school, his boat, fishing and other matters of importance to a lad of that age. It would hardly be worth mentioning had not the postscript on its final page ended: "You said that you would send me some copies for drawing. Shall I send

you the drawings or send them back to you and the copies. Your
nephew C. T. Wells." This is the only reference known connecting
Charles to drawing and art and gives us a hint of his interest and
involvement in drawing at an early age. The location of the original
Wells family letters that Dr. Archer collected are presently unknown,
but photostats and transcriptions of most of them, including this letter
of Charles's, are now in The Francis A. Countway Library in Boston.

37. Dr. Henry D. Epstein of the Harvard dental faculty brought this
underlying picture to our attention. He had had an earlier x-ray of it
in his possession for many years but could not locate it for our use.
In order enable us to illustrate the underlying picture here, the Fogg
Art Museum authorities x-rayed the portrait anew.

11

The Redemption Of Horace Wells Through Public Art

Shirley Stallings and Michael Montagne

Horace Wells, the discoverer of modern anesthesia, became a public icon in 1875 when his bronze image was placed in the city park in Hartford, Connecticut. Information regarding Wells the man has been fragementary, often disdainful, and cloaked in mystery. Out of context documentation has encouraged speculation of a seemingly tragic man out of step with his world.[1] The view of Wells presented by Sykes, for example, is not atypical of this sort of speculation: "we know that he was irresolute, wayward and volatile, for he kept abandoning his dental practice in order to make a living in strange and unusual ways."[2] Wells's journey through life, however, was representative of what was occurring culturally to the people of New England during the early decades of the nineteenth century, as America embarked on a new phase within the framework established by the Pilgrims. Public art dedicated to Wells between 1875 and 1937, particularly in Hartford, constitutes im-

Illustration 37. (left): Front view of the statue of Horace Wells by Truman Howe Bartlett that was placed in Hartford's Bushnell Park in 1875; (right): Side view of the Bartlett statue, showing the book, bag and scroll at Wells's lower right and the base of his walking stick.

portant visual and documentary records of how society has viewed Wells the man and provides a better understanding of his accomplishments.

Perhaps the most instructive commemoration of Wells is the statue of him by Truman Howe Bartlett (1835–1921), which was cast in Paris by the French foundry of Gruet and placed in Hartford's primary public park on Thursday, July 22, 1875 (Illustration 37).[3] This academically unified, detailed, three-dimensional bronze portrays a full-length columnar embodiment of a trousered standing male figure. The head is defined by both the coiffure of bountiful hair with mutton chops down each cheek and a face squarely forward with eyes that are directed resolutely ahead of the figure. At the neck are shirt collar, cravat, stock, and waistcoat details exposed by the large collar of the expansively draped cloak gathered about the body by the left arm braced against the chest. The figure's left leg is placed forward and bent at the knee, while its weight is placed on the rigid straight right leg. Extending down alongside the body, the right arm, barely bent forward at the elbow, continues to where hand and walking-stick converge. The walking-stick persists in the downward angle to the toe of the booted right foot. Adjacent to the right foot, at the base of the walking-stick, is a grouping of objects that generates further impetus to the figure: a book on which is inscribed the word "Anesthesia," a small box, and a scroll imprinted with the words "I was desirous that it should be as free as the air we breathe" (Illustration 37).

Hartford During America's Renaissance

After the cataclysmic effects of the Civil War, a new chapter in the mission to move forward, to improve, and to expand the bounties of a free nation was declared. At a time when invention was transformed from novelty toy to useful tool which pitched American society into the throws of choking industrialism, art rose alongside to counterbalance the resulting social and moral disorder. Artists, scientists, and politicians all began to feel a new imperative to find some solid fundamentals on which to build for the future. That challenge was made easier by advances in scholarship and science which gave an impetus to the arts and put solid ground under them. No longer were the underlying ideas of religion and science as set forth by Isaac Newton almost two centuries before enough to explain the world order. Basic scientific thinking began to yield on every side. While science, utilitarian in its aims and humanitarian in principle, was always a part of American belief and existence, in the latter part of the nineteenth century it thoroughly merged with the American belief of progress. Faith in natural science had been characteristic of modern society for three hundred years, but never was there a time when this faith spread to so many people, or was held so firmly, so optimistically and with so few qualms or mental reservations as in the half-century preceding the First World War. The nation had a destiny, motivated by the new science of Charles Darwin.

Deeply absorbed in the evolving American experience since its early seventeenth century Puritan beginnings, Hartford, a second tier city on the Connecticut River, midway between Boston and New York City, aspired to the same materialistic and cultural flamboyance of the Gilded Age as did its neighbors. By the 1870s, many factors made Hartford, with an estimated population of 50,000 people, an attractive place for manufacturing and living. There were factories, armies of workers, and the sprawling sales forces of big business. National markets were created and supported by railroads and the telegraph. Hartford was the center of the nation's insurance business. There were twelve commercial banks, as well as eight savings banks and trust companies. The principal offices of sixty-four manufacturing companies found Hartford an attractive place of business, although many of their production plants were located elsewhere. The city maintained a paid fire department and a fire-alarm telegraph. And to ensure opportunity for moral and spiritual well-being, there were thirty-six churches in the city, many of them "models of tasteful architecture."[4]

To John Ruskin, the influential English nineteenth century art critic, environment was an imperative to his philosophy. He felt it was necessary "to get your country clean, and your people lovely." Ruskin advocated art to be, "not an escape from, but the way to life." In order for art to be a part of life, "the great business of art," Ruskin said, is "not only to produce things, but to see them, and to enable others to see them."[5] To that end, Hartford, as well as

America, embraced that philosophy as a morally renewing counterbalance to the industrialism that socially and environmentally laid
waste to urban areas in particular.

From 1858 on, cities all across America built large urban parks
designed in a pastoral style based on Hartford native Frederick Law
Olmstead's Central Park in New York City and Boston's Emerald
Necklace. Like Ruskin, Frederick Law Olmstead succinctly stated
his position that a park "should be made interesting by a process of
planting and decoration so that in necessarily passing through them,
whether in going to or from the park, or to and from business, some
substantial recreative advantage may be incidentally gained."[6]

The embryonic process of public art patronage in Hartford was
set in motion when the public park was designed in 1859, as "a
neatly laid-out enclosure of forty acres" by Jacob Weidenmann
(1829–1893), an emigre from Winterthur, Switzerland, who relocated to Hartford in that year.[7] Not until 1876, by a resolution of
the city's common council, was the park officially named for Horace
Bushnell (1802–1876), an advocate of the urban park, as well as the
pastor (1833–1859) of Hartford's North (Park) Congregational
Church.[8] Bushnell was integral to America's religious Second Great
Awakening, based largely on a sweeping change in national perception that God was Nature. Eventually, Richard Mitchell Upjohn
(1828–1903), the son of the architect who designed New York City's
Trinity Church, conceived the unique High Victorian state capitol to
occupy an elevated park site in full view of travelers arriving in the
city by railroad. Built between 1878 and 1885, the capitol was
replete with a glorious conglomeration of Gothic and Roman, Lom-
bard and Palladian stylistic elements, capped by a parade of gables
and turrets. Bushnell Park became associated with the moral, social,
and political health of both people and the city itself as if the park
were the "lungs of the city."

Hartford and Connecticut continued to be deeply committed to
and implicated with the adaptation of America to the future. The
desire to include statuary within the bounds of the public park
demonstrated a dedication to the betterment and dignity of its capitol city. On May 11, 1870, a resolution was presented to the Connecticut General Assembly which stated

That the court of common council, in the city of Hartford, be, and hereby is authorized and empowered, by concurrent vote, to appropriate from the city treasury, a sum of money not to exceed the amount of ten thousand dollars, for the purpose of erecting a monument in honor of Horace Wells, late of said city, and discoverer of anesthesia.[9]

Within two months the resolution was approved. Meanwhile, a second resolution was considered and approved by the General Assembly:

That the comptroller of public accounts, be, and he is hereby authorized and directed to draw his order on the treasurer of this state for the sum of five thousand dollars payable to Hon. Marshall Jewell as trustee, to be appropriated by him to aid in the erection of a monument to the late Horace Wells of Hartford, the discoverer of anaesthesia, when an amount equal to said sum of five thousand dollars shall have been raised by subscriptions for the above named purpose; said monument to be erected on the park, in the city of Hartford, at such place as the city council of said city of Hartford may direct.[10]

With an expected $20,000 contributed by the State, City, and private subscriptions, the first public monument to Wells began to take shape, twenty-three years after the General Assembly had, in 1847, passed resolutions proclaiming that Wells was the discoverer of anesthesia.[11]

Truman Howe Bartlett, the artist commissioned to create the "Horace Wells" statue, considered by some to be his most important work, was born in the town of Dorset, Bennington County, Vermont.[12] When nineteen he learned the trade of a stone cutter, then studied under the Latvian Launitz in New York City, who trained a number of eminent American sculptors and played an important part in the development of this branch of art in America. Bartlett later studied in Paris, Rome and Perugia. He received orders from several sources in Connecticut for monumental work and some bronze pieces. He worked in Waterbury on the Benedict monument in 1862, in New Haven in 1863, and afterwards, with an occasional absence, exhibited at the National Academy between 1866 and 1880, and was for twenty-three years an instructor in modelling at the Massachusetts Institute of Technology. Leaving America, Bartlett wrote in the third person, that he

> went to Rome in 1867 to study & execute work in Sculpture, Rome & Florence, being regarded by Americans at the time as the only good places in the world for such purposes—Staying in Paris 2 months while on his way to Rome he discovered that the city contained the greatest living sculptors & the best schools of art, in the estimation of the most competent judges, & *he resolved to return there* on the first opportunity to continue his studies.[13]

By 1872, one other statue, privately funded, was already in Hartford's public park.[14] Cast by Robert Wood & Co. of Philadelphia, the Connecticut patriot and Revolutionary War hero, "General Israel Putnam," by J.Q.A. Ward, was an academically rendered statue.[15] Based on specifically American subject matter, Ward's work provided history as a vehicle of moral education in terms of nationalistic traits. John Quincy Adams Ward (1830–1910), was born in Urbana, Ohio. He studied in the Brooklyn, New York sculpture studio of Henry Kirke Brown. After working three years in Washington, D.C., Ward set up his own New York studio in 1861. For fifty years thereafter, Ward's late nineteenth century reputation was that of "sculptor laureate" and "the first native sculptor to create, without benefit of foreign training, an impressive body of good work."[16] In 1863, Ward was elected an Academician in the National Academy, and served as its President in 1873–74.

Like Ward's depiction of Israel Putnam, Bartlett similarly portrayed Horace Wells as a representation of American history. Both statues derived significance from their historical Connecticut subject matter, but perhaps more importantly, each statue illustrated a man that played a role in freeing Americans from tyranny. In Putnam's instance it was freedom from the tyranny of distant imperial rule, while in Wells's case it was freedom from the tyranny of physical pain. The American desire for a solid foundation on which to build its future was exemplified in the national history that Putnam and Wells epitomized.

Bartlett depicted Wells in clothing appropriate for a professional man of the early American Republic: trousers, cloak, jacket, black stock, white blouse, boots, and an abundance of hair—the sartorial apparel that was in vogue for professional men during the 1840s. The coats and waistcoats were most generally black and were worn with brown or black trousers, and with a black stock at the neck. In medicine, black was the established color for doctors, as well as the apothecary. [17] In the 1840s, one authority informs us, the high black stock, a military style introduced into the civilian wardrobe by George IV in 1822, was as popular as ever. Several inches deep, stiffened with buckram and fastened with a large buckle, it gave the wearer a stately, if pained, demeanor. The same source relates that "In the Victorian period, a man's neck was one of the few areas which gave him scope for sartorial individuality. Introverts and exhibitionists alike could find patterns and colors to suit them,"[18] as well as many styles of knot. While real gentlemen continued to wear linen shirts, would-be gentlemen wore cotton shirts, with linen fronts and cuffs. And an abundance of hair was much admired throughout the period.

Wells's Journey

During Horace Wells's life the world was changing rapidly. While vast western territories were acquired, urban populations were growing and the rhythm of farm work, dictated by the work itself and by nature, was changing to a time-regulated work dictated by machines and a financial bottom line. In farming, work was a social activity and integrated easily into the daily round of activities—leisure was not a factor. In the cities by 1840, work was not a social activity, but created social activities. Industrialization also affected the income and age of the individual in the work force. Rather than growing up and living with parents until the family farm was divided up and distributed between children as in the seventeenth and eighteenth centuries, nineteenth century workers left home at an earlier age and started out with less property ownership than their forbearers. At first, income was low, but when income started on the upward trend it usually rose rapidly. Once the worker rose to peak income levels, he or she usually stayed at that level for a longer period of time than did persons of earlier generations. Thus, young workers starting out in the work place did not have the fiscal resources to support a family, clearly affecting fertility rates.

Family and kinship were considerable forces that had roots in seventeenth century Massachusetts and extended to Connecticut. Colonial marriages often created powerful kinship ties that enhanced professional and social status; family power and wealth were often expanded by marital ties, and hometown connections were sustained. Many marriages between the initial colonizing families occurred sooner or later through ties of indissoluble friendship based on community, family, battlefield, or intellectual pursuits which created either blood relatives or shirt-tail relatives with many of the other families in the community. As a result, family groups often expanded their affiliations into neighboring or regional communities. The Wells family reflected the historical importance of kinship relations during times of great cultural change.

Hezekiah and Sarah (Trumbull) Wells had ten children between 1770 and 1791, five girls and five boys who grew up in East Windsor, Connecticut.[19] Horace (1776–1829), the fourth child, as well as the fourth son, in 1810 married Betsey Heath. She was a child in an equally large family, being the eighth child of eleven children. Her parents, Stephen Heath (born in England in 1750)[20] and Sarah Osborn (1753–1823) were married in 1770, and resided in East Windsor at Warehouse Point, a "considerable village on the Connecticut River . . . at the head of sloop navigation." [21] Sarah Osborn was a member of an "old" East Windsor family that could trace its roots back to the early settlers of the area. Shortly after their marriage, Horace and Betsey left East Windsor, Connecticut for the town of Hartford in Windsor County in the relatively new state of Vermont (1794).

Hartford, Vermont was incorporated as a town in 1761. Within ten years Dartmouth College was in operation in Hanover, New Hampshire, across the Connecticut River from Hartford. Like so many other small New England villages of the period, Hartford, with the "valuable mill privileges" of water power, was in the throws of believing that developing a manufacturing base would bring riches to the community. Beginning in 1771, a sawmill was the focus of a sell-buy cycle that enlarged the site to include grist and fulling mills. After more than forty years and twelve owners, the operation was abandoned. "The same story was repeated with every other industry in Hartford—the tannery, the bedspring factory, the dyeing and carding mills—all failed."[22]

Horace and Betsey stayed in Hartford, Vermont long enough to begin their small family in a modest house (Illustration 38).[23] Their eldest son, Horace, was born in 1815, the same year his parents purchased farmland downriver in the flourishing and wealthy agricultural river community of Westminster, Vermont. The house on that property was large in so far as the original structure supported a massive rear addition and was reputed to be a "Hotel" for "stages and freight teams which passed up and down the Connecticut valley" (Illustration 39).[24] It was in Westminster that Horace's brother Charles and his sister Mary were born. Once the family moved to Bellows Falls just four miles north of Westminster along the Connecticut River in 1820, Horace, Sr. commenced the operation of the "first Grist Mill . . . at the mouth of Saxtons River."[25]

Schooling for Horace began while the family was in Bellows Falls and entailed private education at Walpole and Hopkinton, New Hampshire, and Amherst, Massachusetts. Horace was fourteen years old when his father died in 1829, at the age of fifty-three. In that same year, Horace began to teach a variety of subjects at several schools.[26] Education was always considered important in New England. A Massachusetts law in 1647, and a Connecticut law in 1650,[27] declared education to be a colonial imperative to which every town with fifty households appoint and pay a teacher to teach all that were interested. It was further proclaimed that a town with one hundred households should set up a grammar school in preparation for the university.[28] However, private schools and academies generally offered a far richer curriculum by approved and licensed schoolmasters than the available public schools, and often met the special or specific interests of the students. In many circumstances, attendance was often considered an extraneous activity compared to the sustenance of daily living.[29]

Almost two years later, Horace's mother Betsey remarried. Abaither Shaw, Jr. of Westmoreland, New Hampshire, widowed not long after Betsey Wells, had seven children, and lived in a late eighteenth century home which his parents had built (Illustration 40). Wells attended school in a small brick structure on the same property and probably taught writing (Illustration 41). Shaw was the eldest son of six children, all of whom were born in Norton, Massachusetts, home to their paternal grandparents. Abaither, Jr. was for "many years a boatman on [the] Connecticut River." At one

Horace Wells's Homestead

On January 21, 1815, Horace Wells was born at Hartford, Windsor County, Vermont. He was the first child of three born to Horace and Betsey Wells.

This is his birthplace and as the house looks today (1993). The original house is that portion seen below (bottom picture) wherein Wells was born. The photo on the left is an addition to the original portion.

Illustration 38. (above): Wells's birthplace at Hartford, Vermont (Courtesy of Dr. Leonard F. Menczer). Illustration 39 (below): The Wells's homestead in Westminster, Vermont, which Horace Wells's father purchased in 1815, the same year that Horace was born.

Illustration 40. (above): The Abiather Shaw, Jr. homestead at Westmoreland, New Hampshire where Horace's mother Betsy lived after her marriage to Shaw in 1831. Illustration 41 (below): The schoolhouse on the Abiather Shaw, Jr. property which Horace attended and where he probably taught writing.

time he was also a farmer owning more than six acres at Britton Ferry which he sold in 1835.[30]

Like his father, Horace Wells chose to leave his family home to seek his fortune. Wells went to Boston and eventually to Hartford, Connecticut at particularly auspicious moments in each city's history. Wells arrived in Boston in 1834 at age nineteen, when its population exceeded 61,000[31] and the city was flourishing. After a year in Boston, Wells wrote his step-sister Susan in Westmoreland, New Hampshire, that, "I think you would like living here in Boston, the advantages are far superior to those in the country."[32] Among the amenities offered in the city were the Massachusetts Medical College, the Boston Lyceum, and the Boston Athenaeum. The Athenaeum provided, in addition to a lending library, an opportunity to experience the world through the eyes of many European and American artists. Painters and sculptors offered their works to the public by means of grand exhibitions that charged only twenty-five cents to get in the door. All the grand institutions were conveniently located within blocks of each other not far from the harbor wharfs. And railroads connected Boston with Lowell, Worcester, and Providence by 1835.

In 1835, Wells wrote to his parents that "I have considerable time to study and improve my mind." His "spare time . . . [was] principally taken up in reading . . . Hervey's *Meditation* . . . My last book was [William Andrus Alcott's] *Young Man's Guide.*"[33] The former author was a prolific writer of meditations and contemplations of religious philosophy. Multitudinous editions of the *Meditation* were published through the 1830s in both London and Worcester, Massachusetts. By the time Wells wrote his parents, Connecticut-native Alcott's 354 page book was in its fourth Boston printing.

By November 1835, Wells discovered the Boston Lyceum to which he indulged a $2.00 membership fee that entitled him the privilege to participate in lectures on cultural subjects. The Lyceum movement began in Millbury, Massachusetts in 1826, as a local self-improvement society which met in the home of neighbors. What started as a simple community exercise in intellectual improvement swept the country to become an enduring successful American enterprise. At first, speakers offered their services for free, but it did not take long to determine that people were willing to pay an admission for cultural improvement. The Boston Lyceum was considered "highly intellectual," perhaps because Daniel Webster was president for several years, and the great minds of the time accepted large honorariums to divulge their secrets. Webster, Oliver Wendell Holmes, Alexander Graham Bell, Louis Agassiz, Henry Ward Beecher, and Horace Greeley were among the speakers on the growing lecture circuit. Europeans such as Charles Dickens also ventured into the competitive realm of Lyceum speakers.[34]

By the spring of 1836, Wells relocated to Hartford, Connecticut, where an advertisement that he "offers himself as a professional Dentist" appeared in the April 4, 1836 *Connecticut Courant*. In the same notice Wells indicated "that he has at length acceded to the wishes of numerous friends in this section of the country, by making arrangements for spending a short time in the City, with a view of becoming a final resident, should present patronage be sufficient to warrant future success."[35] The extended Wells family was undoubtedly quite abundant in the surrounding Hartford region; and perhaps, because of Wells's involvement with the Boston Lyceum, provided the "numerous friends in this section of the country." Hartford, too, enjoyed the popularity of the Lyceum movement.[36]

Hartford, like many other cities, including Boston, was effective in the establishment and maintenance of an early nineteenth century institutional infrastructure which exerted cultural, social and educational forces of its own. Various reform movements were based upon a profound national current of humanitarianism that consisted of a heightened sense of a concern for the well-being of the people of America. A great hope of ameliorating the ills that plagued nascent modernism provided the impetus for reform movements. And it was through the upheaval of cultural transition, from colony to independent nationhood, that beliefs of individual dignity were gaining popular favor within the collective American mind. Concurrently, economic prosperity and materialism rose, while thresholds of misery appeared to decline. The commercialism of the period attracted ambitious entrepreneurs in a variety of callings, not just the Lyceum lecture circuit.

The results were varied and often haphazard. In time, professionalism and bureaucratization began to standardize reform activities. Founded by Rev. T.H. Gallaudet in 1817, the American Asylum for

Deaf-mutes was parent of all similar institutions in the country. The Chinese Educational Commission, founded by a Chinese graduate of Yale was devoted to the education of young men from China for positions within the Chinese government. The Hartford Orphan Asylum began operations, as did the Retreat for the Insane, an institution which was reported to have an almost unparalleled success in the treatment of lunacy. The state prison was "reformed." The Hartford Female Seminary acquired great celebrity under Miss Catharine E. Beecher, who was its principal for several years. Another effort in the betterment of education was the Episcopalian incorporation of Washington (Trinity) College in 1823. Independent of other educational institutions, the Connecticut Historical Society was formed in 1825. There were also several large halls, well adapted for lectures, concerts, and entertainment. [37] Thus, the Hartford which Wells moved to was full of benevolent activity.

With an "[o]ffice in Main-street, nearly opposite the Connecticut Hotel," about a half a block from the Connecticut State House on State Street, and about one block from City Hall, Wells, in 1836, wrote to his sister, who was attending the well respected Mary Lyon's Ipswich Academy in Massachusetts, that "I am here happy as a *clam*." "But," he observed, "the greatest wonder is that I have not got on to some other business before this time; or moved to some other place; I have been here almost six months—that beats all water." [38] In the same letter, Wells mentions that he "joined the church here a short time ago. I am very much pleased with Mr. Haws the pastor . . . It is now a time of general declaration through out New England in regard to religion. . . ." [39] Not only was work favorable, but Wells was expanding his social circle by taking part in Hartford's religious community.

Mr. Hawes's church was the First (Center) Congregational Church; founded by Thomas Hooker, it was the oldest church in Hartford. Its Pastor was noted for dealing with everyday problems instead of the overwhelming theoretical controversies prevalent in theology at the time. And with that distinction, it counted Catharine, Mary, and Harriet Beecher as members, as well as wealthy and prestigious citizens as its lay leaders. Among those who dignified the congregation was Daniel Wadsworth with a costly pew at the front of the church. He was a prominent banker, whose family had distinguished itself since the settlement of Hartford, and himself as a patron of the arts, as well as architecture. Other important members of Hartford society whose genealogical roots were deeply set in Connecticut soil were the Terry family, William Ellsworth, and Thomas Day.[40]

Before years' end, Wells informed his parents that he was still in Hartford rather than removing to a "foreign climate":

> but expect soon to leave, how soon I do not know. I have a work now in the prep, which will be out in a few days, you doubtless wish to know my future prospects. I have only to say that I have not changed my mind since I saw you however I think it rather more probable that I shall continue the publishing business (if I succeed well this winter). . . . [41]

Wells clearly had an active interest in writing which he envisioned as a viable livelihood. His letter to his parents continues and indicates his altruistic purpose in writing: "It is my sincere desire to do as much good as possible. and I hope and pray that no selfish motive may ever influence me to go contrary to this principle."[42]

Following in his father's footsteps, and so many other's, Wells was not depending on dentistry as a single lifetime career to support himself. And perhaps, dentistry did not offer Wells the scientific and spiritual humanitarianism he was searching for. An increased proliferation of proprietary and patent medicine sales addressed issues of health reform and relief from pain by means of a host of concoctions, many of which contained alcohol, cannabis, and opiates such as laudanum—tincture of opium. Popular acceptance and usage of such products was indicative of the changing expectations of the public towards the effects of pain in every sphere of life as reflected in the wide variety of reform movement topics.[43]

Wells certainly would have been familiar with the public's declining pain threshold and growing interest in proprietary drugs through his pharmacist friend, Henry Humphrey who was "selling pills as fast as ever."[44] In 1838, the Hartford firm of Case, Tiffany & Co. published a small work on dentistry which Wells had written and which he titled *An Essay on Teeth*. He wrote:

> So insupportable is the pain of the tooth-ache, and its effectual remedy so revolting to most persons, it is no matter of astonishment that every

nostrum which is offered for sale, with the assurance it will effect a speedy cure, should be grasped with eagerness. . . . I will not specify any particular medicine thus offered for sale, but indiscriminately condemn the whole.[45]

In *An Essay on Teeth*, Wells also examined the practice of dentistry in America and regretted the lack of education, competency, and professionalization that occurred in his line of employment, "especially as no profession is more liable to the abuses of quackery." [46] The term "quack" was used broadly by mainstream and nonestablished practitioners alike. He admitted that ". . . popular errors exist, which, in many instances, arise from deep rooted prejudices. . . ."[47] Perhaps, his brother Charles's choice of pursuing the profession of medicine at Philadelphia's Jefferson Medical College provided particular opportunities for discussion and thought on the topic. Horace Wells contended that anyone "can abandon any trade or profession whatever, and immediately place the word 'Dentist,' for a sign upon their doors, with impunity."[48] Similar invectives were made in Boston and New York City sixteen years prior to Wells's treatise, but yet no true profession of dentistry had emerged during that time which could parallel the traditional professions of law, medicine, and divinity. Rather, dentistry was perceived a trade that required apprenticeship.

Of the possible preceptors that Wells may have studied under in Boston,[49] Josiah Foster Flagg's (1788–1853) reputation was as a "pioneer dentist, anatomical artist, and early experimenter in dental porcelain. . . ."[50] As a student at the Massachusetts Medical College, from which he graduated in 1815, Flagg studied medicine and surgery with Dr. John Collins Warren. Together they published an 1813 edition of Albrecht Haller's *Anatomical Description of the Arteries of the Human Body.* Flagg's part of the project was "reproduc[ing] the copper [engravings] with wood-cuts of his own."[51] In 1822 Flagg published his account of *The Family Dentist* in which he discusses the "structure, formation, diseases, and treatment of the human teeth."[52] The last chapter entitled, "On the Profession of a Dentist," comprises an assertion "that a proper knowledge of this treatment [of the teeth] constitutes an important subject in the healing art." Flagg went on to collaborate with N.C. Keep, also a Boston dentist, in developing "mineral teeth," a boon to dental therapy in 1833. Flagg was also an inventor of specialized tools that were used in both dentistry and general medical procedures. Flagg's specific training for a career in dentistry was unusual. The M.D. degree was the "official" license as society's main basis for judging medical competence. Even Wells did not obtain such a complete education despite his energetic curiosity and inventiveness.

Health reforms during the early nineteenth century not only included dentistry, but affected diverse areas of American life. From Graham crackers to the cult of domesticity, virtually each and every effort to improve the self became a vision to perfect humanity. As an element to the religious Second Great Awakening the distinctions between the Puritanical veneration of the soul and the antebellum concept that morality was dependent upon a healthy body cloaked the transition from theological perfectionism to a more hygienic secular world. It was into this environment that Wells introduced his invention of the perfected stove or fireplace grate, his "coal-sifter," patented on December 31, 1839. Not only did the new gadget help make a filthy chore less so by keeping clothes and rooms cleaner during the necessary process, but also by implication would create less work for the lady of the house. Also a support to both a hygienic secular world, as well as to a more defined professionalism, dentistry became an American institution when the Baltimore College of Dental Surgery was founded in 1840, at the University of Maryland. At the same time, the American Society of Dental Surgeons, the forerunner of the American Dental Society, was founded.

By 1842, Wells was on his way to being a full-fledged member of the Hartford community. Not only was he a married man with a child, but he was having a house built for his small family too, having considered building a house in Hartford since at least 1838. Catharine Beecher's *Treatise on Domestic Economy* was first published in 1841, which among a myriad of other topics, described the building of a house. Her house design was an effort to order the multiplying needs of society and the increasing importance of the home as a temple of family management and healthful development where each room had a definite use. Because of his penchant towards invention and convenience, perhaps the Wells family consulted

Beecher while planning their house to make it "the most convenient house in all creation."[53]

Meanwhile, the Wadsworth Atheneum was initiated due to the philanthropy of Daniel Wadsworth through his generous donation of land on Main Street that was the site of his father's house. Subscribers were called on to support the venture beginning at a $25 level, and the association was incorporated in 1842. Wadsworth led the funding effort which culminated in 133 subscribers giving $31,730. In addition, Wadsworth contributed a substantial financial sum in order to complete the structure. Prior to the decision to build a cathedral to art, Wadsworth utilized his father's house as a "headquarters" for struggling mobile artists in need of sanctuary. Thomas Cole and miniaturist Henry Colton Shumway were among the artists who availed themselves of Wadsworth's interest. At the time, Hartford accommodated a modest active artist community that included many native sons.[54]

Wells evidently became quite comfortable in Hartford by 1843, despite the fact that his otherwise lucrative dental practice included a brief business partnership with his student W.T.G. Morton in Boston which Wells felt to be a poor investment. Col. Thomas Roberts, Manufacturer, had been found to produce Wells's coal-sifter.[55] Wells also joined the Young Men's Institute that had been established in 1838 to provide reading rooms and lectures on the Lyceum circuit. The reading rooms offered a total of 5,620 volumes in its initial catalogue, with more than half offered by the eighteenth century Library Company of Hartford, for an annual fee of $3.00.[56]

In 1844, the first *Catalogue of Paintings now exhibiting in Wadsworth Gallery,* appeared. For the fee of $.25 or an annual fee of $1.00 a person could enter the gallery and experience eighty-two entries that included Biblical subjects, European landscapes by Pousin, portraits by Rubens, "Mount Aetna" by Thomas Cole, and many historical paintings of the American Revolution by John Trumbull. Wells was related to Trumbull, as second cousins, twice removed, through his paternal grandmother. Daniel Wadsworth, the benefactor of the gallery, was also related to Trumbull through marriage. Mrs. Wadsworth was Trumbull's niece.[57] Catalogues were furnished free for use in the Gallery. One could be purchased for the cost of ten cents. Most entries had written descriptions, but in the case of Trumbull's historical paintings, the descriptions occasionally went on for several pages.[58]

In July 1844, Wells announced that: "I am in the enjoyment of good health animal magnetism to the contrary."[59] Perhaps through the Young Men's Institute, or simply motivated by a curiosity in popular health reform topics, or for other reasons, Wells and his wife Elizabeth experienced Mrs. Powers, a magnetized lady. Animal magnetism, first practiced by the flamboyant Franz Antoine Mesmer in Paris during the late eighteenth century, enjoyed a brief popularity. A metal wand and a harmonica were critical to Mesmer's ministrations, as were a wooden tub as a conductor and metal rods. Connected to the metal rods at the points of pain, the patient gripped the tub as the treatment commenced when Mesmer touched the patient with either his wand or his hands to augment the effectiveness of the "electrical fluid" that coursed through the system. A single course of treatment could take hours. Mesmer's regard was short lived in France, and he retired to England. An elaborated form of Mesmerism was taken up by Connecticut physician Dr. Elisha Perkins and his son Benjamin in the 1790s. Again it was not well received by physicians in the United States, and Perkins took his galvanic tractors to England and made his fortune.[60] During the flurry of mid-nineteenth century health reform ideas, electricity still had its advocates.

Hartford subscribed to "eighteenth century regulations that suppressed performances by rope-dancers, tumblers, mountebanks, etc." Requests for special concessions rarely received approval. [61] But with increasing societal pressures, Hartford could not continue to deny its citizen's desires to participate in the popular culture of the period. An opportunity to learn and experience more of the world's wonders was scheduled for December 10, 1844. It was billed as "A GRAND EXHIBITION of the effects produced by inhaling NITROUS OXIDE. . . . The Gas will be administered only to gentlemen of the first respectability."[62]

Buried deep in the newspaper advertisement, in small print, was the statement that "The entertainment is *scientific* to those who make it scientific. . . . The History and properties of the Gas will be explained at the commencement of the entertainment." The exhibition was a private enterprise to which twenty-five cent tickets could be purchased either at the door or "at the principal Bookstores."[63] The scientific aspect to the entertainment was probably the inducement that brought Wells to the exhibition. The following morning, Wells gathered the principals of the "Grand Exhibition" and a colleague for what was to become the experiment that would change the world of surgery. Despite the experiment's initial success, Wells went on with his work day that included filling teeth for "Miss E.," billed to Governor Ellsworth.

In order to bear out the results of the initial experiment, Wells continued to use the gas on willing subjects. After several weeks of success, he felt it an important part of the scientific process to venture into the professional world of Boston to inform others in the medical field of his discovery. Rather than presenting his findings to a full field of peers, the effects of nitrous oxide were introduced to a class of medical students in January 1845. At a time when the term "quack" was used profusely by everyone to either defend or promote competitive ideas in virtually every field, the students of Dr. John Collins Warren were immediate in their negative opinion of Wells' visionary concept. Brief public notice was taken of Wells' efforts in the *Boston Bee* shortly after his classroom presentation: "A dentist in Hartford, Conn., has adopted the use of nitrous oxide gas in tooth pulling. It is said that after taking this gas the patient feels no pain."[64]

With no instantaneous encouragement from orthodox physicians, Wells' discovery seemed destined to hover at the edge of the professional world. To Wells, professionalism in dentistry was the epitome of his practice; it was an over-riding consideration that drove Wells in both his office and his writing. Not long after the Boston demonstration, Wells advertised his "Cottage to let."[65] He then decided to "relinquish my professional business for the present, in consequence of ill health" in April of the same year. Wells stressed professionalism in giving over his practice to "Dr. J.M. Riggs, whose professional qualifications in my opinion are not surpassed by any Dentist in the country. This is strong language. . . ."[66] Perhaps Wells' ill health was from a combination of elements. The onset of illness was possibly a result of his failure in Boston to convince the established medical world that his discovery would be of invaluable service to surgeries of all kinds. And perhaps it was aggrevated by his involvment with exhausting business travel—working on an invention idea or mar-keting,[67] along with the pressure of preparing another venture which he called "WELLS' PANORAMA OF NATURE."

After thoroughly enjoying the instructive entertainments of the Boston Lyceum and the Hartford Young Men's Institute, Wells staged his own lecture on natural history, a subject that had captured the imagination of American artists, writers, and scientists. In the spirit of the times he scheduled "Mr. Hamilton's Brass Band" to herald the opening of his cultural diversion. On June 2, 1845, the *Hartford Courant* advertised the evening's festivities would begin at 8:00 p.m., after the doors opened at 7:00 p.m. Considered a family affair, admission was $.25 for a single ticket; $.37 $1/2$ for a couple; and tickets for children under 12 were half price.[68]

Wells's mother wrote to her daughter Mary on June 17, 1845 and reported news that she had received from Wells a week earlier, telling Mary that "H. says he is neither sick nor well & is at present a loafer, but says he is uneasy as a fish out of water, with nothing to do, but is satisfied it is his duty to give up all care until he is better."[69] Almost simultaneously, an article by Dr. P.W. Ellsworth appeared in the *Boston Medical and Surgical Journal* that gave scant attention to the benefits of nitrous oxide during dental operations. Unfortunately, Ellsworth, a neighbor of Wells in Hartford, made no specific mention of the discoverer's name.[70] By September, Wells began practicing again at an office site on Asylum Street, in the vicinity of his old office on Main Street.[71] In the meanwhile, invention kept Wells busy. Returning to the tin and sheet iron manufacturer who had produced Wells's coal-sifter, Wells persuaded the stove dealer Roberts to col-laborate on a "new and improved shower bath." Hydropathy, also referred to as the water cure, was, after the 1840s, an integral characterization of the hygienic segment of the health reform move-ment. Not only was it supposed to cleanse the body, but it was also reputed to cure it. After a conflict over ownership of the invention, the two men entered another business relationship that resulted in Roberts once again taking charge of product construction and Wells assuming responsiblity for marketing in New England and New York.[72]

By April 1846, Wells's mother confessed worry about her son in a letter to Wells' sister, Mary: "I do feel anxious to know what business that Horace is in I fear he will run to fast." [73] It had been her hope to visit Hartford during the spring of 1845, but she refrained because, "Horace was dodging about so that I knew not where to find him." In another letter, dated May 4, 1846, Wells' mother elaborated on his activities, as well as her concern:

> Horace was here about three weeks ago stayed only one night and part of a day. he appeared to be in pritty good health. he came up as far as Hinsdial on business. he has been studying out some new invention for showering and has sent on for a patant he is going largely into the business he came up to Hinsdail to make a contract for showering bath. he thinks he is now on his way to fortune. but I fear he is building castles in the air which will soon burst.[74]

In the late spring of 1846, Wells wrote to his brother-in-law Joseph Wales of his opportunity to move to his "old office" to resume the dental practice, adding, "how long I shall continue at it is very uncertain." Wells also indicated that he had joined the Odd Fellows fraternal lodge and was "thus far very much pleased with their proceedings." Despite the workload of dentistry, writing, invention, and marketing that Wells had created for himself, he was able to maintain a sense of humor: "I am well aware that I was odd enough before, but this extra touch of oddity will do me no harm. . . ." He continued: "My patent has not come yet and I understand it will not before November and perhaps not then. I wish you would not let Cutler and Robinson know that I have sent you a bath for they might make difficulty in consequence of it."[75]

In his quest for financial success, Wells had become sensitized to the hazards of business relationships and the patent process. At the same time Wells was marketing his shower bath, he continued to work on developing a professional support base regarding nitrous oxide. On a business trip to New York, he visited Dr. Valentine Mott to discuss the "influence of the Nitrous Oxyd or Sulphuric Ether to obliterate all consciousness of pain in surgical operations." [76] While Wells was concerned about certain men creating a "difficulty" for his shower bath, his former student and brief 1843 Boston business associate, W.T.G. Morton, wrote to Wells on October 19, 1846, telling him that he had "discovered a *preparation* by inhaling which a person is thrown into a sound sleep" and that he had patented it, offering Wells a chance to help him profit from it.[77]

Wells made immediate arrangements to travel to Boston to speak to Morton about the particulars of Morton's project, but consequently rejected Morton's offer.[78] By November 9, 1846, Elizabeth Wells wrote to her mother-in-law: "Horace has turned dentist and it seems like old times to have him home again." Morton's activity seemed not to shed a cloak of darkness over Wells' enterprises at the time. Wells however, writing in the same letter discussed how his "$10,000 speculation had turned out." His shower bath had run into snags along the patent process. At the time, he related, "I have not made half that sum, and in the next place I do not know myself yet how much I have made for my business is not yet entirely closed up."[79]

As a self-made venture capitalist, Wells was not expecting to continue his business with "that scamp" Mr. Roberts, the stove dealer who compounded Wells's shower enterprise by undermining large contracts:

> The only way I could get my patent through at this time was to complemise [compromise] the matter with him and have him withdraw his claim, and as I have not yet collected all my dues I cannot say how much is made out of the operation. . . . I would not give a str[a]w for the business next year. . . . I am now getting ready to start for New York and Boston to close up my business there, which was agreed to be settled when I got my patent.[80]

Once the issue of the shower bath was under control, Wells had time to write a letter to the editor of the *Hartford Courant* on December 7, 1846, which was published on December 9. In his letter, Wells claimed priority of discovery over Morton and Dr. Charles T. Jackson who were contesting patent issues over Morton's "preparation." Through a chronologically developed argument, Wells left "it for the public to decide to whom belongs the honor of this discovery." Meanwhile, Wells had received a copy of Morton's claim and immediately wrote Morton on December 10, 1846, to inform him that "I do not wish, or expect, to make any money out of this invention, nor to cause you to be the loser; but I have resolved to give a history of its introduction, that I may have what credit belongs to me."[81] He wrote to his brother-in-law, Joseph Wales in Boston, on December 15, 1846, to continue seeking payment from an errant debtor, presumably Morton, and if Wales was successful in his collections, to send whatever was received to Wells at 117 Main Street, Hartford.[82]

Wells had not been one to wait long for other projects to come along. On December 18, 1846, he applied for a passport so that he could travel to Paris to purchase paintings to sell in America.[83] During the nineteenth century, academic art in America developed alongside the Lyceum circuit and reform movements to become an integral popular enhancement for the morality and spirituality of the age as a reaction to, and commensurate with, industrialism. Art dealers began to sell imported European art in the grand tradition inexpensively, while galleries and academies opened to display European art and sell contemporary American art.[84] Patrons of the arts like Daniel Wadsworth encouraged artists to paint what they saw, and influenced all sorts of citizens to follow his lead. Wells's passport was swiftly issued on December 19, 1846. On the same day he wrote an advertisement regarding his dental copartnership with J.B. Terry at the offices located at 180–1/2 Main Street, and it was published in the *Hartford Courant* on December 22.[85] Within a few days, Wells had completed preparations for his absence and departed for France.

Wells's wife wrote to him not long after his departure for Europe. In her letter of December 27, 1846, she included news that she had "called yesterday at Mr. Churchs and unexpectedly met Frederick, he has sold his large painting. The Emmigration of Hooker to our Institute for $130 and is now painting for Dr. Beresford. He leaves this week for N.Y."[86] The Church family had roots in the original settlement of Hartford at the time that Thomas Hooker led the early seventeenth century settlement from Massachusetts Bay. Joseph Church was a businessman who was successful with a paper mill, bonnet making, and real estate. The Church family was, as were the Wells, members of the Center Church of Hartford. It was not until the well-known artist Thomas Cole, under the patronage of New York merchant Luman Reed, agreed to teach Church's sixteen year old son Frederick in 1844, that the elder Church accepted his son's desire to be an artist. Despite the popularity of art in America, it was not considered an appropriate profession for a gentleman; there were other employments that provided more lucrative incomes and did not imply a lack of motivation. Prior to Cole, Church studied with Hartford artists Benjamin Coe, A.H. Emmons, and the sculptor, E.S. Bartholomew.[87]

By the time Church's "Emmigration of Hooker" was purchased by the fledgling Wadsworth Atheneum, the painting had been exhibited at the National Academy of Design in New York City. The following year, 1847, another of Church's paintings, "Christian on the Borders of the 'Valley of the Shadow of Death,' Pilgrim's Progress," was displayed at the National Academy.[88] The subject matter retained a general popularity despite the overwhelming choice of wealthy patrons to prefer American landscape. American history, specifically that of Hartford, was an important factor and the primary impetus for the Atheneum to purchase the Hooker painting. "Pilgrim's Progress" was apparently a response to the seventeenth century English book of the same title by John Bunyan that enjoyed continued popular interest.

In her December 27, 1846 letter, Elizabeth also informed her husband that "Our Hartford friends are getting quite interested about the gas war. . . . Bigelows piece is copied in the Courrent of this week."[89] The issue of priority of gas discovery reached the House of Representatives where a select committee favored Morton's claims. A supporter of Wells, the Honorable James Dixon, protested against a decision until the committee could hear arguments in favor of Wells. Dixon also blocked Dr. Jackson's Congressional petition for $100,000 as compensation for his part in the discovery of etherization.[90] In March 1847, Wells returned from Europe. Upon his return, various major urban newspapers published articles from the French media. The *Boston Transcript* copied a column from the *New York Journal of Commerce* that had printed the expatriate American dentist Dr. Brewster's letter of support for Wells. Wells' *History of the Discovery of the Application of Nitrous Oxide Gas, Ether, and other Vapors, to Surgical Operations* was published before the end of March by J. Gaylord Wells of Hartford.[91]

On April 2, the *Boston Atlas* published Wells's February 17, 1847 letter to the Parisian *Galignani's Messenger* which again defended his process of discovery and priority to the claim of discovery. By April

12, Wells had returned from a trip to New York City to receive letters of support regarding the gas discovery. The Army and Navy committee sent a letter of inquiry about the gas. His recent publication had been distributed in bulk to New York, Philadelphia, Baltimore, Albany, London, and Paris. And the paintings from Europe had arrived. In a letter to her brother Joseph, Elizabeth related that "They are beautiful in the real sense of the word."[92] Beyond what Wells may have received for his efforts in the delivery of the paintings, the total cost for eleven European pictures for Mr. D. Clark was $82.75.[93]

Imported pictures, considered "old masters," gave unfair competition to native historical art because, in addition to having more prestige, they were cheaper. The fourteen contemporary American paintings owned by the Boston Athenaeum in 1833 had cost $7,523, the thirteen "old masters," $1,815. While a living artist had to be reimbursed for his time, a picture dealer needed only to make a profit over what he had himself paid for "old masters." Since American incomes were still relatively small, only the European canvases that European connoisseurs spurned journeyed across the ocean—but the labels were impressive. Auctioneers commonly offered in a single afternoon "masterpieces" by the dozen, Titians and Raphaels mounting the block between Lancrets and Teniers. New York's leading art dealer, Michael Paff, frequented pawnshops with amazing results.[94]

Wells continued to parry with Morton in the newspapers. He also resumed his dental practice, as well as assisting various physicians in surgical procedures by administering nitrous oxide to their patients, beginning in the summer of 1847 and proceeding into January 1848. By January 17, 1848, Wells placed a notice in the *New York Post* regarding an informal opportunity for interested persons to discuss the uses of various gases in the art of dental surgery. On the same day, he placed an advertisement in the *New York Herald* of the establishment of his professional services, and the fact that he was the discoverer "of the wonderful effect of ether and various stimulating gases in annulling pain."[95]

The remainder of Wells' life was short and tragic. He died in New York City under a cloak of despair. Because of the capricious act of another person whom he implicitly sanctioned, he no longer approved of his own life. Until the final unfortunate turn of events he was, however, successful in terms of both survival and acceptance in society. Wells' life was a story, the story of a pilgrimage, his journey through life. It demanded choices and they were not as autonomous as perhaps supposed; they were conditioned by social and heredity factors, and sometimes, it would seem, by chance or even the stars. The vicissitudes of the journey brought troubles, traumas and tensions whether or not they began with a burden. The goal of the journey? Salvation. To give safety. To find safety. Redemption.

Wells as Pilgrim

The metaphor of Wells as pilgrim provides an understanding of his accomplishments, the collective milieu in which he was bound, and the context in which Wells' legacy was extended by his community and profession. Throughout the entire nineteenth century, John Bunyan's English allegorical book *The Pilgrim's Progress,* first published in 1678, was popular reading. The concept of a journey, or pilgrimage, was a stock metaphor of the Christian life, and it abounded in Puritan sermons and lectures. In America, the evangelical zeal of the Second Great Awakening during the early nineteenth century projected Bunyan's work into unprecedented acceptance.[96] The influence of the pilgrim metaphor on American literature and art was also pervasive, particularly in the writings of Nathaniel Hawthorne, as well as artist Frederick Church's pictorial rendering of the "Emmigration of Hooker," based squarely on the American experience and Bunyan.

The last great paintings that Church's mentor and teacher, Thomas Cole produced at the end of his life were based on Bunyan: "The Pilgrim of the World, at the End of His Journey" and "The Pilgrim of the Cross at the End of His Journey" (1846–1848). [97] Bunyan's inspiration did not decrease in the later nineteenth century. "The Pilgrim's Progress from the City of Destruction to the Celestial City" was a popular engraving from *The Entire Works of John Bunyan,* which was edited by Henry Strebbing, and published at London in 1862.[98] And in 1887, Augustus Saint-Gaudens sculpted a popular bronze image entitled "The Puritan," which incorporated the classic symbols of a pilgrim, the ever-present cloak and walking-stick.[99] Nineteenth century American culture was thoroughly caught-up in the pilgrimage theme.

After Bartlett's statue of Wells was installed in Bushnell Park in 1875, Wells' long-time friend, Connecticut artist, Jared Flagg (1820–1899) commented on the statue:

> Wells would be very much surprised if he could see himself so portrayed. . . . He was nothing of a poseur. He never thought himself great and was of a peculiar, retiring, quiet disposition. He wore a cloak—we all wore cloaks in those days—but he never stood and gathered it about him as in that statue![100]

Flagg and Wells had been Hartford neighbors. When Wells's office was at 117 Main Street, Flagg's studio was located at 115 Main Street, over a hardware store.[101]

Jared Flagg and his son Charles Noel Flagg, also an artist, agreed, however, that the monument to Wells was "a good likeness."[102] The good likeness resulted because the image "was modeled from a plaster cast taken after death, and an old daguerreotype,"[103] a variation on the imperial Roman custom of making a death mask of the subject and modelling the portrait on it, which gave portrait sculpture a particularly true facial rendering. The conspicuous commerciality of the early nineteenth century helped to generate a great age of American pictorial art through increased private patronage of the growing number of artists. An enthusiasm for heroic biographies and patriotic ambitions included paintings, engravings, silhouettes, and miniatures of important persons. After the 1820s, the famous and not so famous indulged in the technological advances of lithography in the form of the ubiquitous and prolific American dictionaries of biography for the sake of posterity. By 1840, the French daguerreotype not only captured personal images but the American imagination as well. "Citizens of prosperous, essentially middle-class republics . . . have always shown a marked predilection for portraiture."[104]

Bartlett's rendering of Wells's posture, attire, and accessories are not only appropriate for an 1840s' businessman, but especially as a businessman following his dreams. Bartlett particularly imbued aspects of the figure with an emphasis that provide interesting commentaries of Wells the man as well. Contrary to Flagg's realistic approach to American art, in that a standing portrait figure would most likely be positioned in a stationary stance, Bartlett posed Wells in a manner that suggests a pause in the midst of a stride. Much of Wells' clothing is covered by a cape gathered and drawn to his body by his left arm as if in protection from the environment. He wears boots and has the aid of a walking-stick. At the foot of the statue are a book, a box, and a scroll. As depicted, the entire figure suggests an image of a traveler on a pilgrimage.[105]

The combination of staff, cloak, and satchel were commonly depicted pilgrim attributes within the context of medieval Christian European culture. The symbolism continued as Christian civilization developed over time. By the early seventeenth century, the term pilgrim was appropriate for the many people seeking refuge from oppression and who were willing to forsake civilization for their beliefs. For those most famous travellers to America, they had to cope with battles against barbarity and wilderness for the sake of Christianity, civilization, and the salvation of their souls. The pilgrims were master craftsmen and organizers. They were reformers of worlds and societies and individuals. To one who lacked the pilgrim's sense of urgency, Wells's desire to go on a strange journey must have been utterly incomprehensible.

Jared Flagg maintained his predisposition toward realism when he continued his critique of Bartlett's statue:

> Men who build statues of persons they never knew often transmit an erroneous impression, just as historians sometimes give their ideals of certain persons who have accomplished something, and the ideal, instead of presenting fact, presents the author's conception of a person who might be capable of the achievements which belong to the man; but we know that great men do not always look as great as they are.[106]

Bartlett used the cloak as a device to suggest Wells's protection against the struggles of his life journey, and perhaps as an allusion to the mysteries of the future had Wells lived. Garments capable of enclosing the entire body such as the cloak, lend optical unity to the human form and render protection of great variety to the person it envelops. A pilgrim required the strength of commitment for protection from the elements of the natural and social environment for his formidable journey. The dedication of a pilgrim to achieve his goal has been regarded as his power. And faith and courage traditionally has been the pilgrim's protection along his uncharted route.

In traditional symbology, the ambience of the wearer of the cloak, be he king or prophet, is conveyed to the garment. Similarly, but more obscure, the concept of aura can also be transmitted to Wells' abundance of hair which can be construed as a halo, an aura of glory surrounding an idealized person, as well as a symbol of salvation. The visual implications of the Wells statue suggest historical pilgrim associations, as did also Augustus Saint-Gaudens's 1887 sculpted bronze image entitled "The Puritan," which incorporated the cloak that seventeenth century Puritans wore, as well as a walking-stick.

The walking-stick has been the most common and most necessary pilgrim attribute throughout history. By augmenting the reach of the arm, it provides an extension of the self. It has had similar meanings of protection and power, as has the cloak. Aesculapius, the Greek god of medicine and healing, had his staff that could drive out spirits and restore health. And the caduceus of the Greek god of commerce and travel, Hermes, also known as Mercury in Roman lore, caused men to fall into the sweetest of sleeps. He was recognized as a "hastener" or messenger of the gods. Symbolizing a journey on foot, especially pilgrimages, the walking-stick is the attribute of St. James, the patron saint of travellers. As an apostle, St. James was a messenger, one of the earliest missionaries in Christendom, who also helped to initiate and advocate reform through his travels.

Also a patron to travellers, St. Christopher, carried a great burden that became too heavy for him to continue his journey and Christ gave him remission of his sins, as well as eternal life. On the ground, adjacent to Wells, the box, the book inscribed "Anesthesia," and the scroll imprinted with the words "I was desirous that it should be as free as the air we breathe," represent symbolic burdens that became too heavy for Wells to bear during his life's journey to salvation. To distinguish Wells from other Americans of the early American Republic, Bartlett used the traditional convention of placing personal attributes and identifying symbols within the context of the sculpted portrait.

Bartlett's "Horace Wells," is perhaps the most instructive imaging of the discoverer of modern anesthesia. Bartlett found a visual language to characterize Wells that combined a sensitive historical portrait with allegorical overtones. The Wells statue was based on the life Wells led, not a hero's life, and not that of a martyr, but a man who had the faith and courage to search for a better life. Bartlett's representation expresses Wells's journey through life, reflecting his values and the values of the society in which he lived, which grew from a complex interaction of life and belief. Bartlett incorporated the visual metaphor of pilgrim as a device to embody late nineteenth century beliefs in concrete form with a realistic aim in the content of its perception.

In 1894, a bronze plaque (5 feet by 29 inches) was sculpted by Enoch S. Woods (1846–1919), and cast by the Chicopee, Massachusetts foundry of Mossman.[107] Woods was an active artist in Hartford during the late nineteenth century.[108] The tablet was placed at Wells' primary office site at 180–1/2 Main Street (now 805 Main Street) to commemorate the discovery of anesthesia (Illustration 42). Divided into two sections, the plaque's upper segment contains a profile of Wells encompassed within a circle, a traditional emblem symbolizing eternity. Similar to the Bartlett statue, Wells is portrayed with an abundance of hair, mutton chops down the cheek, shirt collar, knotted cravat, and coat. On Wells' shoulder rests a wreath of laurel, a conventional symbol of renewal, honor, and eternity. A ribbon bowknot is tied at the wreath's center. The upper left corner spandrel contains the date "1815," and the right corner "1848."

The wreath's ribbon gracefully drapes the bottom section of the tablet. It is inscribed "This tablet commemorating the 50th Anniversary is Placed by 250 American Dentists." And, surrounded by the ribbon, the primary inscription reads "To the memory of the Dentist who on this spot, December 11, 1844, submitted to a surgical operation, Discovered, Demonstrated and Proclaimed the Blessings of Anesthesia." As a traditional memorial to an important personage, the tablet followed imperial Roman preference for relief sculpture. It was another link in the chain that bound the past, present, and future.

Colored glass window memorials became prevalent during the European Middle Ages, as a complement to the grand Gothic architecture of its cathedrals. Unlike medieval Europe, New England was not receptive to colored glass windows in its churches until well into

Illustration 42. (left): Commemorative plaque by Enoch S. Woods which was placed at the site of Horace Wells's office at 180 1/2 (now 805) Main Street, Hartford, in 1894. Illustration 43 (right): The stained glass window by Tiffany Studios, Inc., which was placed in the Center Church at Hartford in 1903 to commemorate Horace and Elizabeth Wells.

the nineteenth century. Louis Comfort Tiffany advertised his late nineteenth century windows as "object-lessons," "consolation," and "historical records" that benefited both the church they graced and all of the eyes that beheld the fine art that rivaled "the best works on canvas."[109]

At Center Church (675 Main Street), the Tiffany Studios' "Wells Memorial Window: Righteousness and Peace" (1903) graces the walls of the early nineteenth century building (Illustration 43).[110] The colorful architectural element has as its focus a seated crowned figure on a throne, in flowing robe, breastplate, and foot and head armor. The throne is surmounted by an arch centered between a pair of flame finials. The figure's right arm is fully extended forward, a sword hilt is grasped by the hand while the vertical implement's blade tip rests on the floor. To the left is a kneeling figure, clothed in robes, holding a dove, and protected by the central figure's left arm which supports a shield. Both figures are framed by vine-entwined corinthian columns supporting a horizontal beam. At the top of the window are the words:

> Mercy and truth are met together righteousness and peace have kissed each other.

The inscription at the base of the image is:

> Neither shall there be any more pain for the former things are passed away.

And, at the window base is the dedication for the memorial:

> In memoriam Horace Wells The Discoverer of Anesthesia and his wife Elizabeth Wales Wells.

Perhaps a more appropriate title for the window can be gleaned from the first words of the inscription, "Mercy and truth are met together."[111] The allegorical image depicts a regal medieval Crusader who has been crowned by honor and achievement that represents Righteousness sitting in the "mercy-seat," the place where mercy is dispensed. Flames of truth, transformation, strength, and fervor are incorporated into the crest of the "mercy-seat." Between the finials of flame, as part of the "mercy-seat" crest, is an arch, or an elliptical form suggesting an aura of glory surrounding Righteousness, as well as signifying salvation. To the side of Righteousness, who conformed to standards of virtue, justice, and duty, is the figure of Truth whose qualities represent faithfulness to the facts of nature, duty, and profession. Truth holds the dove of love and constancy.

Wells as Righteousness, represents the discoverer of anesthesia as one who could, with compassion, show mercy through his heart-felt duty to relieve the pain and suffering of humanity. Combined with the figure of Truth holding the dove, the meaning of the window scene expands to relay the importance of nature, duty, and the dental profession in Wells's life. Wells was faithful to his providential blessing. He felt that a dentist had to "first become acquainted with the nature of these organs, and of their destroying agents. . . ." [112] He wrote to better his profession. He made efforts to make his profession less unpleasant to his clients. And he practiced his profession in terms of high standards. To that end, Wells wanted his anesthesia discovery to "be as free as the air we breathe."

Wells as Crusader, represents the discoverer of anesthesia who fought a philosophical battle regarding the priority of the discovery of anesthesia and its accessibility. The Crusades (1000–1300) took place as a result of European Christians journeying a great distance to recover the Holy Land from Islam. It was a reforming enterprise undertaken with zeal, that eventually went awry because of misfortune, lack of resources, and bad timing. Religious motives dominated at first, but worldly considerations were never absent, and the conflict between spiritual and material aims grew increasingly serious. Thus, Wells as Crusader refers directly to the journey that Wells's life followed after the discovery of anesthesia. In the final analysis however, Wells did journey a great distance to recover the "Holy Land from Islam," in metaphorical terms, but he had reclaimed the Holy Land before his life ended.

The figure of Truth holding the dove beside Righteousness can also be construed to represent Wells's wife Elizabeth, who was his faithful companion. She supported Wells throughout the vicissitudes of his life journey. The dove, representing love and constancy, illustrates her dedication to Wells and his work. After Wells's death, Elizabeth continued her husband's crusade to keep his accomplishment before the public until her death in 1889.

Another example of the medieval ecclesiastical commemoration tradition, a carved pew end dedicated to Wells, was unveiled in the chapel of Hartford's Trinity College in 1937 (Illustration 44). It was presented to the College by the President of the Horace Wells Club.[113] The offspring of the Quonehtacut Dental Club, the Horace Wells Club was formed in 1895 by sixteen Connecticut dentists and was unique in the history of the dental profession. Its object was "to promote professional and social intercourse among the gentlemen of the Dental Profession in Connecticut."[114] The unknown artist used a Gothic architectural vocabulary, similar to Enoch Woods' 1894 bronze plaque portrayal, to describe Wells. The main end panel incorporates an encircled profile of Wells, displaying Wells with his abundance of hair, mutton chops down the cheek, shirt collar with knotted cravat, vest, and jacket. In small lunettes atop the encircled profile border are his birth and death dates. Surmounting the end panel is a three-dimensional carving of Aesculapius. The god of medicine is represented with a staff held by his right hand and his cloak draped over his left arm. The adjacent panel supports the image of the patroness of dentistry, St. Appollonia.

Hartford's Old North Burying Ground was the original site of Wells' grave. In 1908–1909, Wells's son Charles chose to move the family burial plot to Cedar Hill Cemetery and had a large oblong stone monument erected on the site.[115] A more fashionable site, Cedar Hill was designed in 1859, by Jacob Weidenmann, the Swiss landscape architect who created the plans for Bushnell Park. A "rural cemetery," Cedar Hill was an early example of the picturesque fields of paradise, an "antique" landscape of death. Affixed to the stone monument's facade were bronze relief tablets by Louis Potter (1873–1925). Potter was born in Troy, New York, attended Hartford's Trinity College, and studied at the Connecticut Art Students' League under Charles Noel Flagg. He went on to study in Paris under a number of artists, including James McNeil Whistler. His works were exhibited in Paris, Tunis, New York, and St. Louis. He was made an Officer de Nichan Iftikar by the Bey of Tunis.[116]

The relief on the face of the monument portrays a majestic angel suspended in mid-air (Illustration 45). Her arms are extended down in front of her, her hands bearing a vaporous offering to a man in

Illustration 44 (above): Church pew at the Trinity College chapel (artist unknown) which was dedicated to Horace in 1937. Illustration 45 (below): Bronze relief on the stone memorial at Horace and Elizabeth Wells's final gravesite in Cedar Hill Cemetery, Hartford, Connecticut.

a reclined position. His upper body is pushed upward towards the angel as he supports himself on his right elbow, while his head is thrust back and face towards the sky. The man has only a brief cloth covering the lower half of his body. Beneath the image are the words, "There Shall Be No Pain." The guardian angel offers the man, a representation of mankind, the gift of anesthesia. The symbolism suggests that if mankind should accept the gift, civilization would no longer suffer the tyranny of physical pain. Carved into the back of the stone memorial is the dedication, "Horace Wells, 1815–1848, Discoverer of Anesthesia."

On either end of the monument, pictorial reliefs describe the effects of anesthesia. The right relief, with stars and poppies as symbols of sleep, is inscribed, "I sleep to awaken" (Illustration 46). On the left relief, with a resplendent sun radiating its life-giving rays on a vine of morning glory flowers in full bloom as symbols of alertness, the inscription reads, "I awaken to glory" (Illustration 46). Unfortunately, the original panels were removed in 1979–1980, by unknown persons for unknown reasons. They were since replaced with low relief bronze plaques with similar designs by the Horace Wells Club, which took responsibility for the care of Wells' gravesite.

Americans have always been pragmatic and optimistic, as well as inventive, and art has expressed these attitudes. Prior to the 1840s, sculpture was virtually a nonexistent art in America except for tombstone and funerary monuments. However, the early nineteenth century saw the beginnings of formal sculpture, generally depicting allegorical and heroic figures such as war heros and George Washington in particular, imitating the then fashionable white marble historic idealism draped in toga-like swags originally created in classic Greece. But it was not until the 1840s that an American school of sculpture emerged and was dedicated to things American. By the mid-nineteenth century, heros and events became more closely equated with the experiences of ordinary American people. As the 1876 American Centennial neared, the realization that the United States had its own relevant history, science, and art became the focus of public nostalgia and patriotism, and its own Renaissance.

Wells lived at a time when hope and anxiety reflected a sense that fundamental change was taking place in the life of America. It was also a disturbing time because the old Puritanical morality had not

Illustration 46. Wells's gravesite monument bronze reliefs. (left): Right side panel, "I Sleep To Awaken;" (right): Left side panel, "I Awaken To Glory."

disappeared even though it might be banished temporarily to private life and personal affairs. The requirements of economic and political success clashed with the rooted precepts of established religions. Wells was evidence of the age of the common man, a product of Jacksonian America that narrowed the schism between the wealthy and the middle-classes. The new times could not be denied, and the older values and qualities of life required new forms to accommodate the new spirit and direction of America. In his own way, Bartlett's "Wells" relates the spirit of traversing the Jacksonian American Republic. Like the pilgrims arriving on the shores of America in the seventeenth century, Wells was searching for a haven in which to live and work.

At the beginning of the nineteenth century, there was little differentiation among the branches of natural philosophy, as the study of science was then known. The distinction between science and technology was essentially unknown. The philosopher of optics, the astronomer, the discoverer of the Law of Gravity, the lens designer and lens grinder—Isaac Newton—were all one person. So was the kite flyer, moral philosopher, printer, scientific experimenter, stove designer, and diplomat—Benjamin Franklin. As more and more of the objects in the universe were classified, and each class of objects possessed its own "building blocks of knowledge," which had to be mastered in order to be added to, differentiation among the sciences gradually became necessary. Each branch of science began to develop its own techniques and to limit the class of objects it was interested in, as the task of accumulating all the evidence and discovering all the laws became more elaborate and monumental.

Through the art and artists that visually commemorated Wells, beginning in 1875 and continuing throughout and beyond the American Renaissance, it is possible to place into context a multi-faceted man immersed in the nascent Republican Era. Significantly different than the often depicted "irresolute, wayward and volatile" man, the picture of Wells that emerges reveals entrepreneurial patterns of a person trying to reconcile the requirements of livelihood and invention, and the image of an urban pilgrim who began to clear the scientific wilderness, to bridge adaptation, and to make his science accessible to society so that it could become more civilized.

Notes

1. Milton Asbell's article, "The Heroes of Yesteryear," *Journal of the American Dental Association* 111, no. 6 (December 1985): 1038, brings up Wells' propensity for failure. But is it really failure?
2. W. S. Sykes, *Essays on the First Hundred Years of Anaesthesia*, (Edinburgh, E & S Livingstone, Ltd., 1961), v. 2, p. 144. Sykes's view has been quoted in L. F. Menczer, M. Mittleman, and J. A. W. Wildsmith, "Horace Wells," *Journal of the American Dental Association* 110, no. 5 (May 1985): 773–776.
3. *Hartford Daily Courant*, Friday morning, July 23, 1875, v. 39, no. 11453, as cited in W. Harry Archer, "Life and Letters of Horace Wells," *Journal American College of Dentists*, v. 2, no. 2, June 1944, 174.
4. R. H. Howard and Henry E. Crocker, *History of New England* (Boston, Crocker & Co., 1881), v. 1, pp. 318–323.
5. Henry Ladd, *The Victorian Morality of Art*, (New York, Octagon Books, Inc., 1968), 341, 403,fn17.
6. Frederick L. Olmstead, "Needed: A Park Central to All," *Journal of Social Science* 3 (November 1871): 26.
7. William A. Tishler, ed., *American Landscape Architecture* (Washington, D.C., Preservation Press, 1989), 44, 206.
8. R. H. Howard and Henry E. Crocker, *History of New England*, 322.
9. William J. Geis, *Horace Wells Dentist. Father of Surgical Anesthesia. Proceedings of Centenary Commemoration of Wells' Discovery in 1844 and Lists of Wells' Memorabilia* . . . (Hartford 1948), 366.
10. Ibid.
11. W. Harry Archer, "Life and Letters of Horace Wells," 130.
12. Glenn B. Opitz, *Dictionary of American Sculptors* (Poughkeepsie, New York, Apollo, 1984), 25; George C. Groce and David H. Wallace, *The New-York Historical Society's Dictionary of Artists in America* (New Haven, Yale University Press, 1957), 33; Henry Willard French, *Art & Artists in Connecticut* (New York, Kennedy Graphics, Inc., 1970), 145, which is an unabridged republication of the first edition published in Boston and New York in 1879.
13. Truman Bartlett's handwritten notes are in the Paul Bartlett Papers, Department of Manuscripts, Library of Congress, as cited in Michael Edward Shapiro, *Bronze Casting and American Sculpture 1850–1900* (Newark, Delaware, University of Delaware Press, 1985), 190,n35.
14. R. H. Howard and Henry E. Crocker, *History of New England*, 318; W. Harry Archer, "Life and Letters of Horace Wells," 176.

15. M. E. Shapiro *Bronze Casting and American Sculpture, 1850–1900,* 176 reports that J. Q. A. Ward's "General Israel Putnam," which stands in Bushnell Park in Hartford was cast by Robert Wood & Co., the firm's name from 1866 to 1878, it having previously existed as Robert Wood, Philadelphia, 1839–58, and as Wood & Perot, 1859–1865. From 1879 to 1881, it reverted to its original name, Robert Wood.

16. Groce and Wallace, *The New-York Historical Society's Dictionary of Artists in America,* 660–661; Margaret Ferrand Thorp, *The Literary Sculptors* (Durham, North Carolina, Duke University Press, 1965), 177, reports St. Gaudin's thoughts on Ward.

17. Diana deMarly, *Working Dress* (London, B.T. Batsford LTD, 1986), 86.

18. Sarah Levitt, *Victorians Unbuttoned* (London, George Allen & Univen, 1986), 18, 48, 142.

19. Henry R. Stiles, *The History of Ancient Windsor* (Somersworth, New Hampshire Publishing Co., 1976), v. 2, pp. 784–787. It appears Hezekiah Wells changed the spelling of his last name from Wills to Wells which affected all of the family that lived in East Windsor, Connecticut.

20. Ibid., 386.

21. John Warner Barber, *Connecticut Historical Collections* (New Haven, Durrie & Peck and J.W. Barber, 1838), 76.

22. Page Smith, *A City upon a Hill* (Cambridge, Massachusetts, MIT Press, 1966), 89–90.

23. Since Wells' birth, an 1840s Greek revival addition has been attached to the street side of the house. The original house on the site in which Wells was born is now located between that structure and the barn.

24. W. Harry Archer, "Life and Letters of Horace Wells," 85.

25. W. Harry Archer, "Life and Letters of Horace Wells," 84.

26. Henry R. Stiles, *The History of Ancient Windsor,* 786.

27. Jarvis Means Morse, *A Neglected Period of Connecticut's History 1818–1850* (New Haven, Yale University Press, 1933), 143.

28. Thomas Goddard Wright, *Literary Culture in Early New England 1620–1730* (New York, Russell and Russell, 1966), 22–23.

29. Robert Francis Seybolt, *The Private Schools of Colonial Boston* (Cambridge, Massachusetts, Harvard University Press, 1935; reprint edition, Westport, Connecticut, Greenwood Press, 1970), 83–92.

30. *History of Westmoreland, New Hampshire 1741–1970* (Westmoreland, New Hampshire, Westmoreland History Committee, 1976), 537.

31. R. H. Howard and Henry E. Crocker, *History of New England,* 253.

32. W. Harry Archer, "Life and Letters of Horace Wells," 88.
33. Ibid., 87. Horace's letter is dated Nov. 21, 1835.
34. Victoria Case and Robert Ormond Case, *We Called it Culture: The Story of Chautauqua* (Garden City, New York, Doubleday & Co., Inc., 1948), 22–25; A. Augustus Wright, ed., *Who's Who in the Lyceum* (Philadelphia, Pearson, 1906), 10–22.
35. W. Harry Archer, "Life and Letters of Horace Wells," 89.
36. Jarvis Means Morse, *A Neglected Period of Connecticut's History 1818–1850*, 142, 166–168.
37. R. H. Howard and Henry E. Crocker, *A History of New England*, 319–321.
38. W. Harry Archer, "Life and Letters of Horace Wells," 89.
39. Ibid., 90.
40. Kathryn Kish Sklar, *Catharine Beecher: A Study in American Domesticity* (New York, W.W. Norton, 1973), 72–74; Jarvis Means Morse, *A Neglected Period of Connecticut's History*, 129.
41. W. Harry Archer, "Life and Letters of Horace Wells," 90.
42. Ibid.
43. Nancy Knight, *Pain and Its Relief* (Washington, D.C., Smithsonian Institution, 1983), 54–55. See also James Harvey Young, *The Toadstool Millionaires* (Princeton, NJ, Princeton University Press, 1961).
44. W. Harry Archer, "Life and Letters of Horace Wells," 89, 91.
45. Horace Wells, *An Essay on Teeth* (Hartford, Case, Tiffany & Co., 1838), 54–55.
46. Ibid, 64.
47. Ibid., vi.
48. Ibid., 66.
49. W. Harry Archer, "Life and Letters of Horace Wells," 86, indicates that only T. W. Parsons, J. F. Flagg, N. C. Keep and D. Harwood were listed in the Boston directories of 1834, 1835, and 1836 as "dentist" or "surgeon-dentist," but there were others practicing this specialty who were not listed. It is possible that Wells studied with more than one preceptor.
50. "Flagg, Josiah Foster," *The Dictionary of American Biography*, (New York, Charles Scribner's Sons, 1931), v. 6, p. 450.
51. Albrecht von Haller, *Anatomical Description of the Arteries of the Human Body, Illustrated by Several Coloured Engravings, Selected and Reduced from the Icones of Haller. Exhibiting the Parts as They Appear on Dissection. From the Last London Edition. Corrected and Improved* (Boston, Printed by Thomas B. Wait & Co., for the Proprietor, 1813). Josiah F. Flagg is named proprietor on the copyright

slip mounted on the verso of the title-page. Flagg engraved the plates on wood after the steel engravings of the London edition which was first published in 1808 and again in 1811. The plates were reduced copies of selected plates from Haller's *Icones*. This edition was prepared under the supervision of Warren, who improved the references to the plates and made a number of revisions.

52. Josiah Foster Flagg, *The Family Dentist; Containing a Brief Description of the Structure, Formation, Diseases, and Treatment of the Human Teeth* (Boston, Joseph W. Ingraham, 1822).
53. W. Harry Archer, "Life and Letters of Horace Wells," 100.
54. Charles W. Burpee, *History of Hartford County, Connecticut, 1633–1928* (Hartford, S.J. Clarke, 1928), v. 1, pt. 2, p. 381; H. W. French, *Art and Artists in Connecticut* (New York, Kennedy Graphics, Inc., 1970), 10, which is an unabridged republication of the first edition published in Boston and New York in 1879.
55. W. Harry Archer, "Life and Letters of Horace Wells," 102–103.
56. Charles W. Burpee, *History of Hartford County, Connecticut 1633–1928*, 381; see also Willis I. Twitchell, ed., *Hartford in History* (Hartford, 1899), 163.
57. H. W. French, *Art and Artists in Connecticut,* 10; Henry R. Stiles, *The History of Ancient Windsor,* 766.
58. Wadsworth Atheneum, *Catalogue of Paintings now exhibiting in Wadsworth Gallery* (Hartford, Elihu Geer, 1844).
59. W. Harry Archer, "Life and Letters of Horace Wells," 105.
60. James Harvey Young, *The Toadstool Millionaires,* 23–29.
61. Jarvis Means Morse, *A Neglected Period of Connecticut's History, 1818–1850,* 140.
62. W. Harry Archer reproduced the advertisement in facsimile in his "Life and Letters of Horace Wells," 177.
63. Ibid.
64. Ibid., 109.
65. Ibid., 110.
66. Ibid.
67. Ibid., 114.
68. Ibid., 111, 113.
69. Ibid., 111–112.
70. Ellsworth's article, which appeared in the *Boston Medical and Surgical Journal* on June 11 and 18, 1845, is discussed by Archer in his "Life and Letters of Horace Wells," 112.
71. Ibid., 112.
72. Ibid., 113.

73. Ibid., 114.
74. Ibid., 114–115.
75. Ibid., 116.
76. Ibid., 114.
77. Ibid., 116–117.
78. Wells replied to Morton in a letter dated October 20, 1846, is quoted by Archer, "Life and Letters of Horace Wells," 117.
79. W. Harry Archer, "Life and Letters of Horace Wells," 118–119.
80. Ibid., 118–119.
81. Ibid., 121.
82. Ibid., 121–122.
83. Ibid., 122.
84. Margaret Farrand Thorp, *The Literary Sculptors*, 149–169.
85. W. Harry Archer, "Life and Letters of Horace Wells," 122.
86. Ibid., 123.
87. "Church, Frederick Edwin," *The Dictionary of American Biography,* (New York, Charles Scribner's Sons, 1930), v. 4, p. 101.; Gloria-Gilda Deak, *Profiles of American Artists* (New York, Kennedy Galleries, 1984), 56.
88. *National Academy of Design Exhibition Record 1826–1860* (New York, New-York Historical Society, 1943), v. 1, p. 80.
89. W. Harry Archer, "Life and Letters of Horace Wells," 124.
90. Ibid., 125 & 129.
91. Ibid., 127–128.
92. Ibid., 129.
93. Ibid., 135.
94. James Thomas Flexner, *History of American Painting* (New York, Dover Publications, Inc., 1970), v. 2, pp. 240–241.
95. W. Harry Archer, "Life and Letters of Horace Wells," 135–136.
96. Roger Sharrock, *John Bunyan* (New York, St. Martin's Press, 1968), 95.
97. *National Academy of Design Catalogue Twenty-third Annual Exhibition 1848* (New York, 1848). Its last page contains a notice indicating that, "The Exhibition of the Works of the late Thomas Cole, N. A. is now open for a few weeks, only at the Gallery of the American Art Union . . . ," and included "Pilgrims" and "Cross in the World."
98. Ola Elizabeth Winslow, *John Bunyan* (New York, The MacMillan Company, 1961), 148–149.
99. Whitney Museum of Art, *200 Years of Sculpture* (New York, David R. Godine, 1976), 51, 81.
100. Howard Riley Raper, *Man Against Pain* (New York, Prentice Hall, 1945), 164.

101. Helen D. Perkins, *An Illustrated Catalogue of Known Portraits by Jared B. Flagg 1820–1899* (Hartford, Nook Farm, 1972), 5; W. Harry Archer, "Life and Letters of Horace Wells," 122.
102. Howard Riley Raper, *Man Against Pain*, 164.
103. "The Wells' Statue," *Hartford Daily Courant*, July 23, 1875, v. 39, no. 175, as cited in Archer, "Life and Letters of Horace Wells," 174.
104. Jean Lipman and Alice Winchester, *The Flowering of American Folk Art 1776–1876* (New York, The Viking Press, 1974), 17.
105. Dictionaries of mythology and symbolism are numerous, but few are comprehensive. See Steven Olderr, *Symbolism: A Comprehensive Dictionary* (Jefferson, North Carolina, McFarland & Company, Inc., 1986); Sven Tito Achen, *Symbols Around Us* (New York, Van Nostrand Reinhold Company, 1978); Hans Biederman, *Dictionary of Symbolism* (New York, Facts on File, 1992).
106. Howard Riley Raper, *Man Against Pain*, 164.
107. W. Harry Archer, "Life and Letters of Horace Wells," 178.
108. Glenn B. Opitz, *Dictionary of American Sculptors* (Poughkeepsie, New York, Apollo, 1984), 439.
109. Tiffany Studios, *Partial List of Tiffany Windows* (New York, Tiffany Studios, 1910). Reprinted 2nd edition, (Watertown, Massachusetts, Tiffany Press, 1973), 44.
110. W. Harry Archer, "Life and Letters of Horace Wells," 186.
111. Cummings Stained Glass Studios, Inc., "Bid to restore Center Church windows, 1993." Center Church, Hartford, Connecticut.
112. Horace Wells, *An Essay on Teeth*, 70.
113. W. Harry Archer, "Life and Letters of Horace Wells," 182.
114. William J. Gies, *Horace Wells Dentist*, 154.
115. W. Harry Archer, "Life and Letters of Horace Wells," 189.
116. Glenn B. Opitz, *Dictionary of American Sculptors*, 319; Arthur Nicholas Hosking, ed., *The Artists Year Book* (Chicago, Art League Publishing Association, 1905), 157.

Photographic credits: All photographs in this essay are by Shirley Stallings and Michael Montagne, taken on site in 1992–1994, except for Illustration 38, which was supplied by Dr. Leonard F. Menczer.

12

Horace Wells And His Paris Statue

Jacques Fouré

On the Place des Etats Unis, a pleasant garden square in a fashionable section of Paris, stand four monuments commemorating joint Franco-American efforts for common causes. One memorializes Washington and La Fayette and their allied action during the American War of Independence. Another commemorates the participation of the American volunteer "Doughboy" with the French "Poilu" in what we Frenchmen still call "The Great War." The bust of Myron T. Herrick, the American Ambassador during this dramatic period, appears on a high stone column dominating the square. The fourth monument might seem unusual and even out of place, for it is a marble bust of Horace Wells, a modest American dentist, placed on a large stone pedestal, on the side of which appears in relief the profile of an eminent French scientist and statesman, Paul Bert (Illustration 47).

The two men who share this monument were not even contemporaries. But they were associated in a common cause, the spreading of the blessings of a discovery which was to overcome an obstacle that had impeded the progress of surgery until the middle of the

Illustration 47. (Left), Statue of Horace Wells in the Place des Etats Unis, Paris, looking toward its front; (right), view of the side where appears the name of Paul Bert.

nineteenth century: pain. This obstacle was to be overcome by the discovery of nitrous oxide anesthesia by Wells in 1844 and its refinement by Bert about thirty-five years later.

The story has been told in this collection of essays honoring Wells how Priestly discovered oxygen and nitrous oxide in the last decades of the eighteenth century and how Humphry Davy explored in detail the chemical and physiological effects of the latter at the beginning of the nineteenth. But it would remain for Horace Wells, a young dentist of Hartford, to formulate the theory, *and prove it,* that the inhalation of nitrous oxide and similar gases could abolish pain for an interval during which surgical and dental operations could be performed with relative ease. Furthermore, a fraternal spirit imbued with altruism and great generosity seems to have prompted Wells to make known his discovery and share it in order to relieve suffering and revolutionize the surgery of his time.

We have also read how the failure of proving his discovery in Boston in January 1845 had a profound effect on Wells's physical and mental health and how, as a result, his career would be marked by numerous long interruptions due possibly to deep depressions. And we have seen that his discovery was claimed by his former associates Morton and Jackson and that, following his visit to Paris in January and February 1847, the facts of his discovery were presented to the Académie de Médecine.

In a letter dated March 8, 1847, sent to the Academy of Sciences, Wells claimed the priority of the discovery in these terms:

> Gentlemen, with your permission I will make a few suggestions respecting the use of stimulant gases or vapour as a means of rendering the system insensible to pain during the performance of surgical operations, trusting you will pardon me for presuming to address so enlightened a body upon this important subject when it shall appear that I have been the humble instrument of first introducing this subject to public notice.[1]

He continued by giving details of his experiments but also mentioning his setback in Boston. He compared the use of ether with nitrous oxide, and, while speaking of the preparation of these gases, he concluded: "From what I have already said it is apparent that this discovery does not consist in the use of any one specified gas or vapour, but in the *principle* that any exhilarating agent will cause insensibility to pain."

Upon his return to America, Wells's mental health rapidly deteriorated, exacerbated probably by his experiments with chloroform and other stimulating gases, and while under the influence of chloroform, he committed suicide on January 23, 1848. At the time of his death, he had not received the letter reportedly sent on January 12 by his Paris friend, Dr. Christopher Starr Brewster, informing him that the Paris Medical Society and the Academy of Medicine had voted to confer on him the honor due to the inventor of anesthesia, election as an Honorary Member of the Society and the awarding of a doctorate.[2]

There can be no doubt that Wells made a favorable impression on the French during his visit to Paris in 1847. Through the efforts first of Brewster and later of Thomas W. Evans, preeminent and highly respected American dentists in the French capital, and the later scientific work of Paul Bert, Wells would gain a special place in the hearts and minds of French surgeons and dentists and French medical scientists; so that when, in 1910, and American figure was to be honored in the Place des Etats Unis, it would be the effigy of Horace Wells that would be chosen to appear there as a symbol of French-American alliance.

When unveiling this statue, which was sculpted by René Bertrand-Boutée, who ornamented its pedestal with a medallion portrait of Bert, it was pointed out by one of the speakers that Horace Wells's methodical experiments had varying results for a while but eventually were crowned with success, and he was able to affirm to the world that anesthesia was a possibility. And while noting that others had taken credit for Wells's invention and that, soured by his failure to make the world believe his claims, he had committed suicide, the speaker remarked that posterity has since repaired the injustice done to this great American.

The importance of anesthetic sleep, even of short duration, had not passed unnoticed by the dental profession, for extraction was still the principal operating act, dreaded by the patient and distressing to the dentist. Among those daring to try this new means of producing insensibility was André Préterre, who deserves special merit for having sent a report of his experiences to the Academy of

Medicine. It was during a meeting of the Academy on May 29, 1866, that the paper he had sent on the use of nitrous oxide anesthesia was presented.[3] It stressed the importance of the use of this gas to produce anesthetic sleep of short duration. In his conclusion, Préterre said: "When this gas is used totally pure, it can be breathed with no danger and never produces an accident. For all operations of short duration . . . it should be given preference over all known anesthetic agents." Furthermore, Préterre claimed to have done over 20,000 extractions without a single accident.

This paper, or, at least, the repercussions that Préterre's report had made on the general public, was not to be perceived indifferently by the keen mind of Paul Bert, the young French scientist (he had been born in 1833), who had just taken charge of the classes of Claude Bernard at the Faculty of sciences at the University of Pairs and was particularly interested in the problems of respiration. Bert was also assistant to Flourens in the chair of comparative physiology at the Muséum and had chosen as the subject for this course the "comparative physiology of respiration." Bert was to study mountain sickness and the special condition that affected those who dwelt at high altitudes, hence, the influence of decompression. His investigations on respiration and on oxygen would bring him in 1870 the great biennial prize of the Institute.[4]

Paul Bert appreciated the harmless nature of nitrous oxide and knew that American surgeons who had used it were not able to produce an anesthesia of long duration without sensibility recurring for short and repeated phases in-between. He realized that if the patient was made to breathe nitrous oxide for a long period with no input of air, the result was suffocation or asphyxia. The problem, then, was how to obtain a prolonged anesthesia with no threat of asphyxiation. Bert would tackle this problem and solve it. The result would modify the use of this anesthetic agent from that of an uncertain and risky one to one which could be used for long and difficult operations with a minimum of complications due to narcosis.

In a paper he read before the Académie des Sciences on November 11, 1878, Bert reported the results of his experiments:[5]

By placing the patient in an apparatus in which the pressure is increased, let us say to two atmospheres, the patient can be submitted

to the desired pressure by making him breathe a mixture of 50%
nitrous oxide and 50% air. Thus it is possible to obtain the anesthesia,
all the while maintaining a normal quantity of oxygen in the blood
and preserve the normal conditions of respiration.

Bert hastened to add that he had conducted his experiments only
on animals, and he cited an example:

> In a cylinder . . . with a pressure increased by one fifth of an atmo-
> sphere I make the dog inhale a mixture of five sixths nitrous oxide
> and one sixth oxygen, a mixture in which the pressure of the so-called
> "laughing gas" is practically equal to one atmosphere. Under these
> conditions the animal is, in one or two minutes, after a very short
> phase of agitation, under complete anesthesia; the cornea or the con-
> junctiva can be touched without a blink of the eyes, the pupil of which
> is dilated; pinching of an exposed sensory nerve, the amputation of a
> limb can be done without the slightest movement; the muscular reso-
> lution is really extraordinary.

After having made numerous experiments and having obtained a
deep and prolonged anesthesia with no harmful results, Bert concluded:

> I can thus now, after my experiments made on animals, highly recom-
> mend that surgeons use nitrous oxide under pressure in view of ob-
> taining anesthesia of long duration . . . to obtain insensibility and
> muscular resolution as complete as they desire, with the immediate
> return to sensibility followed by perfect well-being.

Encouraged by the results of his experiences, Paul Bert could not
wait to convince the outstanding surgeons to apply his ideas. The
first operation using nitrous oxide with increased atmospheric pressure was made by Labbé for the removal of an ingrown nail. The
set-up necessary for such an operation was not simple, for a large
sheet-iron chamber had to be constructed in order to be able to
increase the pressure of the air. But the use of a mixture of eighty-five
parts of nitrous oxide and fifteen parts of oxygen made it possible
to induce anesthesia without the period of agitation, and the rapid
return to sensibility was made in the absence of secondary effects
such as nausea and vomiting, and the experience proved to be completely harmless to the patient, not to mention the relief of the
surgeon. Later, the fabrication and the storage of the gas would

Illustration 48. Ceremonies marking the restoration of the statue of Horace Wells to the Place des Etats Unis following the liberation of Paris from the Nazis. The ceremony took place on December 10, 1944, on the hundredth anniversary minus one day of Wells's discovery of anesthesia. In the photo are, left to right: Lt. Col. William Ryder, commanding the U.S. Dental Service in the Paris area; Dr. Henri Villain, President of the Féderation Dentaire National; Dr. Daniel Hally-Smith, an American dentist in Paris; Dr. Fourquet, Director of the École d'Odontologie; Dr. Pascal-Dubois, President of the Association de l'École Odontologique.

make it possible to dispense with the complicated fitting-out of a special chamber. The precursors of this new surgical era in France were Labbé, Péan and Rottenstein at the St. Louis and Lariboisière Hospitals.[6]

It had taken forty years between the time that Wells's discovery was made and the general and practical application of nitrous oxide anesthesia. And another thirty years would pass before the work of Wells was officially recognized in France and acknowledged with a monument—the subject of this report. It was in the presence of numerous eminent personalities that the monument was dedicated on March 27, 1910.[7] However, over the years the monument was to suffer various vicissitudes. First, in 1923, it was to forego its forward position on the Avenue d'Iéna in favor of the monument honoring the American volunteers of the 1914–1918 war, and Wells was relocated to the interior of the square and his present position. Later, during the Nazi occupation of Paris in World War II, the statue suffered various outrages; but, thanks to the initiative of the guardian of the square, it was hidden in a small tool shed which then existed on the square.

Following the liberation of Paris, it was again brought out and, after appropriate cleaning, and in spite of some slight visible damage, it was returned to its base where Paul Bert was waiting. A ceremony was held to mark the occasion. This ceremony took place one day short of the one hundredth anniversary to the day that Horace Wells had his tooth extracted by John Riggs, thus introducing a new era of surgery. On this occasion, December 10, 1944, a new inauguration of the monument took place,[8] this time in the presence of an American colonel, the Chief of the United States Army Dental Services in the Paris area, and with numerous government and academic officials on hand (Illustration 48). To further celebrate the centenary, a two-day commemoration had been organized at the Paris Dental School. In America, commemorative ceremonies were also taking place. Thus, the French and Americans were united one more time to bear witness that Horace Wells was really the first to make known to mankind the blessings and benefits of anesthesia.

It is indeed strange that but few traces remain of Horace Wells's visit to Paris in 1847. Of the various professional societies to which he is said to have presented his claim, only the Académie des Sciences and the Académie de Médecine exist today. In the archives of the

Académie des Sciences can be found Wells's long letter or report quoted in its entirety in my paper on Dr. Christopher Starr Brewster. There is no record in the U. S. State Department of Wells's trip abroad in 1846–1847, nor in the American embassy in Paris, which has a policy of destroying documents more than three or four years old. We know that during Wells's stay in Paris his wife Elizabeth addressed at least one letter to him in care of the Banque Hottinguer which, presumably, had taken care of money transfers from America. I asked my friend Baron Jean-Conrad Hottinguer, President of the bank, which still exists today (the bank has been in the Hottinguer family since its foundation early in the nineteenth century), to have a search made in their archives on Wells's account. Despite a conscientious search, no record of Wells could be found.

Furthermore, I have noted in my article on Christopher Starr Brewster that Brewster wrote a letter to Wells on January 12, 1848 (which arrived following Wells's death) in which he informed Wells that he had been awarded several honors in consequence of his discovery of anesthesia. But, once more, I have been unable to find any record of this award. It is true that a biennial prize was decreed and the decree signed by Napoleon III to be awarded for "a work or discovery of outstanding merit." But the decree is dated April 14, 1855 and was not to take effect until 1861. It may have been through the efforts and contacts of Brewster with the French court that a special award was made in Wells's case, but there are no records of such a transaction extant at this time. As is noted in my article on Brewster, the outbreak of the Revolution of 1848 in February of that year probably interfered with the carrying through of this award.

Nor is there mention of Wells's visit, his stay in Paris, nor his discovery in the only English language newspaper published in Paris at the time, the *Galignani's Messanger,* nor in any of the French publications save for the letter which Wells himself published in *Galignani's Messanger* on February 17, 1847 while in Paris (which was reprinted in the *Boston Atlas* on April 2). This was a response to the Article that P. W. Ellsworth had published in the *Boston Medical and Surgical Journal* the previous December and to which Wells was now offering some remarks pertaining to his discovery and the effects produced by the inhalation of nitrous oxide vapor for the performance of surgical operations.[9]

Among the eminent personalities mentioned as being present at the inauguration ceremony of the Wells's monument in 1910 was Dr. N. S. Jenkins, President of the American Dental Club of Paris. The American Dental Club of Paris had been founded on October 13, 1890 at the home of Dr. Thomas W. Evans, who served as its first president. There were sixteen original members, all Americans but for one non-American associate member. Dr. Jenkins came late in life to practice dentistry in Paris with Dr. William S. Davenport, Sr., one of the founding members of the club. Dr. Jenkins, a native of Massachusetts, had retired from practice in Dresden, Germany, where he had resided since 1861. He had enjoyed an exceptional practice in Dresden; emperors, kings, ministers were common in his life, as were eminent men of science and of the arts and letters. When he came to Paris, many of his friends and patients in Germany did not hesitate to follow him, which did not fail to arouse a certain discord between him and his Dresden associate, Dr. MacBride, but which Dr. Davenport tactfully settled.

The year of the inauguration of the Wells monument was also the year of Jenkins's seventieth birthday, and he related in his mémoires, "The climax of my professional career was reached at a banquet which the Paris club gave me upon my seventieth birthday on December 29, 1910,"[10] an occasion which Dr. Davenport says was celebrated in something like regal splendor. But enough of Jenkins. I mention him only to point out the tradition of American dentistry that has existed in Paris up to recent times. Those interested in learning about this tradition can find additional information in my brief history of the American Dental Club of Paris, 1890–1990.[11]

APPENDIX

Sunshine and the Horace Wells Paris Monument
by Howard Riley Raper

Among the papers accumulated by W. Harry Archer was found a single-page report by Dr. Howard R. Raper, the author of the 1945 epic of anesthesia *Man Against Pain*, concerning a photograph of Wells's Paris monument which he had made. Because it has relevance to the paper just presented, and because it has a fresh charm about it, the editors have seen fit to print it here. Dr. Raper's article, or paper, or report, or commentary, entitled "Sunshine and the Horace Wells Paris Monument," and dated "April 1972," now follows:

This picture should have some such title as: *Wells Finds His Place in the Sun*. Or perhaps it should be: *The Sun At Last Finds Horace Wells*. At any rate, here is the story that goes with the picture [Illustration 49].

It was when I was doing research for writing *Man Against Pain* that I first learned that there was a statue to Wells in a small park in Paris. In those days, one of my good friends in Albuquerque had a brother living in Paris. I asked my friend to have his brother hire a photographer to make a picture of the monument for me.

In due time I received word that the photographer had located the park and the statue, but that it was impossible to get a picture because the monument was too obscured by trees and bushes.

I sent word to the photographer that it was my understanding that a really good photographer never let such trifles as trees, bushes and

Illustration 49. Photograph made for Dr. Raper in early 1972 of the Horace Wells monument in Paris. Courtesy of Mrs. W. Harry Archer.

shade stop him from getting a picture. And that was the last I heard from Paris for many weeks.

Then, at last, came urgent word that if I still wanted the Wells picture to say so, and it would be forthcoming. I sent word immediately that I still wanted it, and not long thereafter the picture arrived.

The photographer my friend's brother had contacted was no ordinary fellow, and my comment about "a really good" photographer turned out to be the challenge he needed. He kept the park and the statue under periodic observation for weeks—for about three months, if my memory is not tricking me. And finally he had found the right time of year and the right time of day for the sun to shine on the memory of Horace Wells.

Because of the background of circumstances, and because the whole episode is somehow symbolic of the history of Horace Wells, you will understand why this particular picture is a special favorite of mine.

Stop, and take a look at it again. See how the sun seeks out Wells, as if it had almost gone out of its way to find him, and shine on him. In spite of all the bushes and trees and adverse circumstances justice is finally prevailing—and straight from the heavens! Well, anyway, that's the way I feel about it when I look at this picture. A bit sentimental? Of course. Why not? Especially in these sad and cynical days of universal frustration.

The caption for the Wells Paris monument in *Man Against Pain* reads as follows: "Bust of Horace Wells by Bertrand-Boutee in the *Place des Etats Unis* in Paris. Other monuments in this plaza are the one to Washington and Lafayette and to 'Franco-American Friendship.'" (*Man Against Pain*. Section of Illustrations, pages 10 and 11.)

Notes

1. Wells's report is preserved in the archives of the Académie des Sciences and has been reproduced in full in translation in an appendix to my article on Christopher Starr Brewster (pages 294–296). An extract of the French original appeared in the *Comptes-rendù des Séances de l'Académie des Sciences* 24 (1847): 372. The report to the Académie de Medécine was published in full in the *Bulletin de L'Académie de Médecine* 12 (February 12, 1847): 394–396.
2. These events are discussed in my article on Christopher Starr Brewster.
3. *Bulletin de l'Académie Impérial de Médecine* 31 (1866): 749–752.
4. Paul Bert, *Oeuvres Scientifiques* (Paris, Edgar Berillon, 1887).

5. Paul Bert, "Sur la possibilité d'Obtenir à l'aide du Protoxyde d'Azote, une Insensibilité de Longue Durée, et sur l'Innocuité de cet Anesthétique," *Compte-rendù de l'Académie des Sciences* 87 (1878): 728–730. This article appeared in translation in the *London Medical Press and Circular* n.s. 27 (1879): 99.

6. Hector Defosse, *Paul Bert* (Paris, A. Quentin, 1883), 16.

7. *Dental Cosmos* 52 (1910): 660–679.

8. This description is based on the memories of the author.

9. Wells's letter is printed in full in United States Senate, *Statements, Supported by Evidence, of Wm. T. G. Morton, on His Claim to the Discovery of the Anaesthetic Properties of Ether* (Washington 1853), 118–120, and in W. Harry Archer's "Life and Letters of Horace Wells," 125–127.

10. Newell Sill Jenkins, *Reminiscences* (Princeton 1924). Only forty copies of this work were printed.

11. Jacques Fouré, *American Dental Club, Paris: The First Hundred Years* (Paris, the Club, 1990). This thirty-page pamphlet was reviewed and discussed in the *Bulletin of the History of Dentistry* 40, no. 1 (April 1992): 49–50.

Notes On Contributors

C. Richard Bennett succeeded Leonard M. Monheim as Chairman of the Anesthesia Department at the University of Pittsburgh's School of Dental Medicine.

David A. Chernin practices dentistry in Brookline, Massachusetts. A graduate of Tufts University School of Dental Medicine, he is Clinical Instructor of Endontics at the Harvard School of Dental Medicine and Chairman of the History and Library Services Committee of the Massachusetts Dental Society.

Jacques Fouré practiced dentistry in Paris for forty-eight years and for a period of that time was Chief of Staff of the Dental Department of the American Hospital in Paris. He lived in retirement in Baltimore until his death in June 1994

Sarah H. Gordon is Assistant Professor of History at Quinnipiac College at Hamden, Connecticut, and is the author of histories of two Chicago hospitals

Leonard F. Menczer, a leading Horace Wells enthusiast, trained as a dentist but spent most of his professional career in public health. For twenty years before his death in early 1994 he served as Curator of the Historical Museum of Medicine and Dentistry of the Hartford Medical Society.

Michael Montagne is Associate Professor of Social Pharmacy at the Massachusetts College of Pharmacy in Boston.

Shirley Stallings is an historian and former museum director; she is currently writing about American history based on its material culture.

Leroy D. Vandam is Professor of Anaesthesia, Emeritus, at the Harvard Medical School and formerly Chief of the Department of Anesthesia at the Peter Bent Brigham Hospital, now the Brigham and Women's Hospital, Boston.

W.A.D. Wildsmith is Clinical Director of Anaesthetics at the Royal Infirmary of Edinburgh and associated hospitals. He is author of a number of articles on the history of anesthesia and on Horace Wells.

Richard J. Wolfe is Curator of Rare Books and Manuscripts in The Francis A. Countway Library of Medicine of Harvard University and Joseph Garland Librarian of the Boston Medical Library.

Index

Académie des Sciences, Paris, 280, 283, 284, 303, 408–409, 411; Horace Wells's "Memoir" to, 294–297, 406, 411–412, 416n1

Académie Royale de Médecine, Paris, 282, 283, 406, 407,408, 411

Account book, see ledger

Achen, Sven Tito, *Symbols Around Us*, 403n105

Aetna Life Insurance Company, 191, 247

Agassiz, Louis, 371

Alcohol, 2, 230, 373

Alcott, William Andrus, *Young Man's Guide*, 370

Allen, John 66n89

Alston, Washington, 324, 350n3

Amalgam, Dental, 92, 105; Controversy over, 92, 105, 288, 293n31

Ambler, Louise, 356n35

America, Changing values in, 396–397; Health reform in, 373, 375, 379; Industrialism in, 360–361, 365–366, 382; Puritanism in, 361

American Academy of Dental Surgery, 265

American Asylum for the Deaf and Dumb, Hartford, 190, 371–372

American Dental Association, 268, 274n28; History Committee, 316; Horace Wells Centennial Committee, 316

American Dental Club, Paris, 413, 417n11

American Dental Society, 375

American Institute of Homeopathy, 30

American Journal of the Dental Sciences, 291n3

Ameican Medical Association, 236

American Society of Dental Surgeons, 375

American Therapeutic Association, 70n109

Anderson, Elizabeth Garrett, 304

Anderson, Flavia, 190

Andrews, Kenneth R., *Nook Farm: Mark Twain's Hartford Circle*, 215n85

"Anesthesia in Surgery.—Who Discovered It?," 273n12

Anesthesia, 245; Centennial of discovery of, 65–66n89; Discovery of, 24, 25, 27–28, 198; Introduction of, 25, 42; Of short duration, 407–409, 411; Patenting of, 36–37, 47,

198; Receives its name, 39–40; Spreads to Europe, 40–41, 302

Animal magnetism, 47, 224–225, 377

Appleton's Cyclopaedia of American Biography, 213n50

Archer, "Billie" (Mrs W. Harry Archer), 314, 255n29

Archer, W. Harry, As supporter of Horace Wells, 312–313, 314- 316; Collects anesthesia instruments, 314; Collects Wells's family papers, 293n28, 314–315, 316, 337, 355n29, 414; Commisions portrait of Wells by V. Kirafly, 318, 341; Early life and schooling, 331–314; "Historical notes on Horace Wells: Authorship of an Old Pamphlet Claiming Wells the Discoverer of Anesthesia Established," 233, 320n3; "Life and Letters of Horace Wells," 22, 27–28, 47, 60n65, 64n78, 94n4, 95n17, 113, 116, 120n19, 231, 247, 272n10, 285, 292n21, 316, 328, 335, 349nl, 356n36; Portrait of, 318; Teacher of anesthesia, 316–317; Teacher of oral surgery, 317

Art, And society, 360–361, 382; As a profession, 382–383; Imported, 384; Increased patronage of, 376, 382, 386

L'Art Dentaire, 278, 291n5

Arthur, Robert, 93; *A Treatise on the Use of Adhesive Gold Foil*, 96n38

Asbell, Milton B., "The French Connection," 292n16; "The Heroes of Yesteryear," 398n1; "Vignettes in Dental History: Benjamin Adolph Rodriguez, 1815–1871," 291n4, 201n6

Ash Dental Supply Company, London, 87

Asphyxia, 20

Ayers, Linda, *"The Spirit of Genius:" Art at the Wadsworth Antheneum*, 211n32

Azote, Oxide of, 3, 4, 6, 9, 21

Babock, W.W., "The Uses and Limitations of General Anesthesia," 70n109

Bache, Franklin, 14; *Dispensatory of the United States*, 12, 55n43

Bacon, L.H., 103

Bacon, Leonard, 103

Ball, James Wales, 325

Ballard, James F., 352n9

Baltimore Dental College, 375

Banque Hottinguer, Paris, 412

Barber, John Warner, *Connecticut Historical Collections*, 399n21

Barber, Mr., 230

Barnard, Henry, 119n11

Barrett, Charles E., 334–335, 341, 343

Barrett, Charles E. Jr., 335, 343,

Bartholomew, E.S., 383

Bartlett, Paul Wayland, 352n8

Bartlett, S., 103

Bartlett, Truman Howe, 202–203, 263, 264, 327, 329–330, 351n8, 352n9, 353n10, 353n11, 359, 360, 363–365, 385- 389, 397, 398n13; *The Life of William Rimmer*, 351n8

Barton, William P.C., 9; *A Dissertation on the Chemical Properties and Exhilirating Effects of Nitrous Oxide Gas*, 7–8, 51n13, 52n20; *Vegetable Materia Medica*, 52n20

Baumrind, Sheldon, "Mark Twain Visits the Dentist," 265–266, 274n22

Beck, Lewis C., *Manual of Chemistry*, 16, 56n49

Beddoes, Thomas, 2–3, 5, 6, 20

Beecher, Catharine E., 185, 372, 375; *Treatise on Domestic Economy*, 375

Beecher, Harriet, see Stowe, Harriet Beecher

Beecher, Henry Knowles, "Nathan P. Rice's *Trials of a Public Benefactor*, a Commentary," 71n117; "Some New Letters on Horace Wells Concerning an Historic Partnership," 62n72, 113, 114, 119n14, 119n16

Beecher, Henry Ward, 245, 371

Beecher, Mary, 372

Beers, W. George, 311n4

Bell, Alexander Graham, 371

Bell, Thomas, 93
Bennett, H.J., 285, 286
Beresford, L.B., 28, 31, 32, 65n87, 382
Berkshire Medical Institution, 43, 71n116
Bernard, Claude, 408
Bert, Paul, 404, 405, 406, 407, 408–409, 411, 417n6; *Ouevres Scientifiques*, 416n4, "Sur la Possibilité d'Obtenir à l'Aide d'Azote, une Insensibilité de Lounge Durée," 417n5
Bertrand-Boutée, René, 407, 416
Bichat, Xavier, 9
Biederman, Hans, *Dictionary of Symbolism*, 403n105
Bigelow, Henry Jacob, 243, 383; Announces discovery of anesthesia, 24, 34, 38, 39–40; *A Century of American Medicine*, 46–47, 72n121; "A History of the Discovery of Modern Anesthesia," 72n121; "Insensibility During Surgical Operations Produced by Inhalation," 62n71; Role in introducing surgical anesthesia, 37–38; Supports Morton's claim to the discovery of anesthesia,38; Well's claim denegrated by, 46
Bigelow, Jacob, 239–240, 242–245; "Anesthetic Inhalation," 253n42
Billings, Hammitt, 352n8
"Biographie. Le Docteur Brewster," 291n5, 291n10, 291n14
Birge, F.M. & Co., 188
Birge, Francis, 188
Black, Jopseph, *Lectures on the Elements of Chemistry*, 21, 59n63
Blair, David, see Phillips, Sir Richard
Bletcher, Albert M., "A Ride Through Central Park," 253n40
Bockstoce, Mrs. Clifton, 333, 354n16, 354n19
Bockstoce, John, 326, 333
Bondt, N., 49n5
Bostock, John, *Essays on Respiration,* 4, 51n11
Boston, 370; Advantages of medicine in, 40

Boston Atlas, 383, 412
Boston Athenaeum, 370, 384
Boston Bee, 378
Boston Lyceum, 370, 371, 379
Boston Medical Library, 328, 329, 352n8, 352n9
Boston Medical and Surgical Journal, 27, 28, 29, 30, 42, 239, 282, 283, 286, 292n29, 379, 412
Boston Transcipt, 282, 383
Boswell, John L. 75, 109, 193, 200, 201, 210n12
Bourdet, Etienne, 93, 278; *Operations sur les Dents*, 29ln9
Bousquet, Mr., 279
Brace, Joseph, 209n11
Braddock, John, 79
Braid, James, 20–21, 225
Braine, F. Woodhouse, 304, 307, 309–310; "The Horace Wells Fund," 311n9
Branch, Anthony D., "American Dentist in Paris, Dr. Thomas Evans," 292n16
Brandagee, Robert B., 325, 355n27
Brande, William Thomas, *A Manual of Chemistry*, 8, 53n29
Brewster, Anna Maria Bennett, 288, 290
Brewster, Benjamin, 276
Brewster, Christopher Starr, 412; Birth and early life, 276- 277, Correspondence with W.T.G. Morton, 280, 282; Death and burial, 289, 290; "Dévolopment Abnormal de la Portion Antérieure de l'Os Maxillaire Supérieur," 291n11; Letter to Horace Wells, 284, 293n26, 407, 412; Marriage and family, 288, 290; Practices Dentistry in Paris, 277–79; Supporter of Horace Wells, 275, 280, 282–284, 285, 287, 292n19, 292n21, 292n23, 303, 383, 407
Brewster, Sir David, *Letters on Natural Magic*, 12–14, 16, 22, 56n44
Brewster, Fanny Starr, 276
Brewster, Lewis Seabury James, 288
Brewster, Seabury, 276

Brewster, William, 276
Briggs, Charles P., 345
Briggs, Edward Cornelius, 345, 356n34
Brigham, Amariah, 30, 63n76
Brinley, George, 194
British Journal of Dental Sciences, 245, 247, 304, 305, 306, 307, 309,
Brockett, Linus Pierpont, 60n68, 193, 212n50
Brooks, Mr., 72n122
Brown, F.A., 95n17
Brown, Henry Kirke, 364
Brown, J. Seymour, 109
Brown, John, *Elements of Medicine,* 11
Brown, Mr., 210n12
Brown, Rhonda, 107
Brown & Gross, Hartford, 238
Brown & Parsons, Hartford, 188, 201, 210n12
Brownell, Frances J., 66n91
Brownell, T.C., 66n91
Bryn, Thomas K., *The Development of Anesthetic Apparatus,* 96n23
Buel (Buer), Mrs., 199
Bulfinch, Charles, 325
Bull, John, 110
Bunon, Mr., 93
Bunyon, John, 402n96, 402n98; *Pilgrim's Progress,* 68n98, 383, 385
Burnham, Mr., 194
Burpee, Charles W., *History of Hartford County, Connecticut, 1633–1928,* 401n54
Bushnell, Horace, 74, 324, 362
Butler, Dr., 110

Camp, Henry W., 109
Canada Journal of Dental Science, 316
Cannabis, 373
Caries, Dental, 91, 92
Carrick, Alice Van Leer, *Shades of Our Ancestors: American Profiles and Profilists,* 356n31
Carroll, A.L., 274n70
Cartwright, F.F., *The English Pioneers of Anesthesia,* 5–6, 20, 25–26, 37, 51n16, 58n60, 63n73,

Case, Victoria, and Case, Robert Osmond, *We Called It Culture,* 400n34
Case & Skinner, Hartford, 103, 109
Case, Tiffany & Company, Hartford, 191, 194, 201, 373
"The Case of Mrs. Horace Wells," 310n3
Catching, B.H., 261, 267–268, 273n15, 274n27
Caulkins, Francis M., *History of Norwich,* 291n2
Cavandish, Henry, 21
Center (First Congregational) Church, Hartford, 185–186, 187, 188, 191, 192, 193, 194, 202, 203, 209n11, 215n90, 219, 247, 372–373; Stained glass window commemorating the Wells in, 203, 215n90, 390, 391
Chair, Dental, 83, 88
Channing, Walter, 243
Chaptal, M.I.A., *Élemens de Chemie,* 52n18; *Elements of Chemistry,* 7, 52n18
Cheney, Miss, 110
Chavelier, John D., 86, 87
Chinese Educational Commission, 372
Chloroform, 47, 343, 265–266; Horace Wells's use of, 200, 229, 230–231; Horace Wells's possible poisoning by, 250n24; Use in treating cholera, 10, 67n93
Cholera, Use of anesthetics in treating, 10–12
Christison, Robert, 58n57; *Dispensatory, or Commentary on the Pharmacopoeia of Great Britain,* 58n56; *Treatise on Poisons,* 19, 57n56
Church, Federick Edwin, 185, 191, 198–199, 202, 212n39, 382, 402n87; "Christian on the Borders of the 'Valley of Death,'Pilgrim's Progress," 383; "Hooker and Company, Journey Through the Wilderness from Plymouth to Hartford in 1636," 198–199, 382, 383, 385
Church, Joseph, 185, 191, 193, 198, 201, 382
Church, Richard, 185
Civil War, 237, 328, 35ln7

Clark, D., 384
Clark, F. Le Gros, 304
Clark, John Y., 279
Clarke, William E., 42–43
Clover, Joseph C., 304, 307
Coe, Benjamin, 383
Cole, Arthur Wells, 341
Cole, Mrs. Arthur Wells, 241, 242, 341
Cole, John, 197
Cole, Mary Wells, 183, 185, 186, 187, 193, 196, 197, 210n19, 221, 225, 228, 241, 242, 285, 341, 368, 372, 379
Cole, Thomas, 191, 199, 212n39, 376, 382, 385, 402n97
Colton, Gardner Quincy, 46, 273n15; "Anesthesia," 273n12; Demonstrates nitrous oxide gas, 2, 16, 18, 21, 23, 60n68, 225, 226, 258, 259, 260, 261, 301, 303, 377–378; And the Horace Wells Testimonial Fund, 304; Introduction of nitrous oxide into Europe by, 287–288, 304–305; Purchases Truman Smith book for distribution in Europe, 238; Revives nitrous oxide as an anesthetic, 25, 66n89, 303; Supplies gas for the first dental operation under anesthesia, 2, 88, 260–262, 273n12; Supports Well's claim to discovery of anesthesia, 31, 38, 273n12, 303, 305; *A True History of the Discovery of Anesthesia, A Reply to Mrs. Elizabeth Whitman Morton*, 62n69, 65n88
Comstock, Dr. J.A.G., 101, 110
Comstock, James Lee, 57n50
Connecticut, 362; Education legislation in, 368
Connecticut Antiquarian and Landmarks Society, 110
Connecticut Bicentennial Commission, 110
Connecticut Courant, 73–80, 95n13, 109, 110, 114, 185, 191, 192, 193, 210n12, 258
Connecticut Historical Commission, 110
Connecticut Historical Society,

210n21, 211n30, 233, 238, 315, 334, 372
Connecticut Hotel, Hartford, 189
Connecticut League of Art Students, 325
Connecticut Medical Society, 267
Connecticut River, 183, 368
Connecticut River Bank, 111, 112, 118n10, 120n27, 183, 189, 209n3
Connecticut State Dental Association, 267
Connecticut State Library, Hartford, 210–211n21, 248n3, 333
Connecticut Valley Dental Society, 272n3
Conner, Eugene H., "Anesthetics in the Treatment of Cholera," 10–12, 50n5, 55n40
Conversations in Chemistry, see Marcet, Mrs. Jane
Cooley, Mary A., 215n81
Cooley, Samuel, 2, 23, 24, 49n3, 61n69, 117, 196, 201, 214-215n81, 260, 261, 262, 273n15
Covell, C.L. 95n17
Coxe, John Redman, 7, 54n31; *The American Dispensatory*, 8–9
Crocker, Mr., 101, 193, 194
Crocker, Henry E., *History of New England*, 398n4
Crofoot, Evelyn, 77, 110, 192, 202, 212n46
Cruikshank, George, 16, 17
Cullen, William, 39–40
Cummings Stained Glass Studios, Inc., "Bid to Restore Center Church Windows, 1893," 403n111
Cunard Line, New York, 239n29
Cutler & Robinson, 380
Cuyler, Mr., 77, 110, 192, 212n46

Daboll, Nathan, *Daboll's Schoolmaster's Assistant*, 117nl
Daguerre, L.J.M., 322
Daugerreotypes and daugerreotypy, 321, 322, 328–329, 330, 335, 353nll, 355n31, 386
Dartmouth College, 366
Darwin, Charles, 361

Darwin, Sir Francis, "Thomas Galton," 72n120
Davenport, William S., Sr., 413
Davy, Humphry, 44, 46, 240, 243, 244, 301, 305; Discovers analgesic properties of nitrous oxide gas, 1, 5, 6, 7–8, 21, 23, 41, 49; *Elements of Chemical Philosophy,* 51n15; Gives name to nitrous oxide, 6; "Outlines of Obsevations Relating to Nitrous Oxide," 3–4, 50n7; *Researches, Chemical and Philosophical, Chiefly Concerning Nitrous Oxide,* 1, 24, 49nl, 50n8, 55n42, 58n59; Researches on nitrous oxide, 2–3, 5, 7, 13, 14, 19, 21, 406; Statue of, 305
Day, Thomas, 185, 373
Day book, 101–102, 108; see also Wells, Horace, "Day Book A"
deMarlay, Diana, *Working Dress,* 399n17
Defosse, Hector, *Paul Bert,* 417n6
Dental Rays, 314, 315
Dental Register, 273n12, 274n20
Dentifrices, 90
Dentistry, As a profession, 374; Children's 78, 90–91; Equipment suppliers, 80, 89; Fees charged for, 104–105, 118n4; Lighting in, 76–77, 94n7; Need for alleviating pain in, 24; Nitrous oxide employed in, 21, 25, 32, 66n89, 287–288, 303, 304; Office for, 76–77; Operative, 91–94; Practiced by Horace Wells, 48, 73–74, 75, 90–94, 183, 189, 190–191, 192, 193–195, 200, 219, 226, 228, 232, 302, 379, 380, 381; Practiced by John M. Riggs, 264–267;Preventive, 90; Surgical and prosthetic, 91; Tools used in, 89–90
Dentition, 90–91
Dentures, 84, 85, 106. See also Plates, Dental
Dickens, Charles, 371
Dieffenbach, J.F., *Die Aether gegen die Schmerz,* 71n112
Diemen, J.R., 49n5
Discovery of Anesthesia by Dr. Horace Wells, 252n39

Discovery of Anesthesia by Dr. Horace Wells. Memorial Services at the Fiftieth Anniversary, 66n89
Dixon, James, 287, 316, 383
Dr. Wells, the Discoverer of Anesthesia, 236, 238, 340
"Dr. John M. Riggs," 272n3
Dodge, David, 196, 200, 224
Doolittle, James, 188
Doremus, Robert O., 245, 253n47
Draper, Miss, 186, 187, 190, 191
Drills, Dental, 81–82, 87, 90
Dudet, Mr., 279
Duncan, Andrew, *The Edinburgh New Dispensatory,* 8–9, 53n30
Dwyer, Mr., 230

Eastern Society of Anesthetists, 317
Eaton, Amos, *Botanical Grammar,* 21
Edinburgh Daily Review, 239
Edinburgh Pharmacopoeia, 8
Edouart, Auguste, 331–333, 353n13, 353n14 353n15, 355n31
"Education in the Time of Henry Barnard," 119n11
Edwards, Ralph W., "Horace Wells, Dentist: a Further Contribution to His Life," 95n17, 231, 232, 251n26
Edwards, Robert L., *Genius of Singular Grace, a Biography of Horace Bushnell,* 94n3, 109, 118n8
Elliotson, John, 20–21, 225
Ellsworth, Harriet, 109
Ellsworth, Oliver, 109
Ellsworth, Pickney Webster, 60n66, 63n76, 65n87, 197, 199, 200, 282, 292n19, 292n23; "Amputation of the Thigh Under the Influence of Nitrous Oxide Gas," 65n86, "The Discoverer of the Effects of Sulphuric Ether," 64n77; Early use of anesthesia by, 29–31, 32; "The Life of Horace Wells, M.D.," 201, 215n83, 238; "On the Modus Operandi of Medicines," 27, 63n76, 379; Supports Horace Wells in his claim for the discovery of anesthesia, 27–28, 42, 109
Ellsworth, Governor William W., 27,

109, 185, 186, 195, 201, 209, 373, 378
Emerson, Ralph Waldo, 255, 271
Emmons, A.H., 383
Enclycopaedia Britannica, 243, 253n46
Epstein, Henry D., 357n37
Erhardt, Carl L., 225n40
Erichsen, John, 304, 307
Esdaile, James, 20–21
Ether, Accepted in Europe as an anesthetic, 302; As an anesthetic, 24, 25–26, 67n93, 198; Demonstrated in chemistry classes, 27, 29, 64n79; Early uses in medicine, 26; "Frolics," with 1, 23, 42 303; Used by Horace Wells as an anesthetic, 26–29; Used in the treatment of cholera, 10; versus nitrous oxide as an anesthetic 25–26, 28–31, 33–34, 45, 64n79, 64n80, 244, 406
Eugenie, Empress of France, 279, 280
Evans, Thomas, 279–280, 287–288, 303, 304, 407, 413

Faraday, Michael, 19, 58n48
Fauchard, Pierre, 277, 278; *Le Chirurgien Dentiste*, 29ln8
Ferguson, Sir William, 304
Ferrotype, 329
Fink, Raymond B., *The History of Anesthesia*, 67n92, 71n115
Fire & Marine Bank, Hartford, 200
First Congregational Church, Hartford, see Center Church, Hartford
Fisk, John, 213n50
Fitch, Samuel S., 92, 105, 106, 107; *System of Dental Surgery*, 89, 93, 96n26, 118n5
Flagg, Charles Noel, 355n27, 386, 387, 393; Birth and career, 324–325, 328, 350n3; Paintings by, 325, 328, 349n2; Portrait of Horace Wells, 321–323, 328, 330, 333, 335, 349nl, 356n36
Flagg, Ellen Fannie Earle, 325
Flagg, George Whiting, 324, 345
Flagg, Lieut. Gershom, 350n3
Flagg, Henry Collins (artist), 324
Flagg, Henry Collins (lawyer), 350n3

Flagg, Jared Bradley, 322, 324, 330, 343, 345, 349n2, 356n32, 386, 387
Flagg, John, 350n3
Flagg, John Foster Brewster, 324; *Ether and Chloroform*, 350n4
Flagg, Col. Josiah, 350n3
Flagg, Josiah Foster, the elder, 324, 350n3
Flagg, Josiah Foster, the younger. 62n71, 87, 324, 351n5, 374, 375, 400n49, 400n50; *Anatomical Description of the Arteries of the Human Body*, 374, 400n51; *The Family Dentist*, 374, 401n52
Flagg, Josiah Foster, III, 350n4
Flagg, Lucius C.S., *Family Records of the Desceendents of Gershom Flagg*, 349n3
Flagg, Montague, 324, 325, 355n27
Flagg, Norman Gershom, *Family Records of the Descendants of Gershom Flagg*, 349n3
Flagg, Paulel J., 351n4
Flagg family, 349n2, 349n3
Flagg Night School for Men, 325
Flegg, Thomas 350n3
Flexner, James Thomas, *History of American Painting*, 402n94
Flourens, M.J.P., 408
Forceps, Dental, 84, 89, 106
Ford, Charlotte, "Nathan P. Rice's *Trials of a Public Benefactor*, a Commentary," 71n117; "Some New Letters of Horace Wells Concerning an Historic Partnership," 62n72, 113, 114, 119n14, 119n16
Fouré, Jacques, *American Dental Club, Paris: The First Hundered Years*, 417n11
Fourquet, Dr., 410
Fox, Joseph, 93
Fox, Charles James, 304, 305, 306, 307, 309; "The Late Horace Wells," 310n2
France, Accepts Wells as discoverer of anesthesia, 287; Revolution, 277; Revolution of 1848, 285, 293n27, 412; Status of dentistry in, 277
Francis, Henry, 194

Francis, John Wakefield, 64n79
Franklin, Benjamin, 397
Franklin Institute, Philidelphia, 279
Fremier, Emmanuel, 352n8
French, Henry Willard, *Arts & Artists of Connecticut*, 298n12
French, Joseph S., 75, 185
French & Wales, Hartford, 185, 189
Friedlander, Walter J., "The Bigelow-Simpson Controversy: Still Another Early Argument over the discovery of Anesthesia," 242, 253n44
Frost, Eben, 243
Fulton, John F., *The Centennial of Surgical Anesthesia*, 8, 21, 52n23, 64n78, 249n14

Gabriel, Mary, 65n87
Gaddis, Eugene R., "Foremost Upon This Continent: a History of the Wadsworth Atheneum," 211n32
Galignani's Messanger, 383, 412
Gallaudet Rev. T. H., 371
Gas bag, 46, 87–88, 226–227
"Gas war," 198, 199, 383
Gases, And the alleviation of pain, 6, 19, 44, 49; Used in medicine, 3
Gaslight, 76
Geer, Elihu, 251n28
Geis, William J., *Horace Wells Dentist: Father of Surgical Anesthesia*, 398n9
Genius, 255–256, 257, 268, 271
George IV, 365
Georgia Medical Society, 41, 42
Glass, Stained, 389, 391, 403n109, 403n111
Glenner, R.A., *The Dental Office: a Pictorial History*, 95n18, 96n25
Goethe, J.W., von, 267
Gold, 87, 91, 92, 93, 105, 224; Foil, 85, 92, 93, 269, 279; Leaf, 86, 278
Goodwin, Charles L. 110
Goodwin, Rev. Francis, 322, 325
Goodwin, James W., 110
Goodwin, John H., 108, 110
Goodwin, Williams, 110
Gordon, Sarah, 219

Gorham, John, *Elements of Chemical Science*, 8, 53n28
Gould, Augustus Addison, 39–40
Graham, Sylvester, 375
Grant, Ellsworth Strong and Marian Hepburn, *The City of Hartford, 1784–1988*, 209n10
Gray, J.A., 236
Great Awakening, 185, 362, 375, 385
Great Britian, Introduction of nitrous oxide into, 303
Greeley, Horace, 371
Green, Jacob, *Textbook of Chemical Philosophy*, 10, 55n38
Green, Samuel, *The Practical Accountant*, 102, 118n1
Grimes, Miss, 193
Groce, George C., *The New-York Historical Society's Dictionary of Artists in America, 1464–1860*, 349n2, 356n32
Gruet Foundry, France 360
Gynaecological Society of Boston, 243

Hall, Henry Bryan, 334–336, 338, 340, 344, 354n23
Hall, Henry, Bryan, Jr., 354n23
Haller, Albrecht von, *Anatomical Description of the Arteries of the Human Body*, 374, 400n51
Hally-Smith, Daniel, 410
Hamilton, Frank, H., 245
Harding, Chester, 344–345
Hare, Robert, 54n35; *Compendium on the Course of Chemical Instruction in the Medical Department of the University of Pennsylvania*, 14, 56n47
Harris, Nicholas, *Complete System of Practical Bookkeeping*, 102, 108, 118n2, 118n7
Hartford, Connecticut, Art community in, 372–373, 376, 383; Asylum Street, 189, 194, 196, 197, 201; Bushnell Park, 109, 264, 329, 358, 359, 360, 362–364, 386, 393; Cedar Hill Cemetary, 248, 393; Center Church, 185–186, 187, 188, 191, 192, 193, 194, 202, 203,

209n9, 209n11, 215n90, 247, 372–373, 390, 391; City directories, 204-205, 210n21, Entertainments in, 68n98, 377; Gaslight installed in, 76; Goodwin Park, 110; Growth, 74, 361; Historical Museum of Medicine and Dentistry, 334, 341, 342, 344; Horace Wells's ties to, 182–183; Industry, 74, 210n12, 361; Insurance business in, 74, 190, 361; Lack of medical institutions, 40; Lord's Hill, 194–195, 196, 201; Main Street, 188–190, 200–201, 215n91; Maps of, 207–208, 215n91; North (Park) Congregational Church, 362; Old North Burying Ground, 217, 231, 247, 248, 262, 393,; State House, 191, 325, 362; State Street, 189; Streets, 206; Wadsworth Atheneum, 190, 199, 203, 211n32, 322, 325, 328, 349n2, 356n36, 376–377; Young Men's Institute, 190, 199

Hartford Courant, 199, 200, 201, 210n12, 210n16, 253n50, 322, 325, 328, 379, 381, 382; Advertising rates, 79; "Education in the Time of Henry Barnard," 118n11; Horace Wells's advertising in, 95n13; Publishes Wells's letter claiming discovery of anesthesia, 28, 34, 35, 198, 381

Hartford Dental Society, 100–101, 239, 306

Hartford Female Seminary, 372

Hartford Medical Society, 96, 100–101

Hartford Orphan Asylum, 372

Hartford Public Library, 190

Hartford, Vermont, 183, 366–369

Hartford, Vermont, Historical Society, 209n3

Harvard Medical School (Massachusetts Medical College), 244, 370, 374

Harvard School of Dental Medicine, 267, 345–347, 351n5, 356n36

Harvard University, 267; Fogg Art Museum, 347, 357n37

Harwood, D., 351n5, 400n49

Hasbrouk, Dr., 260–261, 273n14

Havens, H.C., 111

Hawes, Rev. Joel, 187, 372

Hawthorn, Nathaniel, 385

Hayden, William R., "The History of Anesthesia, or Painless Surgery," 32–33, 67n94

Health reform, 373, 375, 379

Heath, Betsy, See Shaw, Betsy Wells

Heath, Stephen, 366

Hender, Sally, see Wales, Sally Hender

Hender, Thomas, 187, 188, 195, 196, 201

Henry, William, *The Elements of Experimental Chemistry,* 50n9, 52n24, 54n35; *Epitome of Chemistry,* 4, 8, 50n9, 52n24

Herrick, Myron T., 404

Hervey, James, *Meditations,* 370

Hewlitt, J.S., 200

Heywood, Charles F., 47, 72n122

Hickman, Henry, 20, 21, 41, 58n60

Hills, Mr., 193

Hine, Charles, 342, 343, 344–345, 356n32

Hindsdale, Mary, 188

Hirsch, Nicholas P., "Gardner Quincy Colton: Pioneer in Nitrous Oxide Anesthesia," 310n1

Historical Museum of Medicine and Dentistry, Hartford, 334, 341, 342, 344

History of Westmoreland, New Hampshire, 1741–1970, 399n3

Hoffman-Axthelm, Walter, *History of Dentistry,* 94n21, 278, 291n12

Holmes, Oliver Wendell, 39, 371

Hooker, Thomas, 185, 199, 202, 372, 382

Horace Wells Club, Hartford, 393, 395

"Horace Wells Testimonial Fund," 245, 310n4

Hosking, Nicholas, *The Artists Year Book,* 403n116

Hosmer, Betsy, 218, 224

Hottinguer, Jean-Conrad, 412

Howard, R.H., *History of New England,* 398n4

Howland, Dr., 260–261, 273n14
Hudson River School of Painting, 199
Humphrey, Frances, 103, 187, 193
Humphrey, Harriet, 190
Humphrey, Henry, 107, 186–187, 190, 193, 211n34, 221, 373
Humphrey Lucy, 190,
Humphrey, Nancy, 190
Humphrey Seyms & Co., Hartford, 189, 200, 201
Hunter, John, 93
Hurlbit, C.S., 271
Hydrotherapy, 379
Hypnosis, 21, 225, 249n14

Index Catalogue of the Library of the Surgeon General's Office, 32
Ingres, J.A.D., 324
Institute for Living, Hartford, 190
Instruments, Dental, 80–90, Case for, 81, 86–87
International Congress of Anesthetists, 317
International Medical Congress, 7th, London, 1881, 267
Ireland, Famine in, 200, 201
Irving, Henry W., *The Connecticut River Banking Co.,* 118n10

Jackson, Charles T., 35, 68n96, 69n99, 112, 244. 282, 283, 286, 287, 381; Aids Morton in developing ether anesthesia, 36–37, 44–45, 245; Credited with the discovery of anesthesia, 41; Death, 239; Dispute with W. T. G. Morton over discovery of anesthesia, 233–34, 237; *A Manual of Etherization,* 33, 237, 252n35; Presses claim for discovery in Europe, 40, 280, 286, 383, 406
Jackson, Samuel, *Principles of Medicine,* 11–12, 35n41
Jacobs, Stephen, *The Student's Chemical Pocket Companion,* 6, 51n17
Jaquesson de la Chevreuse, L. M. F., 324
Jefferson Medical College, Philadelphia, 10, 30, 222, 257, 258, 350n4, 374; Patients anesthetized at, 67n93

Jenkins, Newell Sill, 413, 417n10; *Reminiscences,* 417n10
Jenner, Edward, 233, 251n27
Jewell, Marshall, 363
Johansen Erling, 250n24
Johnson, Judith Ellen, 214n81
Journal of Commerece, New York, 29, 229, 282–283, 292n19, 292n21, 383
Journal of Natural Philosophy, Chemistry and the Arts, 3
The Journal of the Gynaecological Society of Boston, 242–243, 253n45

Kane, Sir Robert, *Elements of Chemistry,* 16, 57n52
Keep, Nathan Cooley, 24, 69n99, 324, 351n5, 374–375, 400n49
Kingsbury, C.A., 116, 237n10
Kirafly, Verona, 318, 335, 341, 355n28
Kirkland, D., 258
Kissam, Richard S., 64n79
The Knickerbocker, or New York Monthly Magazine, 43
Knight, David M., "Humphry Davy," 49n2
Knight, Nancy, *Pain and Its Relief,* 400n43
Koch, Charles R.E., *History of Dental Surgery,* 264, 269, 271n3, 272n5, 272n7, 274n23, 274n29, 350n4

Labbé, Leon, 409, 411
Ladd, Henry, *The Victorian Morality of Art,* 398n5
Lafayette, Marquis de, 404
Lamphrey, Bruce H., 252n40
Lancet, 285, 305
Lancret, N., 384
"The Late Horace Wells," 310n4, 311n8
Laudanum, 373
"Laughing gas," 10, 303
Launitz, R. E., 363
Lauwerenburgh, A., 50n5
Lavoisier, A.L., 21
Ledger, 98, 101–102, 108
Lee, Elizabeth, 5
Lee, Mayo 111

Lerner, Adele A., "The History of Anesthesia at the New York Hospital," 32, 67n92, 67n93, 68n95

Lewis, John, 81, 87

Library Company of Hartford, 376

Lichtman, S.S., *Diseases of the Liver, Gallbladder and Bile Ducts*, 250n24

Lincoln, Abraham, 328

Linnaeus, Carolus, 39

Lipman, Jean, *The Flowering of American Folk Art, 1776–1876*, 403n104

Lister, Joseph, 304

Litchfield, J. G. & U., 195

Litchfield, Mr., 195

Litchfield, Connecticut, 185, 209n11

Litchfield, Law School, 209n11

Lithography, 386

London, Introduction of nitrous oxide in, 243

London Dental Hospital, 304

London Pharmacopoeia, 8

Long, Crawford, And the discovery of anesthesia, 41–42, 43, 301; "An Account of the First Use of Sulphuric Ether by Inhalation as an Anesthetic in Surgical Operations," 71n113

Longbotham, B.T., 93

Longet, F.A., 40; *Expériences Relatives aux Effects de l'Inhalation de l'Éther sur les Systéme Nerveux*, 71n112

Longfellow, Fanny, 351n5

Louis, Philippe, King of France, 278, 279, 286, 288, 293n27

Lyceum movement, 370–371, 376, 382

Lyman, Henry Munson, *Artificial Anesthesia and Anesthetics*, 43, 71n114

Lyons, Mary, 372

Lynch, Daniel F., 320

MacBride, Dr., 413

McClellan, George, 30

McClintock, Elizabeth R., 356n33, 356n36

McHinney, Miss, 107

McKesson, E.I., 316

McLean Assulum, Charlestown, Mass., 239

McManus, Charles, 98, 100–101, 272n3

McManus, James, 100–101, 110, 267, 272n3, 341; *Notes on the History of Anesthesia . . . Early recorda of Dentists in Connecticut*, 116, 118n9, 120n19, 257–258, 272n10

McManus, James Goodwin, 335, 341, 355n27

Macneven, William James, 52n29

Magee Hospital, Pittsburg, 317

Major, A. Hyatt, 354n15

Marcet, Mrs. Jane, 4–5; *Conversations on Chemistry*, 4–5, 16, 51n14, 57n50

Marcy, C.C., 60n66, 65n84, 240; Debates using ether or chloroform, 28–30, 244; Early use of anesthesia, 28–31; Espouses homeopathy, 30, 65n84; "Inhalation of Ether to Prevent Pain," 29, 65n83; "Removal of a Large Scirrhous Testicle From a Man While Under the Influence of Nitrous Oxide Gas," 65n85; "Sulphuric Ether &c., in Surgical Operations," 292n19; Supports Horace Wells in the discovery of anesthesia, 42, 282, 283

Martin, Thomas, 111

Massachesetts, Education legislation in, 368

Massachusetts Charitable Mechanic Association, 86–87; *The Fourth Exhibition . . . September 16, 1844*, 95n20

Massachusetts General Hospital, Boston, Introduction of ether anesthesia at, 25, 31, 36, 38, 39, 45–46, 47, 232, 235, 244; Patients anesthetized at, 67n93

Massachusetts Institue of Technology, 352n8, 363

Massachusetts Medical College, see Harvard Medical School

Maury, J.C.F., 87

Medical College of South Carolina, 277, 291n5

Medical Society of South Carolina, 291n5

Medical Times and Gazette, London, 240

Melainotype, 329

Menczer, Leonard F., 22, 249n7, 334, 354n17; "Horace Wells," 398n2; "Wells's Death and Hartford Burial Sites," 248n2

Mérimee, Prosper, 279; *Correspondence Generale,* 292n15

Merrick, Judge, 103

Merritt, Arthur, "The Historical Background of Periodontology," 264, 272n3, 273n14, 274n18

Mesmer, Antoine, 377

Mesmerism, 11, 225, 226, 249n14, 377

Metropolitan Museum, New York, 325

Miller, Albert H., "Prelude to Surgical Anesthesia," 69n99

Miller, W.D., 91

Mills, George A., "Some Observations From the Life of the Late Dr. John M. Riggs," 262, 266, 272n3, 274n17, 272n26

Miss Pierce's Female Academy, 209n11

Mitchill, Samuel Latham, 3, 6; *Remarks on the Gaseous Oxyd of Azote or of Nitrogene,* 50n6

Mittleman, M., "Horace Wells," 398n2

Monheim, Leonard M., 319

Montijo family, 279

Moorsfield Eye Hospital, 304

Moran, Philip S., 334, 335, 343, 345, 354n18

Morgan, Junius Spencer, 328

Morgenstern, Henri, *La Guerre des Dentistes en France en 1846,* 292n13

Morris, Mary 211n30

Morse, Jarvis Means, *A Neglected Period of Connecticut's History, 1818–1850,* 399n27

Morton, Elizabeth Whitman, 31, 32, 62n69, 69n99, 113

Morton, William James, 38, 70n109; "Memoranda Relating to the Discovery of Surgical Anesthesia," 71n110

Morton, William Thomas Green, 32, 33, 41, 286, 287, 381, 406; Accounts with Horace Wells, 101, 106, 112–113, 114–115, 116–117, 180–181, 200, 382; Advantaged because of location in Boston, 40; Aided by H.J. Bigelow, 37–38, 39–40, 47; Aided be A.A. Gould, 39–40; Aided by C.T. Jackson, 36–37; Aided by luck, 40–41; Attends Harvard Medical School, 69n99; Awarded prize by Massachusetts Charitable Mechanic Association, 86–87; Controversy with C.T. Jackson, 233–234, 237; Corresponds with C.S. Brewster in Paris, 280, 282; Death, 239, 252–253n40; Dental practice, 69n99; And discovery of anesthesia, 25- 26, 43, 49, 198, 240; Financial difficulties, 235; And introduction of anesthesia, 30, 42, 43, 44, 45–46; Instructed in dentistry by Horace Wells, 25, 112, 115, 116; Learns about anesthesia, 34, 35–36, 44, 45, 70n105, 71n114, 244; Marriage, 69n99, 113; And the naming of anesthesia, 39–40; "National Testimonial," for, 235; Offers Wells agency for promoting anesthesia, 36, 70n106, 381; Opposes Wells's claim to discovery of anesthesia, 31, 32, 119n17, 198, 285, 302, 384; Partnership in dental pracrice with Horace Wells, 25, 62n72, 112–114, 223–224, 376; And the patenting of anesthesia, 36, 48, 198, 252n36, 302, 351n5, 381; Personality and character, 62n72, 113–114; Petitions Congress for renumeration for discovery of anesthesia, 232–235, 237, 334, 383; *Remarks on the Comparative Value of Ether and Choroform,* 95n19; *Trials of a Public Benefactor,* 35–36, 37, 70n104, 235, 340, 355n24

Morton Testimonial Association, 235, 252n37

Mossman Foundry, Chicopee, Mass., 389

Mott, Valentine, 33, 68n95, 235, 380
Mount Auburn Cemetary, Cambridge, Mass., 239
Muskens, Louis J.J., 250n24
Napoleon, Louis, (Napoleon III), 279, 290, 412
National Academy of Design, 325, 364, 383; *Twenty-third Exhibition, 1848,* 402n97
National Academy of Design Exhibition Record, 1826–1869, 401n88
National Union Catalog of Pre-1956 Imprints, 5, 22
New York City, 189, 361; Central Park, 362; Horace Wells in, 32–33, 200, 384; Trinity Church, 362
New York Dental Recorder, 69n100, 89, 96n25, 249–250n24, 285; And amalgam controversy, 288, 293n31; "Dentists' fees," 104, 118n4; Editorial on use of chloroform and Horace Wells, 230–231; "Ether and Chloroform," 293n26
New York Herald, 384
New York Hospital, 32; Patients anesthetized at, 67n93
New York Post, 484
New York Times, 245, 253n47
Newton, Issac, 361, 397
Nicholson, William, 52n18; *Journal of Natural Philosphy, Chemistry and the Arts,* 3
Nieuwland, P., 49n5
Nisbit, Robert, "Sociology: Genius," 255, 271n2
Nitrous oxide, 245; Action on living bodies, 3–4, 5, 18, 119n14; Analgesic powers of, 5, 9, 20, 24, 196, 305; Analgesic powers ignored, 5–6, 7–8, 12, 302; Aparatus for making and preserving, 14, 15; Behavior resulting from, 3, 10, 13, 14, 16–18, 23, 119n16; Death allegedly caused by, 309, 311n7; Demonstrated by Gardner Q. Colton, 2, 16, 18, 21, 23, 60n68, 225, 226, 258, 259, 260, 261, 301, 303, 377–378; Demonstrated in chemistry classes, 7, 16–18, 27, 29, 64n79; Depressing powers of, 3, 8; Discovery of, 3, 301, 406; Discovery of analgesic powers of, 1; Discovery of analgesic powers by Horace Wells, 2, 14, 19, 27–28, 41, 42, 44, 45, 46, 61n69, 226, 236–237, 259–260, 261–262, 305–306, 380, 406–407; Early notice of, 4–5, 6–10, 14, 16, 18–19; Early use as an anesthetic, 27–31, 67n93, 262; Employed by Horace Wells in dentistry, 21, 88, 226, 227, 262; Humphry Davy's researches on, 2–3, 5, 7, 13, 14, 302–303; Introduced as an anesthetic into Europe, 287–288, 304; Loses favor as an anesthetic, 31–32, 303; Named by Humphry Davy, 3, 6; Not mentioned in Wells's "Day Book A," 112; Refined in France, 406, 407–409, 411; Revived as an anesthetic, 25, 32, 68n89; Safety of, 10, 19; Stimulating and exhilarating powers of, 3, 8, 10, 11, 12, 13, 19, 27; Used in treating cholera, 10–12; Versus ether as an anesthetic, 25–26, 28–31, 33–34, 45, 64n79, 64n80, 244, 406
Nook Farm Enclave, 202, 215n85
North, Seth, 106
North (Park) Congregational Church, Hartford, 362
Norwich, Connecticut, 276; Vital Records of, 291n1
Norwich Courier, 276, 291n3
Nysten, P.H., *Recherches du Physiologie et de Chime Pathologiques,* 9, 54n33

"Obituary Dr. Christopher Starr Brewster," 291n7
"Obituary, Dr. John M. Riggs," 272n3, 272n6, 272n9, 274n30
Odontological Society of Pennsylvania, 66n89
Olderr, Steven, *Symbolism: a Comprehensive Dictionary,* 403n105
Oliver, Andrew, *Auguste Edouart's Silhouettes of Eminent Americans,* 331, 332, 353n14, 353n15
Olmsted, Frederick Law, 362;

"Needed: Park Central to All," 398n6
Olmsted, G. Howell, 199n17
Olmsted, John & Co., Hartford, 115, 119n17
Opitz, Glenn B., *Dictionary of American Sculptors,* 398n12
Opium, 47, 230, 373
Orfila, P.M., *Practical Chemistry,* 8, 53n27, 54n32; *A Treatise on Mineral Vegetable and Animal Poisons,* 9, 54n32
Osborn, Sarah, 366
Osler, William 45–46; "The First Printed Documents Relating to Modern Anesthesia," 72n119
Owen, Robert, "Report on the Archetype and Homologies of the Vertabrate Skeleton," 72n120
Oxide of azote, see Azote; Nitrous oxide
Oxygen, 3, 406

Paff, Michael, 384
Paget, Sir James, 304
Pain, Early attempts to overcome surgery, 19–21; Eighteenth-century view of, 6; Power of nitrous oxide to overcome in surgery, 19–21
Paris, American dentistry in, 413; C.S. Brewster practices dentistry in, 277–280; Horace Wells's visit to, 280, 282–283, 286, 303, 407, 411–412; International exhibition, 1867, at, 238, 287, 304; And the reception of anesthesia in, 280, 282, 283; Thomas Evans practices dentistry in, 287–288; Use of nitrous oxide in, 243
Paris, John Ayrton, *The Elements of Medical Chemistry,* 55n39; *Pharmacologia,* 55n39
Parker, Willard, 64n79, 235
Parkes, Samuel, *The Chemical Catechism,* 4, 8, 51n12, 53n26, 54n35; *Chemical Essays relating to the Arts and Manufacturers of the British Dominions,* 54n35; *An Essay on the Utility of Chemistry to the Arts and Manufacturers,* 51n12; *The Rudiments of Chemistry,* 51n12
Parkinson, James, *Chemical Pocket-Book, or Memoranda Chemica,* 4, 50n8
Parks, Public, 362
Parmley, E., 288
Parsons, Edward W., 188, 199–200, 201, 231
Parsons, Francis, 188, 197
Parsons, Henry, *Parsons Family: Descendants of Cornet Joseph Parsons,* 211n22
Parsons, T.W., 351n5, 400n49
Pascal-Dubois, Dr., 410
Pasco, Lester, 189
Pasteur, Louis, 24, 267
Patent medicine, 373
Péan, Jules, 411
Pease, Persis, 188
Pease, William, 188
Pennsylvania College of Dental Surgery, 350n4
Pereira, Jonathan, *Elements of Materia Medica,* 19, 26
Perkins, Bemjamin, 377
Perkins, Elisha, 377
Perkins, Helen D., "Charles Noel Flagg, A. N. A., 1846–1916," 392n2; *An Illustrated Catalogue of Known Portraits by Jared Flagg, 1820–1899,* 403n101
Phelps, Daniel, 189
Philadelphia College of Dental Surgery, 350n4
Philadelphia Dental College, 116
Philadelphia Medical Museum, 7
Phillips, Sir Richard, *Grammar of Chemistry,* 21–22, 60n64
Pierce, Sarah, 209n11
Pilgrim, 358, 386; Horace Wells characterized as, 385–389
Pilkington, James, *The Artist's and Mechanic's Repository,* 18, 57n54; *The Artist's Guide and Mechanic's Own Book,* 57n54
Pirogov, N.I., 40; *Recherches Pratiques et Physiologiques sur l'Ethrization,* 71n112

Pittinger, Charles B., "The Anethetization of Fanny Longfellow." 351n5
Plates, Dental, 87, 91, 106, 223, 278. See also Dentures
Pneumatic medicine, 3, 6
Potter, Louis, 393
Poussin, Nicolas, 376
Powers, Mrs., 224–225, 226, 377
Préterre, André, 407–408
Priestly, Joseph, 3, 6, 301, 406
Protection Fire Protection Company, 190
Protoxide of azote, see Azote; Nitrous oxide
Protoxide of nitrogen, see Nitrous oxide
Puritans and puritanism, 361, 386, 396–397
Putnam, Israel, 364, 399n15
Pyorrhoea alveolaris, 264–265

Quonehtacut Dental Club, 393

Rainey, Henry, Dr. Thomas Evans, American Dentist to European Royalty, 287, 292n16, 293n30
Ramette, Russell Donald, The Wales Family of Dorchester, Massachusetts, 210n18, 218, 248n1
Raper, Howard Riley, Man Against Pain, 312, 319, 414, 416; "Sunshine and the Horace Wells Paris Monument," 414–416
Raphael, 384
Reed, Lumen, 382
Reed & Barber, Hartford, 210n12
Reeve, Tapping, 186, 209n11
Renwick, James, First Principles of Chemistry, 16, 57n51
A Representation to Congress by the Morton Testimonial Association, 252n37
Republican Party, 269
The Retreat for the Insane, Hartford, 64n76, 190, 194, 372
Revere, Brig. Gen. Joseph Warren, 328
Rhode Island Medical Society, 350n4
Rice, Nathan P., "A Grain of Wheat From a Bushel of Chaff," 44–45,

71n118; Supports Wells's claim to the discovery of anesthesia, 43–45; Trials of a Public Benefactor, 35–36, 37, 43, 70n104, 235, 354n24
Richmond, Mr., 109, 194
Richmond & Coleman, Hartford, 109. 189, 194
Rider, H.L., 112, 115
Riggs, John, 256
Riggs, John M., 67n91, 69n103, 78–79, 107, 116; Adds middle initial to his name, 257, 272n5; Birth and education, 256–257; Death, 262, 271; "The Discovery of Anesthesia," 261–262; And early use of anesthesia, 28, 29 70n105, 243, 260, 262; Extracts Wells's tooth in first dental operation with anesthesia, 2, 196, 202, 260–262, 273n12, 411; And the filling of teeth, 266–267; "Genius, the Result of Original Mental Superiority," 257; And the hygiene of the mouth, 266; Makes death mask of Horace Wells, 231, 262–264, 329–330, 352n9, 353n10, 353n11, 378; Method of keeping books, 102–103, 269; On committee to erect monument to Horace Wells, 202, 267; Opinion on W.T.G. Morton, 62n72; Personality and philosophy, 267–268, 269; Portrait of, 270; Relationship with Horace Wells, 196, 200, 258–262, 378; Supports Wells's claim to the discovery of anesthesia, 35, 38, 40, 42; "Supparative Inflamation of the Gums and Absorbtion of the Gums and Alveolar Process," 265, 274n21; Training in dentistry, 256–257, 273n10; Treatment of Mark Twain, 265–266; Treatment of pyorrhoea alveolaris, 264–266, 267; Views on dental education, 268–269
Riggs, Mary Beecher, 256
Riggs's disease, 264–265
Rimmer, Caroline, 352n8
Rimmer, William, 352n8
Ring, Malvin E., 22

Roberts, Carolyn, 334–335, 341, 354n18, 354n19
Roberts, Gov. Henry, 333, 334, 343, 354n19
Roberts, Col. Thomas, 119n17, 188, 197, 376, 379, 381
Rodin, Auguste, 352n8
Rodriguez, Benjamin Adolph, 277, 291n3
Rogers, John Kearney, 32, 33
Rogers, Professor, 29
Root canal therapy, 93–94
Ross, John, 332
Rottenstein, J.B., 411
Royal Institution, London, 3
Royal Society of Medicine, 45
Rubens, Peter Paul, 376
Ruskin, John, 361, 362
Ryder, Col. William, 410

Saint-Gaudens, Augustus, 385–386, 388, 399n16
Saltmash, Dr., 224
Saunders, Paul, *Edward Jenner, the Cheltenham Years*, 251n27
Scoffern, John, *Chemistry No Mystery; or, a Lecturer's Bequest*, 16–18, 57n53
Scott, Sir Walter, 12, 22
Sercombe, Edwin, 304, 307
Seybolt, Robert Francis, *The Private Schools of Colonial Boston*, 399n29
Shapiro, Michael Edward, *Bronze Casting and American Sculpture, 1850–1900*, 398n13
Sharrock, Roger, *John Bunyan*, 402n96
Shaw, Abiather, Jr., 183, 186, 368, 369
Shaw, Abiather Lambert, 183, 186, 187
Shaw, Betsy (Elizabeth), 183, 186, 188
Shaw, Betsy Wells, 183, 197, 201, 219, 225, 228, 232, 285, 368, 369, 379, 381
Shaw, Harriet, 183, 186
Shaw, Robert Gould, 332
Shaw, Susanna (Susan), 183, 186, 370
Shumway, Henry Colton, 376

Siemiatkoski, Donna Holt, *The Ancestors and Descendants of Chief Justice Oliver Ellsworth and His Wife Abagail Wolcott*, 211n24
Sigourney, Lydia, 315
Silhouettes, 321; By Auguste Edouart, 331–333; Cut by Horace Wells, 321, 333–335, 349; Of Horace Wells, 321, 331, 334, 335, 339, 355n31, 386
Silliman, Benjamin, 7, 13–14, 16, 52n24; *Elements of Chemistry*, 14, 22, 26, 56n46, 56n47, 63n74
Silver, 92, 105, 288. See also amalgam
Simpson, James Young, 59n62, 302, 306; Controversy with Jacob Bigelow over discovery of anesthesia, 239–240, 242–245; "Historical Letters on the Introduction of Anesthetics in Dentistry and Surgery in America," 253n42; And the introduction of chloroform, 47, 229; "A Reply to Dr. Jacob Bigelow's Second Letter," 253n45; Supports claim of Horace Wells for discovery of anesthesia, 240, 243- 245, 302; Writes article on anesthesia for *Encyclopaedia Britannica*, 242, 253n46
Sims, J. Marion, 245
Skinner, Mr., 109
Sklar, Kathryn Kish, *Catharine Beecher: a Study in American Domesticity*, 400n40
Smith, Gary B., "Gardner Quincy Colton: Pioneer in Nitrous Oxide Anesthesia," 310n1
Smith, J. Eugene, *One Hundred Years of Hartford's Courant*, 95n11
Smith, J.H., 66n89
Smith, Mr., 109
Smith, Page, *A City Upon a Hill*, 399n22
Smith, Truman, 60n66, 61n68, 62n72, 68n95, 225, 259; Advances Horace Wells's claim to Discovery of Anesthesia, 234- 236; "Anesthesia! The Greatest Discovery of the Age," 235- 236, 251n34; Assistance acknowledged by Charles T. Wells,

238; Collects evidence to support Horace Wells's claim, 88, 225, 228, 234; *Dr. Wells, the Discoverer of Anestheia* attributed to, 236m, 238; *An Examination of the Question of Anesthesia*, 60n66, 61n68, 63n72, 65n87, 66n91, 72n123, 96n24, 119n12, 201, 233–234, 235, 236, 238, 242, 251n29, 284, 293n25, 340; *An Inquiry Into the Origin of Modern Anesthesia*, 33, 68n96, 68n97, 94nl, 238, 329–330, 336, 354n18, 354n21

Smith, W.D.A., *Under the Influence: A History of Nitrous Oxide and Oxygen Anesthesia*, 95n22

Smithsonian Institution, 337, 341

Snell, James, 83, 88

Societé de Médecine, Paris, 283, 292n24; Credits Wells with discovery of anesthesia, 407; Elects Wells an honorary member, 284, 285, 407

Society of Hartford Artists, 325

Soifer, Max E., "Historical Notes on Horace Wells," 239, 240, 245, 253n41

Solder, Dental, 87, 112, 224

Southern Dental Journal, 261, 262, 267, 272n3, 273n15

Spear, Dorothea N., *Bibliographies of American Directories Through 1860*, 210n21

Springfield Republican, 254n50

Stanley, F., "Poisoning by the Inhalation of Impure Nitrous Oxide Gas," 58n58

Stanton, Madeline E., "The Centennial of Surgical Anesthesia," 8, 21, 52n23, 64n78, 249n14

Stearns, H.P., "Pickney Webster Ellsworth," 63n76

Stebbins, Theodore E., *Close Observation, Selected Oil Sketches by Frederick E. Church*, 212n39

Steele, Mr., 193, 194

Steele & Crocker, Hartford, 101, 189, 193, 200

Stetson, John B., 43; "William Clarke

and His 1842 Use of Ether," 71n115

Stiles, Henry B., *The History of Ancient Windsor*, 209n1, 211n25, 399n19,

Stockwell, C.T., 267, 268, 274n27

Stone, Darius, 189

Storer, Horatio R., 242–243

Stowe, Calvin Ellis, 209n11

Stowe, Harriet Beecher, 185, 202, 209n11, 372

Strauss, Maurice B., *Familiar Medical Quotations*, 62n70

Strebbing, Henry, 185

Street, Mr., 109

Street & Crocker, Hartford, 109

Stuart, Gilbert, 325, 328

Sulfuric ether, see Ether

Surgery, 7, 19; Painless, 5–6, 19–21, 40, 245

Sykes, W.S., *Essays on the First Hundered Years of Anesthesia*, 358, 398n2

Taft, Dr., 197, 225

Taft, Robert, *Photography and the American Scene: a Social History*, 352n7

Teeth, Brushing of, 90; Filling of, 89–90, 92, 93, 266–267, 277–278; Root canal therapy, 93–94

Teeth, Artificial, 69n99, 86. See also Dentures

Teniers, D., 384

Terry, J.B., 28, 80, 110–111, 198, 199, 382

Terry family 373

Thenard, L.J., 19; *Traité de Chiemie Élementaire*, 58n57

Thomson, Thomas, *A System of Chemistry*, 4, 8, 51n10, 53n25

Thorp, Margaret Ferrand, *The Literary Sculptors*, 399n16

Tiffany, Louis Comfort, 391

Tiffany Studios, *Partial List of Tiffany Windows*, 403n109

Tin, 92; Foil, 105

Tintype, 327, 329, 330, 335, 349, 351n7

Tishler, William A., *American Land-scape Architecture*, 398n7
Titian, 384
Toucey, Issac, 234; *Discovery by the Late Horace Wells, of the Applica-bility of Nitrous Oxyd Gas, Sulphu-ric Ether and Other Vapours in Surgical Operations*, 233, 251n28, 315
Trail, T.S., 253n46
Transatlantic crossing, 293n29
Trinity College, see Washington College
Troostwik, P. van, 49n5
Trumbull, John, 328, 376, 377
Trumbull, Joseph, 119n17
Trumbull, Robert, 115
Trumbull, Sarah, 219
Turner, Edward, *Elements of Chemis-try*, 10, 14, 54n35, 55n37, 56n48; *Elements of Experimental Chemis-try*, 56n48
Twain, Mark, 202, 215n85, 265–266, 325

United States Congress, *Report No. 114, William T.G. Morton - Sulphu-ric Ether*, 67n93
United States Department of State, Passport Division, 315
United States House of Repre-sentatives, *Report . . . Vindicating the Rights of Charles T. Jackson to the Discovery of Anesthesia*, 351n5
United States Naval Academy, 313
United States Patent Office, *List of Patents for Inventions and Designs 1790–1847*, 69n100
United States Senate, *An Examination of the Question of Anesthesia, Aris-ing on the Memorial of Charles Thomas Wells*, 61n68, 70n105, 72n122, 96n24, 212n50, 225, 234, 235, 259, 273n11, 293n25, 293n27; *Statements, Supported by Evidence of Wm. T.G. Morton*, 28, 35, 39n3, 64n78, 65n87, 111, 118n3, 119n13, 119n17, 259, 292n18, 292n19, 292n20, 417n9

University of Pennsylvania, 41; *Com-pendium of the Course of Chemical Instruction in*, 14; Patients anesthe-tized at, 67n93
University of Pittsburgh, School of Dental Medicine, 313, 319, 355n29; Dental Library and Mu-seum, 314
Upjohn, Richard Mitchell, 362
Ure, Andrew, *Dictionary of Chemis-try*, 9, 54n34
Van Buren, William H., 33, 67n94
Vandam, Leroy D., 253n40
Van Poznack, Alan, "The History of Anesthesia at the New York Hospi-tal," 32, 67n92, 67n93, 68n95
Viets, Henry R., "Nathan P. Rice M.D., and His *Trials of a Public Benefactor*, New York, 1859," 71n117, 235, 251n30
Villain, Henri, 410

Wadsworth, Daniel, 199, 372–373, 376, 382
Wadsworth Antheneum, Hartford, 190, 199, 203, 211n32, 322, 325, 328, 356n36, 376, 383; *First Cata-log of Paintings*, 376–377; *Paintings by the Flagg Family*, 349n2
Wainright, Nicholas, "A Philadelphia Forty-Niner," 351n4
Wales, Elizabeth, see Wells, Elizabeth Wales
Wales, Frederick, 193
Wales, Henry, 218, 219
Wales, Joseph, 60n66, 187, 189, 199, 200, 211n30, 218, 228, 233, 235, 248n4, 248n5, 251n28, 356n36, 380, 382, 384
Wales, Dr. Lemuel, 193
Wales, Nathaniel (17th century), 218, 219
Wales, Nathaniel (19th century), 187, 217–218, 248n3
Wales Sally Hender, 187, 217–218, 248n3
Wales, Thomas, 218, 219, 222
Wales, Timothy, 219
Wales, William, 218
Wales family, 217–219; *Bible*, 248n3

Walker, Issac P., 234

Walker, Rev., 247

Wallace, Davis H., *The New-York Historical Society's Dictionary of Artists in America, 1564–1860*, 349n2, 356n32

Waller, John Augustine, 9

Ward, J.O.A., 364, 399n15

Ward, R.B. & W.A., Hartford, 249n5

Waring, Joseph I., *A History of Medicine in South Carolina*, 291n5

Warner, Alfred P., 188

Warner, Charles Dudley, 202, 325

Warren, Edward, 282, 284

Warren John Collins, 34, 378; *Anatomical Description of the Arteries of the Human Body*, 374, 401n51; *Etherization With Surgical Remarks*, 69n100

Washington, George, 325, 395, 404

Washington (Trinity) College, 29, 64n79, 190, 256, 257, 324, 330, 372, 393; Carved pew in chapel dedicated to Wells, 393; *Statement of the Course of Study and Instruction*, 272n4

Webster, John White, *Manual of Chemistry*, 10, 55n36

Webster, Noah, 27

Weidenmann, Jacob, 362, 393

Weigand and Snowden, Philadelphia, 89

Wellcome Historical Museum, London, *Souvenir, Henry Hickman Centerrary Exhibition*, 58n60, 292n24

Welles, Gideon, 186, 328

Welles Leonard T., 190, 200

Wells, Betsy, see Shaw, Betsy Wells

Wells, Charles, 183, 185, 186, 187, 201, 222, 228, 258, 368, 374

Wells, Charles J., "Horace Wells," 248n6

Wells, Charles P., 186, 193

Wells, Charles Thomas, 68n98, 197, 224, 228, 229, 231, 248n3, 315, 322, 333, 334, 353n11; Acknowledges assistance of Truman Smith, 238; Annuity fund for, 304–309, 310; Birth and early life, 191, 222, 223, 228; Commissions C.N. Flagg

to paint portrait of father, 328; Erects cemetary monument for parents, 248; Estate of, 334, 335; Health, 247, 309, 310; Later life and death, 247; Memories of father, 210n17, 213–214n62, 238; Paints portraits of parents, 335, 338, 341, 345, 346, 347, 348, 356n36; Petition presented to Congress on behalf of, 88, 225, 234; Portrait of, 246; Reburies bodies of parents, 248, 393–395; Visits Paris to view casting of statue of father, 309

Wells, Elizabeth Wales, 2, 23, 36, 72n123, 96n24, 189, 191, 196–197, 225, 228, 284, 285, 333, 340, 381, 384; Account of G.Q. Colton's nitrous oxide demonstration, 225–226; Annuity fund for, 304–309, 310; Benefit fund for, 246; Birth and early life, 217, 219; Birth of son Charles, 191, 222; Body reburied, 248, 393–396; Character and personality, 217, 221, 222, 227, 247; Corresponds with Sir James Young Simpson, 240 253n43; Courtship and marriage to Horace Wells, 187–188, 219–222; Death, 247, 253–254n50; Describes the discovery of anesthesia, 226; Effect of husband's death on, 225, 229, 231, 304, 305, 306; Health, 196, 224, 228; Interest in Wales family geneology, 218–219, 247; And the making of gas bags, 88, 227; Portraits of, 222, 240–241, 315, 334, 343, 345, 347, 348; Preserves family bible, 248n3; Promotes husband's claim to the discovery of anesthesia, 232, 233, 235–237, 239–240, 242, 245, 392; Relationship with husband, 196, 228–229; residences of, 201, 215n82; Support and assistance of Truman Smith, 238

Wells, Captain Hezekiah, 219, 366, 399n19

Wells, Horace, 16, 255n29; Accounts with W.T.G. Morton, 101, 106, 112–113, 114–115, 116–117, 180–

181, 200, 382; Administers nitrous oxide in early operations, 31, 32-33, 48, 67n93, 68n95, 88, 200, 302; Advertising of dental practice, 73–80, 183, 212n44; Ancestry, 183, 219, 249n6; Attends G.C. Colton's nitrous oxide demonstration, 2, 23, 225, 226, 259–260; Awarded prize by Massachusetts Charitable Mechanic Association, 86–87; Awarded prize for dentistry, 79; Birth and early life, 183, 219, 367- 370; Body reburied, 248; Bronze tablet commemorating Wells as discoverer of anesthesia, 203, 215n89, 389, 390; Burial, 200, 231; Cemetary monument, 248, 254n52, 393–396; Character and personality, 47, 60n66, 227, 358, 397; Characterized as crusader, 392; Characterized as pilgrim, 385–389; Chloroform addiction and possible poisoning, 229, 230–231, 250n24, 407; Claim supported by British medical and dental professions, 307–308, 310; Claim supported by C.S. Brewster, 280, 282–284, 287, 407, 412; Claim supported by J. Marion Sims, 245; Claim supported by Académie des Sciences, Paris, 303; Claim supported by James Young Simpson, 243- 245, 306; Claims discovery of anesthesia, 198, 228, 234, 235–237, 381; Collaboration with C.C. Marcy in early operations with anesthesia, 28–30; Courtship and marriage, 187–188, 191, 219–222; Daguerrotypes of, 321, 322, 327, 328, 329, 330, 335, 386; "Day Book A," 74, 75, 78, 79, 97–101, 102, 103–112, 114–117, 193–194, 249n7 258, 341; "Day Book A" transcribed, 120–181; Death mask of, 231, 262–264, 329, 330, 335, 352n9, 353n10, 353n11, 386; Dental instruments employed by, 73, 80–90; dental offices, 74, 75, 76, 77, 183, 189, 190–191, 192, 193-195, 197; Dental plates made by, 75, 91, 106, 223; Disadvan-

taged because of his location in Hartford, 40; Discovers analgesic properties of nitrous oxide, 2, 14, 19, 27–28, 41, 42, 44, 45, 46, 61n69, 226, 236–237, 259- 260, 261–262, 305–306, 380, 406–407; Discovers painless dentistry, 22; And discovery of anesthesia, 24, 25, 31, 38, 48–49, 94, 117, 301, 302; "The Discovery of Etherial Inhalation," 28, 64n80; Early dental operations with anesthesia, 24, 88, 243, 302; Early interest in painless surgery, 212n50, 225; Early use of ether anesthesia, 26- 29, 45, 253, 380, 384; Employment of nitrous oxide in dentistry, 21, 88, 226, 227, 262; Engraving of H.B. Hall, 238, 334–336, 340, 344, 354n18; An Essay on Teeth, 90, 92–93, 94n1, 191, 194, 121n43, 373–374; Estate of, 80, 86, 87, 95n14, 115, 117, 200, 214n76, 231, 323; European trip, 48, 72n123, 182, 198–199, 228- 229, 232, 280, 282–284, 285–287, 297–300, 382, 383, 407, 408, 412; Extraction of teeth by, 91, 106; Failure of demonstration in Boston, 34–35, 40, 48, 114, 119n16, 196, 227, 232, 262, 302, 378, 406; Fees charged for dentistry, 104–105; And the filling of teeth, 76, 89, 92–93, 104–106; Finances, 223, 231–232; First published portrait of, 236, 238; Funeral, 200; Gas bags used by, 33, 88, 226; In Hartford, Connecticut, 74–75, 192, 201, 211n36, 371; Has tooth extracted by John Riggs under anesthesia, 2, 226, 260–262, 273n12, 411; Health, 77, 79, 113, 117, 182, 186, 187, 191–192, 196, 198, 224, 225, 228, 232, 302, 378, 379, 380, 407; History of the Discovery of the Application of Nitrous Oxide Gas, 28, 49n4, 64n80, 69n100, 69n101, 200, 214n74, 283, 284, 383; House on Lord's Hill, 194–195, 196, 222, 223, 232, 378; Income from dental practice, 111;

Informs W.T.G. Morton about anesthesia, 34, 35–36, 44, 45, 49; Instructs W.T.G. Morton in dentistry, 25, 112, 115, 116, 194; Interest in animal magnetism, 113, 224–225, 226, 377; Interest in ornathology and natural history, 187, 196, 210n17; Invention of coal sifter, 22, 60n65, 375, 379; Invention of dental instruments, 22, 78, 88, 89, 91; Invention of non-corrosive dental solder, 112–113, 195; Invention of shower bath, 22, 48, 60n65, 119n17, 188, 197, 198, 213n62, 227, 228, 232, 379, 380, 381; Inventory of dental office equipment, 80, 87, 231; Joins the Odd Fellows, 228, 380; Knowledge of Humphry Davy's research on nitrous oxide, 21, 23, 60n68; "Memoir," to the Académie des Sciences, 60n68, 294–297, 406, 411–412, 416n1; Life in Boston, 370; Moves to New York City to introduce anesthesia there, 32–33, 200, 384; Obituaries of, 72n124, 229–231; Opinion on W.T.G. Morton, 113–114; Opposition by W.T.G. Morton to Wells's claim to discovery of anesthesia, 31–32, 198, 232, 381, 384; Parisian statue of, 404, 405, 407, 410, 411, 441–416; Partnership with W.T.G. Morton, 25, 62n72, 112–114, 195, 213n55, 223–224; Partnership with Samuel Cooley alleged, 214–215n81; Passport granted to, 281, 316, 382; And the patenting of anesthesia, 198, 381; Pew in chapel of Trinity College dedicated to, 393; Portrait by C.N. Flagg, 321–323, 328, 330, 333, 335; Portrait by James C. McManus, 335, 341; Portrait by Verona Kirafly, 318, 335, 341; Portrait by son Charles, 335, 338, 341, 345, 346, 347; Portrait in miniature on ivory, 222, 315, 335, 337, 340; Portrait possibly by C. Hine, 342, 344- 345; And the practice of dentistry, 48, 73–74, 75, 90, 228, 232, 302, 379, 380, 381;

Publishes claim for the discovery of anesthesia in *Hartford Courant,* 28, 34, 35, 69n100, 198; Purchase of French paintings for re-sale, 72n123, 182, 198, 199, 227, 232, 280, 382, 384; Puts on "Panorama of Nature" exhibition, 196, 213n59, 227, 232, 379; Relationship with John Riggs, 196, 200, 258–262, 378; Relationship with wife Elizabeth, 196, 200, 224, 227; Restlesness and changes of locations, 77, 79–80, 117, 190–191, 192, 196–197, 198, 227, 373, 380; Schooling, 183, 368, 369; Self-experimentation with anesthetic agents, 48, 227, 229, 232, 305, 407; Silhouettes of, 223, 321, 322, 326, 328–329, 330–331, 333, 334–335, 349, 353n12, 355n31; Son Charles, 191, 222, 223; Stained glass window installed in Center Church, 203, 215n90, 390, 391–392; Statue by Truman H. Bartlett, 199, 201–203, 245, 267, 305, 306, 329, 352n8, 358, 359, 360, 363–365, 385–389, 397; Suicide death, 24, 48, 94, 200, 229–230, 249–250n24, 284, 302, 303, 321, 384–385, 407; Supposed instability of, 113, 227, 358, 380; Testimonial fund, 304–309, 310; As teacher of dentistry, 194, 257, 273n10; Tintype of, 327, 330, 335, 349; Training and apprenticeship in dentistry, 24, 74, 183, 219, 324, 351n5, 400n49; Visits W.T.G. Morton in Boston to observe his anesthesia, 36, 70n106, 380–381; Women patients, 193–194
Wells, Horace, Sr., 183, 366, 368, 370, 373
Wells, Horace, of Weathersfield, 249
Wells, J. Gaylord, 200, 201, 383
Wells, Mary, see Cole, Mary Wells
Wells, Sarah Trumbull, 366
Wells, T. Spencer, 304
Wells, Governor Thomas, 183
Wells & Humphrey, Hartford, 186, 188

Wells & Strong, Hartford, 191, 200

Wells family, 183, 328, 333, 335; Papers, 293n28

"Wells Testimonial Fund," 311n5

Wescott, Amos, 82

Wheaton, Rev. Nathaniel S., 257

Whipple, Anson, 248n3

Whipple George Hoyt, 250n24

Whistler, James McNeil, 393

White, Samuel S., 80; *A Century of Service to Dentistry,* 95n16

Whiting Rising & Co., Hartford, 103, 193

Whitman, Elizabeth, see Morton, Elizabeth Whitman

Whitney Museum of Art, *200 Years of Sculpture,* 402n99

Wildsmith, J.A.W., "Horace Wells," 398n2

Williams, Elizabeth, 70n105

Wills, Hezekiah, 399n19

Wills family, 183

Wilson, James Grant, 213n50

Winchester, Alice, *The Flowering of American Folk Art, 1776- 1876,* 403n104

Windsor, Connecticut, Horace Wells ancestry in, 183

Winslow, Ola Elizabeth, *John Bunyan,* 402n98

Wood, George B., *Dispensatory of the United States,* 12, 55n43

Wood, Henry Erving, "The Discoverer of Anesthesia: Dr. Horace Wells of Hartford," 68n98

Wood, Robert & Co., Philadelphia, 364, 399n15

Woodhouse, James, 6–7, 9; "Observations on the Effects of Nitrous Oxide," 7, 52n19

Woods, Enoch S., 389. 390, 393

Wright, Thomas Goddard, *Literary Culture in Early New England, 1620–1730,* 399n28

Wright, William, *On the Varieties of Deafness and Diseases of the Ear,* 20, 21, 58n61

Yale College, 267, 372

Young, Hugh H., "Long, the Discoverer of Anesthesia," 71n113

Young, James Harvey, *The Toadstool Millionaires,* 400n43

Young Men's Institute, Hartford, 190, 199, 376, 377, 379